WOUNDED CITY

The Social Impact of 9/11

Nancy Foner, Editor

Russell Sage Foundation, New York

The Russell Sage Foundation

The Russell Sage Foundation, one of the oldest of America's general purpose foundations, was established in 1907 by Mrs. Margaret Olivia Sage for "the improvement of social and living conditions in the United States." The Foundation seeks to fulfill this mandate by fostering the development and dissemination of knowledge about the country's political, social, and economic problems. While the Foundation endeavors to assure the accuracy and objectivity of each book it publishes, the conclusions and interpretations in Russell Sage Foundation publications are those of the authors and not of the Foundation, its Trustees, or its staff. Publication by Russell Sage, therefore, does not imply Foundation endorsement.

Library of Congress Cataloging-in-Publication Data
Wounded city : the social impact of 9/11 / edited by Nancy Foner.
    p. cm.
  Includes bibliographical references and index.
  ISBN 0-87154-264-1 (cloth)   ISBN 0-87154-271-4 (paperback)
    1. September 11 Terrorist Attacks, 2001—Social aspects—New York (State)—New York.
2. New York (N.Y.)—Social conditions. I. Foner, Nancy, 1945–
HV6432.7.W68   2005
974.7′1044—dc22   2004051490

Text design by Genna Patacsil.

RUSSELL SAGE FOUNDATION
112 East 64th Street, New York, New York 10021
10 9 8 7 6 5 4 3 2 1

WOUNDED CITY

CONTENTS

CONTRIBUTORS

NANCY FONER is Distinguished Professor of Sociology at Hunter College and the City University of New York Graduate Center.

DANIEL BEUNZA is assistant professor of economics and business at Pompeu Fabra University in Barcelona.

JENNIFER L. BRYAN is a doctoral candidate in sociology at Yale University.

MARGARET M. CHIN is assistant professor of sociology at Hunter College, City University of New York.

MONISHA DAS GUPTA is assistant professor of ethnic studies and women's studies at the University of Hawaii at Manoa.

KAI ERIKSON is William R. Kenan Jr. Professor Emeritus of Sociology and American Studies at Yale University.

SANDRA GARCIA is a doctoral candidate in social work at Columbia University.

IRWIN GARFINKEL is Mitchell I. Ginsberg Professor of Contemporary Urban Problems at the Columbia University School of Social Work.

MELANIE D. HILDEBRANDT is assistant professor of sociology at Indiana University of Pennsylvania.

PHILIP KASINITZ is professor of sociology at the Graduate Center and Hunter College of the City University of New York.

NEERAJ KAUSHAL is assistant professor of social work at the Columbia University School of Social Work.

WILLIAM KORNBLUM is professor of sociology at the City University of New York Graduate Center.

STEVEN LANG is an independent scholar who received his doctorate in sociology from the City University of New York Graduate Center.

BINH POK is a doctoral candidate in sociology at the City University of New York Graduate Center.

FRANCESCA POLLETTA is associate professor of sociology at Columbia University.

JULIA ROTHENBERG recently received her doctorate in sociology at the City University of New York Graduate Center.

KAREN SEELEY teaches at Columbia University and Barnard College and has a private psychotherapy practice.

GREGORY SMITHSIMON is a doctoral candidate in sociology at Columbia University.

DAVID STARK is Arthur Lehman Professor of Sociology and International Affairs at Columbia University and external faculty member at the Santa Fe Institute.

JULIEN TEITLER is assistant professor of social work at the Columbia University School of Social Work.

LESLEY WOOD is assistant professor of sociology at York University.

FOREWORD

IN THE GRIM WEEKS after the terrorist attack on the World Trade Center on September 11, 2001, many New Yorkers asked themselves how they could contribute their talents and abilities to help their fellow citizens and assist in the effort to restore and revitalize the city. As a research organization with a long history of studying social and economic conditions in the city, the Russell Sage Foundation naturally turned toward the idea of using the analytic capacities of social science to assess the shocking blow New York had suffered and analyze the underlying dimensions of what we fervently hoped would be its full recovery. In the following months, the foundation assembled a working group of nineteen experts on New York and supported their coordinated research on the economic, social, and political implications of the terrorist attack on the city. Now, four years later, we are pleased to present the results of their efforts in three volumes.

Resilient City, edited by economist Howard Chernick, assesses the impact of September 11 on the city's economy. By and large, the book tells a remarkable story of recovery. Fears that New York's competitive position in the world economy would deteriorate as firms fled the city proved to be unfounded. The attractions that New York has always offered—high density and a large, skilled labor force—kept most businesses in the city, despite the perceived threat of another attack. Manhattan's enormous commercial real estate market managed to absorb the loss of 10 percent of its available inventory and still accommodate 80 percent of the firms forced to relocate from downtown. While demand for space in tall buildings suffered a temporary slump, occupancy rates for buildings of more than fifty stories returned to near normal levels over the three-year period following the attack. The job market fared less well, suffering a net loss of over 125,000 jobs by September 2004. By some estimates, it may take another five years for the city's job base to return to its pre-attack peak. The attack has also increased New York City taxes by about 8 percent and caused commercial insurance costs to soar. To the extent that these increased costs raise the price of doing business in New York, the city's long run competitiveness could suffer. While no one can predict the eventual consequences of the attack, the price signals in the real estate and financial markets remain positive. Housing prices and rents have risen more steeply than in the rest of the country, and the shares of firms headquartered in New York City are not selling at a discount. Remarkably, four years after the attack, confidence in the city seems fully restored.

Wounded City, edited by anthropologist Nancy Foner, is a book that digs below the aggregate outcomes revealed by economic statistics to look at especially vulnerable neighborhoods and groups of workers. Here the stories are about lasting scars and painful dislocations. The garment industry in Chinatown nearly collapsed due to security restrictions near Ground Zero that prevented the movement of merchandise, leaving thousands of immigrant workers jobless. Cabdrivers in the city, most of them Muslim, suffered from the increased hostility of their customers and the loss of business as tourism declined, leaving many of them in debt to pay the leases for their taxi medallions. The precipitous drop in air travel after September 11 eliminated thousands of New York jobs in the airline industry, stranding many workers with little prospect of regaining their jobs despite massive federal subsidies for the airlines. Communities as disparate as the Muslims in Jersey City and the white ethnic neighborhoods of Belle Harbor in the Rockaways suffered lasting trauma. Belle Harbor endured the double disaster of its many firefighters lost on September 11, followed eight weeks later by the crash of American Flight 587. The Muslim community in Jersey City experienced both an increase in hate crimes and assaults from their neighbors, and the impact of detentions, investigations, and raids by law enforcement agencies in the wake of the attack. *Wounded City* shows how New York communities and workers have struggled to cope with these problems, some more successfully than others. New York is healing, but the process remains uneven and incomplete.

Contentious City, edited by political scientist John Mollenkopf, offers valuable insights into the bewildering contest among the political actors who have grappled with decisions about how to rebuild the World Trade Center site and memorialize those who lost their lives in the attack. Stories of this ongoing political battle have filled the New York press almost daily for the past four years. As *Contentious City* is published, the outcome remains in doubt, but the political experts who contributed to the book do an excellent job of exploring the underlying logic that continues to drive the process. After the veneer of public participation in discussions about the redesign of the site wore off, the decision process revealed itself as a strikingly undemocratic contest among the governor, the mayor, the Port Authority, and the lease holder. In this game, the city and its citizens held very few cards. As a result, the narrow goal of restoring the commercial revenues from the site has generally trumped broader efforts to establish mixed residential and commercial use for the downtown area and to improve its transportation links to the rest of the city. This, despite the fact that commercial vacancies downtown are at a historic peak and demand for commercial space remains distinctly weaker in downtown than midtown. As our books go to press, it appears likely that some version of the Freedom Tower will be built. It is much less certain that tenants will be ready to occupy this space at viable prices, or that the predominantly commercial redevelopment of the site will be best for the city in the long run.

The brutal shock of September 11 caused profound human suffering for the thousands of New Yorkers who lost loved ones, and a new sense of vulnerability still experienced by everyone in the city. It is commonplace to say that nothing will ever be the same after September 11, and in many ways this is true. But the reaction to the attack also revealed much about the persistent character of the city—the enormous strength and flexibility of its economy, the vitality as well as the fragility of its communities, and the byzantine complexities of its power politics. The tools of social science, deftly wielded in these volumes, bring all these underlying constancies of New York life into sharp relief in an effort to probe the deeper dimensions of what has happened in the wake of September 11. As citizens of New York, we would like to contribute these volumes as a small part of the city's ongoing effort to understand and improve itself—and to recover from its darkest hour.

Eric Wanner
President
Russell Sage Foundation

ACKNOWLEDGMENTS

THIS BOOK is the product of the activities of a working group formed by the Russell Sage Foundation to study the impact of the September 11, 2001, terrorist attack at the World Trade Center on the social life of New York City. It is part of a larger project, New York City's Recovery from September 11. Members of the social effects group, as it came to be known, were Nancy Foner (chair), Margaret M. Chin, Kai Erikson, Irwin Garfinkel, Philip Kasinitz, William Kornblum, and David Stark. When the working group was formed in the spring of 2002, we held a series of initial meetings to solicit and evaluate proposals for ethnographic research to be conducted in the coming months. Most of this research built on projects in which working group members (or other established scholars or graduate students) were already involved, but some of these ethnographic projects, usually with working group members in an advisory role, were altogether new. In the fall of 2002, the researchers presented in-progress reports at several meetings; when the final written reports were submitted in the winter of 2003, we began discussions about the organization and shape of this volume. Every member of the social effects group has a chapter—and in one case two chapters—in this book; several are coauthors with one or more of the ethnographic researchers who submitted reports.

I want to thank the working group members for their commitment to the project at every step of the way—for their insights, sage advice, good humor, and, along with the other authors, the quality of their contributions to this volume. On behalf of the group, I would also like to thank all of the ethnographic researchers supported by the Russell Sage Foundation for doing "fieldwork under deadline" for the project, thereby illuminating the impact of the events of September 11 on a wide range of New York groups and communities in the months after the attack: Daniel Beunza, Jennifer L. Bryan, Margaret M. Chin, Monisha Das Gupta, Melanie Hildebrandt, Steven Lang, Setha Low (and her collaborators Dana Taplin, Mike Lamb, and Mirele Goldsmith), Binh Pok, Francesca Polletta, Julia Rothenberg, Karen Seeley, Gregory Smithsimon, and Carolyn Turnovsky.

Thanks, too, to my co-steering committee members on the New York City

Recovery Project for their advice and support: John Mollenkopf, chair of the working group studying the politics of recovery, and Howard Chernick, chair of the working group investigating the economic impact of the attack. The meetings that the steering group organized for all three working groups featured guest speakers and were a source of ideas; the reports presented by members of the politics and economics working groups at various sessions were informative and useful.

I and all the members of the social effects group owe a debt to the Russell Sage Foundation, and in particular its president, Eric Wanner. This book would never have seen the light of day—and many of the research projects on which it is based would not have been conducted or completed—without the Russell Sage Foundation's support and Eric Wanner's vision and encouragement. From the very beginning, when the New York City Recovery Project was established, and throughout its duration, Eric Wanner served as an intellectual guide, a wise counselor, and an unfailing source of support.

I also owe a great debt to Stephanie Platz, the Russell Sage Foundation program officer responsible for the New York City Recovery Project from its inception until she left the foundation in August 2003. Stephanie Platz ensured that all the administrative details went smoothly. More than this, she was a much-valued sounding board and an enormous help in getting the ethnographic research projects off the ground and organizing the reports and working papers that resulted.

Also at the Russell Sage Foundation, Katy Hermann and, later, Bindu Chadaga helped with the arrangements for meetings and dealt with other administrative chores essential to the organization of the social effects working group and the preparation of this book. Last, but certainly not least, I am grateful to those at the foundation who were involved in the actual publication process, including copyeditor Cindy Buck and David Haproff, director of public relations. I owe a special thanks to Suzanne Nichols, the director of publications, for her expertise, thoroughness, humor, and encouragement. It has been a great pleasure to work with her.

PART 1

Introduction

CHAPTER 1

The Social Effects of 9/11 on New York City: An Introduction

Nancy Foner

THE ATTACK on the World Trade Center (WTC) on September 11, 2001, changed New York City forever. The twin towers, which had become one of the symbols of the city and were a workplace for more than 30,000 people, were destroyed. An entire zip code, 10048, is now, as one journalist puts it, in a kind of twilight zone and has not been used since the attack (Haberman 2003). The death toll was shattering. At latest count, 2,749 died in the attack, close to half of them New York City residents and most of the others from the surrounding suburbs. More than 7,000 of the World Trade Center population were injured or hospitalized in the attack. Family members of those who died, were missing, or had been hospitalized and injured numbered about 17,000. And in the days and months that followed, almost 18,000 rescue and recovery workers labored at the site, which almost immediately came to be called Ground Zero.[1]

It was not, of course, only New Yorkers who lost loved ones or worked in or close to Ground Zero who were affected by the attack. There were the residents of neighborhoods near the site as well as those in communities farther away in the city and metropolitan area where large numbers of the victims had lived. There were the thousands displaced from their homes, workplaces, and schools, and the many who lost their jobs or businesses or suffered economic losses. There were the thousands whose adverse physical and emotional reactions hampered their ability to function in their daily lives. And there were those, mostly Muslims, who found themselves subject to a kind of hostility they had not experienced before.

This volume brings together a series of in-depth accounts that explore and analyze how September 11 has affected various social groups and communities in the New York area. It is a product of a working group formed under the auspices of the Russell Sage Foundation to study the impact of the terrorist attack and its aftermath on the social life of the city as part of a larger project, New York City's Recovery from September 11. Concurrently, another working group investigated the economic impact of the attack, including job losses, low-skilled workers' wages and earnings, and the city's public finances, office market, and competitive position. A third working group focused on the politics of recovery and looked at, among other things, the rebuilding of the WTC site and the political calculus of development efforts.

In setting out to examine the social effects of September 11, the social effects working group was faced with a wide array of potential groups, communities, and organizations to study. New York, after all, is a city of eight million people, and the wider metropolitan area is more than twice that size. Many well-known studies of the social consequences of disasters, by contrast, have looked at small communities, such as Buffalo Creek, West Virginia, a place with only a few thousand people made famous by Kai Erikson in *Everything in Its Path* (1976). The working group decided to focus on a set of residential, ethnic, and occupational communities that were thought to have been particularly hard hit by the WTC attack and that had not come in for much journalistic or public attention, unlike the firefighters and police involved in the rescue and recovery effort.

A series of ethnographic studies were commissioned and conducted in the spring, summer, and fall of 2002, based on in-depth interviews and participant observation in a broad array of settings. Several studies built on research already under way for other purposes before September 11. Before the attack, David Stark and Daniel Beunza, for example, were in the midst of an ethnographic study of a trading room in the World Financial Center (directly adjacent to the World Trade Center); Gregory Smithsimon had been conducting fieldwork in Battery Park City as part of another project on public space and community life; and Margaret M. Chin had completed research on Chinese garment workers a few years earlier.[2] After September 11 but before the working group was formed in the spring of 2002, Jennifer Bryan had been engaged in dissertation research on intergroup relations in Jersey City; Monisha Das Gupta had been involved in planning a survey for the New York Taxi Workers Alliance; and Francesca Polletta and her colleagues had begun a study of public deliberations in response to the disaster. Whenever they began, most of the ethnographic studies reported in this volume had ended by the last months of 2002, so that with three exceptions—the chapters by Jennifer Bryan; Philip

FIGURE 1.1   SELECTED SITES IN THE NEW YORK CITY AREA

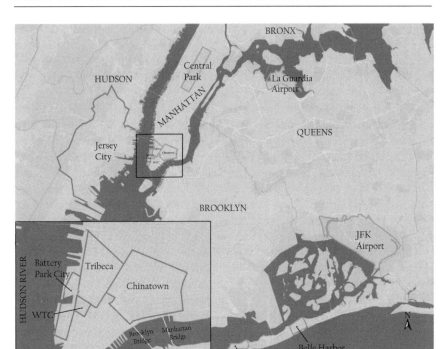

Source: Merih Anil of the CUNY Center for Urban Research.

Kasinitz, Gregory Smithsimon, and Binh Pok; and Francesca Polletta and Lesley Wood, which are based on research that continued into 2003—they discuss responses in the first year or so after the attack.

Although the working group and this volume concentrate on communities
and groups that were deeply affected by the attack, for others the impact was
less dramatic; sometimes in fact it was quite fleeting and superficial. For many
New Yorkers, life in the months after September 11 was mainly business as
usual. This point needs to be emphasized at the very outset. Most New Yorkers did not know anyone personally who was killed in the attack, and their
everyday lives went on much as before. Even in the immediate aftermath of
September 11, New Yorkers responded differently, in large part on the basis of
where they worked and lived in the city. Those living closest to Ground Zero
or working in or near the site, for example, were likely to have experienced

more distress—emotional and in some cases, owing to the very air they breathed, physical—than those living farther away (Low 2002; see also studies reported in Garfinkel et al., this volume). Fortunately, in their chapter Irwin Garfinkel and his colleagues are able to present a picture of the reactions and responses of a broad swath of New Yorkers, gained through an analysis of three waves of the New York Social Indicators Survey, the most recent conducted six months after the attack.

There is also the issue of focusing on the social as opposed to the individual effects of the attack. Clearly, the attack had a devastating impact on the lives of many people, leading to grief, sorrow, and trauma that, even several years later, have made it difficult for some to manage. For others, graphic reminders of the attack continue to trigger emotional responses. When the World Trade Center PATH station reopened in November 2003, the *New York Times* reported that many commuters in the first rush hour since September 11 fought back tears as they remembered fleeing from the site more than two years earlier (Luo 2003). Several chapters in this volume tell of people dealing with distress and anxiety, including residents of the Rockaway community of Belle Harbor whose relatives or neighbors died in the attack, traders who worked in the World Financial Center, and psychotherapists who have been treating patients suffering from trauma. Garfinkel and his colleagues report that adverse reactions to the attack were widespread in the city. In the survey they conducted in the spring of 2002, almost one-third of the adults interviewed reported sleeping poorly since September 11, and one-third had trouble concentrating at work. Almost half of the parents said their children had experienced at least one symptom of anxiety since September 11, such as problems sleeping or concentrating, fear of crowded places, or anxiety that the parent would go away and not return.

Important as these individual reactions are, the analyses in this book nevertheless center on the impact of the September 11 attack on the social level. In his study of the Buffalo Creek flood, Kai Erikson (1976) coins the terms "individual trauma" and "collective trauma" to differentiate between individual reactions to disaster and community-wide responses, but this distinction does not get at what is at issue here. The question here is not so much about collective trauma, although in chapter 4 Melanie Hildebrandt discusses the notion of collective trauma in the context of her analysis of the impact of the WTC attack and the subsequent plane crash in the Rockaways and in chapter 10 Karen Seeley considers it in examining how both therapists and patients were shaken and hurt by the same catastrophic event. Rather, the focus of this book is on how September 11 and its aftermath have affected groups of people who share the same occupation, industry, workplace, religious or ethnic identity, or residential community; how the very nature or structure of these groups and communities shaped their reaction to the attack and its impact on them;

and how the response itself sometimes led to changes in the groups and communities.

It is worth recalling Émile Durkheim's classic study *Suicide* (1951), which deals with that most individual of acts, taking one's own life. Durkheim argues that the concern of the sociologist is not the individual factors—temperament, character, and private history—that lead a particular person to commit suicide, but rather suicide rates. Individual conditions "may perhaps cause this or that separate individual to kill himself, but not give society as a whole a greater or lesser tendency to suicide" (Durkheim 1951, 51). In a similar way, the chapters in this volume, while concerned with an event that affected particular individuals in unique ways, explore the social rather than the psychological impact of the disaster. Indeed, the survey reported by Garfinkel and his colleagues in chapter 2 shows, as they note, that "some groups suffered more than others" in the wake of the attack. Not surprisingly, already vulnerable populations—among them, the least educated, the disabled, Hispanics, and Muslims—were the most likely to report mental health symptoms.

Erikson notes in the epilogue that the early social science literature on disasters emphasized the waves of good feelings and of warmth and fellowship that often follow catastrophes. He offers examples from this volume's chapters of "rituals of gathering" that brought together people in neighborhood communities and efforts to become part of a larger communal whole by joining with other New Yorkers in conversations and projects related to the city's future. Yet as Das Gupta makes clear in her contribution (and Erikson also suggests), the twin towers disaster did not produce a monolithic community of survivors in New York City or a "city of comrades." Class, ethnic, and racial divisions, among others, constitute what has been called the "terrain of disaster" and have structured not only the dilemmas and difficulties New Yorkers faced after September 11, 2001, but the resources available as they sought to cope with the aftereffects.

THE NEW YORK CONTEXT

If this book is about the social effects of the WTC attack, it is also about New York City and urban change. Indeed, it is useful to place the attack in the context of other disasters that have occurred in the city in the past and to note pertinent features—economic as well as demographic—that characterized New York at the time of the September 11 tragedy.

In one sense, the collapse of the twin towers can be seen as the latest in a long line of disasters that have struck the city throughout its history. New York, as historians remind us, has withstood natural and manmade disasters before. In the nineteenth century, for example, the cholera epidemic of 1832 killed 3,513 people over a period of six weeks—at a time when the total population of the city was not much more than 200,000. Half the entire population fled the city for fear of being infected. Three years later a fire destroyed almost seven hundred buildings—virtually all of downtown Manhattan. The insurance claims were so huge that twenty-three of the city's twenty-six fire insurance companies went into bankruptcy (Mandell 2001).

In the early twentieth century several terrible disasters shocked the city. On June 15, 1904, the *General Slocum*, a wooden excursion steamer taking German and German American members of St. Mark's Evangelical Lutheran Church on its annual Sunday school outing, caught fire in the East River. Some fifteen minutes later, when the captain beached the floating inferno off the Bronx shore, the fire had caused the death—mostly by drowning—of 1,021 of the 1,331 passengers on board, most of them women and children. The old and rotten life preservers, fire hoses, and lifeboats proved useless—indeed, rotten life jackets dragged many straight to the bottom—and the crew, untrained in emergency procedures, put up only a token effort to fight the fire (O'Donnell 2003a). Seven years later, in March 1911, the Triangle Shirtwaist Factory fire became, as one historian puts it, "the fire of fires" in New York's memory—or as a recent book on the event states, "for ninety years the deadliest workplace disaster in New York history" (O'Donnell 2003a, 213; Von Drehle 2003, 3). In less than fifteen minutes after the fire began in the garment factory a block from Washington Square Park, 146 women were killed, many having jumped from open windows. And finally, there was what one historian calls "the first Wall Street bomb" on September 16, 1920—until 9/11, the city's worst terrorist disaster. As hundreds of workers poured onto the corner of Wall Street and Broad Street at their lunchtime break, a bomb exploded that killed about 30 people and injured 300; by the end of the year the death toll was up to 40. Radicals were blamed for the bombing, but despite dozens of arrests, the perpetrators were never found (Gage 2002).

The September 11, 2001, attack on the World Trade Center may be only one of many disasters that the city has withstood over time, but clearly it stands out in many ways. It has the distinction of being the worst terrorist disaster in the city's history and, of course, being masterminded by a terrorist organization from abroad and carried out by means of advanced modern technology. Erikson (1994, 141) has coined the term "new species of trouble" to describe a new category of events that specialists have come to call technological disasters, "meaning everything that can go wrong when systems fail, humans err, designs prove faulty, engines misfire, and so on." Erikson is particularly concerned with technological accidents that involve toxins that "pollute, befoul, and taint rather than cause wreckage" (144). One might say that September 11 is yet another, even newer, species of trouble. Given its scale, size, and location in a quintessentially global city, September 11 was also a truly global event as people all over the world were able to watch much of it on television—including the collapse of the towers—as it actually happened. "The iconic image of September 11," the city planner M. Christine Boyer (2002, 119) has written, "may live in the images recycled again and again in 90 hours of nonstop television coverage: two commercial airlines flying into the quarter-mile high Twin Towers, simultaneously causing both towers and planes to explode in an all-consuming fire.... [Then] one tower was no longer there, and then—horror upon horror—the other was gone."

For the analysis in this volume, what is key is that the WTC attack occurred at a specific moment in New York City's development, thereby shaping the responses and reactions to it. By 2000, New York's population had passed the eight million mark—the largest number in the city's history. Given the mass immigration of the past four decades—in the main, from Latin America, Asia, and the Caribbean—the population is now more diverse than ever. Over one-third of New Yorkers are foreign-born, and the city is extraordinarily heterogeneous, home to large numbers from a wide array of nations and cultures. A new ethnic-racial hierarchy is evolving as New York has become what is sometimes called a "majority minority" city. In 2000, 35 percent of New Yorkers were non-Hispanic white, down from 63 percent thirty years before; Asians had reached 10 percent of the citywide total; Hispanics made up 27 percent, and non-Hispanic blacks 26 percent. Virtually every sector of the city has been affected by the huge immigrant influx, from schools to hospitals and churches, and new immigrant neighborhoods have sprouted in all the boroughs, as have new ethnic occupational niches (see Foner 2000, 2001; Waldinger 1996). The particular difficulties facing South Asian taxi drivers and Chinese immigrant garment workers after September 11 are the theme of two of the book's chapters; the hardships endured by Arab Muslims are highlighted in another; and attitudes toward Dominicans, the city's largest immigrant group, come into the analysis of Belle Harbor because Dominicans were the main victims of the plane crash that devastated that community only two months after September 11.

At the time of the attack New York City was a place not only of astounding ethnic and racial diversity but of stark inequalities of wealth, which had grown in recent years to what one historian calls "Brobdingnagian proportions" (Wallace 2002, 213). In 2000, according to census data, more than one-quarter of New York City households had incomes under $20,000 while 14 percent had incomes over $100,000 (Gurian and Gurian, n.d.). Manhattan had the distinction of being the U.S. county with the highest disparity of income in the nation: the top fifth of Manhattan households received more than fifty times as much income as the bottom fifth (Beveridge 2003). September 11 came at the beginning of a recession, after a boom time in the mid- to late 1990s. Just how the attack and the recession are related—and how much employment losses after September 11 were due to the attack or due to the recession—are topics investigated in the volume in preparation by the Russell Sage Foundation economic effects working group. In this volume, several chapters on occupational groups—airline and garment workers, taxi drivers, and artists—suggest that the twin towers disaster exacerbated hardships or declines already being felt as a result of the economic downturn.

Since the recession continued in New York City into 2002 and 2003, we could also say that it accentuated the negative economic effects of September 11 in particular occupations.[3] Yet there were earlier positive trends in the larger city economy that also shaped the reaction to September 11. Garfinkel and his colleagues argue that the long period of economic growth and prosperity and declining crime in the 1990s mitigated the negative effects of the attack. Comparing the three waves of the Social Indicators Survey—1997, 1999 to 2000, and 2002—they find an overall improvement in most indicators of economic and health well-being over time; a higher proportion surveyed rated the city as a good place to live in 2002 than in 1999 to 2000 or in 1997. Despite the economic downturn after 2000 and the WTC attack, many New Yorkers were still feeling the afterglow of the pre–September 11 boom years, a period when they had significantly improved their living conditions. Had New York instead been experiencing a long decline in prosperity and living conditions when the attack took place, chapter 2 suggests, the responses to the survey might well have been very different.

These comments about the economy raise a larger question concerning the way social, economic, and political patterns in neighborhoods, occupations, and organizations shaped reactions to the attack on the World Trade Center—and in turn whether, and how, the attack led to changes in these patterns. In a broad sense, September 11 can be seen as part of an ongoing process of change in New York as societal events—including disasters—continue to transform the city. In the past, to mention three of the disasters previously noted, the *General Slocum* fire accelerated the dissolution of Little Germany in lower Manhattan; the Triangle Shirtwaist Factory fire resulted in the enactment of fire safety regulations, laws mandating improved working conditions, and a boost to the labor movement; and the Wall Street bomb in 1920 justified a renewed campaign against radicals (Gage 2002; O'Donnell 2003a; Von Drehle 2003). Of course, disasters need not lead to change at all, or they may promote only superficial or insignificant changes; they may even encourage resistance to change (Hoffman 1999, 311). For those cases in which substantial change does occur, the anthropologist Susanna Hoffman (1999, 316) sets out a number of key questions: "Do the changes represent simple shifts in old patterns or utter rifts? Did the calamity initiate wholly new developments or merely accelerate processes already underway? Did the changes permeate the entire populace or subsume a certain few?" In her own study of an earthquake on the Greek island of Thera in the 1950s, she finds that the disaster exacerbated the island depopulation that already had been taking place and thereby set in motion a series of additional changes—a scenario echoed in a number of chapters in this volume on the effects of September 11. Whether the WTC attack accelerated ongoing change or led to entirely new developments, and whether it aggravated existing problems or created new ones, are central questions in many of the chapters.

THE IMPACT ON RESIDENTIAL AND ETHNIC COMMUNITIES

A broad range of residential communities in the New York area were hard hit by the collapse of the WTC towers, owing to either their proximity to the site or the large number of victims who had lived in them. In his account of the *General Slocum* fire, Edward O'Donnell (2003a, 214) calls it a concentrated tragedy because the great majority of the victims were from a single parish and lived within a forty-block area in Manhattan. The WTC disaster could be said to be a dispersed tragedy in that clusters of victims were located throughout the five boroughs and surrounding suburbs. Within New York City the area with the most victims was the Upper East Side, home to many high-end employees in the financial industry, followed by several Staten Island neighborhoods where hundreds of firefighters and police officers live (Newman 2002). Outside of the city, several affluent New Jersey communities lost many residents, one of them the focus of the journalist Gail Sheehy's account in *Middletown, America: One Town's Passage from Trauma to Hope* (2003).

Yet it is not just a question of the number of victims. Several neighborhoods in lower Manhattan that bordered or were close to the World Trade Center were badly shaken: residents had been forced to abandon their homes and, on return, had to cope with a variety of strains and disruptions. Clearly, location and geographical contours are important in understanding the effects of the attack on residential communities, as are a host of other contextual factors, including the history of the area, its patterns of development, and its demographic composition.

Two residential neighborhoods were closest to the World Trade Center—Battery Park City and Tribeca. All of the residents of Battery Park City and over one thousand in Tribeca were evacuated on September 11. When they returned days, weeks, or months later, their homes were caked in dust; streets in both neighborhoods were blocked for months. Yet in "Disaster at the Doorstep: Battery Park City and Tribeca Respond to the Events of 9/11," Philip Kasinitz, Gregory Smithsimon, and Binh Pok note that within a year after the attack, the two downtown communities were responding in different ways. One of the great benefits of comparative studies is that they "increase the 'visibility' of one structure by contrasting it with another" (Bendix 1964, 17).

The comparison of Battery Park City and Tribeca dramatically highlights the role of geography as well as the very nature of the communities and their organization in shaping the responses to the disaster.

There were, of course, a number of similarities. In both places there was unity in adversity as residents joined together in the immediate aftermath in face-to-face action and in groups and began to talk to neighbors, in their homes and in public, in ways they had not done before. In both places the response led to a general upsurge in local civic activity as established organizations took on new roles or were revitalized and new groups were created; some of the issues raised were similar too, in particular environmental and cleanup concerns. But there were also marked differences. Tribeca's recovery, Kasinitz and his colleagues argue, was remarkable, especially compared to Battery Park City. Unlike Battery Park City, there was no exodus of residents in Tribeca after September 11. Nor were deep discounts in rents required to lure new residents. After a few months rents and housing prices began to rise; by 2002 they were again among the highest in the city. Moreover, these authors report, a year after the attack September 11 no longer permeated community consciousness in Tribeca the way it did in Battery Park City. The twin towers disaster led to new divisions in Battery Park City between long-term residents and the many newcomers, who did not share the bonding experience of having gone through the disaster; in Tribeca, Kasinitz and his colleagues argue, September 11 gave new focus and energy to what had been a fairly unorganized community of business owners and residents. Post–September 11 developments accelerated the gentrification trends already under way in Tribeca as upscale restaurants expanded and the conversion of lofts to residential spaces continued apace.[4]

One reason for the different recovery process in these two communities had to do with geography: Tribeca residents were not, like those in Battery Park City, cut off from the rest of the city by the destruction of the towers and the excavation efforts. Also, the communities have dissimilar histories. Battery Park City is a brand-new planned neighborhood that prior to September 2001, the authors argue, was functionally a gated community. Because it has few street-level businesses, many residents used to do their shopping in the World Trade Center Mall. In contrast, Tribeca, a community of lofts and expensive apartments in a former manufacturing and wholesaling area, houses many businesses, including restaurants and art galleries. Before September 11, Battery Park City, in the words of the authors, turned its back on the city, while Tribeca generally looked north to Soho and Greenwich Village and turned its back on the World Trade Center. These contrasting features help explain the different reactions in these two communities to post–September 11 policy initiatives. With its many high-end stores and restaurants, Tribeca benefited from the "recovery through shopping" promotions and cultural events sponsored by local government in the weeks and months after September 11, which were seen in the community as healing. In contrast, when urban planners and redevelopment officials attempted to decrease Battery Park City's isolation with increased ferry service and plans to "roof over" West Street with a park, residents objected, as they did to programs intended to draw people to the neighborhood's public spaces and parks. These efforts increased the sense of violation among residents, who sought to maintain the community's isolation and separation from the city—the very reason so many had moved there in the first place.

In "Double Trauma in Belle Harbor: The Aftermath of September 11 and November 12 in the Rockaways," Melanie Hildebrandt offers a different kind of comparison that adds further insights into the response of residential communities to the attack. She examines how the history, geography, and demographic features of Belle Harbor and Breezy Point influenced reactions to September 11, and by comparing the responses to September 11 and to the devastating plane crash that occurred in Belle Harbor eight weeks later, she is able to show that the nature of the disaster itself led to particular results.

As she explains, September 11 hit the western Rockaway neighborhoods hard: over seventy residents (out of some twenty-three thousand) died in the terrorist attack on the World Trade Center, including many firefighters and financial service employees. Hildebrandt argues that despite the tragic losses—and the dozens of funerals and memorial services in the weeks following September 11—the Rockaway communities she studied became more "cohesive, supportive, and unified," largely owing to their cultural and social organization. Breezy Point and Belle Harbor are part of New York City, but these geographically isolated, middle-class, virtually all-white beach communities have a small-town—or as some would say, insular—character. Often dubbed "firefighter country" because so many residents and their relatives have worked for the New York City Fire Department, Hildebrandt notes the informal code of reciprocity and extensive support network that were already in place among firefighter families, as well as the extended kin ties among Irish Americans (the largest ethnic group), who have lived in the area for generations. Furthermore, the Rockaway communities include a web of community organizations, churches, and (in Breezy Point) synagogues.

If, as Hildebrandt contends, the structure and culture of the community helped residents move on after September 11—and strengthened community bonds through shared grieving and memory—the airplane crash that occurred two months later created tensions and divisions. Mainly, the tensions had to do with the nature of the disaster and its aftermath. Unlike the September 11 attack, the crash—which killed all 260 (mostly Dominican) passengers and five on the ground, destroyed a dozen homes, and damaged many others—disrupted the physical space of Belle Harbor. Indeed, the Catholic church, which had played such an important role in healing after September 11, was cordoned off and unavailable for the first days. The community had gained positive recognition after September 11—the firefighters from the community who died were honored as heroes, and the civilians as innocent victims of terrorism—but after the plane crash residents felt treated with disdain by U.S. government officials as they tried to make sense of what had happened. Moreover, resentments developed within the community over lawsuits and insurance settlements for property damage and loss.

Plans for the memorial for the plane crash victims created additional tensions. Memorializing the victims of flight 587 came to be seen as affecting only a few individuals rather than the whole community. Moreover, the plans for the memorial involved not just Rockaway residents but Dominican families who had lost relatives in the plane disaster and were pushing for a memorial on the very site of the crash. Never a racially tolerant place, many Belle Harbor residents resented the incursion of nonwhites into the community. Hildebrandt notes the "declining sympathy" for the Dominican families visiting the site to place wreaths or flowers on a makeshift memorial, as well as angry letters to the local newspaper about building a memorial on the site of the crash. Hildebrandt concludes, however, on a positive note: despite the internal fissures that developed and the emotional strains of dealing with the double trauma, Belle Harbor and Breezy Point, she argues, have not been torn apart or destroyed, but remain, for the most part, cohesive and united. Indeed, "there is nothing to suggest that the glue that has bound these communities together for generations has changed in any fundamental way."

Virtually every ethnic and racial group in New York City was affected by September 11, but Muslims were especially vulnerable. Of course, Muslims were not immune to stereotyping and discrimination before the attack, but as Mehdi Bozorgmehr and Anny Bakalian (2003) point out, the events of September 11, involving Muslim suicide bombers, brought the Middle Eastern conflict to American soil; Arabs and Muslims were seen as a threat to national security and targeted by a series of federal administrative measures. Starting immediately after the attack, Arab and Muslim immigrants became subject to detention. If suspected of terrorism, they could be kept without charge for an extended period of time, denied bond, and their attorney-client communications disregarded. Most of those detained were housed in a Brooklyn detention center and the Passaic County Jail in Paterson, New Jersey, with Pakistanis comprising the largest number of detainees, followed by Egyptians, Turks, and Yemenis. Other federal initiatives included an entry-exit registration system obligating aliens from twenty-six countries, all predominantly Muslim, to be registered, fingerprinted, and photographed on their arrival and periodically afterward; special registration requiring male citizens of a number of predominantly Muslim countries who were older than sixteen to register with the

Immigration and Naturalization Service (INS) if they had entered the United States before September 10, 2002, and planned to remain at least until December 16, 2002; and "voluntary" FBI interviews with several thousand men who had entered the United States between January 2000 and November 2001 from countries suspected of al Qaeda presence or activity (Bozorgmehr and Bakalian 2003).[5]

How these federal initiatives and directives—and new fears of Muslims and hostility toward them—affected Muslims themselves is the subject of chapter 5, "Constructing the 'True Islam' in Hostile Times: The Impact of 9/11 on Arab Muslims in Jersey City." Jersey City, just two miles west of Manhattan across the Hudson River and a ten-minute train ride away, is home to a sizable Arab Muslim community. (Jersey City is, of course, in the state of New Jersey, but its location, commercial and residential development, and close ties to New York City have recently led some to refer to it as a "sixth borough."[6]) The Arab Muslims whom Jennifer Bryan talked with during two years of field research in Jersey City experienced intensified levels of hostility after September 11. She describes the impact of detentions, investigations, and raids, as well as hate crimes and assaults, including physical violence against women and children and attempts in one neighborhood to close down a mosque.

In response to the hostility and hate crimes, Bryan argues that there was a swing toward traditionalism among Jersey City's Arab Muslims. Many emphasized making the Muslim community stronger—and changing the way Islam has been represented and understood in American society—by adhering more strictly to religious practices that reflect their sense of the "true Islam." There was renewed interest among many Arab Muslims in close readings of the Qur'an, traditional weddings, and the religious rules regulating social interactions. The emphasis on practicing "the true Islam," on the one hand, strengthened community ties; on the other hand, it created tensions and exacerbated the rift between more traditional and progressive Muslims. Whether the response of Jersey City Arab Muslims to the aftermath of the WTC attack is typical of Arab Muslims in other parts of the New York area and the five boroughs and whether hostility toward them was as virulent and extensive elsewhere are questions that Bryan's ethnographic study of one community cannot answer. Clearly, further research is required to address these questions as well as to explore whether the turn to traditionalism will persist in Jersey City itself.

THE IMPACT ON OCCUPATIONAL GROUPS

In the weeks and months after September 11, reports about the firefighters and police officers who died in the attack or were involved in the recovery efforts were prominent in the media. Other occupational groups in the city that were hard hit by the event received much less attention, including many businesses located near the WTC site, such as retail stores, restaurants, and a host of corporate firms. The chapters in part III focus on a subsample of the occupational groups that were affected. They give voice to the difficulties experienced by workers in a variety of fields—ranging from immigrant workers in low-skilled, poorly paid, and insecure jobs to high-level professionals—as they coped with the aftershocks of the disaster. To what extent did the WTC attack and its aftermath accelerate changes that were already under way in specific occupational sectors or exacerbate preexisting problems or conflicts? How did the structure of the particular occupation influence the response to September 11 and subsequent recovery? Did September 11 lead to new difficulties or problems among particular groups of workers or professionals who, for example, lost their jobs or income, had to cope with their own and others' trauma, or faced new or intensified hostility, owing to their ethnicity, religion, or national origin?

Airline workers are among the hardest-hit occupational groups discussed in this book. If Belle Harbor residents experienced a double whammy, the airline workers described by William Kornblum and Steven Lang in chapter 6, "The Impact of 9/11 on the New York City Airline Industry," were subject to a triple punch: the restructuring of the airline industry, economic recession, and the attack on September 11. As Kornblum and Lang argue, corporate reorganization and downsizing meant that even before the WTC attack the major carriers were laying off workers; the recession that began prior to September 11 was causing job insecurity and unemployment as well. When the collapse of the twin towers led to additional losses in the industry and even greater unemployment, the economic impact, in Kornblum and Lang's words, was swift and severe. On September 11 itself, the airports were immediately closed; when they reopened, passenger traffic plummeted. By just three months after the attack, approximately 140,000 airline workers in the nation had lost their jobs, some 10,000 of them in the New York area. A year after the event, more than half of the airline workers in the New York metropolitan area who had been displaced were still unemployed.

If the attack on the World Trade Center aggravated existing problems in the airline industry, it also created new ones for the workers, especially for those who were let go after the attack. Kornblum and Lang tell a grim story—the human experiences behind the summary statistics. For those laid off as well as for those who continued on the job, there was grief over lost friends: many of the flight attendants interviewed in the study knew one or more of the flight attendants who had been killed in the attacks. There was the fear of new attacks on the ground or in the air. Displaced workers suffered a loss of income and, for many, loss of medical benefits and health insurance; many suffered from physical conditions associated with increased stress and financial insecurity. Those who found other work generally had to settle for jobs at lower wages. Moreover, displaced workers confronted limits on their eligibility for relief assistance, isolation from their former occupational communities after being laid off, and government unwillingness to assist labor unions' efforts to secure employment for displaced members after the attacks.

Kornblum and Lang's analysis reveals that airline workers' sense of neglect—of being "tainted, isolated, shunted aside, superannuated, not eligible for emergency relief, not considered worthy of special consideration"—has been aggravated by the public adulation of the firefighters, police officers, emergency workers, and other emergency crews at Ground Zero as heroes. The government response to the plight of the airline companies has compounded that sense of neglect. Congressional leaders and members of the Bush administration used the terrorist attacks of September 11 as the primary justification for a massive and highly public bailout of the airline corporations. Airline workers felt left out in the cold. Many of those displaced faced the prospect of being shut out of the airline industry forever or, if rehired, having to work for the new lower-cost airlines—at lower wages and without the benefits they had been accustomed to as unionized workers.

Chinatown's garment workers were also devastated by the twin towers disaster, as Margaret M. Chin shows in chapter 7, "Moving On: Chinese Garment Workers After 9/11." Like the airline industry, Chinatown's garment industry was already in trouble, and September 11 accelerated the downward trends. The industry had long been struggling with overseas competition, and in the 1990s the rapid spread of dot-com firms also pushed out many factories in the area. After September 11, Chinatown's garment industry had to cope with many problems, including delivery delays caused by increased bridge and tunnel security, street closures, and the rerouting of traffic. As a result, a massive number of orders were canceled, continuing through 2002. Six weeks after the attack every Chinatown factory that had contact with the garment workers' union had laid off workers or reduced hours. By September 2002, 75 shops had closed and 3,500 Chinese garment workers were out of work. Gaining access to September 11 relief funds was difficult since those who worked and lived north of Canal Street were ineligible for government aid in the first few months (80 percent of Chinatown's garment shops were north of this disaster zone), and the complicated application procedures were daunting. Chinese garment workers, nearly all women, turned to unemployment insurance, help from children or other relatives, and part-time work in the factories as their incomes fell dramatically. On average, the annual household income of the workers in Chin's study declined by almost half, to $16,000, after September 11. Over half of the husbands were employed in restaurants and a few other businesses that were also hard hit by the disaster.

Chin shows that the garment workers' loss of income had ripple effects throughout the local Chinatown economy. The thousands of Chinese garment workers—about half of whom lived outside of Chinatown—not only worked in the community but also shopped and used services there. In Chin's words, the workers "made the ethnic economy hum." When garment workers lost their jobs or had less income, Chinatown's stores, banks, hair salons, and other services suffered (as they did in other Chinese communities in the city). Moreover, street closings in Chinatown, the elimination of parking spaces to accommodate extra police and security vehicles (still in effect in the spring of 2004), and of course the disappearance of the WTC towers reduced the number of tourists, shoppers, and restaurant patrons so critical to the ethnic economy.

Whether Chinatown's garment industry will rebound or sink further into decline is an open question. Meanwhile, Chin suggests, the disaster has affected how Chinese garment workers look for work and made it clear to them that they cannot depend only on co-ethnic ties. Indeed, her findings about the limits of co-ethnic ties in the period after September 11 lead Chin to reevaluate the ethnic enclave model, which has been prominent in discussions of Chinatown in the scholarly literature. In good times, she argues, the ethnic enclave provided jobs with flexible hours and health benefits for Chinese immigrant women without English skills; when disaster hit, the ethnic enclave proved to be a liability. It fostered dependence on co-ethnic networks that no longer carried useful information, and it did not provide leads to work outside of Chinese neighborhoods or opportunities to learn English.

For the taxi drivers at the center of Monisha Das Gupta's chapter, "Of Hardship and Hostility: The Impact of 9/11 on New York City Taxi Drivers," it was not a question of losing jobs or being forced into part-time work, but of suffering a drop in income, increased financial worries, and a rise in hostility from passengers. Das Gupta analyzes the impact of the WTC attack in the context of structural features of the industry, in particular the leasing system, which requires most drivers to make advance payments to garages or brokers no matter what fares they earn. In the immediate aftermath of September 11, taxi drivers were hurt by bridge and tunnel closings, road closings for security reasons and emergency work, increased traffic, and a downturn in air travel (and trips to the airports) and tourism. A year later the drivers Das Gupta studied still had not recovered from their initial income losses. Partly responsible for their plight was the recession, which reduced demand for their services, but also critical was the leasing system's demand that they pay costs up front without assurance of making back what they paid. In the first weeks after September 11, many drivers depleted their savings and spiraled into debt; with accumulated debt added to depressed earnings, many still had not recovered from the initial blow even many months after the attack.

To make matters worse, taxi drivers, like Chinatown garment workers, confronted numerous obstacles in obtaining disaster assistance, including, initially, being ineligible for FEMA (Federal Emergency Management Agency) aid because their income was not solely dependent on the delineated disaster area in lower Manhattan. Even after the geographical definition of the affected area was changed, other requirements, such as citizenship or legal residency, were problematic for some drivers, and the paperwork was overwhelming. Taxi drivers were disillusioned and discouraged not only when they were turned away for assistance but when they received little public recognition for providing free rides to family members of victims, rescue workers, and other volunteers at Ground Zero.

Far from being praised for their role in the recovery process, taxi drivers, the vast majority of them Muslim, found that, like the Jersey City Muslims in Jennifer Bryan's study, they were victims of an anti-Muslim backlash in the wake of the twin towers disaster. South Asian and Muslim drivers, as Das Gupta puts it, "did not feel drawn into the community of sufferers, even though they responded with a sense of unity, purpose, and service. . . . The 9/11 attacks, seen from the drivers' perspective, solidified rather than dissolved the lines drawn along ethnic, religious, national, and racial difference" (this volume, 234). Many South Asian and Middle Eastern Muslim and Sikh drivers stayed away from work in the first week after the disaster, and some stayed away even longer, out of fear of reprisals for the attack. When they returned to work, the majority of the drivers surveyed between July and November 2002 reported some form of overt hostility, including verbal harassment, physical threats, and damage to their cabs. Drivers were used to being ordered around by passengers, and Das Gupta argues that city policies instituted in the 1990s had promoted negative images of cab drivers. Still, drivers experienced "the overt hostility directed at them by some passengers [after September 11] as new."

Visual artists seem like a world apart from taxi drivers and garment workers, yet as Julia Rothenberg and William Kornblum show in chapter 9, "New York's Visual Art World After 9/11," they too experienced economic losses. In what is by now a familiar theme, when the planes hit the WTC towers, many visual artists were already suffering from the economic recession, which had begun to weaken the art market and the industries, such as graphics and web design, that were sources of employment. The suicide bombings worsened the situation. Admittedly, established artists, commercial art dealers, and auction houses rebounded fairly quickly after the attack. However, gallery owners located near the WTC towers experienced severe losses, and younger, less-established artists were hard hit with a double blow: not only were there further declines in the demand for their art, but, perhaps more important, they faced a loss of job opportunities in the sectors of the economy on which they relied for their daily bread, such as restaurants and bars. Rothenberg and Korn-blum contend that the combination of the events of September 11 and the recession has increased polarization and stratification in the visual arts com-munity: on one end are the most well established artists, galleries, museums, and nonprofit organizations, and on the other end are the more innovative galleries, museums, nonprofits, and artists who depend on them, which fared much worse after September 11.

September 11 also influenced artists' creative work, which was fed by what Rothenberg and Kornblum call an almost insatiable demand for visual repre-sentation of the terrorist attacks. The response has been an outpouring of artwork dealing directly or indirectly with the events of September 11, from painting and sculpture to artworks that incorporate video images. Of course, the creative output following the disaster—and produced in direct reaction to it—went way beyond the visual arts. Given that New York City is the cultural capital of the nation, this is not surprising. In November 2003, theaters in the city (virtually all of them off- or off-off-Broadway) were mounting, were about to mount, or had mounted in the past year some twenty-five productions about the September 11 attacks. Dance productions were created and performed in New York in response to the attack, and more than two dozen film and video documentaries chronicled the attack itself or the reaction to it of New Yorkers and New York institutions. Just a year after the towers collapsed, September 11 had, by one account, spawned more books than any other single news event in American history. By the fall of 2002, Amazon.com had nearly seven hun-dred 9/11-related titles in stock, including anthologies produced by news orga-nizations, memoirs, and children's books.[7]

Given the nature of their work, the mental health professionals who are the focus of chapter 10, "The Psychological Treatment of Trauma and the Trauma of Psychological Treatment: Talking to Psychotherapists About 9/11," faced a different set of dilemmas than the other workers profiled in this volume. Karen Seeley tells a moving story of individual and collective trauma, and also of innovation and change. On a broad institutional level, Project Liberty, a feder-ally funded disaster mental health program designed by the New York State Office of Mental Health, was, as Seeley notes, "strikingly different from its previous initiatives." Among other things, Project Liberty trained thousands of mental health professionals in disaster mental health and community outreach and extended free counseling to anyone affected by the attack. Psychoanalytic institutes and mental health organizations acted as clearinghouses to meet the demand for psychological treatment. But many of the individual psychothera-pists Seeley interviewed had little sense of what to do as they tried to treat survivors and victims' families suffering from trauma (some of whom still suf-fered from severe distress more than a year after the attacks). A number of psychotherapists, especially those who volunteered in the first days after the attack, spoke of making it up as they went along. In general, many therapists whom Seeley interviewed "found themselves delivering mental health services they had never been formally trained to provide, to populations they had never been trained to treat, in a catastrophic situation for which they had never been prepared."

Not only was the work itself emotionally wrenching for these therapists as they listened to tales of anguish, grief, and trauma, but they were in a new kind of situation: the therapeutic boundaries between patient and therapist were blurred by the fact that both had been emotionally affected by the same attack. Indeed, several therapists had family members who had been injured in the attack or witnessed it from their offices. A number of therapists told Seeley that it was difficult for them to keep their composure in front of patients; some talked of being dazed, exhausted, numb, and sometimes left in tears after listening to patients tell their stories. In this context, Seeley notes, many modified their usual mode of practice, and some changed their understanding of the psychotherapist's role. Whether these modifications will lead to longer-term clinical shifts among individual therapists is uncertain. Yet in the end, Seeley suggests, the experience of treating trauma after September 11 may well have long-term effects on the mental health profession, which may rethink the scope and implications of therapy and the role of psychotherapists in times of disaster. Certainly, the experience is likely to stimulate broader and more urgent clinical interest in the treatment of trauma and traumatic loss, the consequences of terrorism for individuals and communities, and finding ways to ensure adequate therapeutic response in the event of future catastrophes.

THE IMPACT ON ORGANIZATIONS

Inevitably, the chapters on residential and ethnic communities and occupational groups discuss the role of organizations in the recovery from the September 11 attacks—from churches and community groups in Belle Harbor and Battery Park City to the labor unions and workers' associations representing airline employees, garment workers, and taxi drivers. The organizations themselves do not occupy center stage in these studies, yet clearly they deserve their own close analysis. Understanding how organizations responded to the disaster in New York is important to a full appreciation of the social effects of the attack. Some organizations changed, if only in subtle ways, as a result of the disaster. Moreover, a number of new organizations and new organizational forms developed, such as Project Liberty, the program created to offer free counseling after the attack.

A dramatic example of organizational response to the disaster—and of organizational resilience—is provided by Daniel Beunza and David Stark in chapter 11, "Resolving Identities: Successive Crises in a Trading Room After

9/11." Their chapter focuses on the trading room of a major international investment bank that they refer to pseudonymously as International Securities; it
was located in the World Financial Center, right next to the World Trade
Center. Beunza and Stark had the unique opportunity to study the organization's response to attack because they had been doing research in the trading
room for two years before September 11. On that day, shortly after the first
terrorist-piloted plane hit Tower One, the 160 traders in the organization evacuated their offices; by the evening of September 11, it was unclear how and
when the trading room could resume operations. In just six days, however,
when the New York Stock Exchange reopened on September 17, the traders at
International Securities were trading again—in a basement in a New Jersey
suburban corporate park that, on the day of the disaster, had contained no
workstations or desks and had no "connectivity."

Responsiveness, Beunza and Stark argue, was a combination of anticipation
and improvisation aided by the structure of the organization, with a flat hierarchy and competing subgroups. Before September 11, this structure, they contend, was a resource in exploiting the uncertainties of the market; afterward,
it was a resource in coping with the more difficult uncertainties created by
the attack (see also Beunza and Stark 2003). In the New Jersey location, the
traders combined old and new technologies and were flexible about changing
roles to solve problems: some became clerks, others worked as manual operators, and still others shared cable to the New York Stock Exchange. At the
same time, the traders sought to reconstruct the familiar order in their New
Jersey outpost: for example, they arranged their desks to reproduce the layout
of their office in the World Financial Center.

Over time, Beunza and Stark note, the exhilaration of meeting the challenges of rebuilding gave way to the realities of long commutes and continued
anxieties. The circumstances in New Jersey began to threaten traders' identities as sophisticated professionals, and in December 2001, with the bank's ap-
proval, a group of them left to establish themselves as a temporary trading
room in midtown Manhattan. What could have caused a serious crisis was
averted, however, by a leadership style that managed ambiguities, as Beunza
and Stark put it. Management presented the midtown trading room as a short-
term policy and emphasized the commitment to return to the World Financial
Center; at the same time, the leaders hedged their bets by setting up a facility
in Hoboken, only a five-minute ferryboat ride from the World Trade Center,
in case it proved impossible to return to Manhattan.

As it turned out, the traders were able to move back to their old trading
room at the World Financial Center in March 2002. They did not, however,
return to the status quo. For one thing, the firm now had a backup facility in
Hoboken, which could be fully operative within thirty minutes of an evacuation from the World Financial Center. Beunza and Stark also hint at some

structural changes in the organization—for example, a decrease in communication across desks. And of course, it was impossible to avoid daily reminders of the attack or the emptiness of the site. The traders now did their jobs in a room that overlooked Ground Zero, and they had to walk alongside or around the WTC site on the way to work.

If the tale of the International Securities trading room is one of organizational resilience and survival in response to the attack, "Public Deliberations After 9/11" analyzes a different kind of organizational innovation. In chapter 12, Francesca Polletta and Lesley Wood focus on "Imagine New York" and "Listening to the City," two public deliberative efforts designed to solicit input into the redevelopment of lower Manhattan. Imagine New York was spearheaded by the Municipal Arts Society, and Listening to the City by the Civic Alliance, a coalition of environmental, planning, and civic groups formed after September 11 and led by the Regional Plan Association. Certainly, organized public forums of this type, set up to influence the rebuilding process, are a new response to disaster in New York. Their emergence was partly a result of the vast scale of the disaster and the various economic and political stakes involved in the rebuilding, but also playing a role were the increase in civic, neighborhood, environmental, and planning organizations in recent decades and a growing interest in deliberative democracy. Whatever the reason for their development, the forums organized by these two groups attracted thousands of participants—over four thousand, for example, attended a daylong Listening to the City event at the Jacob Javits Center on July 20, 2002. Most of the participants did not think they would have much impact on decision-makers; rather, they were seeking an opportunity to talk about issues that were important to them with people different from themselves.

Whether these groups did in fact have any influence on the design process remains in dispute. As Polletta and Wood point out, the lower cost and low-tech format of Imagine New York seem to have made it easier for its organizers to maintain an ongoing campaign for public involvement.[8] Even if, in the end, the groups have little impact on how lower Manhattan is developed, the very fact of their existence and the public deliberation around the WTC site may have long-term effects on what Polletta and Wood call the "landscape of citizen participation in urban planning" in New York City. In one scenario they present, there may be efforts to substitute public deliberative forums for more traditional modes of resident input, such as community board meetings or city council hearings. The danger is that such forums, even if institutionalized, may simply provide the illusion of participation if no mechanisms are provided to keep decisionmakers accountable for the recommendations that come out of them. Another possibility is that civic and advocacy groups will increasingly turn to public deliberative forums to represent the priorities being given short shrift in development plans.

THE LEGACY OF SEPTEMBER 11

Speculation about the future, of course, is a notably risky business. After all, ten years ago no one would have predicted the attack on September 11, 2001, and equally unforeseen social, political, and economic developments—to say nothing of other disasters—may be in store in the years ahead. What the chapters in this volume make clear is that the events of September 11 set in motion a chain of responses and reactions that have altered the New York urban landscape in numerous ways. Unlike some earlier disasters, such as the *General Slocum* fire, September 11 is unlikely to fade rapidly and almost completely from public memory.[9] As time goes on, the practice of dividing the world into pre- and post–September 11 periods will probably disappear, yet the scale of the event, the televised and film and video memories, and the planned memorial are bound to keep the twin towers disaster alive in the public consciousness. It is also likely that some of the social consequences of the attack, including many discussed in this book, will continue, at least in the near future, to shape institutions, organizations, occupations, and residential communities in New York City. The chapters in this volume offer rich insights into the way a broad spectrum of New Yorkers and New York communities were influenced by the September 11 attack in the first year or so after it occurred. It remains for future studies to determine whether—and how—the effects examined in these pages leave a longer-term legacy.

NOTES

1. These figures on injuries and hospitalizations, as well as the number of rescue and recovery workers, are from Gail Sheehy (2003, 330). Some newspaper stories put the estimate of rescue and recovery workers much higher.
2. See also Caroline Tarnovsky (2002), who did research on the impact of September 11 on the day laborers she had been studying at a Brooklyn site.
3. The thirty-two-month New York City recession lasted from January 2001 through August 2003. For an analysis of the economic impact of this recession and 9/11 on low-wage workers in New York City, see James Parrott and Oliver Cooke (2004), a revised version of which will appear in the volume edited by Howard Chernick (2005) on the economic effects of September 11 on New York City.
4. See Setha Low and others (2002), whose report on Battery Park City for the social effects working group detailed, among other things, divisions between new and old residents in the community and the changed organizational landscape.
5. Mehdi Bozorgmehr and Anny Bakalian (2003) and Gary Gerstle (2003) place the current policies against Arab and Muslim immigrants in the historical context of the actions taken against "enemy aliens" in times of war in earlier eras.
6. The title of the 2003 roundtable sponsored by the Steven L. Newman Real Estate Institute at Baruch College, City University of New York, was "Jersey City: New York's Sixth Borough?"

7. For a list of the books, film documentaries, museum exhibitions, theatrical productions, and visual and performance art in New York in response to 9/11, see *Gotham Gazette* (n.d.).
8. On the influence of civic associations in the rebuilding of the WTC site, see Arielle Goldberg (2003), an expanded and revised form of which will appear in the volume being prepared by the working group studying the politics of recovery from September 11.
9. The historian Edward O'Donnell (2003a; 2003b) suggests several reasons why the *General Slocum* disaster was soon all but forgotten, in contrast to the Triangle Shirtwaist Factory fire, which came to be remembered as "the fire of fires" in New York's history, even if it claimed far fewer lives. One was that the Triangle fire was linked with the intense labor struggles of the day. The onset of World War I also contributed to the forgetting process: rabid anti-German sentiment erased public sympathy for anything German, including the victims of the *General Slocum* disaster. Newspaper articles about the annual June 15 memorial for the victims of the *General Slocum* fire stopped abruptly in 1914 and did not reappear until 1920, at which time the Triangle fire was achieving "iconic status as the city's most memorable blaze" (O'Donnell 2003b). In fact, O'Donnell notes, it was the attack on the World Trade Center that renewed interest in the *Slocum* story.

REFERENCES

Bendix, Reinhard. 1964. *Nation-Building and Citizenship*. New York: John Wiley.

Beunza, Daniel, and David Stark. 2003. "The Organization of Responsiveness: Innovation and Recovery in the Trading Rooms of Lower Manhattan." *Socioeconomic Review* 1: 135–64.

Beveridge, Andrew. 2003. "The Affluent of Manhattan." GothamGazette.com. Available at: www.gothamgazette.com/article/demographics/20030611/5/421 (accessed November 8, 2004).

Boyer, M. Christine. 2002. "Meditations on a Wounded Skyline and Its Stratigraphies of Pain." In *After the World Trade Center: Rethinking New York City*, edited by Michael Sorkin and Sharon Zukin. New York: Routledge.

Bozorgmehr, Mehdi, and Anny Bakalian. 2003. "The Impact of Post-9/11 Government Initiatives on Middle Eastern and South Asian Americans." Paper presented to the conference "Transcending Borders: Migration, Ethnicity, and Incorporation in an Age of Globalism." New York University, New York (November).

Chernick, Howard, ed. 2005. *Resilient City: The Economic Impact of 9/11*. New York: Russell Sage Foundation.

Durkheim, Émile. 1951. *Suicide: A Study in Sociology*. New York: Free Press.

Erikson, Kai. 1976. *Everything in Its Path: Destruction of Community in the Buffalo Creek Flood*. New York: Simon & Schuster.

———. 1994. *A New Species of Trouble: The Human Experience in Modern Disasters*. New York: W. W. Norton.

Foner, Nancy. 2000. *From Ellis Island to JFK: New York's Two Great Waves of Immigration*. New Haven, Conn., and New York: Yale University Press and Russell Sage Foundation.

————, ed. 2001. *New Immigrants in New York*. 2nd ed. New York: Columbia University Press.

Gage, Beverly. 2002. "The First Wall Street Bomb." In *After the World Trade Center: Rethinking New York City*, edited by Michael Sorkin and Sharon Zukin. New York: Routledge.

Gerstle, Gary. 2003. "The Immigrant as Threat to American Security: A Historical Perspective." Paper presented to the conference "Transcending Borders: Migration, Ethnicity, and Incorporation in an Age of Globalism." New York University, New York (November).

Goldberg, Arielle. 2003. "Civic Associations and the Rebuilding of the World Trade Center." Paper presented to the Working Group on New York City's Recovery from September 11. Russell Sage Foundation, New York (December).

Gotham Gazette. N.d. "The Focus on 9/11 in Art and Culture." GothamGazette.com. Available at: http://www.gothamgazette.com/rebuilding_nyc/topics/culture (accessed November 8, 2004).

Gurian, Craig, and Nico Gurian. N.d. "Wealth and Income Inequality." Antibiaslaw.com, a project of the Anti-Discrimination Center of Metro New York. Available at: http://antibiaslaw.com/demographics/wealthinequality.html (accessed November 9, 2004).

Haberman, Clyde. 2003. "NYC; Twilight Zone for ZIP Code at Ground Zero." *New York Times*, November 14, p. B1.

Hoffman, Susanna. 1999. "After Atlas Shrugs: Cultural Change or Persistence After a Disaster." In *The Angry Earth: Disaster in Anthropological Perspective*, edited by Anthony Oliver-Smith and Susanna Hoffman. New York: Routledge.

Low, Setha. 2002. "Spaces of Reflection, Recovery, and Resistance." In *After the World Trade Center: Rethinking New York City*, edited by Michael Sorkin and Sharon Zukin. New York: Routledge.

Low, Setha, Dana Taplin, Mike Lamb, and Mirele Goldsmith. 2002. "Battery Park City: An Ethnographic Field Study of the Community Impact of 9/11." Unpublished report submitted to the Social Effects Working Group on New York City's Recovery from September 11. New York: Russell Sage Foundation.

Luo, Michael. 2003. "At Ground Zero, a Stream of Commuters and Tears." *New York Times*, November 25, p. B1.

Mandell, Jonathan. 2001. "Looking to History." GothamGazette.com. Available at: www.gothamgazette.com/commentary/103.mandell.shtml (accessed November 8, 2004).

Newman, Andy. 2002. "Zones of Devastation from 9/11: Mapping the Victims by ZIP Code." *New York Times*, August 21, p. B1.

O'Donnell, Edward. 2003a. *Ship Ablaze: The Tragedy of the Steamboat General Slocum*. New York: Broadway Books.

————. 2003b. "The Fire, and the Forgetting." *New York Times*, June 8, p. 3.

Parrott, James, and Oliver Cooke. 2004. "The Economic Impact on Low-Wage Workers of 9/11 and the 2001 to 2003 Recession, with Comparisons to the 1989 to 1992 Recession in New York City." Paper presented to the conference "The Attack on the World Trade Center: Economic and Fiscal Impact on New York City." Russell Sage Foundation, New York (May).

Sheehy, Gail. 2003. *Middletown, America: One Town's Passage from Trauma to Hope.* New York: Random House.

Tarnovsky, Caroline. 2002. "Subjects for Anonymous Reasons: A Study of the Day Labor Community in Post-9/11 New York City." Unpublished report submitted to the Social Effects Working Group on New York City's Recovery from September 11. New York: Russell Sage Foundation.

Von Drehle, David. 2003. *Triangle: The Fire That Changed America.* New York: Atlantic Monthly Press.

Waldinger, Roger. 1996. *Still the Promised City? African Americans and New Immigrants in Postindustrial New York.* Cambridge, Mass.: Harvard University Press.

Wallace, Mike. 2002. "New York, New Deal." In *After the World Trade Center: Rethinking New York City*, edited by Michael Sorkin and Sharon Zukin. New York: Routledge.

CHAPTER 2

Vulnerability and Resilience: New Yorkers Respond to 9/11

Irwin Garfinkel, Neeraj Kaushal, Julien Teitler, and Sandra Garcia

THE TERRORIST attack on the World Trade Center (WTC) took the lives of nearly three thousand people in New York City, resulted in huge economic losses, intensified fears of international terrorism, and launched the "American war on terrorism."[1] The 9/11 attack and its continuing aftermath have disrupted, traumatized, and upturned the lives of many around the world.

In this chapter, we quantify a few of the effects of the WTC attack on the well-being of adults and children who live in New York City. Our study is based on the New York City Social Indicators Surveys (NYSIS), the third wave of which was conducted six months after the attacks. We cannot gauge the extent of loss or grief of the families who lost relatives in the attacks. The Social Indicators Survey sample is too small to capture the effects on those who suffered most directly and grievously. Similarly, the sample is too small to characterize the impact of 9/11 on residents of the small geographic areas that were most directly affected. The sample is better suited to describe the effects of the attack on representative New Yorkers and to quantify some of the effects on their well-being. More specifically, we use the survey results to answer the following questions: What proportion of adults suffered adverse effects? How many people lost jobs or had family members who lost jobs because of the attacks? How were children affected? Were the effects widespread or limited to particular groups? Did the effects persist half a year later?

Most important, this chapter places the effects of the attacks within the context of recent trends in the well-being of New Yorkers. We use data from the NYSIS conducted in 1997, 1999 to 2000, and 2002 to analyze the trends over time and special modules of the 2002 NYSIS to describe the effects of the WTC attack on New York City.

SURVEY DESCRIPTION

The New York Social Indicators Survey is a biennial survey of New York City residents. The survey is conducted by telephone with a representative sample of approximately 1,500 families from the five boroughs of the city. The first wave of the survey was conducted in 1997, followed by a second wave in 1999 to 2000 and a third wave in 2002. Each wave of NYSIS consisted of two parts. A core survey was designed to document individual and family well-being across multiple domains—economic, social, behavioral, and environmental. These core elements of the survey were kept identical from year to year to allow comparability over time. The second part of the survey consisted of a supplemental survey intended to address issues specific to each wave.

Six months after the attacks, the well-being of New York City residents could not be separated from the tumultuous event. The supplemental survey in the third wave therefore included questions about whether adults or children experienced any new health problems as a result of 9/11, and questions were also asked of those affected about whether they sought help and whether these effects persisted at the time of the 2002 interview. We also asked adults if they or their children experienced particular symptoms of anxiety and insecurity, such as having trouble sleeping and preferring to stay home. The supplemental survey investigated the immediate employment effects of the attacks on our representative sample.

The core survey is rich in individual characteristics such as age, race, ethnicity, immigration status, religion, income, marital status, family size, number of children, and place of residence. It also provides information on whether the respondent was a single parent. We use this information to identify more vulnerable groups.

The 2002 NYSIS was conducted between March and June 2002. In total, 1,501 adults were interviewed by telephone. Of them, 791 had children; they were asked about the health, behavior, and academic performance of one randomly selected child.[2] Interviews lasted an average of twenty-four minutes for families without children and thirty-four minutes for families with children. The final sample we obtained accurately reflects the New York City population in terms of sociodemographic composition. To adjust for sampling design and minor discrepancies in sample composition, the data were weighted to 2000 census data.[3]

New York City is a microcosm—a mini-replica of the world. People from countries all around the world live and work there. Our survey reflects the cultural richness and diversity of the Big Apple. In our wave 3 sample, we interviewed adults from eighty-five different countries. Forty percent of the sample consisted of immigrants. The first and second waves of the survey were conducted in English and Spanish and the last wave in five languages: English, Spanish, Mandarin, Cantonese, and Korean.

NEW YORKERS' REACTIONS TO 9/11

In this section, we present the main results from the third wave of the NYSIS study. First, we present the prevalence of adverse reactions to the WTC attack. Next, we present those who were most likely to be affected, and last, those whose problems persisted and who sought help.

How Widespread Were the Adverse Affects?

The third wave of the NYSIS study reveals high levels of adverse physical, emotional, and economic reactions to the World Trade Center attacks (table 2.1). A sizable minority of respondents—14 percent—reported that they or a family member had lost work as a result of 9/11. Fifteen percent of adults reported new health problems, including sleep problems, depression, anxiety, fear, headaches, stomachaches, breathing problems, coughing, skin problems, allergies, emotional problems, eating problems, and stress. Though only 15 percent of adults reported new health problems, much larger percentages reported specific symptoms of anxiety and mental health problems when asked about them directly. About one-third reported sleeping poorly, one-third reported having problems concentrating at work, and 37 percent also said that since 9/11 they preferred to stay home and not go to work or other places. Slightly over half (55 percent) of the adults interviewed reported having experienced at least one of these health problems since 9/11.

Clearly, 9/11 changed many people's sense of security. Not only did more than one-third of adults report that they preferred to stay at home and not go to work or other places, but 43 percent of parents also cut back on their children's freedom to travel around the city.

A number of parents reported that their children experienced problems as a result of 9/11. Eight percent of adults with children reported that their child had a new health problem attributable to 9/11. Twelve percent reported that their child had trouble sleeping as a result of 9/11, and 14 percent said that their child had problems concentrating as a result of the attacks. Slightly higher percentages of parents reported other symptoms of anxiety: 17 percent of children were afraid in crowded places, and 19 percent often wanted to stay at home and not go to school or other places without a parent. Most striking, 28

TABLE 2.1   NEW PROBLEMS FACED BY ADULTS AND CHILDREN SINCE THE 9/11 TERRORIST ATTACK

Problems	Weighted Mean
Economic hardship since 9/11	
Respondent or family member lost job	14%
Adult health since 9/11	
New health problems	15
Problem sleeping	30
Problem concentrating at work	31
Prefers to stay at home	37
Any health problem	55
Cut freedom of children	43
Child's health since 9/11	
New health problems	8
Problem sleeping	12
Problem concentrating	14
Prefers to stay at home	19
Is worried that parent might go away	28
Is afraid of crowded places	17
Any health problem	45
Sample size	
Adults	1,501
Children	791

Source: Authors' compilation.

percent of parents reported that their child was afraid the parent might go away and not come back. In all, 45 percent of parents reported that their child experienced at least one of these outcomes.

Who Experienced the Adverse Affects?

The analyses reported in table 2.1 are based on means, and therefore they describe the problems faced by New Yorkers on average. Did 9/11 have different effects on people with different ethnicity, age, religion, or immigration status? To answer these questions, we turn to a multivariate regression analysis. Regression analysis enables us to isolate the effects of one variable on vulnerability while holding constant all other variables. For example, we can study the vulnerability of respondents from different religions, but with the same other personal characteristics such as age, race, education, immigration status, family size, gender, and income.

The results of the multivariate analysis are presented in table 2.2. The three column headings describe the three dependent variables—whether the respondent or a family member lost a job, the number of ill-health symptoms experienced by adults, and the number of ill-health symptoms experienced by children. The number of symptoms experienced by adults ranges from zero to four, and the number experienced by children ranges from zero to six. The samples for the first two columns are adult respondents. The sample for the last column is limited to adults with children.

Each column is a separate regression and controls for the respondent's gender, age, education, race-ethnicity, religion, family type, family size, immigration status, place of residence, whether the respondent had a work-limiting disability (or the child had an activity-limiting disability), and family income. We define four categories of education: less than high school, high school, some college, and at least a bachelor's degree, with the last as the category of comparison. The sample is distributed into six groups on the basis of religion: Protestant (comparison category), Roman Catholic, other Catholic, Jewish, Muslim, and others. Families are grouped in four categories: married or cohabiting with kids, married or cohabiting with no kids, single with kids, and single with no kids (comparison group). We have five age groups—eighteen to twenty-four, twenty-five to thirty-four, thirty-five to forty-four (comparison group), forty-five to fifty-nine, and sixty and above—and four categories of race: non-Hispanic white (comparison group), non-Hispanic black, Hispanic, and others. Family income is divided into five categories—below poverty level; between the poverty level and twice the poverty level; between two and three times the poverty level; between three and five times the poverty level; and more than five times the poverty level (comparison group).

The coefficients in the first column indicate that the effect of September 11 on whether a respondent (or family member) lost a job did not differ by respondent's age, gender, religion, family type, or whether the respondent had a work-limiting disability. (We did not include family income in this regression because losing a job is expected to lead to lower family income and therefore we cannot isolate the effect of income on job loss.) Three groups of people most adversely affected on this account were those without a college degree, immigrants, and Hispanics. High school dropouts and those with some college education were about 6 percentage points more likely to lose a job than college graduates. Similarly, immigrants and Hispanics were each about 5 percentage points more likely to lose a job compared to native-born and white adults.

The findings on reports of health problems or symptoms (column 2) are similar in a few respects to those on job loss. Adults with less than a high school education also reported a greater number of 9/11-related health problems than college graduates. Marital and parental status and number of children had no effect, controlling for other factors, on the number of health prob-

TABLE 2.2   PREDICTORS OF NEW PROBLEMS FACED BY ADULTS SINCE THE 9/11 TERRORIST ATTACK

Explanatory Variables	Respondent or Family Member Lost Job	Number of Ill-Health Symptoms Experienced by Adults	Number of Ill-Health Symptoms Experienced by Children
Parent's education (omitted: B.A. plus)			
Less than high school	0.057	0.262	0.431
	(0.031)*	(0.118)**	(0.180)**
High school	0.036	0.030	0.270
	(0.025)	(0.094)	(0.153)*
Some college	0.060	0.012	0.178
	(0.025)**	(0.090)	(0.142)
Work- and activity-limiting disability	−0.007	0.551	0.296
	(0.028)	(0.104)***	(0.171)*
Religion (omitted: Protestant)			
Roman Catholic	−0.010	0.214	0.449
	(0.031)	(0.109)*	(0.182)**
Other Catholic	0.031	0.093	0.314
	(0.034)	(0.121)	(0.200)
Jewish	−0.026	0.089	0.303
	(0.041)	(0.145)	(0.258)
Muslim	0.010	0.806	0.899
	(0.060)	(0.216)***	(0.286)***
Other	0.015	0.028	0.159
	(0.032)	(0.113)	(0.188)
Family type (omitted: single, no kids)			
Married or cohabiting, with kids	0.023	−0.193	
	(0.039)	(0.142)	
Single, with kids	−0.006	−0.058	0.159
	(0.035)	(0.123)	(0.134)
Married or cohabiting, no kids	0.003	−0.071	
	(0.029)	(0.107)	
Family size	−0.001	0.023	0.023
	(0.011)	(0.040)	(0.045)
Immigrant	0.045	0.023	0.141
	(0.020)**	(0.072)	(0.111)

(Table continues on p. 34.)

TABLE 2.2   *Continued*

Explanatory Variables	Respondent or Family Member Lost Job	Number of Ill-Health Symptoms Experienced by Adults	Number of Ill-Health Symptoms Experienced by Children
Age of the respondent (omitted: 35 to 44 years)			
18 to 24 years	−0.017	−0.157	
	(0.033)	(0.119)	
25 to 34 years	0.003	0.068	
	(0.024)	(0.086)	
45 to 59 years	−0.025	−0.078	
	(0.026)	(0.092)	
60 years or older	−0.015	−0.511	
	(0.034)	(0.124)***	
Child's age (omitted group: 0 to 10 years)			
11 to 14 years			0.219
			(0.119)*
15 to 18 years			−0.027
			(0.132)
Respondent is male	0.016	−0.367	−0.333
	(0.019)	(0.069)***	(0.113)***
Child is male			0.021
			(0.097)
Race (omitted: non-Hispanic white)			
Non-Hispanic black	−0.008	−0.010	0.246
	(0.028)	(0.101)	(0.169)
Hispanic	0.048	−0.001	0.218
	(0.028)*	(0.100)	(0.160)
Other	0.043	0.148	−0.054
	(0.039)	(0.138)	(0.227)
Borough of residence (omitted: Manhattan)			
Bronx	−0.038	−0.074	−0.172
	(0.031)	(0.110)	(0.175)
Brooklyn	0.007	−0.220	−0.260
	(0.028)	(0.098)**	(0.167)
Queens	−0.024	−0.118	−0.317
	(0.028)	(0.098)	(0.167)*
Staten Island	−0.011	−0.198	−0.368
	(0.043)	(0.156)	(0.241)

TABLE 2.2   *Continued*

Explanatory Variables	Respondent or Family Member Lost Job	Number of Ill-Health Symptoms Experienced by Adults	Number of Ill-Health Symptoms Experienced by Children
Family income (omitted: 500 percent of poverty line or more)			
Below poverty line		−0.062	−0.467
		(0.111)	(0.193)**
0 to 200 percent of poverty line		−0.138	−0.226
		(0.113)	(0.175)
200 to 300 percent of poverty line		−0.183	−0.539
		(0.122)	(0.183)***
300 to 500 percent of poverty line		−0.133	0.012
		(0.098)	(0.159)
Respondent or family member lost job		0.417	0.244
		(0.099)***	(0.141)*
Sample size	1,416	1,327	678

Source: Authors' compilation.
Note: Standard errors are in parentheses.
*p < .10   **p < .05   ***p < .01

lems. On the other hand, although immigrants and Hispanics were more likely to lose a job, neither group reported a significantly greater number of health problems. But a more detailed analysis of particular questions (see tables 2A.1 through 2A.7) indicates that Hispanics were significantly more likely to have problems concentrating at work, more likely to prefer to stay home, and more likely to limit the freedom of their children. (The more detailed results also indicate that blacks were more likely than whites to report preferring to stay home.) Furthermore, when we do not control for employment in the regressions, Hispanics were more likely than whites to report health problems, suggesting that they did suffer disproportional health effects *because* of job losses. What differentiates the findings on job loss and health effects is the large number of significant group differences in the prevalence of health problems. Adults with a work disability, adults who lost a job, Catholics, and especially Muslims reported a significantly greater number of symptoms. Male respondents, those over age sixty, and residents of Brooklyn reported significantly fewer problems.

That those with a work disability would have suffered disproportionately from 9/11 is understandable. Their disability was likely to make them more vulnerable in general to dislocating events. Similarly, we expect—and the results confirm—that losing a job or having a family member who lost a job provoked stress and anxiety. The largest negative health effects are for Muslims. They reported nearly one problem more than Protestants. Increased hate crime and ethnic and religious profiling of Muslims and Arabs and those perceived to be like them, such as South Asians (particularly Sikhs), have triggered additional worries and fears among these groups.[4] The effect for Roman Catholics is more difficult to explain. The coefficient for Roman Catholics is only about one-fourth the size of the Muslim coefficient, but it is significant at the .10 level. One possibility is that because police and firefighters are disproportionately Catholic, Catholics may have been more likely to know someone who died in 9/11.[5] Unfortunately, we did not ask a question to ascertain whether or not respondents knew someone who had died. Another possibility is that we are picking up a difference between Protestants and other groups. Jews and other Catholics were also more likely to report symptoms of distress, but the sample sizes of these groups are quite small and the differences are not statistically significant. Still, more detailed analyses indicate that Jewish adults were significantly more likely (at the $p < .10$ level) to prefer staying at home than Protestants. We did not measure pain and suffering directly, so we cannot tell whether the lower levels of reported health problems among Protestants reflects actual differences in how much they suffered ill effects of 9/11 or differences in levels of stoicism (how they report these experiences). Though the differences between Protestants and Catholics and Jews may approach and even be statistically significant, the magnitude of these differences is swamped by the difference between all three groups and Muslims.

That male respondents reported fewer mental health symptoms is consistent with previous literature. The extent to which this is a real or reporting phenomenon is considered later in conjunction with the discussion of children. Surprisingly, people age sixty or older were also less adversely affected. One possibility is that problems related to being able to concentrate at work or deciding to stay home may be less relevant to older people. But older people also reported fewer new health problems in general and reported fewer problems sleeping as a result of 9/11. Perhaps older people are more used to handling adversity and therefore endured the 9/11 trauma with greater resilience. It is also possible that many of them were already experiencing prior to 9/11 the types of health symptoms they were asked about. Hence, they would have been less likely to report that the problems were *new*. Finally, adults in Brooklyn suffered significantly less than adults living in Manhattan. However, closer inspection indicates that residents of all the other boroughs also suffered less, though not significantly so in this regression. Note also that all of the other borough coefficients for the children's regression in column 3 are negative, but in this case the coefficient for Queens is statistically significant. These results suggest that controlling for other characteristics, residents of the island of Manhattan, the site of the World Trade Center bombing, experienced more distress.[6]

Many of the patterns for ill effects on adults are echoed with children. Children of adults with less than a high school education, children with family members who lost a job, Catholic and Muslim children, and children with a disability experienced significantly more symptoms than their counterparts. Once again, more detailed analyses produce evidence that Jewish children were more affected than Protestant children, that Hispanic children were more af-fected than non-Hispanic white children, and that black children were more likely than non-Hispanic white children to prefer to stay at home after 9/11. And as with adults, being a Muslim had the single largest effect. As noted earlier, children who lived in Manhattan also appear to have suffered more than children who lived in the other boroughs, but only one of the coefficients (for living in Queens) approaches statistical significance.

Early adolescents appear to have been more vulnerable to 9/11 than their younger or older counterparts. This is not surprising because child develop-ment research suggests that this is a particularly vulnerable age. That male respondents reported that their children suffered fewer problems than female respondents suggests that part of the gender difference in the effects of 9/11 is due to reporting rather than actual differences, though it is also possible that children in households in which men were more likely to be home and answer the phone suffered fewer symptoms than children in other households. An investigation into this question, based on the subset of families in which the parent was randomly selected, suggests that both factors contributed to the parental gender effects.

The most surprising result in table 2.2 is that children of high-income par-ents (income greater than 300 percent of the poverty level) were more likely to report symptoms than those in poorer families. Why were children in high-income families particularly vulnerable? One possibility is that children in upper-income groups were less resilient to the effects of environmental traumas be-cause they had been less exposed to hardship and adversity and therefore had a greater sense of security generally. The 9/11 World Trade Center attack was so vivid and such an equal opportunity reaper of death that children from the most privileged backgrounds may have had the most to lose in terms of their sense of security, and they may have been the least well equipped to handle adversity. Another possibility is that wealthier parents may have been more likely than others to perceive or report effects on their children.

To sum up, the results of the NYSIS 2002 supplemental survey show that 9/11 created new health problems and anxieties for New York City residents. Some groups suffered these problems more than others. In general, the greatest suffering occurred among already vulnerable populations—the least educated, the disabled, Hispanics, to some extent immigrants, and to a very limited extent blacks, and first and foremost Muslims. The children of vulnerable adults were the most vulnerable, and early adolescents were the most affected. Two exceptions to these conclusions were the relative invulnerability discovered among those over age sixty and the relative vulnerability of children in high-income families.

Whose Problems Persisted and Who Sought Help?

Unfortunately, we asked questions about the persistence of problems and efforts to seek help only of the 15 percent of adults who reported experiencing new problems and the 8 percent of parents who reported that their children had experienced new problems. As indicated earlier, we know that the general question about new problems painted a more favorable view of the impact of 9/11 than the questions about specific problems. In light of the underestimate of problems that our filter question yielded, it is probably safe to assume that we also underestimated the proportion of adults and children who sought and received treatment for 9/11-related symptoms.

One indication of the severity of the problems reported is their perseverance. Overall, 65 percent of adults who reported having experienced new problems after 9/11 said that those problems were still persisting at the time of the interview—about six months after 9/11. Many parents (44 percent) also reported that their child's problem was persisting. There is some indication that persistent problems were more common among children whose parents sought treatment for them than among those who did not (59 percent and 36 percent, respectively), but not among adults. A *New York Times* survey conducted two years after 9/11 indicated that about one-third of New Yorkers continued to feel nervous or edgy because of the attack (Kleinfield and Connelly 2003).

The results from the questions about seeking help also point to the severity of the new problems that were reported. Among adults reporting new problems, two-thirds said that they had sought help for those problems; among parents reporting that their child experienced new problems, 40 percent had sought help. Overall, 6 percent of adults reported having sought help for new problems, and 4 percent of parents reported having sought help for their children. These proportions, which are likely to be underestimates, represent a considerable number of people in the city—about 350,000 adults and 57,000 children—and confirm anecdotal reports from health and social service agencies that they experienced sharp increases in the number of client visits subsequent to 9/11. Adults sought help for themselves and their children from a wide variety of professionals, including social workers, psychologists, psychiatrists, counselors, and therapists.

Table 2.3 presents an analysis of those whose problems persisted and who sought help that is parallel to the analyses presented in table 2.2. Because the persistence and help-seeking questions were limited to the 15 percent of adults and 8 percent of parents who responded affirmatively to the new health problems question, the samples are much smaller in table 2.3 than in table 2.2. Consequently, we expect many fewer statistically significant results. Columns 1 and 2 present results for children and adults, respectively, in terms of the degree to which problems persisted. The results for the persistence of problems among adults parallel the results in table 2.2. The disabled, the poorly educated, Muslims, those living outside Manhattan, and those living in a family that experienced a job loss were more likely to report that problems persisted, and those over age sixty were less likely to report such persistence. Note, however, that less than half of these coefficients are statistically significant. The story is the same for the persistence of problems among children, but here the sample size is even smaller and the statistical significance even weaker.

Although several of the more vulnerable groups also disproportionately sought help, there are some notable exceptions. Adults and children with a disability, most non-Protestant adults, and adults in families that experienced job loss were more likely to seek help. On the other hand, though they were more vulnerable in terms of experiencing problems, immigrant adults and Hispanic adults were significantly less likely than native-born and white adults to seek help. Similarly, although older adults were less likely to suffer from 9/11 and single parents were no more likely to experience suffering than adults of other ages and family types, both the elderly and single parents were more likely to seek help. We suspect that both sets of anomalies are explained by the degree to which the different groups were already integrated into social service networks where help was readily accessible. Immigrants and Hispanics are less likely, and single parents and the elderly more likely, to be already served by social service agencies.

COMPARISON TO OTHER RESEARCH

A number of other studies have attempted to measure a wide variety of direct and indirect effects of the WTC attack. Some have focused on behavioral responses, including coping, time use, volunteering and charitable activity, and religiosity. Others have looked at attitudes toward national security, government, and work. Finally, a few studies have measured the financial and economic impact of 9/11 on the nation and on New York City (see appendix 2.2). Our purpose here is not to summarize this rich literature but to point out whether its findings are similar to those from the NYSIS. Nearly all of the previous research is consistent with and therefore reinforces our NYSIS findings. Consistent with our finding of widespread job loss as a result of 9/11,

TABLE 2.3   PREDICTORS OF HELP-SEEKING AND PROBLEM PERSISTENCE
SINCE THE 9/11 TERRORIST ATTACK

Explanatory Variables	Adult Problem Persisted	Child Problem Persisted	Adult Sought Help	Child Sought Help
Parent's Education (omitted: B.A. plus)				
Less than high school	0.052	−0.060	0.052	−0.401
	(0.117)	(0.475)	(0.120)	(0.498)
High school	0.005	0.298	0.119	−0.283
	(0.103)	(0.526)	(0.105)	(0.552)
Some college	0.082	−0.152	0.007	−0.124
	(0.093)	(0.351)	(0.096)	(0.368)
Work- and activity-limiting disability	0.322	0.047	0.138	0.214
	(0.082)***	(0.255)	(0.085)	(0.278)
Religion (omitted: Protestant)				
Roman Catholic	−0.161	−0.258	0.281	0.139
	(0.122)	(0.585)	(0.125)**	(0.614)
Other Catholic	−0.230	−0.813	0.298	−0.083
	(0.140)	(0.593)	(0.144)**	(0.622)
Jewish	−0.022	0.032	0.192	0.188
	(0.166)	(0.487)	(0.170)	(0.511)
Muslim	0.127	0.225	0.289	−0.436
	(0.190)	(0.560)	(0.195)	(0.588)
Other	−0.036	0.174	0.248	0.158
	(0.131)	(0.560)	(0.134)*	(0.588)
Family type (omitted: single, no kids)				
Married or cohabiting, with kids	−0.111		0.118	
	(0.133)		(0.137)	
Single, with kids	0.097	0.627	0.269	0.249
	(0.125)	(0.279)**	(0.129)**	(0.292)
Married or cohabiting, no kids	0.114		−0.048	
	(0.110)		(0.113)	
Family size	0.009	−0.028	−0.014	0.086
	(0.035)	(0.093)	(0.036)	(0.097)
Immigrant	−0.086	−0.262	−0.200	−0.074
	(0.076)	(0.227)	(0.078)**	(0.239)

TABLE 2.3   *Continued*

Explanatory Variables	Adult Problem Persisted	Child Problem Persisted	Adult Sought Help	Child Sought Help
Age of the respondent (omitted: 35 to 44 years)				
18 to 24 years	−0.111		0.128	
	(0.146)		(0.150)	
25 to 34 years	0.066		0.159	
	(0.091)		(0.094)	
45 to 59 years	−0.045		0.227	
	(0.085)		(0.087)***	
60 years or older	−0.318		0.234	
	(0.133)**		(0.137)	
Child's age (omitted group: 0 to 10 years)				
11 to 14 years		−0.433		−0.354
		(0.273)		(0.286)
15 to 18 years		0.086		−0.295
		(0.269)		(0.282)
Respondent is male	0.088	0.018	−0.014	−0.079
	(0.070)	(0.322)	(0.072)	(0.337)
Child is male		0.132		−0.120
		(0.189)		(0.199)
Race (omitted: non-Hispanic white)				
Non-Hispanic black	−0.113	−0.054	0.044	−0.179
	(0.113)	(0.381)	(0.116)	(0.400)
Hispanic	0.002	−0.158	−0.285	−0.058
	(0.108)	(0.313)	(0.111)**	(0.329)
Other	−0.116	0.017	−0.112	−0.164
	(0.137)	(0.535)	(0.141)	(0.561)
Borough of residence (omitted: Manhattan)				
Bronx	0.186	0.009	−0.034	0.219
	(0.107)	(0.298)	(0.110)	(0.312)
Brooklyn	0.004	0.015	−0.086	0.201
	(0.105)	(0.332)	(0.108)	(0.349)
Queens	0.132	−0.146	−0.170	0.024
	(0.100)	(0.346)	(0.103)	(0.363)

(Table continues on p. 42.)

TABLE 2.3   *Continued*

Explanatory Variables	Adult Problem Persisted	Child Problem Persisted	Adult Sought Help	Child Sought Help
Staten Island	−0.017	0.121	−0.394	0.107
	(0.161)	(0.549)	(0.165)**	(0.576)
Family income (omitted: 500 percent of poverty line or more)				
Below poverty line	−0.101	−0.220	0.070	0.389
	(0.117)	(0.410)	(.121)	(0.430)
0 to 200 percent of	−0.073	0.107	−0.159	0.094
poverty line	(0.115)	(0.287)	(0.118)	(0.301)
200 to 300 percent of	−0.043	−0.021	−0.183	0.490
poverty line	(0.129)	(0.377)	(0.132)	(0.396)
300 to 500 percent of	0.045	0.005	−0.086	0.009
poverty line	(0.114)	(0.335)	(0.117)	(0.352)
Respondent or family member	0.140	0.339	0.235	−0.177
lost job	(0.086)	(0.282)	(0.088)***	(0.296)
Sample size	216	56	216	56

Source: Authors' compilation.
Note: Standard errors are in parentheses.
*p < .10   **p < .05   ***p < .01

estimates from other sources have indicated that the number of jobs lost in the fourth quarter of 2001 in New York City ranged from 74,000 (Fiscal Policy Institute 2002) to 100,000 (New York State Assembly 2002).

Similarly, many other studies have documented widespread indirect adverse physical and mental health effects among adults, including post-traumatic stress disorder (PTSD), depression, and anxiety. Two months after the attack, 9.7 percent of adults in New York City reported symptoms consistent with depression (Galea et al. 2002), 7.5 percent reported symptoms consistent with a diagnosis of current PTSD (Galea et al. 2002), and one-third were at increased risk of PTSD (ARCGNY 2002). A study from the Center for Urban Epidemiologic Studies conducted five to eight weeks after the attack found that 29 percent of Manhattan residents below 110th Street reported an increase in the use of cigarettes, alcohol, or marijuana, and that persons who increased their smoking of cigarettes and marijuana were more likely to experience PTSD than those who did not (Vlahov et al. 2002). Of course, the effects of 9/11 on mental health were not limited to New York. A series of polls documented high rates of depression and sleep problems nationally (Huddy, Khatib, and Capelos 2002).

Other studies also showed that only a minority of those with symptoms sought help. The American Red Cross in Greater New York (ARCGNY) reported that in February 2002, 76 percent of New Yorkers were willing to seek help for support services but only one-third actually did. At the national level, only one in five who said they were depressed or anxious as a direct result of the terrorist attack reported having seen a mental health professional (APA 2002). And one study showed that the adverse effects persisted: as noted earlier, a *New York Times* survey conducted two years after 9/11 indicated that about one-third of New Yorkers continued to feel nervous or edgy because of the events of that day (Kleinfield and Connelly 2003).

The American Red Cross in Greater New York found that proximity to Ground Zero increased the severity of the impact and the risk for trauma-related distress and behavioral changes (Galea et al. 2002; ARCGNY 2002). This study found that residence below Canal Street was a significant predictor of PTSD. Unfortunately, NYSIS data do not include a sufficient number of cases to look at such a specific area; it is also possible that many of the most affected residents of lower Manhattan had moved away by the time we were in the field. It should be noted that the Red Cross study defined proximity very broadly to include people who worked below Canal Street, members of the downtown business community, and volunteers in the recovery efforts.

Other studies, like the NYSIS, indicated that children in New York City were affected by the World Trade Center attack. A Citizens' Committee for Children of New York study revealed that immediately after the attack parents observed fears and symptoms of stress in their children. Although these symptoms decreased over time, one year after the attack more than one-third of children in the city were still worried about their parents' safety, 21 percent were anxious about leaving home, and 16 percent were having sleep disturbances (Citizens' Committee for Children of New York 2002). Interviews with students in grades 4 through 12 conducted six months after 9/11 by Applied Research and Consulting (2002) for the New York City Board of Education indicated that somewhat less than 30 percent of students reported mental health symptoms.

Finally, in spite of all these negative outcomes, a national survey of Americans indicated that the attack of 9/11 did not destroy confidence in America or elicit shame and national self-denigration. To the contrary, anger was the most profound response (Smith, Rasinksi, and Toce 2001). This is consistent with a finding reported later in this chapter that after 9/11 New Yorkers became even more positive about the city.

With the exception of some economic impact studies, most reports have relied on data collected only after the World Trade Center attack. Using New York City Social Indicators Survey data, we report in the next section on *changes* in a variety of social indicators among New Yorkers before and after September 11 of 2001.

BEFORE AND AFTER 9/11:
CHANGES IN INDICATORS OF WELL-BEING

In this section, we compare indicators of New Yorkers' well-being in the spring of 2002 to indicators of New Yorkers' well-being in 1997 and 1999 to 2000. The national and local economy and labor markets changed profoundly during this period. In response to the longest national economic boom in U.S. history in the 1990s, unemployment in New York City continued declining until January 2001 to a low of 5.2 percent, at which point the trend reversed (U.S. Department of Labor 2003). By the spring of 2002, employment and unemployment rates had reached levels very similar to those in 1999. In fact, by the time wave 3 interviews were conducted, employment had dipped slightly below the levels seen during wave 2 interviews. All else being equal, we would therefore expect New Yorkers to have been faring similarly in 2002 as in 1999. Of course, not all else was equal. On the one hand, there was the tragic destruction of the World Trade Center on 9/11. We interviewed respondents about six months after that, and as the data discussed earlier demonstrate, the collapse of the World Trade Center had a widespread impact on adults' and children's sense of security. On the other hand, the long decline in crime rates in the city extended into 2002 and reduced insecurity. Data from all three waves of NYSIS allow us to investigate the extent to which indicators of well-being changed during this period and the extent to which the prior trends (from 1997 to 1999) were modified. We look specifically at several indicators in three areas of well-being: health, economic well-being, and perceptions of New York as a place to live. First we examine changes in well-being for the entire population of New York adults and children. Then we examine whether there are departures from the general trend among those New Yorkers identified earlier as being particularly vulnerable.

What Are the Trends in the Well-Being of
All New Yorkers?

Table 2.4 presents the changes in indicators of well-being over the three waves of the survey—1997, 1999 to 2000, and 2002. Column 1 presents the mean value of the well-being measure in 1997, while columns 2 and 3 present, respectively, the regression adjusted mean value for 1999 to 2000 and 2002. The

TABLE 2.4   CHANGE IN INDICATORS OF WELL-BEING OF NEW YORKERS, 1997 TO 2002

	Mean Value (1997) Weighted	Wave 2 (1999 to 2000) Adjusted	Wave 3 (2002) Adjusted	Sample Size[a]
Adult indicators				
Respondent and partner income	$35,309	$38,767***	$38,086**	4,149
Adult is in good to excellent health	81.32	76.12***	81.48	4,144
Family has at least one full-time worker	45.72	47.12	44.15	4,143
Family members did not experience hunger	91.64	92.05	95.61**	1,941
Family can borrow $1,000	60.67	68.55***	67.85***	4,045
Family members were not victims of crime	89.56	91.65*	91.93**	4,142
Adult rates New York City as a good to excellent place to live	60.60	70.96***	80.55***	4,120
Adult rates neighborhood as good or very good	70.13	70.45	71.77	4,138
Adult rates police protection as good or very good	63.74	65.83	71.22***	3,989
Child indicators				
Child is in good to excellent health	93.58	92.25	93.30	2,392
Child was suspended from school	5.62	5.68	3.72	1,718
Child often or sometimes doesn't get along with others	19.03	16.93	13.01***	2,083
Child often or sometimes feels sad or depressed	19.76	21.52	21.82	2,071

Source: Authors' compilation.
[a]Combined sample size of the three waves.
*p < .10   **p < .05   ***p < .01

estimates are derived from pooling all three waves of the survey and regressing the dependent variable on the same set of demographic control variables as in tables 2.2 and 2.3.[7]

What stands out in the table is an overall improvement in most indicators of well-being over time. Incomes and ability to borrow increased significantly between 1997 and 1999, then dipped very slightly by 2002 but remained significantly higher than 1997 levels. Though not statistically significant, the percentage of families with at least one full-time worker exhibits an even more pronounced curvilinear trend, such that employment levels, alone among our indicators, were lower in 2002 than in 1997. Despite lower employment, hunger declined steadily during the entire period, from just over 8 percent to less than 5 percent. Adults rated their health as better in 2002 as compared to 1999, reversing a previous trend.[8] The proportion of New Yorkers who reported being victims of robbery, housebreaking, or mugging declined significantly between 1997 and 2002. Ratings of New York as a place to live also improved by a substantial and significant amount. Over 80 percent of New Yorkers rated the city as a good to excellent place to live in 2002, compared to about 70 percent in the period 1999 to 2000 and about 60 percent in 1997. Though perceptions of neighborhoods did not change during this period, the proportion of New Yorkers who believed the police were doing a good job in the city continued to improve after 1999 to 2000 (by over five percentage points).

Two of the four indicators of child well-being also show improvement from the period 1999 to 2000 to the year 2002. Neither overall child health nor the prevalence of depression or sadness changed significantly during this period. Though not statistically significant, suspensions from school declined by two percentage points between 1997 and 2002. And the proportion of parents reporting that their child did not get along with others declined substantially after the 1999 to 2000 interviews. Finally, although not shown in the table because we did not start measuring these variables until 1999 to 2000, the proportions of children with behavioral problems and with D's and F's on their report cards declined significantly between 2000 and 2002.

In sum, despite some evidence that employment suffered after 2000, on other indicators New Yorkers appeared to be better off after 9/11 than they had been two and a half to five years earlier. Is there an incongruity between the large proportions of New Yorkers who reported experiencing negative symptoms of anxiety and distress from 9/11 and these positive trends in the social indicators? Upon reflection, we think not. The economy of the late 1990s was so strong that its effects on individuals' well-being persisted into the economic downturn at least through 2002. Incomes and ability to borrow were higher, and hunger was lower, in 2002 than they had been in 1997. Similarly, crime rates were lower in 2002 than previously, and confidence in the police and the city increased steadily and more broadly between 1997 and 2002. In short, despite the recession that began in late 2000, many good things were happening in New York City, even into 2002. On balance, for New Yorkers as a whole, six months after 9/11 the effect of positive changes seems to have more than countered some of the negative effects of 9/11 on the indicators that the Social Indicators Survey measures.

Do the Trends Differ for Vulnerable Groups?

These findings combined with our findings on vulnerability to the effects of 9/11 suggest another hypothesis: that the vulnerable groups identified may have benefited less from the positive trends of the late 1990s compared to other groups and to themselves before 9/11.

To determine how vulnerable populations fared over this period relative to others, we estimated interactive models to assess the extent to which particular groups diverged from the overall trends in well-being using our social indicators. We did this by interacting the wave 2 and wave 3 dummy variables with variables representing the vulnerable population subgroups and controlling for the demographic characteristics in tables 2.2, 2.3, and 2.4, as well as wave dummies. These models measure the extent to which trends in the outcome measures between the first two waves and between the first and last waves differ across subgroups. Table 2.5 provides the OLS and regression coefficients of the interactions from these regressions and the tests of statistical significance. (The full regressions are available upon request from the authors.) Results are presented for five different vulnerable groups: immigrants, Muslims, the poorly educated, the disabled, and "all vulnerable groups." A negative coefficient in the wave 2 column indicates that the trend between 1997 and 1999 was less positive (or more negative) for the vulnerable group than for others. A positive coefficient indicates that the trend was more favorable (or less unfavorable) for the vulnerable population than for others. Similarly, the coefficients in the wave 3 column compare trends from 1997 to 2002 among vulnerable and nonvulnerable populations. Children of vulnerable adults plus children ages ten to fifteen are considered vulnerable.

Table 2.5 indicates that vulnerable adult groups generally gained less than others after 2001. Seven of the thirty-six wave 3 interaction coefficients for the individual groups among adults are negative and significant. Furthermore, all but one of the coefficients for *any* vulnerable adult group comparing 2002 to 1997 (last column) are significant and negative for the adult outcomes indicators. In other words, there is strong evidence that the groups most vulnerable to 9/11 either reaped fewer benefits of the positive economic momentum and decline in crime than did nonvulnerable populations or were more greatly affected by the economic downturn after 2000. That all but one of the wave 3 coefficients are more negative than the comparable wave 2 coefficients and that two of these differences are statistically significant also provides evidence that the vulnerable adults as a whole fared worse after 9/11, relative to other adults, than they had previously.

TABLE 2.5   INTERACTION EFFECTS FOR SURVEY WAVE BY VULNERABILITY OF FIVE GROUPS OF NEW YORKERS, 1997 TO 2002

	Immigrants		Muslims	
	Wave 2	Wave 3	Wave 2	Wave 3
Adult indicators				
Respondent and partner income	$–2,253	$–6,148**	$9,341	$1,005
Adult is in good to excellent health	0.22	–0.23[a]	–0.41	–0.77
Respondent works	0.08	–0.04	0.32	–0.02
Family members did not experience hunger	0.15	0.32	0.62	–0.45
Family can borrow $1,000	0.52***	–0.17[a]	0.27	–0.90*[a]
Family members were not victims of crime	–0.25	–0.24	–1.28	–1.02
Adult rates New York City as a good to excellent place to live	–0.41**	–0.32*	–0.71	0.01
Adult rates neighborhood as good or very good	–0.17	–0.28	–0.56	–0.31
Adult rates police protection as good or very good	–0.24	–0.12	–0.58	–0.003
Child indicators				
Child is in good to excellent health	0.78*	0.61	1.01	
Child was suspended from school	0.02	0.42	–0.39	
Child often or sometimes doesn't get along with others	0.20	–0.10	–0.59	–0.23
Child often or sometimes feels sad or depressed	0.11	0.18	–0.95	–1.80**

Source: Authors' compilation.
[a]The coefficients for wave 3 and wave 2 interactions are statistically different at the 10 percent significance level.
*p < .10   **p < .05   ***p < .01: Wave 1 is the category of comparison.

The picture for children is different. The second panel in table 2.5 provides no evidence that children from vulnerable populations experienced smaller improvements in the indicator outcomes than did children from other populations. Indeed, one of the few significant differences in the table indicates that Muslim children gained ground, relative to non-Muslims, in terms of our mental health indicator ("often or sometimes feels sad or depressed"). Bear in mind, however, that our data on Muslim children and children more generally are limited. Only thirty-four Muslim children were included in wave 3, only three

Education		Disability		Child Age 10 to 15		All Vulnerable Groups	
Wave 2	Wave 3	Wave 2	Wave 3	Wave 2	Wave 3	Wave 2	Wave 3
$-6,075	$-8,952**	$-4,018	$-5,201			$-3,144	$-6,910***
-0.50*	-1.17***[a]	0.30	0.22			-.02	-0.65***[a]
0.12	0.16	-0.57**	-0.51*			-.20	-0.33**
-0.28	-0.03	0.37	-0.05			-.40	-0.59
-0.04	-0.256	-0.35	-0.16			.10	-0.39**[a]
0.74*	0.10	-0.12	-0.66*			-.18	-0.61**
-0.22	-0.45*	-0.16	-0.25			-.34**	-0.41**
0.29	-0.08	-0.14	-0.10			-.26*	-0.34**
-0.52**	-0.33	-0.54**	-0.34			-.48***	-0.25*
-0.44	0.08	0.43	0.39	0.12	0.25	0.29	0.47
-0.22	-0.21	0.07		0.06	-0.56	1.63***	0.25[a]
0.02	-0.20	0.34	0.27	0.40	0.10	0.21	0.01
0.32	0.03	0.07	0.38	0.22	0.07	0.14	0.11

of whom reported sadness or depression, so little weight should be given to this result. More generally, recall from table 2.1 that the sample size for the children's analyses in wave 3 is about half the sample size for the adult analyses—791 versus 1,501. In addition, a smaller proportion of children than adults reported adverse reactions to 9/11. Thus, our data have less power to detect group differences among children compared to adults. This lack of power helps explain our failure to find that children in groups more vulnerable to 9/11 gained less from the positive effects of the economic boom and decline in crime. Note also that four of our adult indicators—increase in family income, increase in ability to borrow, reduction in hunger, and reduction in crime—apply to children as well as to adults.

SUMMARY AND CONCLUSION

The New York City Social Indicators Survey assesses the impact of the attack on the World Trade Center on a variety of indicators. The NYSIS indicates that, in addition to dealing a severe economic blow to the city, the destruction of the World Trade Center heightened anxiety and insecurity among slightly more than half of New York City adults and slightly less than half of New York City children. The single most widespread indicator of anxiety for adults was not wanting to leave home. For children the most common expression of anxiety was fear that their parents would go away and not return.

Some groups suffered more than others. In general, already vulnerable populations—the least educated, the disabled, Muslims, Hispanics, immigrants, and, to a limited extent, blacks—experienced more mental health symptoms. The children of vulnerable adults were themselves the most vulnerable, and early adolescents were the most affected. Also proving surprisingly vulnerable were children in high-income families. The least affected—that is, the relatively invulnerable—were those over age sixty.

The NYSIS indicates that the negative effects of 9/11 occurred in the context of a city undergoing many positive changes. The long period of economic growth and prosperity and declining crime immediately preceding 2001 had significantly improved the living conditions of many New Yorkers. The overall positive effects of these improvements appear to have largely offset the negative impact of 9/11 on many indicators of well-being. Had New York been experiencing a long decline in prosperity and living conditions when the attacks took place, it is likely that the change in indicators pre- and post-9/11 would have told a very different story. In the absence of 9/11, the NYSIS indicators might have improved even more between 2000 and 2002. Similarly, if 9/11 had been only the first of many attacks, the NYSIS indicators probably would have deteriorated more than they did. Finally, it is possible that our analyses of changes over time would have picked up stronger negative effects had we conducted the interviews immediately after the event. Time is a great healer. Thinking about these hypothetical alternatives helps to reconcile what may appear at first blush to be inconsistent findings. That the groups who were most vulnerable to 9/11 benefited less from the positive trends after 9/11, compared to other groups and to themselves before 9/11, also helps to make sense of these findings.

Although much of this chapter has focused on the differential impact of 9/11 on vulnerable populations, we could characterize the entire population of New York as having been particularly resilient at the time of the attack because of a general sense that the city was on an upward trajectory. In fact, the attack may well have brought the city's population closer together and fostered a greater sense of community, a more positive view of city institutions, and generally greater satisfaction about being part of New York. In other words, despite having a clear negative impact on mental health, the attacks may also have had *positive* effects on other indicators of well-being.

APPENDIX 2.1: MORE DETAILED ANALYSIS OF SOME NYSIS QUESTIONS

TABLE 2A.1   NEW PROBLEMS FACED BY ADULTS AND CHILDREN IN NEW YORK CITY SINCE THE SEPTEMBER 11 TERRORIST ATTACK

Problems	Number	Sample Mean
Economic hardship		
Respondent or family member lost job	184	12.6%
Respondent did not work at time of survey	66	
No family member worked at time of survey	42	
Adult health		
New health problems since 9/11	223	15.1
New post-9/11 health problems continue	152	10.1
Problem sleeping since 9/11	394	27.6
Problem concentrating at work since 9/11	465	31.3
Any health problem	770	51.3
Adult anxiety		
Cut freedom of children after 9/11	329	42.0
Prefers to stay at home after 9/11	590	39.6
Child's health		
New health problems since 9/11	65	8.4
New post-9/11 health problems continue	30	3.9
Problem sleeping since 9/11	85	11.1
Problem concentrating since 9/11	97	12.6
Any health problem	284	35.9
Child's anxiety		
Child prefers to stay at home	151	18.7
Child is worried that parent might go away	219	28.5
Child is afraid of crowded places	128	16.8
Sample size		
Adults	1,501	100
Children	791	100

Source: Authors' compilation.

TABLE 2A.2   OLS ESTIMATES OF THE DETERMINANTS OF NEW PROBLEMS FACED BY NEW YORK CITY ADULTS SINCE SEPTEMBER 11 TERRORIST ATTACK

Explanatory Variables	New Health Problems
Education (omitted: B.A. plus)	
Less than high school	0.027
	(0.036)
High school	−0.018
	(0.029)
Some college	0.016
	(0.028)
Work-limiting disability	0.206
	(0.031)***
Religion (omitted: Protestant)	
Roman Catholic	0.028
	(0.034)
Other Catholic	0.000
	(0.037)
Jewish	0.025
	(0.045)
Muslim	0.096
	(0.065)
Other	−0.013
	(0.035)
Family type (omitted: single, no kids)	
Married or cohabiting, with kids	0.005
	(0.043)
Single, with kids	−0.006
	(0.037)
Married or cohabiting, no kids	0.028
	(0.032)
Family size	−0.003
	(0.012)
Immigrant	0.024
	(0.022)
Age (omitted: 35 to 44 years)	
18 to 24 years	−0.083
	(0.036)**
25 to 34 years	−0.031
	(0.026)

TABLE 2A.2   *Continued*

Explanatory Variables	New Health Problems
45 to 59 years	−0.010
	(0.028)
60 years or older	−0.084
	(0.038)**
Respondent is male	−0.026
	(0.021)
Race (omitted: non-Hispanic white)	
Non-Hispanic black	−0.013
	(0.031)
Hispanic	0.051
	(0.031)*
Other	0.053
	(0.042)
Borough of residence (omitted: rest of Manhattan)[a]	
Proximity to Ground Zero	−0.001
	(0.039)
Rest of Bronx	0.035
	(0.035)
Rest of Brooklyn	−0.033
	(0.033)
Rest of Queens	0.002
	(0.032)
Rest of Staten Island	0.004
	(0.058)
Family income (omitted: 500 percent of poverty line or more)	
Below poverty line	−0.031
	(0.034)
100 to 200 percent of poverty line	−0.013
	(0.034)
200 to 300 percent of poverty line	−0.010
	(0.037)
300 to 500 percent of poverty line	−0.035
	(0.030)
Respondent or family member lost job	0.098
	(0.029)***

Source: Authors' compilation.
[a]In Manhattan, but not in the proximity of Ground Zero.
*p < .10   **p < .05   ***p < .01

TABLE 2A.3 OLS ESTIMATES OF THE DETERMINANTS OF ANXIETY AMONG NEW YORK CITY ADULTS SINCE SEPTEMBER 11 TERRORIST ATTACK

Explanatory Variables	Any Problem[a]	Problem Sleeping Since 9/11	Problem Concentrating at Work Since 9/11	Prefers to Stay at Home After 9/11	Cut Freedom of Children After 9/11
Education (omitted: B.A. plus)					
Less than high school	0.056	0.123	0.072	0.079	0.108
	(0.049)	(0.045)***	(0.046)	(0.048)*	(0.067)
High school	-0.020	-0.005	0.014	0.047	0.138
	(0.039)	(0.036)	(0.037)	(0.038)	(0.057)**
Some college	-0.026	0.032	0.003	-0.015	0.099
	(0.038)	(0.035)	(0.035)	(0.037)	(0.053)*
Work-limiting disability	0.159	0.173	0.073	0.096	0.127
	(0.043)***	(0.040)***	(0.040)*	(0.042)**	(0.064)**
Religion (omitted: Protestant)					
Roman Catholic	0.048	0.060	0.075	0.106	0.013
	(0.046)	(0.042)	(0.043)*	(0.045)**	(0.067)
Other Catholic	0.023	-0.009	0.028	0.112	0.036
	(0.051)	(0.046)	(0.048)	(0.050)**	(0.075)
Jewish	0.009	0.049	0.015	0.117	0.126
	(0.061)	(0.056)	(0.057)	(0.060)**	(0.095)
Muslim	0.229	0.233	0.275	0.270	0.298
	(0.089)**	(0.082)***	(0.084)***	(0.087)***	(0.108)***

	(1)	(2)	(3)	(4)	(5)
Other	0.018	0.054	-0.007	0.018	0.016
	(0.048)	(0.043)	(0.045)	(0.047)	(0.070)
Family type (omitted: single, no kids)					
Married or cohabiting, with kids	-0.049	-0.073	-0.063	-0.009	
	(0.060)	(0.055)	(0.056)	(0.058)	
Single, with kids	0.030	-0.025	-0.043	0.057	0.003
	(0.052)	(0.047)	(0.048)	(0.050)	(0.050)
Married or cohabiting, no kids	-0.006	-0.061	0.028	0.000	
	(0.045)	(0.041)	(0.042)	(0.044)	
Family size	0.006	0.002	-0.002	0.003	0.024
	(0.017)	(0.015)	(0.016)	(0.016)	(0.018)
Immigrant	-0.010	-0.012	0.025	-0.004	0.008
	(0.030)	(0.028)	(0.028)	(0.029)	(0.042)
Age (omitted: 35 to 44 years)					
18 to 24 years	0.007	-0.036	-0.060	-0.051	-0.139
	(0.050)	(0.046)	(0.047)	(0.049)	(0.075)*
25 to 34 years	0.076	0.009	0.022	0.029	-0.050
	(0.036)**	(0.033)	(0.034)	(0.035)	(0.044)
45 to 59 years	-0.019	-0.000	-0.002	-0.039	0.005
	(0.038)	(0.035)	(0.036)	(0.037)	(0.049)
60 years or older	-0.216	-0.151	-0.175	-0.144	-0.209
	(0.052)***	(0.047)***	(0.049)***	(0.050)***	(0.147)
Respondent is male	-0.143	-0.145	-0.074	-0.137	-0.109
	(0.029)***	(0.026)***	(0.027)***	(0.028)***	(0.042)***

(Table continues on p. 56.)

TABLE 2A.3 *Continued*

Explanatory Variables	Any Problem[a]	Problem Sleeping Since 9/11	Problem Concentrating at Work Since 9/11	Prefers to Stay at Home After 9/11	Cut Freedom of Children After 9/11
Race (omitted: non-Hispanic white)					
Non-Hispanic black	0.005	−0.035	−0.061	0.122	0.058
	(0.043)	(0.039)	(0.040)	(0.042)***	(0.064)
Hispanic	−0.008	−0.040	−0.062	0.093	0.116
	(0.042)	(0.038)	(0.039)	(0.041)**	(0.061)*
Other	−0.020	−0.015	0.007	0.112	0.149
	(0.058)	(0.053)	(0.054)	(0.057)**	(0.084)*
Borough of residence (omitted: rest of Manhattan)					
Proximity to Ground Zero	−0.059	−0.016	−0.083	0.021	0.053
	(0.054)	(0.049)	(0.050)*	(0.052)	(0.081)
Rest of Bronx	−0.025	−0.041	−0.021	−0.020	0.109
	(0.048)	(0.044)	(0.045)	(0.047)	(0.070)
Rest of Brooklyn	−0.087	−0.088	−0.137	−0.049	0.019
	(0.046)*	(0.042)**	(0.043)***	(0.044)	(0.070)

	Model 1	Model 2	Model 3	Model 4	Model 5
Rest of Queens	-0.061	-0.049	-0.050	-0.017	-0.035
	(0.044)	(0.040)	(0.041)	(0.043)	(0.068)
Rest of Staten Island	-0.130	-0.077	-0.078	-0.008	-0.086
	(0.078)*	(0.072)	(0.074)	(0.076)	(0.107)
Family income (omitted: 500 percent of poverty line or more)					
Below poverty line	-0.028	-0.014	0.008	-0.047	-0.072
	(0.047)	(0.043)	(0.044)	(0.045)	(0.071)
100 to 200 percent of poverty line	-0.034	-0.046	0.008	-0.068	0.029
	(0.047)	(0.043)	(0.044)	(0.046)	(0.065)
200 to 300 percent of poverty line	-0.040	-0.062	-0.029	-0.064	-0.025
	(0.051)	(0.047)	(0.048)	(0.050)	(0.069)
300 to 500 percent of poverty line	-0.043	-0.036	-0.022	-0.066	-0.062
	(0.041)	(0.038)	(0.039)	(0.040)	(0.059)
Respondent or family member lost job	0.124	0.116	0.146	0.179	0.151
	(0.040)***	(0.038)***	(0.038)***	(0.039)***	(0.052)***

Source: Authors' compilation.
[a] An index of physical and mental health problems that goes from 0 to 4.
*p < .10 **p < .05 ***p < .01

TABLE 2A.4 OLS ESTIMATES OF THE DETERMINANTS OF NEW HEALTH PROBLEMS FACED BY NEW YORK CITY CHILDREN SINCE 9/11

Explanatory Variables	New Health Problems Since 9/11	Sought Help for New Health Problems	New Post-9/11 Health Problems Continue	Any Health Problem Since 9/11	Number of New Health Problems[a]
Parent's education (omitted group: B.A. plus)					
Less than high school	0.018	-0.296	-0.012	0.097	0.420
	(0.040)	(0.495)	(0.029)	(0.068)	(0.180)**
High school	-0.012	-0.159	-0.019	0.092	0.250
	(0.034)	(0.549)	(0.025)	(0.058)	(0.153)
Some college	0.005	-0.087	-0.025	0.038	0.190
	(0.032)	(0.381)	(0.023)	(0.054)	(0.142)
Activity-limiting disability	0.104	0.242	0.052	0.027	0.295
	(0.038)***	(0.279)	(0.028)*	(0.065)	(0.171)*
Religion (omitted group: Protestant)					
Roman Catholic	0.067	0.054	0.033	0.080	0.446
	(0.041)*	(0.662)	(0.029)	(0.069)	(0.181)**
Other Catholic	0.038	-0.169	-0.001	0.072	0.320
	(0.045)	(0.679)	(0.032)	(0.076)	(0.200)
Jewish	0.146	0.167	0.089	0.069	0.315
	(0.058)**	(0.533)	(0.042)**	(0.076)	(0.257)
Muslim	0.073	-0.412	0.046	0.180	0.918
	(0.064)	(0.624)	(0.046)	(0.108)*	(0.287)***
Other	0.044	0.103	0.016	0.037	0.174
	(0.042)	(0.662)	(0.031)	(0.071)	(0.189)

	(1)	(2)	(3)	(4)	(5)
Family type (omitted group: two-parent family)[b]					
Single-parent	0.005	0.313	0.024	0.102	0.150
	(0.030)	(0.310)	(0.022)	(0.050)**	(0.133)
Immigrant	−0.008	0.085	−0.009	0.018	0.021
	(0.010)	(0.099)	(0.007)	(0.017)	(0.045)
Family size	0.032	−0.078	−0.001	0.109	0.149
	(0.025)	(0.239)	(0.018)	(0.042)**	(0.112)
Age (omitted group: 0 to 10 years)					
11 to 14 years	0.024	−0.412	−0.007	0.133	0.231
	(0.027)	(0.298)	(0.019)	(0.045)***	(0.119)*
15 to 18 years	−0.011	−0.280	−0.019	−0.004	−0.024
	(0.030)	(0.293)	(0.022)	(0.050)	(0.132)
Responding parent is male	−0.037	0.004	−0.024	−0.154	−0.348
	(0.026)	(0.318)	(0.019)	(0.043)***	(0.114)***
Child is male	0.003	−0.087	0.007	0.008	0.028
	(0.022)	(0.218)	(0.016)	(0.037)	(0.097)
Parent's race (omitted group: non-Hispanic white)					
Non-Hispanic black	0.007	−0.233	0.022	0.067	0.239
	(0.039)	(0.416)	(0.028)	(0.065)	(0.172)
Hispanic	0.006	−0.096	0.014	0.118	0.205
	(0.036)	(0.337)	(0.026)	(0.061)*	(0.162)
Other	−0.035	−0.111	0.015	0.014	−0.088
	(0.051)	(0.556)	(0.037)	(0.086)	(0.228)

(Table continues on p. 60.)

TABLE 2A.4 Continued

Explanatory Variables	New Health Problems Since 9/11	Sought Help for New Health Problems	New Post-9/11 Health Problems Continue	Any Health Problem Since 9/11	Number of New Health Problems
Borough of residence (omitted: rest of Manhattan)					
Proximity to Ground Zero	0.008	-0.092	0.024	0.056	0.034
	(0.049)	(0.412)	(0.035)	(0.082)	(0.218)
Rest of Bronx	-0.036	0.189	-0.033	0.064	-0.126
	(0.042)	(0.388)	(0.030)	(0.071)	(0.188)
Rest of Brooklyn	-0.078	0.048	-0.046	-0.076	-0.237
	(0.042)*	(0.413)	(0.030)	(0.071)	(0.187)
Rest of Queens	-0.037	-0.110	-0.040	-0.051	-0.264
	(0.041)	(0.385)	(0.030)	(0.069)	(0.182)
Rest of Staten Island	0.018	0.002	0.006	-0.127	-0.478
	(0.064)	(0.634)	(0.047)	(0.109)	(0.288)*

Family income (omitted 500 percent of poverty line or more)

	(1)	(2)	(3)	(4)	(5)
Below poverty line	-0.049	0.262	-0.021	-0.205	-0.455
	(0.043)	(0.424)	(0.031)	(0.073)***	(0.193)**
100 to 200 percent of poverty line	0.020	0.060	0.014	-0.079	-0.217
	(0.039)	(0.309)	(0.028)	(0.066)	(0.175)
200 to 300 percent of poverty line	-0.013	0.461	-0.004	-0.155	-0.518
	(0.041)	(0.396)	(0.030)	(0.069)**	(0.183)***
300 to 500 percent of poverty line	0.036	0.003	0.033	-0.017	0.018
	(0.036)	(0.351)	(0.026)	(0.060)	(0.159)
Parent or other family member lost job	0.028	-0.220	0.024	0.049	0.258
	(0.032)	(0.313)	(0.023)	(0.053)	(0.141)*

Source: Authors' compilation.

[a]An index of physical and mental health problems that goes from 0 to 6.

[b]Married or cohabiting, with kids, as the omitted group.

*p < .10 **p < .05 ***p < .01

TABLE 2A.5 OLS ESTIMATES OF THE DETERMINANTS OF ANXIETY AMONG NEW YORK CITY CHILDREN SINCE 9/11

Explanatory Variables	Problem Sleeping Since 9/11	Problem Concentrating Since 9/11	Child Prefers to Stay at Home	Child Worried That Parent Might Go Away	Child Is Afraid of Crowded Places
Parent's education (omitted group: B.A. plus)					
Less than high school	0.062	0.041	0.028	0.168	0.104
	(0.047)	(0.048)	(0.057)	(0.065)***	(0.055)*
High school	0.043	0.051	0.008	0.149	0.040
	(0.039)	(0.041)	(0.048)	(0.055)***	(0.046)
Some college	−0.005	0.027	0.017	0.084	−0.016
	(0.037)	(0.038)	(0.045)	(0.051)*	(0.043)
Activity-limiting disability	0.113	0.054	0.055	0.093	0.107
	(0.044)**	(0.046)	(0.055)	(0.061)	(0.052)**
Religion (omitted group: Protestant)					
Roman Catholic	0.090	−0.006	0.133	0.000	0.041
	(0.047)*	(0.048)	(0.058)**	(0.065)	(0.055)
Other Catholic	0.058	0.041	0.085	−0.004	0.035
	(0.051)	(0.053)	(0.064)	(0.072)	(0.061)
Jewish	0.062	0.071	0.086	0.031	0.078
	(0.067)	(0.069)	(0.081)	(0.092)	(0.078)
Muslim	0.200	0.060	0.127	−0.012	0.259
	(0.074)***	(0.077)	(0.090)	(0.103)	(0.086)***
Other	0.095	−0.015	0.028	−0.049	0.042
	(0.049)*	(0.050)	(0.060)	(0.068)	(0.057)

	(1)	(2)	(3)	(4)	(5)
Family type (omitted group: two-parent family)					
Single-parent	0.015	-0.016	-0.063	0.081	-0.032
	(0.035)	(0.036)	(0.042)	(0.048)*	(0.041)
Family size	0.004	-0.007	0.002	0.011	-0.012
	(0.012)	(0.012)	(0.014)	(0.016)	(0.014)
Immigrant	0.012	0.036	-0.008	0.131	0.082
	(0.029)	(0.030)	(0.035)	(0.040)***	(0.034)**
Age (omitted group: 0 to 10 years)					
11 to 14 years	0.057	0.083	0.083	0.126	0.121
	(0.031)*	(0.032)***	(0.038)**	(0.043)***	(0.037)***
15 to 18 years	0.031	0.095	-0.024	-0.026	0.014
	(0.034)	(0.035)***	(0.042)	(0.047)	(0.040)
Responding parent's gender	-0.084	-0.050	-0.085	-0.093	-0.063
	(0.029)***	(0.030)*	(0.036)**	(0.041)**	(0.034)*
Child is male	0.003	0.007	0.035	-0.006	0.021
	(0.025)	(0.026)	(0.031)	(0.035)	(0.029)
Parent's race (omitted group: non-Hispanic white)					
Non-Hispanic black	0.056	0.049	0.122	0.013	0.018
	(0.044)	(0.046)	(0.054)**	(0.062)	(0.052)
Hispanic	0.017	0.110	0.062	0.087	0.051
	(0.042)	(0.043)**	(0.051)	(0.058)	(0.049)
Other	-0.079	-0.011	0.053	-0.048	-0.028
	(0.059)	(0.061)	(0.072)	(0.082)	(0.069)

(Table continues on p. 64.)

TABLE 2A.5 Continued

Explanatory Variables	Problem Sleeping Since 9/11	Problem Concentrating Since 9/11	Child Prefers to Stay at Home	Child Worried That Parent Might Go Away	Child Is Afraid of Crowded Places
Borough of residence (omitted: rest of Manhattan)					
Proximity to Ground Zero	-0.105	-0.003	-0.025	0.047	-0.122
	(0.056)*	(0.058)	(0.069)	(0.078)	(0.066)*
Rest of Bronx	-0.089	-0.119	0.003	0.031	-0.067
	(0.048)*	(0.050)**	(0.059)	(0.067)	(0.057)
Rest of Brooklyn	-0.076	-0.095	-0.086	-0.016	-0.118
	(0.048)	(0.050)*	(0.059)	(0.067)	(0.057)**
Rest of Queens	-0.075	-0.070	-0.040	-0.008	-0.136
	(0.047)	(0.049)	(0.058)	(0.065)	(0.055)**
Rest of Staten Island	-0.061	-0.074	-0.037	0.082	-0.141
	(0.076)	(0.078)	(0.091)	(0.105)	(0.088)

Family income (omitted: 500 percent of poverty line or more)

Below poverty line	-0.085	-0.021	-0.007	-0.143	-0.011
	(0.050)*	(0.051)	(0.061)	(0.069)**	(0.058)
100 to 200 percent of poverty line	-0.085	0.019	0.026	-0.084	-0.011
	(0.045)*	(0.047)	(0.055)	(0.063)	(0.053)
200 to 300 percent of poverty line	-0.126	-0.066	-0.024	-0.104	-0.070
	(0.048)***	(0.049)	(0.058)	(0.066)	(0.055)
300 to 500 percent of poverty line	-0.025	0.029	0.019	0.026	-0.014
	(0.041)	(0.043)	(0.050)	(0.057)	(0.048)
Parent or other family member lost job	0.062	0.075	0.009	0.185	0.064
	(0.036)*	(0.038)**	(0.045)	(0.051)***	(0.043)

Source: Authors' compilation.

*p < .10 **p < .05 ***p < .01

TABLE 2A.6   ESTIMATES OF TRENDS IN INDICATORS OF ADULT WELL-BEING IN NEW YORK CITY SINCE 9/11

Explanatory Variables	Adult in Good to Excellent Health	Respondent Works	Family Members Did Not Experience Hunger
Wave 3	0.002	−0.016	0.040
	(0.014)	(0.016)	(0.018)**
Wave 2	−0.052	0.014	0.004
	(0.014)***	(0.016)	(0.018)
Education (omitted: B.A. plus)			
Less than high school	−0.184	−0.260	−0.059
	(0.019)***	(0.023)***	(0.025)**
High school	−0.070	−0.0147	−0.035
	(0.015)***	(0.018)***	(0.023)*
Some college	−0.020	−0.058	−0.033
	(0.015)*	(0.018)***	(0.024)
Activity-limiting disability	0.455	0.315	0.125
	(0.017)***	(0.020)***	(0.018)***
Religion (omitted: Protestant)			
Roman Catholic	−0.004	−0.014	0.005
	(0.017)	(0.020)	(0.022)
Other Catholic	−0.014	0.002	−0.020
	(0.019)	(0.024)	(0.024)
Jewish	−0.040	−0.060	0.038
	(0.025)*	(0.029)**	(0.039)
Muslim	0.036	−0.048	−0.006
	(0.031)	(0.037)	(0.039)
Other	−0.009	0.012	0.024
	(0.020)	(0.024)	(0.026)
Family type (omitted: single, no kids)			
Married or cohabiting, no kids	0.028	0.077	−0.010
	(0.019)	(0.023)**	(0.028)
Single, with kids	0.002	0.092	−0.032
	(0.020)	(0.025)***	(0.025)
Married or cohabiting, with kids	0.009	0.076	0.039
	(0.023)	(0.028)***	(0.030)
Immigrant	−0.024	0.024	−0.008
	(0.012)**	(0.014)	(0.015)

Family Can Borrow $1,000	Family Members Were not Victims of Crime	Adult Rates NYC as Good to Excellent Place to Live	Adult Rates Police Protection as Good or Very Good	Adult Rates Neighborhood as Good or Very Good
0.072	0.024	0.199	0.075	0.016
(0.018)***	(0.011)**	(0.018)***	(0.019)***	(0.018)
0.079	0.021	0.103	0.021	0.003
(0.018)***	(0.011)*	(0.018)***	(0.019)	(0.017)
−0.244	−0.019	−0.068	0.016	−0.118
(0.025)***	(0.016)	(0.025)***	(0.027)	(0.025)***
−0.137	−0.014	−0.069	−0.020	−0.084
(0.020)***	(0.012)	(0.020)***	(0.021)	(0.019)***
−0.116	−0.004	−0.016	−0.011	−0.052
(0.019)***	(0.012)	(0.019)	(0.021)	(0.019)***
0.117	0.048	0.052	0.055	0.058
(0.022)***	(0.014)***	(0.022)**	(0.024)**	(0.022)***
0.025	0.017	0.021	0.015	0.030
(0.022)	(0.014)	(0.022)	(0.024)	(0.022)
0.028	0.020	0.009	0.040	0.019
(0.026)	(0.016)	(0.026)	(0.028)	(0.026)
0.060	−0.010	0.055	−0.017	0.085
(0.032)**	(0.020)	(0.032)*	(0.035)	(0.032)***
−0.087	−0.005	0.042	0.032	0.065
(0.040)**	(0.025)	(0.040)	(0.043)	(0.039)
0.014	−0.017	0.006	−0.0001	0.056
(0.026)	(0.016)	(0.026)	(0.028)	(0.025)**
0.026	0.024	−0.017	0.048	0.048
(0.025)*	(0.016)	(0.025)	(0.027)*	(0.025)**
−0.039	−0.007	−0.096	0.015	−0.076
(0.027)	(0.017)	(0.027)***	(0.029)	(0.026)**
0.056	0.023	−0.060	0.016	0.040
(0.030)	(0.019)	(0.031)**	(0.033)	(0.030)
−0.069	−0.012	−0.047	0.003	−0.069
(0.015)***	(0.010)	(0.016)***	(0.017)	(0.015)

(Table continues on p. 68.)

Table 2A.6   *Continued*

Explanatory Variables	Adult in Good to Excellent Health	Respondent Works	Family Members Did Not Experience Hunger
Family size	0.004	−0.041	−0.008
	(0.006)	(0.008)***	(0.008)
Age (omitted group: 35 to 44 years)			
18 to 24 years	0.042	−0.107	0.031
	(0.020)*	(0.024)***	(0.024)
25 to 34 years	0.030	−0.025	0.028
	(0.014)**	(0.017)	(0.019)
45 to 59 years	−0.021	−0.029	0.022
	(0.016)	(0.019)	(0.022)
60 years or older	−0.065	−0.456	0.071
	(0.022)	(0.026)	(0.027)***
Responding parent is male	0.029	0.175	−0.021
	(0.012)**	(0.014)	(0.016)
Parent's race (omitted group: non-Hispanic white)			
Non-Hispanic black	−0.007	0.035	−0.015
	(0.017)	(0.020)	(0.024)
Hispanic	−0.081	−0.013	−0.023
	(0.016)***	(0.020)	(0.023)
Other	−0.081	−0.012	0.011
	(0.016)***	(0.029)	(0.034)
Borough of residence (omitted group: Manhattan)			
Bronx	−0.029	−0.033	−0.094
	(0.026)	(0.031)	(0.038)**
Brooklyn	−0.015	−0.040	−0.047
	(0.024)	(0.029)	(0.037)
Manhattan	−0.009	−0.025	−0.084
	(0.026)	(0.031)	(0.040)
Queens	0.004	−0.007	−0.062
	(0.024)	(0.029)	(0.037)*

Source: Authors' compilation.
*$p < .10$ **$p < .05$ ***$p < .01$

Family Can Borrow $1,000	Family Members Were not Victims of Crime	Adult Rates NYC as Good to Excellent Place to Live	Adult Rates Police Protection as Good or Very Good	Adult Rates Neighborhood as Good or Very Good
−0.007	−0.011	0.002	−0.008	−0.014
(0.008)	(0.005)*	(0.008)	(0.009)	(0.008)
0.079	−0.023	0.038	−0.001	0.016
(0.026)***	(0.016)	(0.026)	(0.028)	(0.026)
0.043	0.009	−0.0005	−0.0008	0.009
(0.018)**	(0.011)	(0.019)	(0.020)	(0.018)
0.008	0.021	0.046	0.014	0.070
(0.020)	(0.013)	(0.020)**	(0.022)	(0.020)***
−0.126	0.040	0.022	0.043	0.029
(0.029)***	(0.018)**	(0.029)	(0.031)	(0.028)
0.039	−0.012	−0.001	0.0008	0.016
(0.015)***	(0.010)	(0.015)	(0.017)	(0.015)
−0.146	−0.020	−0.126	−0.264	−0.173
(0.022)***	(0.014)*	(0.022)***	(0.024)***	(0.022)***
−0.194	−0.027	−0.134	−0.224	−0.212
(0.021)***	(0.013)**	(0.022)***	(0.023)***	(0.021)***
−0.067	−0.024	−0.046	−0.139	−0.077
(0.031)***	(0.019)	(0.032)*	(0.034)***	(0.031)***
−0.040	−0.020	−0.078	−0.084	−0.133
(0.034)	(0.021)	(0.034)**	(0.036)**	(−0.033)***
−0.047	−0.051	−0.085	−0.115	−0.116
(0.032)	(0.020)**	(0.032)***	(0.034)***	(0.031)***
−0.043	−0.037	−0.008	−0.052	−0.100
(0.034)	(0.021)**	(0.034)	(0.037)	(0.034)***
−0.035	−0.011	−0.046	−0.067	−0.031
(0.032)	(0.020)	(0.032)	(0.034)**	(0.031)

TABLE 2A.7   OLS ESTIMATES OF TRENDS IN INDICATORS OF CHILD WELL-BEING IN NEW YORK CITY SINCE 9/11

Explanatory Variables	Child in Good to Excellent Health	Child was Suspended from School	Child Often or Sometimes Doesn't Get Along with Others	Child Often or Sometimes Feels Sad or Depressed
Wave 3	−0.003	−0.019	−0.060	0.021
	(0.012)	(0.014)	(0.021)***	(0.021)
Wave 2	−0.013	0.0006	−0.021	0.018
	(0.012)	(0.014)	(0.021)	(0.021)
Parent's education (omitted group: B.A. plus)				
Less than high school	−0.059	0.043	0.065	0.069
	(0.018)***	(0.020)**	(0.030)**	(0.030)**
High school	−0.019	0.032	0.039	0.057
	(0.014)*	(0.016)**	(0.024)	(0.024)**
Some college	−0.017	0.029	−0.013	0.018
	(0.014)	(0.016)**	(0.024)	(0.024)
Activity-limiting disability	0.190	−0.054	−0.188	−0.155
	(0.021)***	(0.023)**	(0.035)***	(0.035)***
Religion (omitted group: Protestant)				
Roman Catholic	−0.029	−0.009	−0.014	−0.022
	(0.016)*	(0.017)	(0.027)	(0.027)
Other Catholic	−0.061	0.028	0.079	−0.031
	(0.018)***	(0.021)	(0.031)**	(0.031)
Jewish	−0.035	−0.002	0.021	0.011
	(0.025)	(0.028)	(0.044)	(0.044)
Muslim	0.009	−0.0003	−0.012	−0.005
	(0.027)	(0.032)	(0.047)	(0.047)
Other	−0.014	−0.002	0.024	−0.003
	(0.019)	(0.022)	(0.033)	(0.033)
Family type (omitted group: two-parent family)				
Single, with kids	−0.024	−0.009	0.033	0.104
	(0.013)*	(0.014)	(0.021)	(0.021)***
Immigrant	−0.019	−0.025	−0.003	0.012
	(0.011)*	(0.012)**	(0.019)	(0.019)
Family size	−0.019	0.0008	0.001	0.001
	(0.011)	(0.005)	(0.008)	(0.008)

TABLE 2A.7   *Continued*

Explanatory Variables	Child in Good to Excellent Health	Child was Suspended from School	Child Often or Sometimes Doesn't Get Along with Others	Child Often or Sometimes Feels Sad or Depressed
Age				
10 years or younger	0.027	−0.031	0.074	−0.101
	(0.013)	(0.013)***	(0.022)***	(0.021)***
11 to 14 years	0.017	Dropped	0.070	Dropped
	(0.016)		(0.025)***	
15 to 18 years	Dropped	0.032	Dropped	0.038
		(0.015)		(0.025)
Child is male	−0.011	0.037	0.042	0.012
	(0.010)	(0.011)***	(0.017)**	(0.017)
Parent's race (omitted group: non-Hispanic white)				
Non-Hispanic black	−0.014	0.057	0.017	−0.067
	(0.017)	(0.019)**	(0.029)	(0.029)**
Hispanic	−0.027	0.016	−0.017	−0.031
	(0.016)*	(0.018)	(0.027)	(0.027)
Other	−0.038	0.007	0.026	−0.005
	(0.024)*	(0.028)	(0.041)	(0.041)
Borough of residence (omitted group: Manhattan)				
Bronx	−0.007	0.047	0.043	−0.015
	(0.023)	(0.026)	(0.039)	(0.039)
Brooklyn	0.011	0.009	0.020	0.009
	(0.022)	(0.024)	(0.037)	(0.037)
Manhattan	0.013	0.033	0.050	0.067
	(0.025)	(0.028)	(0.042)	(0.042)
Queens	0.012	0.013	0.010	0.007
	(0.022)	(0.024)	(0.037)	(0.037)

Source: Authors' compilation.
*p < .10   **p < .05   ***p < .01

APPENDIX 2.2: STUDIES ON THE EFFECTS OF 9/11

9/11 United Services Group: A study of the ongoing needs of people affected by the World Trade Center disaster

American Psychological Association (APA) and National Public Radio's "The Infinite Mind": National survey on depression, anxiety, post-traumatic stress, and coping behavior after September 11

American Red Cross in Greater New York (ARCGNY) and Strategic Surveys International: Survey to assess critical needs in the aftermath of September 11 two months and five months after the attacks

Asian American Federation of New York (AAFNY): Economic impact of 9/11 on Chinatown

Center for Urban Epidemiologic Studies: Use of cigarettes, alcohol, and marijuana among Manhattan residents after the 9/11 terrorist attacks

Centers for Disease Control: Survey of Manhattan residents living below 110th Street on asthma and the psychological impact of the attacks (life stressors, depression, risk for PTSD)

Citizens' Committee for Children of New York and Belden, Russonello, and Stewart Research and Communications: Survey about the responses to 9/11 of New York City children and families

City of New York Office of the Comptroller: Fiscal impact of 9/11 on New York City

Fiscal Policy Institute (FPI): Impact of 9/11 on employment

Fiscal Policy Institute: Impact of 9/11 on wage workers

The Food Bank for New York City—Food for Survival: Changes in food assistance after 9/11

Hunter College Graduate School in Social Research on behalf of the New York City Coalition Against Hunger: Changes in food pantry demand in the six months following 9/11

McPheters & Company and Beta Research: "Changing American Lives," a national survey on use of time, religious behavior, attitudes toward media, attitudes toward work, leisure activities, financial behavior, and fears and concerns after September 11

Milken Institute: The impact of September 11 on U.S. metropolitan economics

National Opinion Research Center (NORC) at the University of Chicago: "National Tragedy Study" on reactions after the attacks, physical and emotional responses to the tragedy, psychological well-being, and items included in the General Social Surveys (GSS)

National Public Radio, Henry Kaiser Foundation, and Harvard University John F. Kennedy School of Government: "Civil Liberties Study," a national survey on trust and confidence in government; privacy, civil liberties, and press freedom; and fears and worries

New York Academy of Medicine, Columbia University School of Public Health, and Schulman, Ronca & Bucavalas Inc.: Research program to assess the psychological consequences of the WTC attacks in the entire New York metropolitan area

New York City Board of Education: Effects of the WTC attack on New York City public school students

New York City Partnership: Analysis of the economic impact of 9/11 and exploration of ideas on accelerating New York City's recovery

New York Governor and State Division of the Budget: Current estimated cost of rebuilding New York City

New York State Senate Finance Committee: Financial impact of the WTC attack

Rand Corporation and University of California: National survey on reactions to the terrorist attacks and parents' perceptions of their children's reactions

Southern University: Survey of African American college students' reactions to the terrorist acts of 9/11

Urban Justice Center: "Ripple Effect," a study of the crisis in New York City's low-income communities after September 11

United Way of New York City: "Beyond Ground Zero," a study of the challenges and implications for human services in New York City after September 11

University of Michigan Institute for Social Research (ISR): "How Americans Respond," a survey of attitudes toward homeland security measures and civil liberties; attitudes toward immigrants and racial and ethnic groups; confidence in institutions; volunteering and charitable activity; use of time; and depression, anxiety, and distress

NOTES

1. Jason Bram, James Orr, and Carol Rapaport (2002) have computed the economic cost of the 9/11 attacks for New York City at $33 billion to $36 billion, which includes the lifetime earnings loss for the workers killed in the attacks, the employment impact in the key affected sectors—such as finance, air transportation, hotels, and restaurants—and the cost of repairing and replacing the damaged physical capital stock and infrastructure. Earlier, more quickly assembled estimates were higher: New York City Partnership estimated a total economic impact of $83 billion (including a lost gross city product [GCP] of $39 billion), and the New York City Office of the Comptroller estimated a total economic impact of $82.8 billion to $94.8 billion (including a lost GCP of $52 billion to $64 billion).
2. The child with the most recent birthday prior to the interview was selected as the focal child for the interviews.
3. For 1997 and 2002, we interpolated and extrapolated, respectively, population distributions from the 1990 to 2000 trends in census figures.
4. According to the 2001 FBI hate crimes report (U.S. Department of Justice 2001), the number of anti-Muslim hate crimes rose from 28 in 2000 to 481 in 2001. A Human Rights Watch (2002) report cites data from local and state agencies that indicate growing hate crime against Muslims. In Chicago, for instance, the police department reported 51 anti-Muslim hate crimes from September to November 2001, compared with only four such cases during the entire year 2000. In Los Angeles County there were only 12 hate crime cases against people of Middle Eastern descent in 2000, compared with 188 in 2001 (Human Rights Watch 2002).
5. Unfortunately, our data do not permit us to explore this hypothesis.
6. In results not reported in the table, we identified subsamples of Manhattan residents and of other borough residents who lived close to the site of the World Trade Center, but we could find no significant differences between nearby residents and other city residents. The Social Indicators Survey sample size is too small to detect such small neighborhood effects.
7. Income and employment measures are not included in the regressions.
8. That overall health should be countercyclical appears at first to be counterintuitive. But Christopher Ruhm (2000, 2003; Ruhm and Blank 2002) presents evidence that physical health is countercyclical and suggests that the effect may be explained by on-the-job injuries. Ruhm also finds that changes in behaviors such as a drop in tobacco use, a fall in body weight among the severely obese, and an increase in exercise among the completely inactive supply one mechanism for the pro-cyclical variation in mortality and morbidity observed in recent research.

REFERENCES

American Psychological Association (APA). 2002. "Many Americans Still Feeling Effects of September 11; Are Reexamining Their Priorities in Life." Press release, February 11.
American Red Cross in Greater New York (ARCGNY). 2002. *Findings from Surveys: Two Months and Five Months Later.* Available at: http:/nyredcross.org/wtcrecovery/wtcrecovery_execsummary.htm (accessed May 20, 2002).

Applied Research and Consulting. 2002. *Effects of the World Trade Center Attack on NYC Public School Students*. Initial report to the New York City Board of Education. New York: Columbia University Mailman School of Public Health and New York State Psychiatric Institute (May).

Bram, Jason, James Orr, and Carol Rapaport. 2002. "Measuring the Effects of the September 11 Attacks on New York City." *Economic Policy Review—Federal Reserve Bank of New York* 8(2): 5–20.

Citizens' Committee for Children of New York. 2002. *Children and Crisis: NYC's Response After 9/11*. Report. New York: Citizens' Committee for Children of New York (September 5).

Fiscal Policy Institute. 2002. *The Employment Impact of the September 11 World Trade Center Attacks: Updated Estimates Based on the Benchmarked Employment Data*. Report. New York: Fiscal Policy Institute (March 8).

Galea, Sandro, Jennifer Ahern, Heidi Resnick, Dean Kilpatrick, Michael Bucuvalas, Joel Gold, and David Vlahov. 2002. "Psychological Sequelae of the September 11 Terrorist Attacks in New York City." *New England Journal of Medicine* 346(13): 982–87.

Huddy, Leonie, Nadia Khatib, and Theresa Capelos. 2002. "The Polls-Trends: Reactions to the Terrorist Attacks of September 11, 2001." *Public Opinion Quarterly* 66(3): 418–50.

Human Rights Watch. 2002. *"We Are Not the Enemy": Hate Crimes Against Arabs, Muslims, and Those Perceived to Be Arab or Muslim After September 11*. Report. New York: Human Rights Watch (November 14).

Kleinfield, N. R., and Marjorie Connelly. 2003. "Two Years Later: Public Opinion; 9/11 Still Straining New York Psyche." *New York Times*, September 8, p. A1.

New York State Assembly. Ways and Means Committee. 2002. *New York State Economic Report*. Albany: New York State Assembly (March).

Ruhm, Christopher J. 2000. "Are Recessions Good for Your Health?" *Quarterly Journal of Economics* 115(2): 617–50.

———. 2003. "Good Times Make You Sick." *Journal of Health Economics* 24(4): 637–58.

Ruhm, Christopher J., and William E. Blank. 2002. "Does Drinking Really Decrease in Bad Times?" *Journal of Health Economics* 21(4): 659–78.

Smith, Tom W., Kenneth A. Rasinski, and Marianna Toce. 2001. *America Rebounds: A National Study of Public Response to the September 11 Terrorist Attacks, Preliminary Findings*. Report. Chicago: National Organization for Research, University of Chicago (October 25).

U.S. Department of Justice. Federal Bureau of Investigation. 2001. *Hate Crimes Statistics*. Washington: U.S. Department of Justice. Available at: http://www.fbi.gov/ucr/01hate. pdf (accessed November 5, 2004).

U.S. Department of Labor. Bureau of Labor Statistics. 2003. "Seasonally Adjusted Unemployment Rates from Local Area Unemployment Statistics." Series LASPS36040003. Washington: U.S. Department of Labor. Available at www.bls.gov (accessed November 5, 2004).

Vlahov, David, Sandro Galea, Heidi Resnick, Jennifer Ahern, Joseph A. Boscarino, Michael Bucuvalas, Joel Gold, and Dean Kilpatrick. 2002. "Increased Use of Cigarettes, Alcohol, and Marijuana Among Manhattan, New York, Residents After the September 11 Terrorists Attacks." *American Journal of Epidemiology* 155(11): 988–96.

PART II

The Impact of 9/11 on Residential and Ethnic Communities

CHAPTER 3

Disaster at the Doorstep: Battery Park City and Tribeca Respond to the Events of 9/11

Philip Kasinitz, Gregory Smithsimon, and Binh Pok

ALTHOUGH IT is usually thought of as a place where people work, lower Manhattan is also a place where tens of thousands of people live. The World Trade Center (WTC) site is bordered by two residential neighborhoods: Battery Park City, directly to the west, and Tribeca, which abuts it to the north. In many ways these communities are superficially similar. The residents of both neighborhoods are predominantly white, highly educated, and affluent. Both are, by New York standards, new communities created in the spatial reorganization of lower Manhattan that followed the construction of the twin towers. Both have an unusually strong sense of corporate identity and clear boundaries. Both are defined, to a considerable degree, by their physical appearance, although one could hardly imagine two more different-looking neighborhoods. And both were traumatized by the 9/11 attack and its aftermath. In both communities residents witnessed horrifying sights as the towers burned, and both communities were engulfed in the gray cloud of dust, ash, and debris when they fell. Battery Park City was completely evacuated that day as its normally largely recreational waterfront became New York's Dunkirk and tens of thousands of lower Manhattan workers were ferried to New Jersey. Tribeca was only slightly less affected. Over one thousand residents were evacuated, and an unknown number left voluntarily, joining the panicked throng that filled its streets, heading north.

In the weeks that followed both neighborhoods were placed in the "frozen zone." Most businesses were shuttered, and both foot and vehicular traffic were severely curtailed. For months after the attack streets in both areas were blocked, first by debris, then by the demolition and clean-up efforts. Residents had to decide whether to return to homes now caked in what many feared was toxic dust. Even today (we write in July 2004), the absence of the towers that dominated the local skyline can be felt in large and small ways. Without the light that reflected off them, the streets of both communities are noticeably darker at night.

Despite these many similarities, within a year after the attacks it was clear that these two communities were responding in markedly different ways.[1] In Battery Park City the crisis was, in many senses, ongoing. Many saw recovery efforts and rebuilding plans as a continuation of the assault on a community that, despite its high-rise buildings and location near the heart of the metropolis, had been designed to feel private and almost suburban. Efforts to bring life back to its streets were often seen as an invasion by outsiders, and plans to reestablish links between the community and the rest of the city were greeted with skepticism and sometimes outright hostility. Even within the increasingly close-knit community, divisions became apparent. People who returned to the neighborhood after 9/11 sometimes found relations with former neighbors who had moved out to be strained, and people who had lived in the neighborhood before September 2001 were divided from the newcomers who took advantage of the discounted rents that building owners offered to entice people back to the community after 9/11. Disagreements over minor matters of daily life— whether, for example, it was now safe to let children play in the playground sandbox—kept 9/11 in the forefront of people's minds.

In contrast, Tribeca, although less directly affected by the attack, embraced the post-9/11 recovery efforts. The terrorist attack gave a new focus and organizational energy to what had been a fairly unorganized community of business owners and residents. A major film festival was established, world-famous architects designed new retail spaces, and restaurant reopenings were greeted as public events. Efforts to bring tourists and shoppers back to the area were generally applauded. There was concern that in the rush to reestablish commercial life the "wrong" kind of businesses—chain stores and moderately priced hotels—might move into the exclusive area. Yet most residents and business owners of Tribeca applauded efforts to reestablish the neighborhood's place as a trendsetter in the commercial and cultural life of the city. If anything, both the economic devastation that followed the attack—many businesses were closed for two months or more—and the recovery efforts accelerated trends that had been well under way for a decade.

The differences in how Tribeca and Battery Park City reacted to the events of 9/11 reflect the different relationships the two neighborhoods had had to the World Trade Center prior to the attack. Yet they also tell us a great deal about the nature of two very different communities. Although both are home to mostly white, upper- and upper-middle-class New Yorkers, they represent very different slices of contemporary New York. Indeed, Battery Park City and Tribeca might be said to epitomize different ideas about urban life. The tragic events of 9/11 and the responses of these two communities place these differences in sharp relief.

BATTERY PARK CITY: VERTICAL SUBURBIA?

Battery Park City was, in a very real sense, a by-product of the creation of the World Trade Center. The land the neighborhood sits on was created when rubble from the World Trade Center's excavation was dumped on old piers in the Hudson River. Although it was generally agreed that this "new" land would be used to create a planned residential community, what sort of community that would be was the topic of debate for decades. Plans calling for a mix of low- and moderate-income housing were proposed throughout the late 1960s and 1970s as several governmental agencies wrangled for control over the site. However, by the time the city effectively surrendered control of the site to the newly created Battery Park City Authority in 1979, this social vision was effectively off the table. The authority, a public-private partnership whose head is appointed by the governor, was charged with creating a lively and attractive neighborhood and maximizing income from the development of the site (Dunlap 1999). Between 1982 and 2001 (construction was still going on at the time of the attack), the authority oversaw the creation of parks and playgrounds, a waterfront esplanade, a recreational harbor and ferry terminal, new streets, a major four-tower office complex known as the World Financial Center, several smaller office buildings, two small museums, two hotels, a new home for New York's premier magnet high school, several commercial spaces (although surprisingly few by New York City standards), and high-rise housing for eight thousand residents.

In contrast to most planned communities, care was taken to ensure that Battery Park City did not look like a housing development. Buildings were designed by different architects in different styles and built by different private developers over a period of time, with the idea that neighborhood would thus appear to be an "organic" part of the city. In a nod to the postmodern fashions of the 1980s, some design elements of many of the buildings make reference to the conventions of early-twentieth-century high-rise architecture. The authority points with particular pride to the community's street plan, which, in contrast to the typical development, is supposed to echo the grid pattern of the existing city streets. Yet, as early critics of the project noted, while the postmodern design of Battery Park City's streets and public spaces pays homage to the outer appearance of Manhattan's street grid, in fact the community stands in sharp contrast to the dense urbanism of the rest of lower Manhattan (Trilling 1985). Separated from the rest of the city by West Street—which in spite of its name is an eight-lane highway—Battery Park City was functionally a gated community prior to September 2001 (Low 2003; 2004). The connections to the Manhattan street grid, so clear on a planner's map, completely disappeared for the pedestrian on the ground. In fact, the community could be entered on foot at only a few crossing points—most of them at the extreme southern and northern ends of the neighborhood—either by sprinting across the highway or by taking one of three footbridges over the highway, two of which were destroyed in the 9/11 attack.

Once inside its boundaries, one sees clearly that Battery Park City looks less to the city than to the river. Its large office complex, the World Financial Center, is set back from the street, separated from it by a broad stretch of grass and narrow sidewalk more typical of suburban development than a central business district. There are few street-level businesses—indeed, much of Battery Park City's scarce retail space is *inside* the World Financial Center, whose atrium resembles an upscale shopping mall far more than a New York street. Further, in contrast to Manhattan's usual street grid, Battery Park City is hard for the casual visitor to navigate. Even after crossing West Street, the design is not transparent to the intrepid explorer. The pedestrian bridges linking the development to the World Trade Center led into buildings with no indication that the bridges or the passageways were intended for public use. Once on the street, a "you can't get there from here" feeling prevails for the first-time visitor. No street runs through Battery Park City north to south, and walking is further frustrated because the north-south passages that do exist are poorly marked. The area is as hard to navigate by car as by foot: drivers often find themselves, with little warning, in a cul-de-sac, with no idea where to go next. Although street names like South End Avenue and North End Avenue mimic other parts of the city, there is no street equivalent to Upper Manhattan's Riverside Drive, which allows drivers to see the park and orient themselves to the river.

Even the neighborhood's most important amenities, its parks and public spaces with views of the river, are often difficult to get to or even find. Indeed, one might ask just how truly public these spaces are, as one often must walk through a private office building to reach them. As the writer Phillip Lopate (quoted in Fainstein 1994, 183) asked in 1989:

How public *is* public space, when it has been embedded in a context that raises such formidable social barriers that the masses of ordinary working people (not to mention those out of work) would feel uncomfortable entering it? How many poor families may be expected to cross the raised bridge in that citadel of wealth, the World Financial Center, and wander through the privileged enclaves of South End Avenue and Rector Place before reaching their permitted perch along the waterfront?

This isolated, semiprivate quality is the major feature noted by both Battery Park City's fans and its critics. "The development . . . has an insular quality that attracts those seeking a respite from Manhattan and bothers those who wish it were more public," (Dunlap 1994, 1). "The project essentially turns its back to the city," concedes Stanton Eckstut, one of the main architects of the 1979 master plan, though he argues that this is because at the time of the design process the land faced the then-elevated West Side Highway (Dunlap 1999). Whatever the reason, the design of Battery Park City has created not only a well-defined community but one that has a sense of itself apart from the hub-bub of Manhattan.

This isolated community thus attracted many who sought to combine its convenience to the downtown financial district with a degree of distance and privacy from the rest of the city. By the year 2000, these residents were 75 percent non-Hispanic white, 18 percent Asian, 5 percent Latino, and 3 percent African American, and they reported a median household income of $111,854. One of the attractions of Battery Park City was its proximity to the financial district and the World Trade Center. More than half of residents' jobs were located downtown, and 20 percent worked in Battery Park City's own World Financial Center. According to the public use microdata samples (PUMS) of the 2000 census, an astounding 37.8 percent of Battery Park City residents walked to work.

Residents often comment on the neighborhood's strange combination of walking distance convenience to and psychological distance from the rest of the city. Some moved there because of this, while others bridle against it. "It has always felt like the suburbs of New York," one resident noted, while another reported that she had heard her fellow residents call her neighborhood "suburbia in Manhattan." Indeed, one woman who has lived in Battery Park City for eight and a half years observed: "I absolutely love it here; there's nowhere else to live as far as I'm concerned. . . . It's a small town that's gotten much closer together since September 11. I think it's a beautiful neighborhood. The parks, the water, the esplanade, all of that, it's just a great place to live—because you have the amenities of the city, but you're separate from it." Residents who value the seclusion of Battery Park City from the rest of the city reported the fear that now the permanent loss of this seclusion would be added to their losses from the 9/11 tragedy itself.

Of course, Battery Park City does not *look* much like the typical American suburb. Indeed, for all of its postmodern touches, it realizes many of the modernist ideals of Le Corbusier's "tower in the park." Its residents live in high-rise buildings, and while their apartments are spacious by Manhattan standards, their homes are much smaller than those of most Americans of their income levels. Unlike typical suburbanites, Battery Park City residents have traded large private spaces for outstanding public ones. And yet, prior to September 11, 2001, even these public spaces had a distinctly private feel. And as in Le Corbusier's vision ("We must," he famously wrote, "kill the street"), Battery Park City has little street-level commercial space, particularly when contrasted to the rest of lower Manhattan. Thus, in an unanticipated development, residents began to use the shopping mall beneath the World Trade Center, whose suburban-style chain stores and restaurants were originally envisioned as a place where WTC workers and commuters could conveniently shop as well as socialize.

Battery Park City is rich in public spaces, and there are many planned activities in those spaces, from lunchtime concerts in the World Financial Center atrium to swing dancing under the stars in a plaza. However, while there are a few local bars and cafés—mostly in the hotels—there are far fewer of these sorts of "hanging-out" spaces than is typical for New York. Most of the handful of restaurants are in the hotels and the World Financial Center and cater to the business lunch trade. In contrast to Tribeca, none of the restaurants tend to draw people from outside the community. There are two grocery stores and a few small convenience stores but no pharmacies, and there are no bookstores or many other examples of what Ray Oldenburg has called "third spaces"—those places that are neither private nor, strictly speaking, public but where the unplanned, serendipitous encounters that are the building blocks of public life usually happen (Oldenburg 1990). Indeed, the fact that many Battery Park City residents used the mall in the World Trade Center for such purposes only increased their isolation after the towers were destroyed. Although there was an increase in local discussion and political activity after 9/11, residents were often at a loss as to how to organize. Battery Park City has almost no bulletin boards and no place to post a flyer. For parents of small children, often the community's most mobilized group, the playgrounds are sometimes a point of contact. Tellingly, however, much of Battery Park City's local political organizing takes place on the Internet—a medium that does not require people to share physical space.

We should of course be wary of explaining the relationship between a community's physical structure and its social organization as spatially determined. We are not suggesting that Battery Park City's design *causes* its residents to have certain attitudes toward urban life or led them to respond in certain ways to the events of 9/11. If anything, the relationship is the other way around— many people choose to live in Battery Park City at least in part because of its physical structure. However, the type of social and physical community that Battery Park City was prior to 9/11 undoubtedly played a role in shaping its residents' response to the attacks.

TRIBECA: NEIGHBORHOOD AS BRAND

Tribeca—the *tri*-angle *be*-low *Ca*-nal Street—is the second-closest residential community to the World Trade Center site after Battery Park City. This community of industrial-buildings-turned-upscale-lofts was established in the early 1970s, and the twin towers were effectively its southwestern border. Officially known as the Lower Manhattan Mixed-Use District, a zoning designation established in 1976 to legalize retroactively the conversion of industrial lofts to residential use (a trend that was already well under way), Tribeca is both an old and a new community—old in the sense that this piece of land has been settled since the seventeenth century, and new in that the vast majority of its housing units came into being in the twenty-five years prior to 9/11 and the idea of Tribeca as a distinct place and as a lifestyle also arose during that time. And yet, while Tribeca came into being at the same time as Battery Park City, the process could hardly have been more different. Battery Park City involved the construction of a planned community, on literally new land, but Tribeca was one of the latest examples of the unplanned (if in some senses predictable), postindustrial reuses of spaces at the heart of the old industrial city.

First settled as a wealthy residential enclave just north of the center of the city (much of its original housing stock was destroyed in the great fires of 1777 and 1835), by the midnineteenth century the area had become a center of food and commodities wholesaling, particularly after the piers of the Lower West Side replaced those of South Street as the city's main cargo port. (Some of these were the piers that are today *under* Battery Park City.) With the advent of automobile traffic, the crowded streets of lower Manhattan were increasingly impractical for industry and warehousing, although it was not until the early 1960s, with the planned construction of the World Trade Center, that the last food wholesalers finally left the area for Hunts Point in the Bronx. Left behind were an extraordinary collection of large, nearly empty warehouses, underused industrial lofts, and desolate streets that effectively shut down after business hours.

While businesses were moving out of Tribeca in the 1960s, the empty industrial buildings just to the north were being converted into living spaces. Loft conversion was first legalized in SoHo (*So*-uth of *Ho*-uston Street). Originally only working artists and their families were legally allowed to live in buildings zoned for industrial use. However, with demand for housing high and the demand for industrial space in lower Manhattan on the wane, the definition of "artist" became increasingly flexible, and eventually the provision was dropped altogether. Once seen as the garrets of starving artists, by the 1970s these loft spaces had become increasingly fashionable. By 1976 rental rates for living lofts were on a par with those for traditional apartments (Zukin 1982).

SoHo also brought into the public consciousness the new role that artists (loosely defined) were coming to play in the New York real estate market. In this respect, artists were probably less important as actual consumers than as signifiers of an "artistic" lifestyle. Whereas previous famous artists' enclaves had been associated with bohemian poverty, SoHo was a bohemia for a new era in which the lines between art, design, fashion, and entertainment had been blurred, if not obliterated. For perhaps the first time, avant-garde cultural style was now completely compatible with celebrity and wealth. Further, in terms of urban design, SoHo's success created a look and a style marked by huge open spaces (perhaps the ultimate conspicuous consumption in crowded Manhattan), high ceilings, floor-to-ceiling windows, and massive columns that was soon widely imitated. This in turn created a new demand for nineteenth-century industrial buildings to be recycled into residential spaces.

Because of these changes that had taken place in SoHo, Tribeca, directly to the south, came into existence with a clear model of what it could become. Despite its central location, Tribeca was still a desolate place in the 1970s, lacking any supermarkets or shopping conveniences. Among the first new residents of Tribeca were artists who came in the late 1960s and early 1970s: some had been pushed out of SoHo by rising housing costs, and others had sold SoHo lofts at large profits and thus found themselves suddenly flush but homeless. These pioneers began moving into the empty warehouses in Tribeca; the exodus of manufacturing and wholesaling had left behind expansive, airy, light-filled spaces ready for conversion to residential housing, albeit with a great deal of work.[2]

The legislation that legally established Tribeca in 1976 conceived of it as a mixed-use area—one in which, as in SoHo, many existing industrial buildings would be converted to residential use but other industrial and commercial businesses would remain. Although the provisions that legalized loft living in Tribeca were more complicated than those for SoHo and NoHo (the area No-rth of Ho-uston Street), the point of the law was simple: anyone, artist or not, could legally convert a loft to residential use in Tribeca. And whereas living lofts in SoHo could not be smaller than 1,200 square feet, those in Tribeca could be as small as 1,000 square feet (still spacious by New York City standards). The smaller apartment sizes encouraged commercial developers and investors. Further, by the time people started moving into Tribeca, loft living had become fashionable. Recognizing this, financial institutions that had been wary and slow to participate in SoHo's early residential conversion were quick to invest in Tribeca. A few of Tribeca's present lofts were converted by "shoe string entrepreneurs" (Zukin 1982), but most of its conversions were undertaken by established real estate developers.

The subsequent population growth was dramatic. By 2000 Tribeca had four times the number of housing units that it had twenty years earlier, and fewer than 1 percent of local residents lived in the same home they had lived in prior to 1970.

Although developers were largely responsible for the growth of Tribeca, it was celebrities who gave the area its cache. John F. Kennedy Jr., Robert De-Niro, Bette Midler, Meryl Streep, Cyndi Lauper, and Martin Scorsese all moved to Tribeca between the late 1970s and early 1990s. Whereas upper-class and upper-middle-class New Yorkers began to frequent SoHo art galleries and performance spaces well before the area was known as a home for celebrities, Tribeca's celebrity residents played a key role in bringing nonresidents to the area's still quiet streets. DeNiro's presence and identity with Tribeca culminated in the establishment of his Tribeca Film Center in 1989 as well as his partial ownership of two high-profile restaurants, Tribeca Grill (1990) and Nobu (1994). Artists were also prominent among early Tribeca residents. SoHo had at least initially been populated by rising and struggling artists, but it was the already famous who first moved into Tribeca, including the performance artist Laurie Anderson and the painter James Rosenquist. Today there are seventeen art galleries in Tribeca, although restaurants, bars, and specialty antique and designer stores are far more numerous. Indeed, it is the merger of art and commerce that is central to the Tribeca style. This is perhaps exemplified by Issey Miyake's new flagship store designed by Frank Gehry, which opened with a champagne reception for the famous architect only a few months after 9/11.

The restaurant industry also played a central role in establishing Tribeca. The famous restaurateur Drew Nieporent owns or is partial owner of several high-profile restaurants located in Tribeca, including Montrachet, Tribeca Grill, Nobu, and Layla. Along with other restaurants such as Chanterelle, Le Zinc, and Odeon, these are all among the city's most fashionable and most expensive restaurants. Indeed, their names often recall the extravagances of the 1980s, a fact made clear when the paperback version of Jay McInerney's 1980s novel *Bright Lights, Big City* featured a picture of Odeon on the cover. Today seven of fifty top-rated New York restaurants in the Zagat's restaurant guide are in Tribeca—and all except one are in the "over $70.00 per person" price category. With one of the highest concentrations of multi-star restaurants in the city, Tribeca has become a destination spot for food lovers from New York and beyond.

Most of these restaurants opened when the residential population was still low. They prospered in part by taking advantage of the grand spaces and light available in the former warehouse buildings, but then played a central role in drawing tourists, Hollywood stars, people from the fashion industry, and wealthy New Yorkers down to this previously underutilized area, particularly at night. Thus, for people who lived there, but especially for people from *outside* the community, Tribeca was fast becoming identified as a chic destination spot synonymous with celebrities, high fashion, and very expensive food. Whereas in Battery Park City a strong sense of community emerged out of the sharp sense of separation from the rest of the city, in Tribeca, only a few blocks away, the sense of a distinct local style was marketed for consumption primarily by people who did not live there. Tribeca became, in some senses, as much a concept or a brand as a traditional neighborhood of face-to-face interactions. As such, it depended on being open to outsiders in a way that Battery Park City never did. Tribeca is notably lacking in official public space, and one legacy of its industrial origins is the dearth of parks or playgrounds. It abounds, however, in bars, cafés, and other haunts and hangouts.

In *The Death and Life of Great American Cities* (1961), Jane Jacobs famously argues that successful urban life requires a balance of reliable networks of neighbors and openness to strangers. Prior to 9/11, Battery Park City was extremely successful at creating bonds between neighbors despite its high-rise architecture, which is often seen as not conducive to neighborliness. It did so, however, largely by keeping strangers at bay. Tribeca was largely created by its openness to strangers. Its strong sense of identity had little to do with knowing the people next door. Yet Jacobs would probably see it as too much a place of strangers, with no reliable neighborly bonds. Interestingly, when the events of 9/11 did bring the community together, the effort was largely organized by business owners.

Local residents seem to have a clear, if not exactly accurate, image of themselves as Tribecans. Almost all of our informants viewed themselves as "creative," as "entrepreneurs," or as "pioneers." In demographic terms, however, Tribecans resemble residents of other affluent areas of New York, including Battery Park City. They are predominantly white (77 percent) and well educated (73.5 percent of residents age twenty-five or older had at least a bachelor's degree). Nearly 38 percent of households reported annual incomes above $125,000, and 25 percent reported over $200,000. Thirty-five percent owned their own homes, as opposed to 20 percent in Manhattan generally. Moreover, 47 percent reported being employed as a professional or working in the finance industries, while only 12 percent reported being in the arts or entertainment industries. One telling statistic is the high percentage of residents who reported working from home (16 percent) and walking to work (21 percent). Yet these statistics seem to miss some subtle differences between Tribeca residents and those in Battery Park City. In eight months of Tribeca fieldwork, we did not run across a single resident who had worked in the World Trade Center, and we found only a few who knew anyone who had. And despite its proximity, none of the Tribecans we spoke to would admit to having shopped in the World Trade Center's ground-floor mall. By contrast, many of our Battery Park City informants knew several World Trade Center workers, and several had worked there themselves.[3] Thus, Tribeca residents reported far fewer direct links to victims of the attack. As one respondent noted: "In the first days, we expected to lose a lot of people. But we were surprised to find how few of us knew victims or [knew anyone] even in terms of degrees of separation."

Although the sheer size of the World Trade Center made it a constant presence in the community, it played little substantive role in the daily lives of Tribeca residents. The contrast in how the two neighborhoods related to their mammoth neighbor goes deeper than the fact that many Battery Park City residents worked there and most Tribecans did not. The World Trade Center was designed to be a testament to human ingenuity and dominance over the environment. It symbolized new technologies and a new future of possibilities. For all of its self-consciously referential touches, Battery Park City, a development of new buildings on new land, is in many ways part of that same project and an equally history-free environment. Tribeca's brick industrial buildings, on the other hand, look to the past. As if in opposition to the World Trade Center, Tribeca's appeal is a revalorization of urban history. Urban grit and contemporary glamour are mixed in deliberate juxtapositions. The look of the former factories and markets and the occasional cobblestone streets stands in ironic contrast to the buildings' current high-fashion uses.

Indeed, wandering the streets of Tribeca, one might never guess that its residents are so affluent. The buildings are not very high. Standard Tribeca lot-buildings have six to ten stories with a twenty-five- to fifty-foot frontage on the street and about one hundred feet in depth. Unlike SoHo's fairly unified composition of continuous blocks of cast-iron fronts, Tribeca's architecture reflects its mixed history: giant masonry structures with Italianate storefronts in white or gray-blue marble sit next to sturdy cast-iron storefronts. Businesses and offices usually occupy the first floors of the low buildings, but the remaining floors have two, three, and sometimes four tall windows running across, the curtains and pets peering out testifying to their residential use. A few warehouses still operate in Tribeca. More often, however, restaurants are now using the former loading platforms as sidewalk cafés. Meanwhile, art galleries, restaurants, and design and entertainment businesses, along with stunning loft apartments, are housed in many former warehouses that are often invisible at street level. Large floor-length windows, some creatively hidden by screens or carefully decorated with a few objects, only hint at the impressive spaces found inside. It is a distinct look, a distinct style. And style is the major commodity available in Tribeca.

WHAT HAPPENED ON 9/11

In both Battery Park City and Tribeca, the memory of the 9/11 attack most seared into people's minds is one of fear and chaos mixed with moments of bizarre, "this is not really happening" calm. Many residents in both communities actually saw the planes hit, the towers burn, and the bodies fall from the sky. Then, when the towers fell, both neighborhoods were engulfed in a cloud of dust and ash. In Battery Park City and the southern end of Tribeca, the morning turned dark, and the first instinct was often to flee. One elderly woman from Battery Park City recalled:

> One of my neighbors came by and said, "What should we do?" By this time it had become dark. You couldn't see a foot in front of you [from clouds of black dust—her windows were open]. Every leaf of grass, every leaf of the tree was covered with this gray—I don't know what you call it—pulverized building material. We went down to the lobby, and they advised us to walk south on the esplanade.... What struck me when walking south on the esplanade, what really hit me, were shoes. *Shoes* scattered on the esplanade. I don't know why it made an indelible impression on me. And paper.

Along Battery Park City's waterfront esplanade, boats were pulling up to collect people. With the Hudson's strong current and nowhere to dock properly, boat captains could only jam the prow of their boat against the wall of the esplanade. Two men hoisted her over the railing and onto a boat, where two more people caught her.

> I met six other people on that boat from this building, and we just stuck together. We arrived in New Jersey. I don't think we had a dollar among us. We were not welcomed, we were not expected. They did not know we were coming. A woman offered us change, and said, "I hope this helps." We hitched a ride in a utility service truck. There were no seats in there, just coils of wire. Spools. And we were just going to a hotel, because one of the ladies accidentally found a credit card [in her pocket] and she got the rest of us in. I had no ID, I didn't have a penny. I had nothing else. I didn't move back into my apartment until the end of October.

In Tribeca it took slightly longer for the reality of what had happened to sink in. Some residents were just waking up or drinking their morning coffee. Then a phone would ring and the resident would be taken aback when the caller sighed with relief and asked if he or she was okay. For many, the next few hours were spent dividing their attention between staring out a window in disbelief and watching the television set as the nightmare grew steadily worse. Soon a layer of powdery gray ash was coating everything and everyone in the apartments. One resident reported sudden fear when she realized that she had no idea what the ash contained and that there might be more to it than just burnt paper, glass, and other building materials. Within a few hours nearly all of lower Manhattan had been cordoned off by police blockades, and it would remain so for several weeks. All of Battery Park City and the southern end of Tribeca were evacuated that afternoon, and residents who had already left for work at the time of the attack found that they could not return home. Many residents of northern Tribeca stayed in their homes, although most were without water, electricity, or phone service. No one knows how many Tribeca residents actually left the area—as one community activist put it, "Things were a lot less organized then [prior to 9/11]. We didn't have as many organizations as we do now, and no one was really keeping those statistics."

In both communities some of the most striking memories were of the frantic attempts to locate loved ones—especially children. At the local schools students were just settling into classrooms. The school year had just begun. When the first plane hit North Tower, many parents had just dropped off their children at PS 234, which stands more or less on the border between Battery Park City and Tribeca, just below the tower. Some ran back into the school in a panic to claim their children. Teachers tried to remain calm as they herded the remaining children to the basement. Only with the collapse of the second tower was PS 234 ordered to evacuate. Younger children described a day when they did not quite know what was happening but felt the air charged with the tensions and fears of those who normally soothed their worries. Older children at nearby Stuyvesant High School described the time before the evacuation as an eerily calm period. These surreal moments of false calm as they continued the routines of their schoolday—eating lunch in the cafeteria, reading from textbooks, conducting science experiments—were marked mainly by concern for their own safety as well as that of their parents. But both younger and older children recalled the cacophony of images and sounds that greeted them when they finally left the safety of their school buildings and the feeling of terror when they became a part of the crowd rushing to evacuate downtown.

Teachers and day care workers described feeling fear but also a sense of calming strength as they became aware that their first priority was to keep their young charges safe. The children and staff of the Battery Park City Day Nursery were among the first people evacuated to New Jersey. By the end of the day the nursery's owner and her assistant still had three young children with them. As evening neared they found themselves in the lobby of a strange hotel in New Jersey debating what to do for the night and how they were going to locate the parents of the remaining three children. Of course, in the back of their minds was the fear that the parents were dead. Suddenly, the owner recalled, one child's greatly relieved father came running through the crowd toward the small group, explaining loudly to anyone who would listen that he had been searching for them all day. Eventually both teachers and the two remaining children were invited to a relative's house in New Jersey to spend the night; parents were located the next day.

Over the next few days, as the rest of the country tried to make sense of the tragedy, many lower Manhattan residents found themselves dealing with the added burden of homelessness. A bitter, acrid smell permeated the area as the remains of the World Trade Center continued to smolder. The layer of dust and ash grew thicker. No matter how tightly a window was closed, residents recalled, dust still penetrated their homes. Soon even many Tribeca residents who stayed after September 11 had decided to leave. Like their neighbors in Battery Park City, most moved in with friends and family. Others took refuge in hotels. Within only a few days after the attack, about one hundred families had moved into the chic Tribeca Grand Hotel, occupying about half of the hotel's 203 rooms. The hotel, whose rooms normally cost between $350 and $1,000 a night, charged the families "only" $90 a night and by the second week was offering complimentary telephone calls and 25 percent off food and beverages. While most Tribecans were able to go home two to three weeks after the attack, most Battery Park City residents could not return to their homes until late October. Residents of one Tribeca loft building that directly faced the World Trade Center were not able to return to their homes for more than a year.

BATTERY PARK CITY RETURNS

Battery Park City residents have had many occasions to tell the story of what happened to them on September 11, 2001. Less often discussed, but almost as traumatic, is the memory of the day—weeks or months later—when they first returned to Battery Park City. Seeing Ground Zero—the smoldering blank space where the towers had stood—assessing the damage in their apartments, and having to show identification to police and soldiers in order to enter the neighborhood caused many to relive the events over again.

Inspecting the damage and arranging for cleaning was often less urgent than reconnecting with neighbors. This, most reported, was an overwhelmingly positive experience. "There was more hugging and kissing than you can imagine," one resident remembered. They gravitated to public spaces in a way they never had before. As one noted:

> When you see your neighbors grieve, and everybody's stunned and in grief and in trauma, I found that when I came back people were talking in groups. That never happened in Battery Park City unless you knew people. And I would walk down the street and see all these people talk-

ing who didn't know each other. We had an opportunity to create something very special—something we didn't have. It was always very beautiful. But because of this horrible experience, we had the opportunity to create something beautiful here.

Another noted:

It was different [before 9/11] than it is now. You would see people on the street, and you would say hello . . . but you would just keep on going. But now it is more or less a real community. You see someone, you stop, you talk, you listen.

From the time they returned, residents reported, they interacted much more in the plazas, streets, and parks of Battery Park City. "We'd just go up to each other and hug each other. It was just really great." In the first months this was reinforced by the difficulties of daily life in Battery Park City, which truly seemed like a neighborhood under siege. If the neighborhood had always had a slightly "gated" feel, the main "gate" was now gone. The two footbridges that had been the most convenient way to enter the area had been destroyed in the attack, and residents now had to come and go through inconvenient checkpoints at the southern and northern ends of the neighborhood. Once they did manage to get across West Street, all direct routes into the rest of the city were blocked off, forcing residents to walk around Ground Zero to get virtually anywhere. The closest subway and PATH stations were also closed. With almost all local businesses shut down and the World Trade Center mall now gone, basic shopping became an ordeal. What had once seemed like a suburb in the city was now, residents quipped, something more like a very isolated rural village. Yet these inconveniences served to bond the neighborhood with a strong sense of common purpose and a common project. Indeed, this period is remembered almost nostalgically, and as life gradually returned to something resembling normal, local activists sought to keep some of this spirit alive.

This was epitomized by Battery Park City's "First Annual Block Party" in September 2002. Plans for this event began as a casual conversation among a group of strangers who were gathered at a celebration for the reopening of one of the hotels. Part of their motivation for organizing the event was simply to celebrate the community and its survival. Yet organizers also soon recognized that promoting community connections would help organize the community for the coming political battles over rebuilding on the World Trade Center site. As one resident noted, "This is the acknowledgment of our unshakable spirit. . . . Through it all, what has emerged is the strongest sense of community we have ever experienced. Planners have to understand that this community is very much alive, very much unified, and as the plans roll out and construction begins we want to be recognized as a strong voice" ("Celebrate the Spirit" 2002, 1). The block party and other events during the first year after the attack (particularly around the time of the first anniversary) created connections between people that translated into a loose political organization of residents, who were soon attending community board meetings and other public forums on the rebuilding of lower Manhattan. The residents' shared trauma had made casual interactions easier, and this new openness in turn translated into a small organization, a community-wide event, and aspirations for greater community involvement in future public decisions. People's interactions in public spaces not only were initially therapeutic but began to have long-term effects on their social networks and community political involvement.

Of course, this "small-town" unity had its limits. Under the stress of evacuating, returning, and then living next to a nearly yearlong effort to recover thousands of bodies, it is not surprising that tensions arose in Battery Park City. Residents quickly became sensitive to those topics on which their personal decisions could imply criticism of their fellow "survivors." One woman who did not move back to her home until January 2002, in part because of concerns about the effect of pollutants and environmental hazards on her young daughter, found that she could not talk to others, even friends, about when they decided to return. To families who had moved back in November, her decision implied that they were neglectful parents who had put their children at risk. "We didn't even talk about it. They thought I was being over the top. I didn't think they were being conscientious enough." When this woman kept her child out of the popular playground sandbox (out of concern that, although the sand had been replaced, it could have trapped still-circulating contaminants), it was inevitably perceived as a public statement. When another parent asked her why she was not allowing her child in the sandbox, she answered, "I don't ask you why you put your child in the sandbox, so don't ask me why I don't!"

In general, however, residents remembered the first year back in Battery Park City as a sort of "golden era" of public discussion—a time when issues about the sort of community they wanted and how to organize politically animated casual encounters in the streets, parks, and playgrounds. Over time the intensity of these public interactions diminished, in part because, with the reopening of Battery Park City to nonresidents and then of the World Financial Center, they could no longer assume that everyone they saw in the neighborhood was a local resident. Discussions about the neighborhood's future continued, however, and may have intensified on the Internet, which soon replaced face-to-face meetings as the primary medium for political organizing and information about the various community meetings and public forums on rebuilding that were held almost weekly during 2002.

Divisions also emerged between people who had lived in Battery Park City before September 11 and those who moved in after the attacks. Residential vacancy rates in Battery Park City reached 40 percent in the fall of 2001 (Leland 2002). Landlords offered deep discounts to attract new tenants, and co-op owners cut prices. These strategies brought in a significant number of new residents who had not shared in the community's bonding experience. Most longtime residents minimized the significance of this difference, but most acknowledged that they saw differences in the newcomers: they seemed younger, stayed out later, may have been louder, and were seen as less likely to be married or have children. "The laundry room looks like a dorm on some nights," one pre-9/11 resident noted. True or not, the notion that the newcomers were more transient and less committed to the community added to the feeling that Battery Park City's unique qualities were now at risk. Moreover, those who moved into the community post-9/11 may have been harder to mobilize politically. Local environmental activists, for example, reported that the newcomers were considerably less likely to have serious concerns about environmental problems. Organizers seeking to build a unified response to what they saw as inadequate government proposals for the testing and cleaning of apartments found it difficult to engage new residents. A woman who had arrived in 1993 commented that it was "sort of strange. At first you feel angry at the new people, not having that connection," yet she also noted that older residents had a responsibility to initiate newcomers into the group.

Both Battery Park City and Tribeca saw an upsurge in local organizational and political activity in the wake of 9/11. Environmental and cleanup issues and questions of rebuilding mobilized residents, and federal, city, and state programs to redress the losses, deal with lingering psychological effects, and promote local business called forth a loose collection of new organizations to speak for the neighborhoods. In Tribeca business owners took the lead in creating these groups and were particularly prominent in the largest of them, the Tribeca Organization. (This business association has become, in many ways, the organizational voice of the community.) In Battery Park City, by contrast, it was residents and residential concerns that dominated the political response. Block associations were revitalized, and preexisting organizations, like the PTA, took on new roles while new groups, most notably Battery Park City United, were formed.

After dealing with the immediate issues of cleanup and environmental impacts, the major concern of these mobilized residents is now the still-unresolved debate over the plans for rebuilding on the World Trade Center site and creating a memorial for the victims of 9/11. Discussions of memorials often put Battery Park City residents in an awkward position. On the one hand, as victims of the attacks, they too feel a need to remember. On the other hand, there is a tension for them between the desire to remember and the desire to get back to normal. The needs of grieving family members and tourists, who want a solemn and sacred site to visit, are quite different from those who will have to live with these memorials and see them every time they walk out their front door. One resident worried about the difficulties that a large memorial could pose "as we drop our children off at school, carry our clothes to the dry cleaners, and attend the festivals celebrating the rebirth of Battery Park City.... Contractors and political leaders must remember that when making the decisions that will deeply affect our daily lives" (Davis-Chanin 2002, 4). A plan to install a sculpture recovered from the World Trade Center's central plaza (Fritz Koenig's *Sphere*) in Battery Park City was opposed by residents, who did not want a constant reminder just outside their doors. The sculpture was instead installed in Battery Park, the southern tip of Manhattan just below Battery Park City.

Residents' concerns go beyond their own emotional toll and reflect Battery Park City's long-standing aversion to use of the area by outsiders. In the first year after the attack a temporary memorial was set up under a tent beside a pre-9/11 monument to fallen police officers. Here people visited and left flowers and small items in memory of the uniformed personnel who had died. Some residents were unhappy about the crowds this memorial drew. Others mentioned having to navigate through the crowds that gathered on the street between the southern side of Ground Zero and Engine 10/Ladder 10, a firehouse just east of Battery Park City that lost many men on 9/11. As one woman stated, "I just want the tourists to go. That's what I want when it's ninety-five degrees out and they're out in front of Engine Company Ten and they're ten people deep." Another added, "Most [Battery Park City residents] are here because it's a very quiet neighborhood. So it's very ironic." Residents recognized of course that the area around the World Trade Center is important to many people who want and need to visit it. But they also insisted that their ability to move on depended on not being drawn back into the full emotional impact of the event at every turn. The preference for isolation that had already characterized the neighborhood accentuated this tension.

More surprising than residents' reactions to the memorials were their reactions to rebuilding plans. Battery Park City clearly had suffered from being cut off from the rest of Manhattan by the 9/11 attack. The urban planners seeking to reconnect it were caught off guard by local resistance. The first example came with local opposition to ferry service from Battery Park City's North Cove. Limited ferry and water taxi service had operated between the cove and New Jersey before the attack, but with the PATH train connection to the World Trade Center now gone, ferry service had been greatly increased. As a result, thousands of office workers were walking daily across Battery Park City. Far from seeing the service as an amenity, residents held protests against it, citing pollution, noise, and, most important, an increase in foot traffic. As a result of the protest, ferry service was not permitted to return to North Cove but continued to operate from a temporary terminal slightly farther from the residential buildings. Fences were installed to keep commuters moving directly toward the World Financial Center and the bridges across West Street and to deter them from walking through the neighborhood's park and playground.

A more protracted resistance met the plans to reconstruct the World Trade Center complex itself. In the years since Battery Park City was originally conceived, urban planning fashions had changed, and the moat-like effect of West Street was now widely seen as a mistake. Thus, most of the proposals for reconstruction included a plan to reconnect Battery Park City to lower Manhattan by burying or roofing over the highway, using the "new" land on top of the highway for a park or part of a memorial and otherwise making it easier to walk to Battery Park City at ground level. This was generally a minor feature of the many proposals, and planners assumed that the replacement of a noisy highway by a park would be applauded. It thus came as a surprise when the proposal was strongly opposed by Battery Park City residents. Local activists derided the plans, and letters published in the local *Broadsheet* were consistently opposed to the reconnection proposal.

It was not simply that residents objected to the noise, dirt, and inconvenience that would be caused by the construction. Living around a major construction project *is* certainly an inconvenience, as area residents often noted. But it was hardly a new or unexpected problem in this neighborhood. "I get a headache if I *don't* hear the sound of pile drivers," quipped the chairman of the Battery Park City Authority. Residents' vehement opposition seemed rather to stem from the desire to maintain Battery Park City's separation from the rest of the city. For many the barrier between themselves and the rest of lower Manhattan was an amenity, not a problem to be overcome. As one of the leaders of Battery Park City United put it:

We're kind of not really in favor of [burying West Street] simply because, what is the major reason justifying it? To reconnect Battery Park City to the rest of Manhattan? Hello? We have been living here for ten years, we've been connected to the rest of Manhattan. . . . We had the best of both worlds, really. . . . People living in Battery Park City had that sense of community simply because there was a barrier dividing Battery Park City from the rest of lower Manhattan. What was the nature of that barrier? It was a simple highway. And there was no reason for traffic to go through Battery Park City. If you look at any other neighborhood in Manhattan, you're talking about traffic going through the neighborhood.

There were even local objections to post-9/11 efforts to bring more people to Battery Park City's parks and public spaces. While long-term residents were happy that the area had more street life than it did when they first arrived, many were wistful for a time when the waterfront park was even better hidden and even less well known. This feeling also played a role in their objections to a new park over West Street.

If it's all park land, you'll have half of Manhattan right there. Just over the last five or six years the promenade has become very popular with people from all over Manhattan. Ever since the *New York Times* started writing about it, more people started coming by on weekends. It's not the same thing. If you want to take your kids and walk around the promenade, which is why a lot of people wanted to come here in the first place . . . it's very cramped and crowded, you have Rollerbladers streaking past, you have cyclists ringing their bells, going by at fifty miles an hour. I think that gives us an idea of what's in store if West Street is turned into either a park or office buildings, because either way it changes the relation to the barrier. . . . The problem with articulating these things, at least for me, is, "You're just being elitist, not-in-my-backyard idiots." . . . But there are some things worth preserving.

TRIBECA REBOUNDS

Although Tribeca was not as directly affected by the attacks as Battery Park City, the losses suffered there were hardly trivial. In addition to environmental concerns, police barricades prevented many residents from returning to their homes for days, weeks, and in a few cases, months. Residents complained about what they perceived as the city's incoherent response to their needs. Many reported sneaking past police barricades out of necessity in order to return home to feed pets. As one respondent recalled: "It was like living in a war zone—the barricades, uniformed soldiers, empty streets, the dust, the dirt everywhere, everywhere. And of course the emotional scars. We look okay, but none of us are the same. But we're still here."

Local businesses also suffered. Most were in the frozen zone—where no movement was permitted in the weeks after the attack—and many were inaccessible for weeks or months thereafter. According to a report by the Tribeca Organization (2002, 2), "over 60 percent of the businesses were at risk of closing or moving out of the area either immediately or within six to twelve months if business did not improve." Moreover, an additional 35 percent of businesses feared that they might have to make a similar decision if the economy did not improve in the next six or twelve months.

As in Battery Park City, the first response of many people was to try to come together. The first community-organizing efforts were ad hoc or informal. The first weekend after 9/11, hundreds of residents gathered at a basketball court on Canal Street. This initial gathering was more about touching base and finding familiar faces than about community organizing. Given the chaos reigning in their streets, it was easy to understand Tribecans' desire for social contact. In the following weeks many more such informal gatherings took place, and on September 24 about five hundred residents met in a New York University auditorium. Their primary concerns were returning to their homes, the air quality, and their children's schools. An even larger meeting took place on October 3. Thousands of residents packed the Regent Wall Street to meet with city officials.

Some of the issues raised—particularly the environmental concerns—were similar to those voiced on the other side of West Street. Indeed, at a community meeting a year after 9/11, one local activist spoke about the area's continuing concerns over long-term health consequences and the possibility of lingering poor air quality. She also noted, however, that the subject was not discussed often by Tribeca residents. She explained that residents had many complex reasons for choosing to stay, and this choice had necessitated a degree of acceptance of the environmental risks. A year after the attack only about 26 percent of the 5,547 households in Tribeca had requested the free cleaning offered by the Environmental Protection Agency (EPA).[4] The EPA's offer, she noted, had come only in May 2002 and was a reversal of the EPA's original position that residential homes did not need to be professionally cleaned. For many residents who had moved back into their homes long before, this reversal was more alarming than anything else. "What can you do *now?*"

Nevertheless, a year after 9/11 Tribeca's recovery seemed remarkable, especially in contrast to Battery Park City's. The expected exodus of residents did not occur. Indeed, after a few stagnant months, housing prices and rents began to rise—by late 2002 they were again among the highest in the city. Although the revenues of most Tribeca businesses were markedly down, few went bankrupt. In fact, a surprising number of businesses opened in Tribeca after 9/11, including the Issey Miyake flagship store and art gallery specializing in modern Vietnamese art, at least fifteen new restaurants and lounges, and, in the spring of 2003, a large new luxury condominium complex. This spate of recent openings provides some indication that at least one aspect of Tribeca's businesses—the business of luxury—was not adversely affected by either 9/11 or the general economic downturn in the city.

Less tangible, but equally striking, was the sense that, a year after the attack, 9/11 no longer seemed to permeate community consciousness. Of course, small reminders of the attack were everywhere. In both public and private conversations, Tribeca residents often invoked "what we all went through on 9/11" as a kind of all-purpose preface to the discussion of community issues, ranging from the need for waterfront access to questions about the appropriateness of the location of a new moderately priced hotel. Yet for all of that, Tribeca no longer seemed to be a community in shock or mourning or a community at risk of being defined by its proximity to the site of a historic tragedy. Discussions of the World Trade Center rebuilding plans excited little more interest than they did in other parts of the city.

Part of the explanation lies in simple geography. Although some Tribeca residents lived as close or closer to the twin towers as many Battery Park City residents, they were not cut off from the city by the destruction of the towers or the excavation efforts. Living in an organic part of Manhattan's mainland, with the multiple entry and exit points of the grid system, Tribeca residents were able to come and go relatively easily within a few weeks of the attack. Yet there was also a symbolic dimension to the geographic orientation. If Battery Park City had turned its back on the city, Tribeca generally looked north to SoHo and Greenwich Village and had long turned its back on the World Trade Center.

Beyond this difference in orientation between the two communities, however, Tribeca was otherwise far more in sync with the tenor of the recovery efforts. In the weeks after 9/11 both Mayor Giuliani and President Bush urged people back to the streets to shop, to recreate, to spend money. Residents of Battery Park City were hard-pressed to respond, however, since their community was still under virtual lockdown and in any event had few stores or restaurants that would attract dollars from elsewhere. Nor were the public concerts held in Battery Park City parks a few months later always seen as helpful—they brought in more outsiders and raised residents' anxiety levels.

In Tribeca, however, the newly incorporated Tribeca Organization was quick to jump on the "recovery through shopping" bandwagon. The group organized Tribeca Week, a festival that included one night when all the art galleries and design and furniture stores remained open late. Those who came out were exhorted to take out their credit cards and "shop, buy [your] Christmas presents now from these shops," to show their support for businesses in the area. It was curious that in a time of tragedy and impending war, the battle cry was "Shop!" Yet it was an easy idea to accept in an area that had always identified itself with high-end consumption. Local residents also did not seem to mind—outsiders had always been central to Tribeca's vibrant mix. Residents had always expected to see more strangers than neighbors on the streets.

Robert DeNiro's Tribeca Film Center launched the first annual Tribeca Film Festival in May 2002 as a show of support for the neighborhood and to help revitalize downtown New York's economy (Brook 2002). The five-day event drew at least 40,000 people. Tickets for one screening, intended as a fundraiser for the community, sold for $500. Two smaller venues were set aside for screenings for 3,000 children who had lost a parent in the attack. Some local businesses complained that they did not make enough out of the festival, but we did not come across any residents who were upset that the festival would create crowding or get in the way of local efforts to "heal."

The festival continued to grow, and by 2004 it featured screenings of 250 films from 42 countries and drew more than 250,000 visitors, not only to watch films but to shop and participate in other local activities. Opening ceremonies drew a host of politicians and celebrities who reminded visitors of the moral imperative to spend money in the area. Honorary festival patron Archbishop Desmond Tutu compared New York's—and Tribeca's—recovery to South Africa's recovery from apartheid: "Our country has risen like a phoenix from the ashes and we believe it is possible for your city to rise from the ashes of 9/11" (*New York One News* 2004a). Senator Charles Schumer (D-NY) was no less effusive: "[For] anyone who doubted New York would come back after 9/11, this is proof positive we're back, bigger, better and stronger than ever" (*New York One News* 2004b). One local restaurant owner put it more pragmatically: "It's brought a lot of people in, and we're quite full. I think it's done a lot for the neighborhood" (*New York One News* 2004a). That the festival was drumming up business for some of the city's most expensive restaurants and bringing money into what was already one of its most affluent neighborhoods was rarely noted. Nevertheless, even if the crowds and street closings annoyed some local residents, few expressed such sentiments publicly, and most seemed happy with all the activity.

Similarly, restaurateurs played a role in Tribeca's recovery efforts. Under the direction of Drew Nieporent, workers at Tribeca Grill initially responded to 9/11 by serving sandwiches to recovery workers for several weeks immediately following the attacks. Meanwhile, the restaurant's executive chef, Don Pintabona, created Chefs With Spirit to provide services for the recovery workers. After commandeering a four-deck ship within three days after the attacks—friends helped him make the arrangement with Spirit Cruises—he set it up to serve up to fifteen thousand people a day. Its four decks acted as restaurant, sleeping quarters, and rest stop for thousands of relief and cleanup workers. Hundreds of kitchen workers, several famed chefs, and dozens of volunteers took part in preparing and serving food as well as distributing donated foods. A few months later Chefs With Spirit refocused its efforts on the recovery of the industry. Only six months after 9/11, the Annual Taste of Tribeca went ahead as planned and restaurants drew people back to Tribeca through special promotions such as lowering fixed-price menus and discounted lunches.

As the major community organization in the area, the Tribeca Organization is primarily a business association (although many of its members and most of its leadership are also local residents), so it is not surprising that most of its efforts were focused on business promotion. However, the group also spon-sored activities for residents, many of which were expressly for local children. Indeed, the child-centeredness of many of Tribeca's noncommercial recovery efforts was striking. High-fashion, celebrity-laden Tribeca is hardly thought of as a child-friendly part of town. Yet in the decade prior to 9/11 it had under-gone a small, largely unnoticed baby boom, and by 2000, according to the census (PUMS), 17.5 percent of Tribeca's population were children. This had led to increased interest in supporting the schools and addressing the lack of playgrounds, but prior to 9/11 these concerns were rarely voiced publicly. The attack, however, focused attention on the neighborhood's youngest members and their very local needs. Just two weeks after the attacks parents pooled their efforts to throw a party for the community's children. Meanwhile, local PTAs, concerned over the physical and mental health of neighborhood chil-dren, came together almost immediately. All schoolchildren had been relocated to schools north of Canal Street or in Brooklyn, but parents were already considering the issues involved in their return to local schools. For its part, the Tribeca Organization was soon putting on a children's fashion show and other entertainment activities for youngsters. There were even efforts to orga-nize outdoor recreational and sports activities, most of which took place on the ball fields, parks, and playgrounds a short distance away—in Battery Park City.

Thus, while the events of 9/11 increased Tribeca's organizational density and local public activity, in the long run post-9/11 developments accelerated trends already under way. Although the remaining wholesale and business service firms suffered and some closed, upscale restaurants and high-fashion retailing generally survived and expanded, despite almost two months of no business. The conversion of lofts to residential spaces also continued, and new construc-tion actually increased. Residents became more organized largely in response to the needs of children. Yet, despite its initial coming together, Tribeca re-mains a community connected more by common tastes, lifestyles, and ideas than by the bonds forged by face-to-face communication.

CONCLUSION

Social scientific views of urban neighborhoods often draw on different images of community in the modern world. At one extreme are notions inherited from Georg Simmel (1903/1994) and Louis Wirth (1938/1994), who saw modern ur-ban life as highly individualistic and urban neighborhoods as having weak social bonds and boundaries—they were more perhaps than simply places for people to sleep, but barely communities in more than the geographical sense. At the other extreme is the cohesive, strongly bounded "urban village"; Herbert

Gans's (1962) phrase is now so ubiquitous that we often forget that it was a deliberate oxymoron. Studies of neighborhoods usually find that the degree of closure and the importance of local social bonds vary greatly, although they are almost always somewhere between these two extremes.

Comparing the responses of Battery Park City and Tribeca to 9/11 puts the question of the nature of these urban communities into sharp focus. To be sure, much of the initial reaction of local residents was similar. In the immediate aftermath of the attack, people in both neighborhoods showed a need for collectivity and face-to-face interaction. They began to talk to neighbors, in their homes and in public, in ways they had not done before. Residents of both communities displayed a need to come together in groups to share, discuss, and just make contact with people who had gone through the same experience. And in both cases this initial response soon crystallized into formal organizations and a general upsurge in local civic activity, which, as of this writing, continues.

Yet both the formal and informal responses took different forms, and those forms make clear not only the two neighborhoods' different modes of organization but also the different ideas about urban life that they embody. This is perhaps obvious but nonetheless worth remembering, as it has important policy implications. Well-meaning planners and redevelopment officials did not initially grasp how central Battery Park City's isolation from the rest of lower Manhattan was to its sense of corporate identity and how important that sense had become in the face of the disaster. They saw their attempts to decrease Battery Park City's isolation, by increasing ferry service or roofing over West Street with a park, as obvious and uncontroversial urban amenities of which Battery Park City would be the primary beneficiary. They were caught off guard when these attempts were met with protest and staunch resistance. Similarly, attempts to bring life back to downtown with cultural events and shopping promotions made complete sense and were even seen as healing in Tribeca, where a strong neighborhood identity drew less on face-to-face interaction among residents than on a common self-image based largely on modes of consumption and tastes in entertainment. Yet these same attempts often only furthered the sense of violation in an already wounded Battery Park City.

Part of this difference is due to spatial and architectural factors. It is also due, however, to the cultural preferences that led people in the first place to choose certain spatial and architectural forms. As lower Manhattan is rebuilt over the next decade or more, both of these neighborhoods will no doubt be transformed in ways that cannot yet be predicted. To understand how they react to these changes, it is vital that we recognize the cultural logics that shaped both communities in those now seemingly long ago days before the towers fell.

This chapter is dedicated to the memory of Captain William Burke Jr., FDNY, "Awesome Strike Force" partner of co-author Kasinitz: "A working-class hero is something to be."

NOTES

1. Greg Smithsimon conducted fieldwork in Battery Park City as part of a larger project on public space and community life. His first observations of Battery Park City were conducted in the spring of 1999. For this project, he conducted ethnographic fieldwork, spatial mapping and observations, and formal and impromptu interviews with people who lived, worked, or were involved in community organizations in Battery Park City in the summer and fall of 2002. He would like to thank the people in Battery Park City, whose generosity and openness made this project possible.

   Binh Pok was commissioned to undertake ethnographic fieldwork in Tribeca by the social effects working group of the Russell Sage Foundation's New York City Recovery Project. Her work began in the late summer of 2002 and continued through the fall of 2003.

2. The average size of a Manhattan apartment co-op or condo is 1,100 to 1,354 square feet. In contrast, even as loft sizes have shrunk in the last few years, the average size of a loft apartment in 2001 was still 2,009 square feet.

3. The main exception to all of these generalizations about Tribeca's population is Independence Plaza, a forty-story, Mitchell-Lama middle-income housing complex on the community's western edge that opened in 1975. Although few residents would consider Independence Plaza to be a part of Tribeca socially, its residents lower the median income statistics.

4. This figure was up-to-date as of early January 2003. At the time of this writing, about 2,027 households had requested cleaning. These figures are based on the EPA's count by zip codes, since the EPA division of lower Manhattan into quadrants made each quadrant more expansive than just the Tribeca area.

REFERENCES

Brook, Tom. 2002. "DeNiro Festival Lifts Ground Zero." *BBC News* (May 4).

"Celebrate the Spirit of Battery Park City at the First Annual Block Party." 2002. *Battery Park City Broadsheet*, October 6.

Davis-Chanin, Laura. 2002. Letter. *Battery Park City Broadsheet*, October 21.

Dunlap, David W. 1994. "Opening New Fronts at Battery Park City." *New York Times*, September 4, sect. 9, p. 1.

———. 1999. "Filling in the Blanks at Battery Park City." *New York Times*, February 7, sect. 11, p. 1.

Fainstein, Susan S. 1994. *The City Builders: Property, Politics, and Planning in London and New York*. Cambridge, Mass.: Blackwell.

Gans, Herbert. 1962. *The Urban Villagers*. New York: Free Press.

Jacobs, Jane. 1961. *The Death and Life of the Great American Cities.* New York: Random House.

Leland, John. 2002. "For Residents, New Life Near Ground Zero." *Chicago Tribune,* March 31, p. 5D.

Low, Setha. 2003. *Behind the Gates: Life, Security, and the Pursuit of Happiness in Fortress America.* New York: Routledge.

———. 2004. "The Memorialization of September 11: Dominant and Local Discourses on the Rebuilding of the World Trade Center Site." *The American Ethnologist* 31(3, August): 326–39.

New York One News. 2004a. "Tribeca Film Festival Kicks Off." Television broadcast, May 1.

———. 2004b. "Tribeca Film Festival: Chinese Filmmaker Takes Top Honors." Television broadcast, May 10.

Oldenburg, Ray. 1990. *The Great Good Place: Cafés, Coffee Shops, Community Centers, Beauty Parlors, General Stores, Bars, Hangouts, and How They Get You Through the Day.* New York: Paragon.

Simmel, Georg. 1903/1994. "The Metropolis and Mental Life." In *Metropolis: Center and Symbol of Our Time,* edited by Philip Kasinitz. New York: New York University Press.

Tribeca Organization. 2002. "Tribeca One Year Later." Report. New York: Tribeca Organization (July).

Trilling, Julia. 1985. "A Future That Looks Like the Past." *Atlantic* 256(July): 28.

Wirth, Louis. 1938/1994. "Urbanism as a Way of Life." In *Metropolis: Center and Symbol of Our Times,* edited by Philip Kasinitz. New York: New York University Press.

Zukin, Sharon. 1982. *Loft Living: Capital and Culture in Urban Change.* Baltimore: Johns Hopkins University Press.

CHAPTER 4

Double Trauma in Belle Harbor:
The Aftermath of September 11 and
November 12 in the Rockaways

Melanie D. Hildebrandt

SEPTEMBER 11, 2001, began as a picture-perfect day: crystal-clear skies, beautiful ocean waves, warm temperatures, and best of all, no crowds on Rockaway's beaches. This was the kind of day that many Rockaway residents looked forward to, a day when the summer crowds were gone and the streets, sands, and surf belonged to the locals. Yet this particular day would forever change the way the local residents of the close-knit, predominantly Irish American and Jewish American communities on the west end of the Rockaway peninsula felt about September.

On that day residents stood along the seawall facing Jamaica Bay, watching helplessly as the twin towers burned in the distance. Off-duty firefighters from Rockaway grabbed their gear, said good-bye to their children, and rushed to downtown Manhattan. By day's end, over seventy people from this remote seaside community in southern Queens had died in the terrorist attack on the World Trade Center. Among the dead were firefighters whose families had lived in Rockaway for generations. Others were employees of Cantor Fitzgerald, a financial services firm that lost nearly half its workforce; many of them lived in the Rockaway neighborhoods of Belle Harbor and Breezy Point.

The sound of church bells and bagpipes marked the days and weeks following the September 11 attacks. Dozens of funerals and memorial services were held, many at the St. Francis de Sales Church, a Catholic church located in the de facto town center of Belle Harbor. Monsignor Michael Gallagher (pseudonym), the church's senior pastor, delivered dozens of eulogies, and the streets of Belle Harbor were frequently lined with elaborate funeral processions for firefighters and civilians alike. Not surprisingly, it was a relief that by November the processions and funerals were becoming less frequent. With children back in school and commuters returning to work in downtown Manhattan, many residents began to feel that normalcy was resuming.

Then, on the morning of November 12, American Airlines flight 587, with 260 passengers bound for the Dominican Republic, was taking off from Kennedy International Airport when its tail broke off, sending the plane plummeting into Belle Harbor. Everyone on board and five people on the ground were killed. The vibrations from the crash and the ensuing inferno destroyed a dozen homes at the intersections of Newport Avenue and Beach 130th and Beach 131st Streets. Many other houses were damaged. One engine fell at a gas station on Beach 129th Street, barely missing pumps and fuel tanks. A second engine burned in the backyard of a home on Beach 128th Street.

Initially, local residents had no idea what had happened. Thoughts such as "They're bombing us!" and "Not again! Not another attack!" raced through the minds of virtually everyone living on the Rockaway peninsula. Panic-stricken mothers snatched children from their beds and ran down the street away from the smoke and fumes. In a manner reminiscent of September 11, off-duty firefighters grabbed their gear and rushed to the scene, initially using lawn hoses and shovels to fight the blaze. The crash took out phone and cable service throughout the area. Rumors began to spread. Will the sewers explode? Are more planes coming? How can this be happening to Rockaway? Who even knows that Rockaway exists?

As horrible as September 11 was, many Belle Harborites would assert that the trauma of a plane nosediving into their backyards was worse. In fact, two years later suspicion and resentment still lingered surrounding the flight 587 investigation. Plans for a memorial for crash victims divided the Belle Harbor community, and there were tensions with the Dominican families of the deceased passengers. Lawsuits and insurance settlements made neighbors uneasy with each other. Whereas the September 11 attack unified the entire Rockaway community and reinforced the core values of local culture, the crash of American Airlines flight 587 put a strain on those core values, revealing internal fissures and the limitations of the community's ability to cope with a double dose of trauma, grief, and painful memories.

QUESTIONS AND METHODS

When I began this research in the Rockaways in June 2002, my objective was to understand whether social solidarity in two particular communities had markedly changed in the year following September 11. Specifically, I wanted to know whether divisions or tensions resulting from the terrorist attack and/or the plane crash were threatening the structure or functioning of the historically cohesive New York enclaves of Belle Harbor and Breezy Point. I also wondered whether—and how—local community leaders and cultural institutions were meeting the needs of grieving, traumatized individuals.

These central questions were derived from my familiarity with the work of the sociologist Kai Erikson (1976; 1994) and his extensive investigations into trauma, disaster, and community upheaval. Erikson (1994) asserts that the fabric and functions of tightly knit communities can be damaged or destroyed by disasters, and he makes a distinction between the effects of *individual trauma* and *collective trauma* on the social system. Individual survivors of catastrophes withdraw into themselves, Erikson argues, and feel vulnerable and isolated from their community. Because of its smaller scale, individual trauma rarely affects the nature or structure of community life. With collective trauma, however, the very sociocultural fabric of the community is weakened or destroyed.

This study provides an opportunity to expand on these ideas. Belle Harbor's double tragedy demonstrates how individual and collective traumas interact and how the emerging social context shapes the coping strategies of victims and their community. Indeed, while Belle Harbor's *trauma within a trauma* seems to be unique, the events there are remarkably similar to other tragedies, such as the crash of Pan Am flight 800 in Lockerbie, Scotland, and catastrophes documented by Erikson (1976; 1994) and others.

Owing to the sensitivity of the topics and the nature of the close-knit communities in western Rockaway, I felt compelled to adopt a multifaceted approach. Between July and November 2002, I conducted two dozen interviews with local residents, community leaders, and social service providers and closely followed and developed a content analysis of local newspapers.[1] I also attended a wide range of events, services, and ceremonies, all of which offered insights into the community that otherwise might not have been possible.

"A HISTORY CARVED BY FIRE"

Longtime resident and writer Kevin Boyle (2002, 27) notes that Rockaway "has had its history carved by fire." Indeed, fires plagued the peninsula throughout the nineteenth and twentieth centuries, taking the lives of neighbors and destroying treasured landmarks. The great Seaside Fire of 1892, which devastated the entire middle section of the peninsula known as Arverne, is credited with starting the tradition of firefighting among the many Irish American families in the area. In those days the city's feeble firefighting apparatus was consigned to the mainland, and many Rockawayites relate stories of their grandfathers fighting fires with bucket brigades. According to Boyle, Rockaway firefighters were responsible for pressuring the city to improve firefighting equipment and techniques.

Located on the western end of the Rockaway peninsula, the neighborhoods of Rockaway Park, Belle Harbor, Neponsit, and Breezy Point, flanked by the Atlantic Ocean to the south and Jamaica Bay to the north, are virtually isolated from the rest of the city. Throughout this chapter, when I use the terms "Rockaway" and "the Rockaway community," I am referring to these four West End neighborhoods. For simplicity, I also use the term "Belle Harbor" to refer to the neighborhoods of Rockaway Park, Belle Harbor, and Neponsit, since the borders between these neighborhoods are vague and their residents have similar ethnic, religious, and socioeconomic profiles. Taken together, Breezy Point and Belle Harbor constitute a community where social, occupational, and geopolitical interests frequently overlap, and extended kin group ties closely bind the two neighborhoods. Unless otherwise specified, "the community" refers to both Breezy Point and Belle Harbor and their shared culture, social networks, and resources. However, Breezy Point and Belle Harbor are also distinct communities, with varied demographic profiles and somewhat different worldviews. When such differences are relevant, I refer to each community separately.

By car, Rockaway is connected to the mainland by two toll bridges and a meandering land route leading to Long Island; a single subway line connects the entire peninsula to the rest of New York City and terminates at Beach 116th Street. Commuters must walk or rely on buses to reach destinations west of Beach 116th Street. By contrast, along the East End of the Rockaway peninsula, low-income neighborhoods and housing projects surround the public transportation corridors. Since the 1960s the East End has become densely populated and predominantly black and Latino, while the middle- and upper-middle-class neighborhoods of the West End have remained virtually all white and relatively secluded.

According to census figures for 2000, the total population of Rockaway was 106,638, with the four West End neighborhoods totaling 23,504.[2] While many East End neighborhoods are over 75 percent African American, the Breezy Point neighborhood is 99.4 percent white, with 60 percent claiming Irish heritage, 21 percent Italian, and 16 percent German.[3] Few Jews live in Breezy Point and no people of color. Belle Harbor is scarcely more "integrated," with whites constituting 88.5 percent of the population in 2000, among whom 36 percent were Irish, 12.9 percent were Italian, and 6.5 percent were German. Unlike Breezy Point, Belle Harbor has a sizable Jewish population: there are at least three synagogues west of Beach 116th Street. There are also a handful of Protestant churches, but by far the majority of the population is Catholic.

The West End communities are home to a mix of civil servants (including fire and police personnel) and white-collar professionals (lawyers, doctors, traders, educators, and nurses). For the upwardly mobile, Rockaway tradition

FIGURE 4.1   THE ROCKAWAY PENINSULA

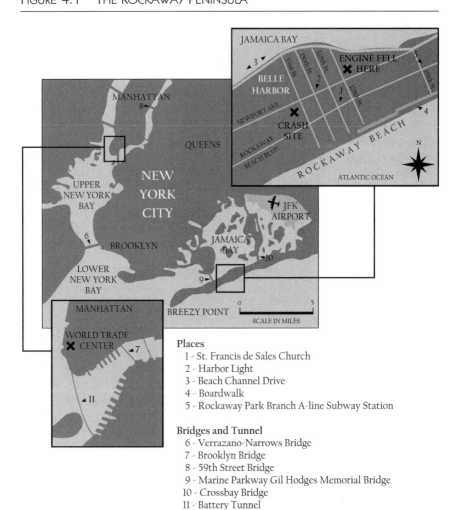

Places
  1 - St. Francis de Sales Church
  2 - Harbor Light
  3 - Beach Channel Drive
  4 - Boardwalk
  5 - Rockaway Park Branch A-line Subway Station

Bridges and Tunnel
  6 - Verrazano-Narrows Bridge
  7 - Brooklyn Bridge
  8 - 59th Street Bridge
  9 - Marine Parkway Gil Hodges Memorial Bridge
  10 - Crossbay Bridge
  11 - Battery Tunnel

Source: Map reprinted courtesy of Rising Star Press, Scotts Valley, California. Originally printed in Boyle (2002). Artist: Greg Tomer, Eternal Designs.

has had it that young (Irish American) men who decided not to work for the Fire Department of New York (FDNY) could always find a job with Cantor Fitzgerald, a financial services firm. (Indeed, it was this tradition that brought so much tragedy on September 11.) The neighborhoods of Belle Harbor and Breezy Point have a distinctly middle-class, almost suburban aspect, boasting, according to the 2000 census, average household incomes of $48,604 and $58,491, respectively.[4]

When I arrived in Belle Harbor on a sunny summer day in July 2002, I was impressed by how *unlike* New York City this neighborhood was. Teenagers rode their bicycles freely up and down streets, with beach towels draped over their shoulders. Middle-aged men, home in the middle of the day, were holding animated conversations on their front lawns. By New York City standards, the houses seemed large and well-kept, and many had front porches, garages, and yards. As I drove through the area I noted that nearly every house was adorned with an American flag. Several longtime residents later assured me that Belle Harbor has always been a patriotic community with many veterans, so "only a few" of the flags were new since the September 11 attack.

The West End of Rockaway has maintained its small-town character by restricting access to the beaches and streets and through zoning restrictions on real estate. Zoning laws limit the number of multifamily units west of Beach 116th Street, and only single-family homes are allowed in the most exclusive neighborhoods of Belle Harbor. Decades ago local residents won strict regulations to prohibit on-street parking during summer weekends. Ostensibly these restrictions were put into place to protect the property of homeowners who complained that DFDs—"Down For the Day" beachgoers—were littering, defecating, and urinating on their yards. Howard Schwach, editor of the weekly community newspaper *The Wave*, further suggests that these parking restrictions were instituted because local residents believed "that the beach at the end of the block that they lived on was indeed 'theirs,' for their pleasure only. They did not want the DFDs crowding 'their' beaches, making noise, listening to loud music, leaving behind garbage and generally causing problems for the residents" (see Schwach 2001, n.p.).

In Breezy Point the parking restrictions are even more stringent. This private, cooperatively owned community at the far western tip of the Rockaway peninsula keeps its boundaries tightly patrolled. Gates, barricades, and security guards make it impossible for visitors to park without obtaining a pass from the gatehouse. Passes are available only to people with official business or a scheduled appointment with a local resident. Uninvited visitors or sightseers must drive through the cooperative without stopping. Clearly this policy is not popular with outsiders. Some Jewish respondents who lived in Belle Harbor said they refused to go to Breezy Point because they disapproved of the checkpoints and felt unwelcome. Breezy Point residents were impervious to this criticism.

"Breezy," as the locals call it, was established in 1960 as a private seasonal community for the "chic Brooklyn Irish" as well as some German and Italian families. Approximately four hundred acres of land, including prime beachfront property, was collectively purchased from the Atlantic Improvement State Corporation to form the Breezy Point Cooperative (BPC) (see *The Wave* n.d.). Since then, approximately 60 percent of the homes have been occupied year-round, many by the original owners.

The houses in Breezy Point range in style from elegant, multistory homes to narrow, single-floor bungalows. Religion and firefighting have been exceptionally strong elements of the local culture: there are three Catholic churches, one Protestant church, and no fewer than three volunteer fire stations ready to serve the cooperative's 2,854 homes, even though a FDNY station is only two miles away.

If Breezy Point is more overtly restrictive and secluded than Belle Harbor, residents of both neighborhoods have similar backgrounds and a shared desire to preserve their way of life by excluding others. Both Belle Harbor and Breezy Point have also been dubbed "firefighter country" by local residents.[5] Community social workers, mental health professionals, and journalists described the resident firefighters and their wives as "a service-oriented group of people" with an unspoken understanding that they should be ready to lend assistance to each other in times of need, whatever the circumstance.

The strength of the connection among firefighters was evident in their frequent and affectionate use of the term "brother" (Boyle 2002). Firefighters often greeted each other by saying, "How's it going, brother?" or, "What's up, brother?" In similar fashion, their wives helped each other in times of stress, even when they were not the closest of friends. Among firefighter families there was an informal code of reciprocity and an extensive support network in which information about schools, tutoring, sports, children's activities, social events, and other services was exchanged.

These values and expectations were transmitted across generations. Andrea and her firefighter husband lived in Belle Harbor. She explained how she acquired her sense of responsibility to the community.

You just get it from growing up in the community, that you're supposed to help the other wives, the other families, when something happens. It's just part of how you're raised. I mean, my brother is a firefighter, my uncle was a firefighter. We just were brought up to know—that's just what you do.

One counselor noted that because many of the women strongly identified with their firefighting husbands, there was "acute attention given to male children" in the local culture. This counselor pointed out how patriotic firefighter families are and noted that families assumed they were "bringing up future firefighters."

In general, there is a sense among residents of both Belle Harbor and Breezy Point that the residents are like "family" and responsible for helping each other. Many of these predominantly Irish Catholic families have lived in the area for generations and have extended kin ties with others in the community, creating a sense of shared history and tradition. "Our networks are very close," said one resident, "and through intermarriage, many people are related or one step removed from literally being family. To the point where, if you have a gripe with someone, you have to be careful who you complain to. You could be speaking about someone's [family member]."

Many observers noted a community-wide commitment to service and activism as well. As one longtime resident of Breezy Point put it, "This is a community that votes," and indeed, Rockaway constituents are in frequent contact with their elected government representatives. Moreover, there are active branches of national organizations like the Rotary Club and Knights of Columbus, as well as several homegrown charities. A local men's organization known as the Graybeards hosts fund-raisers for college scholarships, sponsors youth and adult basketball leagues, and organizes blood drives for the Red Cross. The nonprofit Rockaway Artists' Alliance serves the community through summer camps, after-school programs, and adult art classes. Likewise, organizations such as the weekly newspaper *The Wave*, the *Breezy Point News*, and the Rockaway Chamber of Commerce are vital sources of information and assistance.

A strong "service orientation," as one social worker described it, is juxtaposed with a closed community that places tremendous importance on privacy and self-reliance. Rockaway is known by New Yorkers as an "enclave" and as an "insular" community notorious for overt prejudice against minorities and suspicion of outsiders.

Indeed, residents of Belle Harbor and Breezy Point cherish their isolation from New York City, seeing their beachfront community as the city's "best-kept secret." Yet maintaining the small-town character of their community has come at a price. Residents also see their community as New York City's "forgotten stepchild"; they complain bitterly that city services are poorly delivered or nonexistent and that promises made to the people of Rockaway are easily broken. Locals feel slighted by the lack of business investment during the economic boom of the 1990s. They have frequently voiced their concerns about aging sewers, unrepaired streets, the absence of a hurricane evacuation plan, and low-flying air traffic from JFK International Airport. In addition, there has long been friction between New York firefighters and the city government over job security and pay raises (Boyle 2002).

On the one hand, West End residents, as several respondents put it, "resented anyone coming and telling us how to live our lives." On the other hand, they felt entitled, as taxpayers and civil servants, to having their demands met by city and state governments. As it happens, it is the East End of the Rockaways—Far Rockaway—that has historically suffered from decades of neglect, worsening socioeconomic conditions, poorly performing schools, and high dropout, teen pregnancy, and crime rates. In contrast, Belle Harbor's elementary school is one of the best-performing schools in its district. Belle Harbor residents were aware, of course, that their community fared much better than Far Rockaway. Still, they complained that Far Rockaway was able to get special services and programs while "we get nothing."

The tension between feelings of privilege and entitlement and resentment and neglect has long been an integral feature of Rockaway life, and it is important in understanding the response to the unprecedented double trauma in 2001. The insularity and privacy enjoyed by the middle-class, West End communities provided a network of emotional and social support to trauma sufferers but at the same time impeded the recovery of others.

THE IMPORTANCE OF COMMUNITY SPACE AND LEADERSHIP IN THE AFTERMATH OF 9/11

Immediately after September 11, Rockaway residents drew on the strengths of their community, dropping superficial conflicts and becoming more cohesive, supportive, and unified. If there was anything easy about the recovery from September 11 it was the fact that the community was already culturally and structurally organized to deal with disaster. Leaders praised the community for "pulling together" and "stepping forward," while community members praised the leaders for their wisdom and guidance. Even the racial boundaries dividing the peninsula seemed less important as memorials, fund-raisers, and festivals drew people from all religious, socioeconomic, and ethnic groups. Many respondents gave credit to the "entire community," meaning the entire Rockaway peninsula, for supporting them as they navigated the various waves of emotion following September 11.

Immediately following the collapse of the World Trade Center, Rockaway residents congregated in various places throughout the peninsula. Worried individuals gathered along the seawall facing Manhattan, parishioners prayed on the steps of St. Francis de Sales Church, and neighbors congregated on porches, sidewalks, and stoops, trying to assess the scale of what was happening. Family members tried to make and maintain telephone contact with loved ones working in the towers. As Monsignor Gallagher, the priest at St. Francis de Sales Church, recollected: "There was a gradual buildup of awareness, a spreading fear throughout the day. We knew that what was happening had tremendous implications for the nation and the city. But it became very personal out here very quickly."

From the start, the church played an important role. As the day unfolded, Monsignor Gallagher "got the sense" that people in his parish and throughout the community needed a place to assemble. Realizing that he had no way to communicate with his parishioners, he resorted to "what they did in the old days": ringing the church bells to call people to prayer. At around 7:15 P.M., Monsignor Gallagher rang the church bells. By 7:35 over one thousand people had assembled, filling the five hundred seats inside the church and spilling out onto the adjacent sidewalks and driveways.

Andrea, a firefighter's wife, recalled hearing the church bells ringing from her home. She decided to walk to the church. Her husband was alive and safe (he had called around 4:00 P.M. from Ground Zero), but in the church "I was hearing names of people I knew [who had died] and people I hadn't thought about in years. People I went to school with, someone from camp, and people from the neighborhood." Retelling this story was painful for Andrea, even ten months later. But gathering together for a Catholic mass, in shared prayer, mourning, and support, provided some solace. Many Belle Harbor residents relied on rituals of gathering together with friends and neighbors and attending Mass every night at 7:30 for the first week.

Other religious leaders also used the reassuring power of ritual to help their congregations, and themselves, deal with the tragedy. One Protestant minister immediately incorporated candle lighting and bell ringing into her prayer and memorial services. Although her denomination, United Church of Christ, did not traditionally include much ritual in its services, the minister recognized the need for it at this time.

Each house of worship—synagogues as well as churches—offered special prayer services and made it clear that its doors were open to the community. In Breezy Point several people spoke of how important shared prayer and gathering were during those early days. A senior pastor at one of the Catholic churches in Breezy Point held a special Mass on the night of September 11, and about two thousand people showed up. On the following night all three Breezy Point churches (two Catholic and one Protestant) organized a candle-light vigil on the centrally located baseball field "to pray for the people lost or missing at the World Trade Center and hope for survivors."

The secular leaders of Rockaway responded in similar fashion to what they sensed was the community's need "to do something." Linda Reedstrom, the executive director of the Rockaway Chamber of Commerce, described the early days after September 11:

Immediately after the disaster, people just wanted to help. They wanted to do something—even people who had lost someone wanted to do something. So we set up a program called Rockaway Reaching Out. It was a relief fund to raise money for the tribute [memorial] and other needed things for the recovery. We raised $40,000 for the tribute. One thing we did was we sold pins in the shape of small flags. People could glue the pin to the flag for $1. We had this activity set up on tables all over town, and people loved them—in the beauty parlors, in stores, everywhere. They could wear the pin and donate money at the same time. And it gave everyone something to do.

We also mobilized a system for providing meals for the cops and firemen who were working so hard at the site during the recovery effort at the World Trade Center. We enlisted people to deliver meals two times a day to the firehouses because they were working so hard downtown and were taxed to the limit and devastated.

Similar activities were arranged in Breezy Point to keep children and families busy while many men worked at the World Trade Center site. Knowing that teenagers might attempt to visit Ground Zero and witness horrifying scenes of death, concerned adults deliberately assigned them the task of tending the three local volunteer fire stations.

Perhaps because of the inexplicable and terrifying nature of the terrorist attack, people of all faiths relied heavily on their religious leaders. Particularly important was Monsignor Gallagher, who had served as parish priest in Belle Harbor for fourteen years. Like so many others, he was "challenged to do things [he] never imagined doing," including performing funerals for dozens of members of his parish and their relatives. His ability to listen, empathize, and reassure parishioners was crucial during the early phases of grieving and recovery in Belle Harbor.

Monsignor Gallagher provided a critical form of leadership in the struggle to make sense of an unthinkable tragedy. He responded ably to the feelings of guilt and remorse among firefighters and their wives who felt that they had somehow failed to "look out for each other" on September 11. He granted innumerable interviews to the mainstream press, a responsibility he took on despite his initial inclination to avoid it. From the pulpit he preached peace and healing to counteract the lust for vengeance. When asked how he responded to any anti-Arab sentiment he overheard, Monsignor Gallagher responded, "I would tell them, it's normal to be angry and to want to punish those who did this. I feel that way too sometimes. But if we are to stay true to the words of the Gospel, we must work to be tolerant and not take out our anger on another person or group." Likewise, he encouraged parishioners to confront their fears rather than bury them. Monsignor Gallagher recalled observing two big, brawny firefighters talking after a church service. One man turned to the other and said, "I'm strong, but I'm not this strong." The two men embraced and burst into tears.

Monsignor Gallagher continues to be seen as a pillar of the community. Unfortunately, his leadership was significantly hampered if not lost following the crash of flight 587. With the church so close to the point of impact, the sanctuary and the ritual of church services were unavailable to those in need.

THE CHAOS AFTER THE CRASH

Only eight weeks after the attack on the World Trade Center, on November 12, 2001, American Airlines flight 587, an Airbus 300–600 aircraft, nosedived into the heart of Belle Harbor, destroying a dozen homes, damaging dozens more, and killing all 260 passengers and five local residents on the ground. The initial response to the plane crash in Rockaway was remarkably similar to what happened after September 11. Friends and neighbors, local merchants, and organizations all responded to the disaster with generosity and concern for those most seriously affected. Memorials and tributes were well attended, and special attention was paid to the disaster's impact on local children. Free mental health and counseling services were extended to people traumatized by the crash of flight 587. Once again, racial and ethnic boundaries were crossed as white Rockaway residents joined with the Dominican families of the passengers in grief, memory, and a quest for answers. There were even discussions of a shared memorial honoring the victims of September 11 and November 12. Over time, however, the two events became distinct in the hearts and minds of the Rockaway community. The crash of flight 587 raised some very sensitive, polarizing issues, many of which remain unresolved at the time of this writing. A rift was growing between some trauma sufferers and their neighbors who had grown impatient with the pace of recovery.

In the first few minutes after the plane crashed, no one knew what had happened. Understandably, some residents thought New York was under attack and that terrorists had crashed another airplane into the Rockaway peninsula. Panic spread rapidly as residents fled their homes in fear of toxic fumes, sewer explosions (a long-standing concern among residents), and spreading fire. Elderly people were rescued by a telephone repair crew working in the area, and one ailing couple struggled to the steps of the St. Francis de Sales rectory in their pajamas. Within minutes, rescue personnel had flooded the area, barricades were erected, and an evacuation plan was implemented. Monsignor Gallagher later asserted that such a rapid response was unusual for the Rockaways and was most probably due to the city's preparedness after September 11.

The experience was the worst for the children and the parents of children who witnessed the crash or were evacuated as a result. A woman whose house was damaged by the vibrations of the impact described the unfolding of events as she pulled her frightened children down the street to safety.

I had been lying in bed when I heard the plane. It was really loud, and then I saw the shadow. The shadow went right over the window, and then I felt the house shake and shift. So I jumped out of bed and ran to the window. There was dark black smoke billowing up, but I couldn't see anything, so I shouted to the kids to get dressed. I got my son up first, and he got dressed, but my daughter was having a hard time. So I got my son to help her. But she kept screaming, "I'm not dressed." She still, to this day, wakes up with nightmares screaming, "I'm not dressed."

I went downstairs to figure out what was going on. People were saying that we had to evacuate because they thought the sewers might explode. I had to keep myself together for the kids, so they wouldn't panic. But I remember pulling them down the street—we still didn't know what had happened—and a lady, my neighbor whose son lives in the house next to the crash site, she had fainted in the middle of the street. I just stepped over her. I had to get my kids out of there, so I just stepped over her. I still feel guilty about that. I normally would have helped her, but I was focused on getting my kids out of there. And the smoke, we didn't know what was being released into the air. I don't know. I still feel guilty. But my neighbor, she doesn't even remember it now.

As the immediate crisis subsided some residents were permitted to reenter their homes, where they were greeted by media personnel surveying the scene from rooftops and windows. Rescue workers had also entered the homes in search of sheets and blankets to cover dead bodies found in the wreckage. Garbage cans had also been taken for use in the cleanup efforts.

As if fleeing a fallen airplane and inferno were not traumatic enough, Belle Harborites were deeply resentful of the callous invasion of their personal space and indifference to their needs. Matt Lauer and the NBC crew were broadcasting live from the scene, as were reporters from CNN, ABC, CBS, and other television stations. The media, which had so sensitively brought forth tales of September 11 heroes from Rockaway, were now seen as "swarming the neighborhood" and aggressively pursuing different camera angles of the crash. In addition to trespassing on their property, journalists alienated residents by reporting false or inaccurate stories and breaking promises of anonymity. Then, almost as suddenly as the crash had happened, the reporters and cameras departed, leaving behind an isolated, media-shy community to confront yet another traumatic loss.

Unlike September 11, the plane crash disrupted the physical space and traditional sanctuaries of Belle Harbor. With the St. Francis de Sales church and school cordoned off behind police tape and barricades, there was nowhere to congregate safely. Access to local streets was limited to rescue or FBI vehicles. People were afraid to spend time on their porches or stoops for fear of fumes in the air. Residents who lived closest to the impact were either evacuated or told not to leave their homes. Children, many of whom remain deeply troubled by what they saw, were kept home from school for the entire week. People avoided traveling down the streets near the crash site, afraid of spotting the bodies and luggage of victims. Not only was the physical space altered, but the means to give and receive emotional support were altogether missing during the first week. Monsignor Gallagher noted that with the church unavailable and telephone service disrupted, it was difficult even for him to reach out to the community at large.

Meanwhile, civic leaders from all levels of government seemed to misread the needs of the residents, further fueling their resentment and frustration. For instance, days after the crash, residents on one block gathered to discuss the immediate issues they were facing. Primarily they needed garbage cans, bed sheets, and counselors for their children. After calling a local official who was serving as liaison to American Airlines, they were told that "garbage cans can be claimed on your insurance forms"; the community leadership was not prepared to assist more directly. One woman explained how she took matters into her own hands:

> There are widows living on this block who can't get over to Home Depot to toss a big garbage can in their trunk. So I took it upon myself to call Home Depot. They connected me to the home office, I explained who I was, and within days we had our garbage cans. I also made arrangements through St. Francis de Sales to get real counselors over here. We needed counselors. Our kids needed counselors. But [the local official] said there were counselors at the site and flyers all around. I don't know, but those counselors weren't really there for us. I didn't see any. How could I? They wouldn't let us leave the block.

Many residents felt that local leaders placed the needs of rescue workers above those of civilians. Tables of food and beverages to feed the cleanup crews were donated by local restaurants and delis. Phone banks were set up to allow rescue personnel and investigators to make calls. Meanwhile, traumatized children and their parents remained at home, fearful that their tap water was contaminated and that another plane would come crashing down.

The crash of flight 587 was a dramatic confirmation of a long-standing concern among Rockaway residents. As one person said, "We've always known that it wasn't a matter of *if* a plane will crash in Rockaway, but *when*." Scores of flights leaving JFK airport continue to fly over the Rockaway peninsula on a daily basis. One woman remarked that she thought the planes fly even lower now, "just to show us how safe they think it is." As she said this, the shadow of a roaring jumbo jet crossed her porch, and she shuddered. "It's the shadow," she said. "That's what gets me—I remember the shadow."

The disappointment in local officials was mild in contrast to the frustration and distrust that Belle Harborites felt when dealing with U.S. government agencies. In the wake of September 11, the citizens of Rockaway expected more support from federal officials than they received. Americans were being urged by President Bush to be vigilant and to report "anything unusual" to police or federal authorities. Taking that duty seriously, eyewitnesses to the crash reported their observations to federal investigators. Many people who saw the plane in the air have consistently maintained that it was in trouble long before the tail fell off. Several Rockaway residents insist that a major explosion or fuel eruption occurred while the vertical stabilizer and tail were still attached. Two men fishing from a boat in Jamaica Bay described debris falling and flames bursting from the rear of the plane before the tail plunged into the water. For most parties, the central issue is not *whether* the tail separation caused the plane to crash, but *why* and *when* the fatal events occurred.

According to witnesses, FBI agents were generally dismissive of their accounts of an explosion or fire on board, placing greater importance on fragments of twisted metal than on what Rockaway residents were reporting. One retired firefighter was told by an FBI investigator, "You don't know what you were seeing." Several other eyewitnesses wrote detailed letters to the National Transportation Safety Board (NTSB), only to have them ignored. Members of the Dominican community were also eager for answers. As they began visiting the Belle Harbor site and reading and hearing accounts of the crash, they grew skeptical of the official explanations that pilot error or wake turbulence caused the crash.

What was initially most upsetting to local residents was being brushed off by investigators as if they were attention-seekers who had watched too many disaster movies. A number of the witnesses were firefighters and retired police officers who were trained to observe and report unusual events. Other witnesses were teachers, priests, flight attendants, and lawyers who, as one man put it, "have no reason to make this up." As time passed, however, the official investigation drew the attention of a small group of aviation experts who felt that government agencies were covering up inconsistencies in the instrument data to protect the airline industry. A handful of these experts joined with Rockaway residents in voicing their objections to the investigators' methods and hasty conclusions. They pointed to other occasions when Airbus 300–600 planes had nearly crashed owing to similar rudder malfunctions. One expert asserts that "the NTSB will attempt to blame the copilot for overuse of the rudder.... But no overuse of the rudder can develop the extreme inertia forces required to shear the engine from its support structures" (see Schwach 2004, n.p.). These expert opinions reinforce the cynicism and distrust that Rockaway residents felt toward the federal agencies involved in the investigation.

Three years after the crash, the citizens of Rockaway and the Dominican community were still awaiting an official explanation for the crash, and there was concern that pending lawsuit settlements might end their "search for the truth." To add insult to injury, the NTSB not only continued to disregard their eyewitness accounts but publicly called them "unreliable." An article in *The Wave* strongly criticized the NTSB and defended the credibility of witnesses. The evidence "prove[s] that the Flight 587 witnesses were generally careful to not affirm something they were not sure of" (Trombettas 2002, n.p.).

The bravery of Rockaway firefighters and the losses suffered on September 11 brought the kind of positive recognition and validation that the community so badly craved. After the crash of flight 587, it seemed unfathomable that the heroes of September 11 were suddenly being treated with disdain. How could the National Transportation Safety Board, the Federal Bureau of Investigation, and the American Airlines Corporation publicly call residents of this patriotic, self-sacrificing, service-minded community "unreliable" and attention-seeking? Erikson (1994) argues that in man-made disasters profound damage is done when victims feel that they are offered no apology, no explanation, no sense of compassion, and no acknowledgment of their trauma. Such damage was done to the citizens of Rockaway. In fact, grief counselors concur that the fear and stress generated by September 11 more than quadrupled after the plane crash on November 12, delaying recovery indefinitely for many local residents. Part of the reason is that local residents continued to live within the same set of circumstances that led to and followed the plane crash. Each time a plane passed overhead the trauma was relived; the street corners and landmarks surrounding the crash site were constant reminders of death and lost neigh-bors; government agencies remained unresponsive to local demands to change flight patterns; and no credible explanation for the crash was offered. To make matters worse, those suffering from the trauma of the crash of flight 587 found themselves taking a backseat to the victims, heroes, and bereaved families of the September 11 terrorist attack.

Some of the characteristics that have made residents so proud of their com-munity also impeded some people's recovery from the trauma of the plane crash. The emphasis on privacy and self-reliance made it difficult for outside organizations to reach the most severely traumatized individuals. Suffering in isolation, some trauma suffers experienced feelings of guilt and failure. For many in Rockaway the blanket of security surrounding their secluded, middle-class neighborhood had been shredded, and no one, not the federal govern-ment, not the local leadership, not even old friends and family, seemed willing or able to stitch it back together. Their growing sense of isolation and betrayal led some individuals to see themselves as having an altered relationship with their community and with humanity more generally. While the shared trauma of September 11 deepened the sense of "spiritual kinship" (Erikson 1994, 231) among the citizens of Rockaway, the crash of flight 587 disrupted the spiritual moorings of many individuals, setting them apart from their community support systems.

COMMUNITY ORGANIZATIONS STEP UP TO THE PLATE

Despite the suffering in Rockaway, strong community-based institutions helped to fill the voids created by the two disasters. Not only did religious institutions offer ritual and comfort, but groups such as the Rockaway Chamber of Commerce and the Graybeards organized fund-raising, food drives, and stress-relieving activities. Two local organizations stand out in particular for their contributions to community recovery: *The Wave* newspaper and its editorial staff and the Rockaway Artists Alliance (RAA). Both of these organizations were highly respected throughout the peninsula prior to the double tragedy and were therefore well positioned to reach the most traumatized members of the community. Their effectiveness underscores the importance of community-based organizations during disaster recovery. Neither, of course, cured the suffering or fixed the pain of Rockaway residents, but they were instrumental in beginning the process.

The Voice of *The Wave*

Following the collapse of the twin towers on September 11, *The Wave* took an approach that earned the newspaper much community praise. As an alternative to the in-depth stories of death and tragedy covered by New York City's daily newspapers, *The Wave* offered families the chance to place a full or half-page ad, free of charge, in tribute to lost loved ones. Several families took advantage of this opportunity and were grateful to *The Wave* for making the space available.

After the plane crash, *The Wave*'s role in community dialogue and recovery was even more significant. With so much frustration and anguish in the community surrounding the crash investigation, the newspaper served as a local lightning rod, fielding stories and complaints from a variety of perspectives, sifting through conspiracy theories, and lending support to people who felt voiceless despite efforts to report what they had seen. Recognizing the escalating need, Howard Schwach called a meeting in early July 2002 in which witnesses to the crash explained what they saw to an audience of reporters, aviation experts, and passengers' families. Schwach also invited officials from the

NTSB, although they did not attend. At the meeting witnesses and experts exchanged recollections and opinions about what had brought down flight 587, and community members complained of the planes that were constantly overhead. It was obvious that residents were shaken—even traumatized—by what they had witnessed; they were most emotional about having their "good word" and credibility besmirched by what they saw to be a dehumanizing federal bureaucracy.

One of the New York City daily newspapers printed a story on the meeting. U.S. Congressman Anthony Weiner (D-NY) later demanded that the Federal Aviation Administration (FAA) reroute planes away from the Rockaways, but little changed in the first two years following the crash. Still, the meeting hosted by *The Wave* was considered successful because it gave voice to the concerns and anxieties of local residents. The federal government remained under suspicion for covering up the truth, and some Rockaway residents were deeply invested in the investigation process. Yet, by validating the credibility of witnesses in a public forum, *The Wave* achieved what the NTSB and the FBI could not: they facilitated the recovery process for the people of Rockaway.

The Rockaway Artists Alliance Responds

For weeks after September 11, funeral processions, high-flying fighter jets, and the sight of a battleship on the horizon served as vivid reminders of the trauma that had befallen the community. Just as these images began to dissipate, they were replaced by memories of a plane nosediving into the neighborhood, leaving behind charred ruins of houses. It quickly became clear to community leaders in Belle Harbor and Breezy Point that the emotional well-being of local children and their parents was at risk. Children who had lost a parent in the World Trade Center were understandably depressed and withdrawn. I heard even more accounts of children traumatized by the plane disaster: a ten-year-old boy who would not go outside; a five-year-old girl with persistent nightmares who developed a lazy eye following the plane crash; teenage boys who, months after the crash, were sharing a bedroom with their mother; and children playing outside who stopped and visibly shuddered as an airplane passed overhead.

Everyone—not just children—looked up at the sky when planes passed overhead. However, it was children's suffering and sadness that caused the most distress for the parents I met. "Every time I see her [lazy] eye, it reminds me of that day," said the tearful mother of the five-year-old. Parents struggled to reassure their children that they were safe and protected, but the parents themselves did not feel safe. As one resident of Breezy Point observed, "I think a lot of adults project their own fears onto their children."

The Rockaway Artists Alliance, a not-for-profit organization committed to making art a vital element of community life, recognized that events aimed at children would ultimately benefit adults in the community as well. The RAA integrated an art therapy component into many of its preexisting programs and organized an exhibit for community members to display their drawings, photographs, and poetry related to the disasters. The KidsmART after-school enrichment program and its summertime camp equivalent, Camp KidsmART, gave children the opportunity to express their feelings through art in a safe environment. Many children of Rockaway, according to RAA's education director (a former psychiatric nurse and bereavement counselor), were worried about their parents and did not feel comfortable talking about their feelings at home. Some parents encouraged their children "not to cry, as a way of putting it all behind them, and moving on." Art became a therapeutic vehicle allowing children to express their feelings and share them with others.

The instructors at KidsmART and Camp KidsmART were trained to handle issues of grief and anxiety. The importance of that training became clear one day when a little boy raised his hand and announced, "My daddy is dead." Under normal circumstances, this remark might have made an instructor uncomfortable. Instead, the counselor asked whether anyone else had lost a parent or a family member on September 11. Eight other children raised their hands. The counselor recalled that the boy's face brightened when he realized that he was not the only person to have lost a parent and "that there were other kids just like him."

Following the lead of the RAA, other community institutions incorporated art therapy into their outreach services to help children and adults deal with the traumas of September 11 and November 12. As the minister of the First Congregational Church explained, "When you hear of children sleeping with their clothes folded at the end of the bed in case another plane crashes, you know the need is still there."

The RAA also provided an organizational model for local churches, schools, and other community groups trying to help children cope with loss and trauma. The Chamber of Commerce, for example, held especially elaborate Christmas holiday celebrations. Catholic Charities of Brooklyn and Queens organized a day for the children of Belle Harbor to write their wishes on paper; the wishes were then inserted in balloons that were released, in unison, on the beach. In September 2002, Project Liberty organized a school fair on the grounds of PS 114, complete with carnival games and moon bounces for the children. Such child-centered activities also brought parents together and provided some relief in their stress-filled lives.

These child-centered programs paved the way for the acceptance of the counseling services offered by national, state, and city organizations. The counseling services that had been established by the Red Cross, Project Liberty, and Catholic Charities in response to September 11 were expanded to include any child or adult affected by the plane crash. The three organizations made concerted efforts to penetrate Rockaway's tight-knit social networks by patiently developing social relationships with trusted individuals in the community. Community leaders in Breezy Point would set up their community center as a safe and private place for Catholic Charities' counselors to meet with residents.

Remembering the Two Traumas: Consensus, Conspiracy, and Controversy

My research turned up countless examples of the trauma of September 11 and the crash of flight 587 becoming merged in experience, interpretation, and response. Not only were the two events chronologically and geographically related, but they coalesced into one gigantic traumatic experience for the people of Belle Harbor. Inevitably, stories about one event included mention of the other. Many times I heard about the double tragedy experienced by a man whose twenty-three-year-old son died in the World Trade Center. The man was reported to have said, "They're out to get me," when the plane crashed one block from his restaurant, killing his son's best friend. Local firefighters who had witnessed the horrors of Ground Zero were reputed to have said that the plane wreckage two months later was "worse than anything they had seen."

Stories also circulated that explained the plane crash as revenge for the events surrounding September 11. A number of people told me that the plane crash might well have been payback for a televised challenge to Bin Laden during a benefit concert for the victims of September 11 held at Madison Square Garden. Onstage between band performances, a firefighter who had lost his brother in the attack, shouted into the microphone: "Osama Bin Laden, you can kiss my royal Irish ass. And I live in Rockaway." As it turned out, this firefighter lived, as one resident told me, "two houses from where the engine dropped. At first some people wondered if the plane crash was payback for him saying that on TV." *The Wave* even printed an elaborate cryptogram in an August 2002 issue that purported to link the crash with the assassination of John F. Kennedy, the murder of the Colorado six-year-old Jon Benet Ramsey, and the destruction of the World Trade Center. This and other conspiracy theories dissipated over time, but others may well surface if the cause of the crash is not identified and confirmed by the federal government. In fact, at the end of the summer of 2002 there were stories that flight 587 had been brought down by a shoe bomber.

Given the connections between the two disasters, it is not surprising that initial plans for a September 11 memorial also included the local victims of flight 587. In fact, a website depicting the now-famous image of three firefighters hoisting the American flag at Ground Zero (one of them was George John-son from Rockaway) also bore the names of the five Belle Harborites lost in the plane crash. Then, at some point during the summer of 2002, a decision was made by the memorial planning committee to include only the names of September 11 victims on the Rockaway memorial. This change in plans went unnoticed.

The ground-breaking for Tribute Park, as it is named, took place in mid-September 2002 on a small plot of land overlooking Jamaica Bay; a call for design submissions was placed by the Rockaway Artists Alliance, and commu-nity feedback was solicited prior to the final memorial design selection. Mean-while, four separate memorials were established in Breezy Point to commemo-rate "their own" twenty-four residents who died on September 11, including memorial gardens and plaques near each church on Breezy Point property and a large, permanent memorial sculpture on the sand dunes overlooking the Manhattan skyline. The sculpture is in the shape of a Christian cross built from steel girders removed from Ground Zero, surrounded by handmade wooden crosses bearing the names of lost loved ones and a single Star of David fashioned of small twigs.

If September 11 memorials took shape without controversy, this was not the case when it came to memorializing the victims of the flight 587 crash, which increasingly came to be seen as affecting only a few individuals rather than the whole community. Although many residents saw connections be-tween the two events, some began to urge their traumatized neighbors to "get over it" and "move on." Perhaps more important, there was declining sympathy for the Dominican families visiting the site to place wreaths or flowers on a makeshift memorial. At least one property owner with a house adjacent to the memorial publicly stated, "This is my home, it's not a cemetery," and she re-sisted plans to install a plaque or memorial marker near her home. Another neighbor expressed dismay that "this memorial is being rammed down our throats."

By early December 2003, the Belle Harbor community remained divided on the issue of where to construct a memorial to the plane crash victims. In an effort to resolve the issue, the Rockaway Chamber of Commerce offered to incorporate a memorial to flight 587 victims into the already established Trib-ute Park memorializing September 11 victims. The Dominican community po-litely declined this offer, noting that the Rockaway residents deserved a sepa-rate place to memorialize their loved ones. Congressman Weiner got involved in delicate negotiations between his Belle Harbor constituents and representa-tives of the Dominican families, who felt strongly that the land beneath the crash site was hallowed ground. A majority (60 percent) of Belle Harbor resi-dents supported this plan and were angered by what they saw as selfishness on the part of their neighbors who resisted the plan.[6] For nearly two years, the issue elicited dozens of letters to the editor of *The Wave*: most were in favor of the memorial, but many were angrily against it.[7]

Given Rockaway's history of racial intolerance, it is likely that many local residents resented the incursion of nonwhites from a "different culture" into "their" neighborhood. Also, there was resistance to having the memorial for the crash on private property, where, as one resident put it, the neighborhood would be constantly reminded of the trauma every day: "People don't want hundreds of people crossing their lawns, leaving roses and pictures." Moreover, opposition to a memorial site at the center of the neighborhood no doubt reflected the tradition of community isolation. The community's summer parking restrictions, for instance, have long made it clear that Belle Harborites, as a group, do not welcome outside visitors (see, for example, *The Wave* 2000).

In early 2004, however, New York City Mayor Michael Bloomberg's office circumvented Congressman Weiner's efforts by unilaterally installing a memorial plaque beneath a tree at the corner of Newport Avenue and Beach 130th Street. Subsequently, flight 587 families requested that a larger memorial be installed in a vacant city-owned lot in Belle Harbor. With most local residents either indifferent or opposed to the matter, the mayor is unlikely to make a decision on this memorial site until after the 2006 election, for fear of angering both his Dominican and Belle Harbor constituents.

Conflict over the flight 587 memorial was not the only issue dividing the community. As collective support for those still experiencing trauma symptoms began to wane, some witnesses to the plane crash said that they could no longer even talk to their friends or neighbors about it:

> Honestly, the only people I can talk to anymore are the people who lost someone in the World Trade Center. No one else can understand why I'm still so upset. It's like they want me to move on, to get over it. I've had to avoid some of my old friends because I don't want them to say that stuff to me.

There were also festering resentments over insurance and other settlement payments made to residents displaced by the crash. As one woman said:

> Now my neighbors look at me every time we get something new. My lease ran out on our old car, so we got this new van. Now they think I've gotten some money and haven't told them about it. I haven't gotten anything, and I'm told that we're not likely to ever get anything. But this sort of thing never used to happen.

Indeed, litigation and lawsuits were still in their early stages when I did my research, and it was unclear whether the settlements would create additional conflicts. If so, this will certainly postpone the healing process for the individu-als involved.

The traditional lifelines of emotional and social support so embedded in firefighter and Rockaway culture have clearly not been adequate for everyone. The formal and informal support networks that were credited with helping Rockaway residents "move on" after September 11 have been insufficient to handle the additional trauma experienced by some Belle Harbor residents on November 12. Because the people whose homes were damaged and those who witnessed the crash still feel invalidated, there is a growing sense for them of disconnection from the Rockaway community. Perhaps, then, the cultural predisposition to lean on "the community" has become a liability for those individuals, since their community itself has grown weary from the pain.

CONCLUSION: THE STRENGTHS AND LIMITATIONS OF COMMUNITY

Despite the overwhelming personal pain and loss inflicted on September 11, available evidence suggests that, as communities, Belle Harbor and Breezy Point have remained, for the most part, united and cohesive. Although there is abundant evidence of what Erikson (1994) identifies as individual trauma, there is nothing to suggest that the glue that has bound these communities together for generations has changed in any fundamental way. The kind of collective trauma that so often destroys communities faced with a natural or man-made catastrophe has not surfaced in Rockaway—at least, not yet.

One reason for this, I suspect, is that the September 11 disaster was an occasion for community bonds to be strengthened through shared grieving and memory. The terrorist attack was immediately defined by government leaders as an act of war against the United States, not, as with the crash of flight 587, an act of corporate malfeasance or incompetence. As such, the people who died on September 11 were defined as casualties of war and hailed as heroes, regardless of their occupation. The firefighters who died, many of whom lived in Breezy Point or Belle Harbor, perished in the line of duty, bravely and selflessly trying to rescue countless civilians. The civilians were heroic in their innocence. Within this context of war and heroism, the Rockaway community drew on its strengths, lending financial, emotional, and physical support to those families who suffered personal losses. The socioeconomic and cultural homogeneity of the community made memorial planning relatively easy and part of the healing process. The individuals who died are still sorely missed and the grieving process continues for dozens of families, but many residents give credit to "the community" for pulling them through the most difficult times during that first year.

Sadly, as this research has shown, the same cannot be said of the families and individuals traumatized by the crash of American Airlines flight 587. The plane crash forced Rockaway into the national spotlight. Many respondents resented that this single event "put [them] on the map" and drew attention to their idyllic, "secret" neighborhood as the site of the second-worst airline disaster in U.S. history.[8] Likewise, the ongoing dispute with the Dominican families over the placement of a memorial continued to draw unwanted media attention as the second anniversary approached. For a community that cherishes its isolation and privacy, these events have presented a tremendous challenge, to say the least.

The flames of the crash also tested the resilience of individuals raised to put aside their own needs to assist others. Because the physical space of the community was altered, neighbors could not help each other in the immediate aftermath. The visible reminders of the crash remained for more than two years, deepening the wounds of the people most troubled by it, including local children. Firefighters' wives continued to struggle to fulfill their perceived obligations to comfort and support the widows of September 11. A bereavement counselor noted that the "collective sense of mission failure was tremendous," as the people of Belle Harbor were forced to wrestle with the limits of their own strength. Cracks in the local culture were beginning to show: the trauma of pulling their children to safety amid flames and fumes left a few women questioning the tradition of raising their sons to be firefighters.

There are some interesting parallels between the crash of American Airlines flight 587 and the bombing of a plane over Lockerbie, Scotland, in 1988. On December 21 of that year, a terrorist bomb exploded aboard Pan Am flight 103, which was filled with 259 people, most of them Americans. The burning debris ignited several fires and explosions in the town of Lockerbie, killing eleven people on the ground. In the days, months, and years following that night, Lockerbie and its people have struggled to move forward with their lives, despite constant reminders of the tragedy. They converted a workman's shed in a churchyard into a memorial for the families of the passengers who died. Many loved ones make pilgrimages to the town, seeking answers from townspeople who witnessed the aftermath and leaving artifacts and letters behind at the memorial.

Yet despite the ever-present reminders of pain and grief, the town of Lockerbie seems to have found a balance between moving forward and honoring the dead. A bond developed between the people of Lockerbie and the plane victims' families. In addition to shepherding visiting family members through the town and memorial sites, Lockerbie participates in student scholarships and exchanges with Syracuse University, which lost thirty-two students aboard flight 103.

At the same time, there are rifts tearing at the Lockerbie community, most of them revolving around issues of money and settlements. By one account, "a young man attacked a neighbour's car bought, it was said, with compensation money [from Pan Am]" (Braid 2001). The honors bestowed on local residents who were heroically involved in the rescue efforts following the crash have sprouted similar jealousies.

It is clearly too soon to know whether any sort of positive relationship will emerge between the people of Belle Harbor and the Dominican families whose loved ones perished on flight 587. Certainly the racial and ethnic differences have made dialogue between the two communities awkward, if not downright uncomfortable. The politically and emotionally charged conflict over how and where to memorialize the dead remains unresolved, further delaying the community's recovery. If a positive outcome is possible, it may come only after Belle Harbor has adjusted to its new, albeit regrettable, identity as the site of a high-profile tragedy.

Perhaps more importantly, the healing process for the people most deeply affected by the crash—eyewitnesses, victims' families, and local children in particular—would be best served if they were to receive a plausible explanation of its cause. In the Lockerbie case, the cause of the explosion was quickly identified. So too were the people responsible for the attacks of September 11. However, the emotional recovery from the flight 587 disaster has been hampered by the investigators' lack of sensitivity and the absence of a clear, identifiable cause or "enemy." In the current climate of skepticism and fear, Rockaway's residents feel at sea without an explanation or apology. Such feelings, according to Erikson, can cause irreparable damage to an individual's, and ultimately a community's, well-being. Moreover, though the citizens of Rockaway are familiar, even emboldened, by their identity as New York City's "forgotten stepchildren," the local predilection for privacy and self-reliance threatens to impede the recovery process for many individuals still suffering the effects of the double trauma.

NOTES

1. The weekly community paper in Rockaway, *The Wave*, and several daily New York newspapers—the *New York Daily News*, *Newsday*, and the *New York Times*—provided important background information. Equally valuable was the book authored by Rockaway native Kevin Boyle, *Braving the Waves: Rockaway Rises and Rises Again* (2002), a chronicle of the two disasters and their aftermath in Rockaway. Names of interviewees have been changed to ensure confidentiality.
2. Population figures are available online through U.S. Census Bureau Fact Finder (http://factfinder.census.gov). Beach 102nd Street is the boundary of the zip code 11694 and marks the border between Rockaway Park and Rockaway Beach. Much of the U.S. census data used in this chapter is sorted by zip code as well. Throughout the chapter, when I refer to the West End I am referring to neighborhoods west of Beach 102nd Street.

3. Ethnicity statistics are available online through U.S. Census Bureau (http://www. census.gov/cgi-bin/gazetteer).
4. Income figures are available online through U.S. Census Bureau Fact Finder (http:// factfinder.census.gov).
5. It should be noted that prior to 9/11 the FDNY was predominantly white; blacks comprised 2.8 percent and Hispanics 2.9 percent of all firefighters. Women constituted 0.33 percent of the FDNY (see Thomas 2002).
6. This was one result of an online poll taken by *The Wave* (results posted September 15, 2003).
7. See, for example, letter to the editor of *Breezy Point News*, September 6, 2002. See also *The Wave* (2002a; 2002b).
8. As quoted in *The Women of Rockaway*, a film by Kevin and Rosemary Breslin, broadcast on the Oxygen Channel, September 11, 2002. At the time of this writing, the crash of an American Airlines DC-10 outside Chicago in 1979, in which 273 people were killed, remains the single deadliest airplane crash on U.S. territory. See "Top Ten Fatal Events by Total Fatalities," http://www.airsafe.com/events/mostfat.htm (revised October 5, 2001).

REFERENCES

Boyle, Kevin. 2002. *Braving the Waves: Rockaway Rises and Rises Again.* New York: Rising Star Press.
Braid, Mary. 2001. "Ghosts of Grief Haunt a Town That Became a Place of Pilgrimage: Lockerbie Verdict; the Town." *The Independent* (London), February 1.
Erikson, Kai. 1976. *Everything in Its Path: Destruction of Community in the Buffalo Creek Flood.* New York: Simon & Schuster.
———. 1994. *A New Species of Trouble.* New York: W. W. Norton.
Schwach, Howard. 2001. "From the Editor's Desk." *The Wave*, November 24. Available at: http://www.rockawave.com/news/2001/1124/Columnists/From_the_Editor's_Desk1124.html (accessed November 8, 2004).
———. 2004. "Aviation Pro: AA587 in 'Horizontal Tornado,'" editorial, *The Wave*, June 11. Available at: http://www.rockawave.com/news/2004/0611/Community/004.html (accessed November 9, 2004).
Thomas, Myra A. 2002. "Minority Recruitment Remains a Struggle for the FDNY." *Northstar Network*, September 30. Available at: http://www.thenorthstarnetwork.com/news/specialreports/181518-1.html (accessed September 3, 2003).
Trombettas, Victor. 2002. "Flight 587 Update: 'Witness Reliability.'" *The Wave*, July 6. Available at: http://www.rockawave.com/news/2002/0706/Community/Flight_587_Update0706.html (accessed November 9, 2004).
The Wave. 2000. "A Local's Viewpoint." Letter to the editor of *The Wave*, August 26. Available at: http://www.rockawave.com/news/2000/0826/Letters/A_Local's_Viewpoint0826.html (accessed November 9, 2004).
———. 2002a. "Shouldn't Complain." Letter to the editor of *The Wave*, November 16. Available at: http://www.rockawave.com/News/2002/1116/Letters/Shouldnt_Complain1116.html (accessed November 9, 2004).

————. 2002b. "Crash Site Is Hallowed Ground." Letter to the editor of *The Wave*, November 23. Available at: http://www.rockawave.com/News/2002/1123/Letters/Crash_Site_Is_Hallowed_Ground1123.html (accessed November 9, 2004).

————. N.d. "Rockaway . . . Place of Waters Brights." History files of *The Wave*. Available at: http://www.rockawave.com/common/history/history.html (accessed November 8, 2004).

CHAPTER 5

Constructing "the True Islam" in Hostile Times: The Impact of 9/11 on Arab Muslims in Jersey City

Jennifer L. Bryan

THE ATTACK of September 11, 2001, on the World Trade Center in New York had an enormous impact on Arab Muslims in Jersey City, New Jersey. In particular, it sparked a critical turning point in the construction of Muslim identities, in-group community cohesion, and intergroup relations in Jersey City. It was not the attack itself so much as its aftermath—the state war on terrorism (with its transnational and local variations), the media images and stories linking Arab Muslims with terrorists, and the social and economic backlash against Arab Muslims—that caused such profound social effects.

In the immediate aftermath of 9/11, the Federal Bureau of Investigation (FBI) and local law enforcement officials questioned and arrested hundreds of Arab men, raided dozens of Arab businesses and homes, and surveyed several local mosques. Jersey City was a particular target of investigation because of its association with the 1993 bombing of the World Trade Center, which Sheik Omar Abdel-Rahman was convicted of planning there. After 9/11, the Immigration and Naturalization Service (INS) and the Office of Homeland Security (OHS) detained nearly eight hundred Arab men in jails just outside of Jersey City. Journalists and media crews from all over the United States and the world ran leading stories depicting Jersey City as a "Terror Town."[1] Employers were reluctant to hire Arab Muslims. Landlords imposed large increases in rent on Arab Muslim tenants. Black, white, Latino, Asian, and Arab Christians formed an unprecedented alliance to "watch" Arab Muslims for "suspicious activities"; some organized patrols of public space near mosques and elementary schools, while others used telescopes to monitor Arab Muslims in the privacy of their homes. Afraid and angry that Arab Muslims in Jersey City could be involved in terrorist "sleeper cells," some residents reported the activities of Arab Muslims to the FBI; some intimidated, embarrassed, and even hurt Arab Muslims by verbally or physically assaulting them.

Given the post-9/11 climate of Jersey City, the objective and subjective risks of going to the mosque, wearing Islamic clothing, and practicing Islam in public space were high. Yet in the face of intense scrutiny by the FBI, detentions by the INS, hostility from employers, and hate crimes by neighbors, many Muslims in Jersey City, paradoxically, did not attempt to blend into American life and hide their Muslim-ness. On the contrary, they embraced a more traditional adherence to the religious practices of Islam, striving to represent what they called "the true Islam."

The analysis in this chapter is part of a broader project examining the impact of September 11 on social interactions among diverse groups in Jersey City. Here I draw on two years of ethnographic research (September 2001 to September 2003) to discuss some of the most urgent social effects of 9/11 on Arab Muslims in Jersey City. My aim is threefold: to identify the challenges facing Arab Muslims; to document the ways in which Arab Muslims have responded to these challenges; and to consider the implications of their responses for community cohesion.

SETTING THE STAGE: JERSEY CITY BEFORE 9/11

As a case study, Jersey City presents an important opportunity to evaluate the impact of 9/11 on Arab Muslims. It is impossible to appreciate the scale of this impact without considering several unique characteristics of Jersey City: its close proximity to Manhattan; its diverse population, including large numbers of Arab Muslim immigrants; and its history of a link between a few Jersey City residents and the planning of the 1993 World Trade Center attack.

Jersey City is located in Hudson County, along the Hudson River in northeast New Jersey. It is about two miles west of Manhattan, separated by a short stretch of the Hudson River. On a normal day the commute from Jersey City to lower Manhattan is less than ten minutes; it is easily accessible by PATH train or car through the Holland Tunnel, as well as by ferry across the Hudson River. Jersey City is so widely recognized for its clear view of the lower Manhattan skyline that before 9/11 movie producers often chose Jersey City's waterfront as the ideal place from which to photograph and film the World Trade Center.

Although Jersey City suffered tremendous economic losses with the decline in manufacturing during the postindustrial 1970s and 1980s, its waterfront view and easy access to Manhattan rendered it a prime site for massive revitalization and gentrification in the 1990s.[2] Today downtown Jersey City's newly developed Harborside Financial Center, nicknamed "Wall Street West," is home to corporate giants like Merrill Lynch, Morgan Stanley, and Goldman Sachs. Despite this revitalization, the disparity between the silver skyscrapers and trendy boutiques lining Jersey City's downtown waterfront and the half-burned-out, decaying buildings in its working-class neighborhoods is stark. The 2000 census revealed that almost 19 percent of Jersey City's population reported living below the poverty level (U.S. Department of Commerce 2000a).

Like New York City, Jersey City has long been a key point of entry for immigrants from diverse lands. With a total population of 240,055, Jersey City is the second most populous city in New Jersey, just behind the city of Newark (U.S. Department of Commerce 2000a). Out of all cities in the United States with a population over 100,000, Jersey City is the fourth most densely populated, with over 16,111 persons per square mile (U.S. Department of Commerce 2000b).[3] Although Jersey City's population is twenty-five times smaller than that of New York City, it is similar to New York City in terms of its racial-ethnic diversity. In 2000 the racial composition of Jersey City was approximately 28 percent Hispanic or Latino, 27 percent non-Hispanic black, 24 percent non-Hispanic white, 16 percent non-Hispanic Asian, 4 percent from two or more races, and 1 percent other (U.S. Department of Commerce 2000a).

In addition to its racial-ethnic diversity, Jersey City is home to a very large number of recent immigrants. In 2000, in fact, 34 percent of Jersey City's total population was foreign-born. Of the foreign-born, 49 percent immigrated to the United States between 1990 and 2000, and a total of 79 percent immigrated between 1980 and 2000 (U.S. Department of Commerce 2000a); thus, recent immigrants make up a significant proportion of the population. In the 1980s Arab Muslims from Egypt began immigrating to Jersey City in large numbers. Spurred on by political and economic turmoil in Egypt, Egyptian Muslims were attracted to Jersey City for its proximity to New York City and to Newark Airport and its reputation as a place with affordable rents, good employment opportunities, and a large Egyptian population.

It is difficult to know exactly how large the Muslim community is in Jersey City because the census does not ask a question on religion; however, Muslim community leaders estimate it to be in the tens of thousands. Although the city's Muslim community comprises people from diverse backgrounds, including Pakistani, Moroccan, and African American, a steady stream of Arab immigrants has formed its core for several years. In the year 2000, 6,764 persons in Jersey City reported having Arab ancestry; this made Arabs the fourth-largest ancestry group in Jersey City. Of those 6,764 persons reporting Arab ancestry, 4,820, or almost three-quarters, were Egyptian (see figure 5.1; U.S. Department of Commerce 2000a). Of course, not all persons in Jersey City reporting Arab and/or Egyptian ancestry were Muslim; the city was home to a significant number of Egyptian (Coptic) Christians in 2000. Nonetheless, Jersey City's Muslim population is large enough to support the city's nineteen mosques, three Islamic centers, two Islamic schools, and over two hundred Muslim-owned businesses.

Arab Muslims reside in neighborhoods throughout Jersey City, but more recent Arab Muslim immigrants have tended to rent apartments in the densely concentrated neighborhoods near the city's old central business district and transportation hub, Journal Square. At the time of the 2000 census, the Journal Square area was composed of census tracts that were heavily immigrant—some tracts were about 60 percent foreign-born, and more than half of the population were not U.S. citizens. Persons of Arab ancestry made up 14 percent of the Journal Square area census tracts, and more specifically, immigrants from Egypt made up 11 percent of these census tracts. These figures are no doubt undercounts, given that many undocumented Arab Muslim immigrants were likely to have been missed by census takers.

Before September 11, Arab Muslims in Jersey City, like other immigrants, were focused on earning money to support their families and provide better lives for their children. With financial support, usually from business partners overseas, a number of Arab Muslims were running businesses—including travel agencies, restaurants, check-cashing hubs, beauty salons, and pharmacies—along Journal Square and throughout the city. Some were operating taxi and bus services to accommodate the large number of commuters making their way to work in New York City. Still others provided services in construction and electrical engineering.

Like other recent immigrants in the postmodern era, Arab Muslims in Jersey City maintained close communication with families, friends, and business partners in Egypt and other countries by way of cell phones, e-mail, fax, and regular mail. Many also followed the time-honored practice of sending money back to relatives in their home country. In turn, these relatives often reciprocated by sending specialty food items and clothes, as well as antibiotics and other medicines, which most immigrant workers could not afford given their minimal access to health care in the United States. Many Arab Muslims in Jersey City also traveled back to their home countries for visits and sent money home to allow relatives to visit New Jersey. In short, Arab Muslims were doing what most immigrants have done throughout history: working long hours for little pay; spending time with their friends and loved ones; enjoying specialty foods from their home countries; and saving money to make a better life for their children.

FIGURE 5.1   JERSEY CITY'S ARAB COMMUNITY

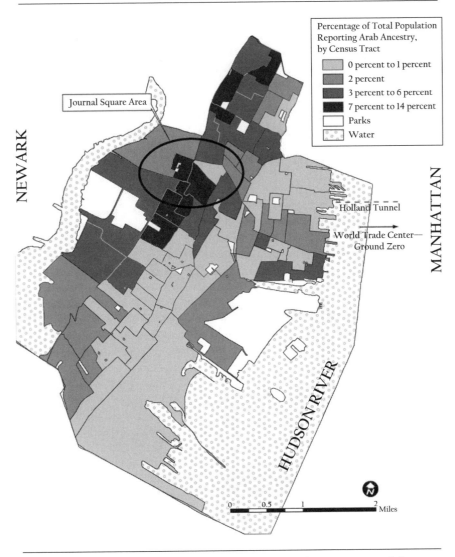

Source: Jersey City Planning Division; data source: 2000 census (U.S. Department of Commerce 2000a).

Jersey City After 9/11

And then the sky fell in on September 11. As this chapter shows, the terrorist attack on September 11 had a devastating impact on Jersey City's Muslim community, shaking loose the foundation they had worked to build and unleashing a wave of hostility toward them. In addition to feeling outrage themselves over the attacks of 9/11, mourning the tragic loss of lives, and seeing on a daily basis the gaping hole that once held the twin towers, Arab Muslims in Jersey City had to contend with public scorn and blame for the attacks. Indeed, the heightened FBI investigations and media publicity in Jersey City opened up the old wounds of 1993, when Jersey City's Muslim community came under intense suspicion after Sheik Omar Abdel-Rahman, who spoke at Al Salam Masjid in Journal Square, was convicted of planning the 1993 World Trade Center attack. The post-9/11 investigation built on these preexisting suspicions of Arab Muslims and as a result exacerbated Jersey City residents' fears. Jersey City's Arab Muslims thus felt targeted not only by the FBI, the INS, and the local police but by their non-Muslim neighbors, who began monitoring their behavior and reporting them to the FBI as suspected terrorists. Needless to say, these factors made Jersey City a hostile place for Arab Muslims after 9/11.

RESEARCH METHODS

Given the large number of Arab Muslims living in the Journal Square area and the highly publicized FBI investigations there, I decided to focus on understanding the experiences of Arab Muslims who prayed at the mosques and/or lived in the neighborhoods in or near this area. I set out with a basic question: *what did it mean to be Arab Muslim in Jersey City after 9/11?* As a non-Muslim American woman conducting an ethnography of a community understandably suspicious of outsiders, I was fortunate to be able to rely on my past experiences growing up in Jersey City and working at an Arab Muslim–owned restaurant from 1990 to 1993 while attending high school. Although many Arab Muslims I knew well had already left Jersey City when I started this project, the fact that many people still recognized me greatly facilitated the establishment of trust.

During a two-year period, from September 2001 to September 2003, I did extensive participant observation and conducted informal interviews with over sixty Muslim women and men. I also gathered in-depth life histories from twelve Muslim women and eight Muslim men. To gain an understanding of how Arab Muslims were getting along with their neighbors, I engaged in participant observation, conducted interviews, and gathered oral histories from dozens of non-Muslims, including Italian Americans, African Americans, Latinos, Egyptian Christians, and others living in the Journal Square area. I began as a casual participating observer of community meetings, protests, prayers at mosques, family celebrations, neighborhood festivals, picnics, weddings, and public spaces such as parks, malls, and transportation centers. Over time I focused more closely on the experiences of three Muslim women and their families. This involved accompanying the women as they worked and shopped, wearing the hijab (Islamic headscarf), eating meals at participants' homes, learning Arabic, and tutoring children in English.

Consistent with the demographics of the larger Journal Square area, most of the Muslims I met and interviewed were recent immigrants from Egypt, Tunisia, or Morocco, or they were Egyptian Americans. Most of them were between eighteen and sixty-five years old. Many of the men worked seventy to ninety hours per week as taxi or bus drivers, restaurant or travel agency owners, construction workers, or electrical engineers. Their goals were to support their families and to save money to buy a house and travel back to their home country. Many of the women I met or interviewed were married with more than two children and worked part-time as salon stylists, as nursing assistants, or in restaurants. Some were full-time mothers who sold Islamic clothing and goods outside mosques. Most of the nonworking women were looking for jobs but confronting discrimination against women who wore the hijab—a point I return to later in the chapter.

LIVING IN TERROR: THE IMPACT OF 9/11 ON ARAB MUSLIMS IN JERSEY CITY

FBI Investigations

Almost immediately following the attack on the World Trade Center, the FBI and the Department of Justice began an unprecedented investigation targeting Arab men for questioning. Under the rubric of "national security," Attorney General John Ashcroft ordered the FBI to interview five thousand Arab and/or Muslim men between the ages of eighteen and thirty-three for information relating to terrorism. Given the history linking the planning of the 1993 World Trade Center bombing to Sheik Omar Abdel-Rahman, who prayed and spoke at Al Salam Masjid in Journal Square in Jersey City, the FBI focused a good part of its investigation on Jersey City and nearby Paterson and Bayonne. The post-9/11 investigation in Jersey City also heated up after the arrest of two men, Ayub Ali Khan and Mohammed Jaweed Azmath, who lived in an apartment building in the Journal Square area. Khan and Azmath were detained on September 12 while on board an Amtrak train in Texas after their flight from Newark to San Antonio was diverted. At the time of their arrest they were carrying $5,000 in cash, hair dye, and box cutters, which were thought to have been used as weapons by the 9/11 terrorists (Kovaleski and Kunkle 2001).

Though the two were later cleared of any wrongdoing, in the immediate after-math of 9/11 their arrests were enough to justify the subsequent arrests of five of their neighbors as well as raids of dozens of apartments in Jersey City.

As a result of the heightened investigations in Jersey City, local Muslims had to contend with the fear that at any point the FBI or local police would enter their homes, question their families, and seize their belongings. An American Muslim woman who was married to a Palestinian Muslim man and lived in an apartment building rented almost entirely by Arab families told me that the FBI came to her apartment three times, showing her photos of Arab men and asking whether any of them looked familiar. On the first occasion she and her husband examined the photos and answered the questions as best they could, but they were unable to offer any information.

The second time the FBI came back when the woman was alone. This time the officers attempted to measure her allegiance to America, to Islam, and to her Palestinian husband. They asked repeatedly what she thought of the World Trade Center attack, her opinion of Osama bin Laden, what she did on the days prior to and after 9/11, and whether her husband had any ties with Palestinians or "political" Muslims. She answered their questions, trying to reassure them that although she and her husband sympathized with the plight of Palestinians, they despised Osama bin Laden and were "angry as hell" about what the terrorists did. As proof, she pulled out a red, white, and blue "We Will Not Forget" T-shirt and matching button, displaying them proudly. Still, the officers continued to ask questions: "Are you *sure* you have never seen any of these men . . . at any point in time? Are you sure your husband has not seen any of them? Remember what happened on September 11." Recalling how upset she was by this questioning, this woman told me:

> Now, I go on Kennedy Boulevard every day. Do you know how many Arab men I see? You try it. There are thousands in Jersey City! Thousands just on Journal Square alone. How am I supposed to know if I saw any of these men? I don't know them any more than you do. And I'm a *Muslim* woman. I don't make eye contact. I don't even look at men.

As a practicing Muslim, this woman avoided contact with men other than those in her immediate family. In fact, her devotion to Islam was so strong that in her job she specifically requested not to be assigned to work with any men, since it is forbidden for a woman to be alone with a man outside her immediate family. Thus, being alone with the male FBI agents was a violation of her religious beliefs.

When the FBI came back to her house for a third time, once again she was shown a book of photographs but could not provide any information. When she asked why the FBI kept coming to her apartment, the officers said that neighbors had called the FBI and reported that the entire apartment building threw a huge party right after 9/11, in celebration of the tragedy. This woman was stunned and dumbfounded. She had thought her non-Muslim neighbors were friendly. She recalled having long talks with some of the elderly women about the "good old days." True, after 9/11 she did not have much contact with her neighbors, but she attributed this to her own decision to not go out as much. This woman did not want to believe her neighbors would do something malicious; she thought the FBI had fabricated this story. Yet I subsequently confirmed that her neighbors had in fact called the FBI to investigate her apartment, thereby illustrating a clear change in neighborly relations after 9/11.

INS Detentions

In its exploratory report released in March 2002, Amnesty International (2002) estimated that nearly eight hundred of a total of twelve hundred detainees were held in two New Jersey jails located just outside Jersey City: the Hudson County Jail and the Passaic County Jail. In other words, by early 2002 the state of New Jersey had held approximately two-thirds of all persons detained in the United States as a result of 9/11-related investigations.[4]

Although the vast majority of those detained, both in New Jersey and throughout the United States, were arrested because of expired visitor or student visas and accepted the court's offer to be voluntarily deported out of the country, many were not released until months afterward. Tragically, one man even died, allegedly of a heart attack, while in custody at the Hudson County Jail (Morrill 2001). The *Jersey Journal* published a letter from one detainee to the director of the INS; it was hand-lettered in neat capital letters on lined yellow scratch paper:

WE ARE SOME PRISONERS HUDSON COUNTY C-CENTRE IN SEC-TION A3W. WE WERE DETAINED AFTER TUES. SEP. 11–2001, THE F.B.I. TOOK US IN CUSTODY AFTER THEY QUESTING US. THEY TRANSFER US TO I.N.S. SOME OF US ARE HERE FOR 50 DAYS AND MORE EVEN THOUGH SOME OF US DIDN'T EVEN SEE THE JUDGE YET AND THE ONES WHO ALREADY WENT TO THE COURT AND THEY ALREADY GOT THE DECISION LIKE DEPORTA-TION. THEY ARE STILL HERE WAITING FOR MORE THAN A MONTH COULD YOU BE PLEASE KIND ENOUGH TO LET US KNOW WHAT'S GOING ON AND HOW LONG THE I.N.S. INTEND TO HOLD US. AND WHEN WE WILL BE DEPORTED.
THERE ARE TO MANY GUYS WHO ARE ALL HERE AFTER THE SEP. 11 AS YOU KNOW 16. NOV IS THE BEGINNING OF HOLY MONTH (RAMADAN). WE HAVE FAMILIES BACK HOME WE

CAN'T REACH THEM ON PHONE. AND OUR CHILDREN & FAM-
ILY MEMBER'S ARE SUFFERING.

As this letter suggests, the experience of being detained by the INS took an incredible toll not only on those detained but, perhaps more importantly, on entire families.

Muslims in Jersey City after September 11, experiencing the fear and uncertainty of not knowing what might happen next, lived in a state of terror—constantly and quite literally. The husband of one Egyptian woman I interviewed had "disappeared." This woman, who was four months pregnant at the time, did not know whether her husband had fled the state, whether he had been detained by the INS, or whether he was lying on the side of a road somewhere, a victim of a hate crime. As a recent Egyptian immigrant with limited economic capital and American social networks, she was unable to get any information about him from the INS; such information had become a matter of "national security." Understandably, she was worried and upset, she was angry with the INS, and she was distraught because her husband was her only source of income:

> I don't know where is my husband. My husband, he disappeared. I think INS has him. He had the expired visa. I don't care if they're going to send him back, but I don't know *where* he is. They don't let me know. And for this I am scared. For this I don't like America. I am in terror every day. I am in terror.

Although her friends urged her to remain in the United States and get a lawyer, and a number of fellow Muslims offered food and shelter, she was petrified of being thrown in jail herself and having something terrible happen to her child. In the end she traveled back to Egypt, hoping that her husband would somehow find his way back there as well.

Fear of Hate Crimes and Hostility

Arab Muslims also had to contend with the fear of hate crimes and hostility in public space. Hate crimes are always difficult to measure, primarily because the victims are often reluctant to report incidents, the definition of hate crimes is subject to change, and law enforcement agencies are not consistent in keeping track of hate crimes across time and location. Nonetheless, according to the FBI Uniform Crime Reporting Program (FBI 2001), the number of anti-Islamic religious bias incidents grew nationwide from 28 in 2000 to 481 in 2001; this reflects a 1,600 percent increase. Of all the states reporting bias incidents to the FBI, New Jersey was second only to California in the number of reported hate crimes, with 804 (U.S. Department of Justice 2001, 20). Nine of the 804 were in Jersey City. Since the Federal Emergency Management Agency (FEMA) allocated funds to the Jersey City police to monitor mosques and watch out for hate crimes, indeed, the relatively low number of reported offenses in Jersey City suggests that some crimes were successfully deterred. Still, this vigilance did not eliminate hostile acts.

Nearly all of the Muslims I interviewed mentioned feeling hostility from employers, coworkers, store clerks and bank tellers, police officers, neighbors, random passersby, and even former friends. The women talked more openly than the men about experiencing various kinds of hate crimes, especially face-to-face assaults. It is difficult to determine whether women were more likely to be targets of hate crimes than men or were simply more willing to talk about harassment, particularly to a female researcher. One reason women may have been more likely to experience hate crimes than men was that so many Arab men were detained or fled Jersey City after the 9/11 attack that they were not as visible as Arab women in public spaces. Also, perpetrators of hate crimes might have been more afraid of Arab men than Arab women, given widespread notions about Arab male terrorists. Nonetheless, regardless of the reasons for physical violence against Muslim women, the effects were dramatic.

Most of the physical violence I learned about was directed at women wearing the hijab and Islamic dress while shopping around the area of Journal Square. For Muslim women it became a daily struggle to reconcile their desire to maintain religious traditions and their fear of coming to harm. The attacks ranged from children throwing rocks at Muslim women to teenagers throwing beer cans to adult men and women punching Muslim women in the face while attempting to rip off their clothes and tear their veils. Speaking of her sister who was badly beaten in Journal Square, one woman explained:

I know a lot of sisters who got beat up. One sister got beat up very, very bad on Journal Square. They tore her dress, pulled off her hijab. Al Hamd li Allah [praise to Allah], some store owner helped her. . . . I told her you have to report this, but she doesn't want to cause trouble. A lot of people don't want to cause trouble. A lot of people are afraid because they don't have papers.

As this account suggests, Muslims were reluctant to report hate crimes because they were afraid of "causing trouble." This was especially true when they lacked proper immigration documents and had overstayed their visitor's visa. Many of these women were dealing with a complex mix of emotions.

They feared being physically assaulted; they were angry at the perpetrators of such violent crimes; they worried that their undocumented immigration status would be found out, and they felt guilty about not having papers; and they were ashamed if their bodies were uncovered. At the same time they were grateful to Allah, the good people who helped them, and the chance to stay in America.

Compounding Muslim women's trauma and fear of physical assaults in public was their need to come to terms with their own feelings of grief over the attack on the World Trade Center. When I asked an Egyptian Muslim woman who had lived in Jersey City for two years about her experiences after 9/11, she paused for a few seconds to hold back tears. Then, composing herself, she began in a strong but emotional voice:

> It's hard. When you feel it, when you see it. I was cry [sic]. Every week I go to the World Trade Center. I love this place. Love this place. Every week I go Monday or Tuesday because that's my day off. I go to the World Trade Center and I get my fish on Canal Street. I love this place.

When I asked if she had experienced any backlash after 9/11, she continued: "One day I was on the bus, and this lady tried to [take] my cover from my head. She tried to pull off my cover. She told me: 'You people, you killed my daughter,' and something like this. . . . I guess she's sad. I believe that. I believe her. I give her time like that because she's going to do it."

This woman had been wearing a cover for the past twenty years and had never gone out in public without it. As a former elementary school teacher and one of the few Egyptian women who had learned to read Arabic, she took great pride in being able to teach Muslim girls about the importance of covering. Yet when faced with the emotions of a woman who was grieving for her daughter and suffering the symbolic association of Muslims (and Islamic clothing) with the devastation on 9/11, she allowed the woman "time" to yell at her and pull at her cover. Later on she made a difficult decision to take off her cover to avoid future conflicts. She explained:

> I ran home and I told my husband I want to take my cover off because it's so sad when you do this stuff, when you see this stuff. I don't like anybody to bother me on the street, and I don't like to bother anybody. He told me, "Okay, you take your cover off." At least for a little while I'll do this.

When I asked how she felt about taking off her cover, she said: "It's sad. Now my kids ask me: 'Why don't you have your cover? Why do you tell us your cover, that's your religion, it's something you must do? Not like a choice

... you must do!'" This woman's decision to take off her cover not only produced an internal conflict but made it difficult to teach the practice of covering to her children.

Employment Discrimination

After 9/11, many Muslim women had to choose between wearing the hijab and risking discrimination in the workplace. Many of the Muslim women I spoke with who had jobs before 9/11 were not fired for choosing to wear the hijab. However, a number of employers did encourage them to take off their covers to avoid potential conflicts. The women most likely to agree to do this were recent immigrants who reported having amicable relationships with their employers and coworkers before 9/11. These women told me that they saw taking off their covers as a temporary way to maintain job security and as a sign of trust to coworkers and friends who were "good" to them. However, the situation for Muslim women who entered the job market after 9/11 was different. One American Muslim woman told me:

After September 11, things got bad. No one wants to hire me because I wear the hijab. I went to the ninety-nine-cents store. I went all on Journal Square. No one would hire me. They said it's too sensitive right now. Another Muslim woman said I shouldn't wear the hijab until I get a job. Then when I start I could wear it. I said no. I'm not gonna pretend. If they don't like me because of this, too bad. I'm not gonna hide my religion.

This woman made a decision not to hide her religious identity by choosing to continue to wear the hijab even if it meant not being hired. Of course, it is an economic luxury to be able to *choose* to wear the hijab in this situation. Indeed, it was not an accident that the poorest Muslim women, who were overwhelmingly recent immigrants from Egypt, did not make the same choice as this American Muslim woman. Yet, even in her case, she sometimes opted to take off the hijab for fear of discrimination. She explained: "The only time I took off the hijab was when I went to the INS with my husband to apply for the green card. They're very hostile in there."

Fear of Violence Against Children

After 9/11, Muslim families in Jersey City had to take extra care in watching after their children. One reason Muslim children came under intense suspicion by their peers had to do with a widely circulated rumor that a Muslim boy warned his classmates not to come to school on September 11 and laughed about the tragedy after it happened. This rumor was so widespread that the *New York Times* reporter Dexter Filkins (2001) opened his article on national 9/11 myths with reference to it: "Did you hear? Arab schoolchildren in Jersey City told their classmates ahead of time that the World Trade Center would be attacked." The school in question was one where students claimed to have seen Muslim men dancing on rooftops of buildings, celebrating as they watched the towers crumble. In part, because of stories like these, all schools in Jersey City remained closed for two days after September 11.

Nearly every mother I talked with shared a story of a child being beaten up or picked on. Most of these acts went unreported because parents were afraid to "cause trouble." They feared that if they made waves in the school or among neighbors, someone would call the FBI about them, a prospect that was especially worrisome for undocumented immigrants. Even when Muslim families did report acts of violence against their children, they often dropped the charges or asked the judge to be lenient to perpetrators. An Egyptian American Muslim woman told me:

My son, he was beat up on September 26. In school they act like everything is okay. But after school they chase him, they call him a terrorist, they throw rocks at him, and they beat him up. I report this to the police. We caught one boy, and we had the trial. But I told the judge to go easy on him. It's not that I'm afraid, because Islam makes me strong. But I know he's young and it's hard. It's a very difficult time right now, a very difficult time.

As a result of hostile acts like this after 9/11, many Muslim parents made arrangements to leave work early in order to walk their children home from school. They also limited their children's outdoor play activities and encouraged them to befriend other Muslim children to avoid being teased by non-Muslims. In fact, many Muslim children I spoke with told me that they had been "abused" by kids in school every day for being Muslim.

Harassment in the Bank

After 9/11, Muslim women and men had a difficult time making transactions at local banks. In part, harassment of Muslims at local banks stemmed from rumors that terrorists were planning to target banks for anthrax and bomb attacks. At least one local bank was evacuated owing to one of the *seventeen hundred* anthrax scares to which the Jersey City Police Department responded (Lieutenant Michael R. Louf of the Jersey City Police Department, personal communication, August 2002). Harassment at banks also stemmed from the new bank guidelines for monitoring "suspicious" monetary transactions that might be linked to terrorist activity. An Egyptian American businessman who was not a practicing Muslim told me:

> It's very hard to move money around now because you have to show an ID. For me, my business is cars. I buy cars and sell them: that's my business. Now, whenever you buy cars, you have to deal in money orders or certified checks. But if it's anything over $3,000, it has to be a certified check. Now, I don't need to be harassed. So instead of getting a certified check, I get multiple smaller money orders. It's a pain, but there's a lot of flagging that goes on, a lot of profiling. I could get picked up easily. You can be arrested for selling fertilizer—fertilizer!

Compounding the issue of "flagging" was the change in how bank employees treated Arab Muslims. Many Arab Muslims pay for safe-deposit boxes to store money and belongings in banks because Islam prohibits collecting interest in bank accounts. However, to use a safe-deposit box requires face-to-face interaction with bank employees, which became very difficult after 9/11. An Egyptian American woman told me: "The worst is when I go to the bank. They look at me like I am the most dirty, filthy thing they've ever seen in their life. Always I am showered. I am dressed. I am patient. I am polite. But they look at me like I am an evil, evil person."

This woman had been going to this bank at the same time every Tuesday for the past seven years. Before 9/11, she was friendly with the bank teller and looked forward to the weekly visits. After 9/11, the bank tellers looked at her as though she were a loathsome outcast. Still, every Monday night she ironed her clothes with care and prepared her bath so as to minimize any chance of humiliation on Tuesday.

Harassment on the Road

A number of people spoke of being stopped by police on the road and being treated unfairly because they were "Arab from Jersey City." A twenty-eight-year-old Arab American man who had not practiced Islam since the age of eight attributed his experience of racial profiling to his last name and his Jersey City address:

> I was pulled over in Atlantic City with my mother and sister in the car. . . . As soon as she [the policewoman] saw my last name and address, she asked me to get out of the car. Then I was arrested. I wasn't read my

rights. They asked me where I was born and questions like that. Then they threw me in a cell by myself for four hours. I had no phone call or anything. . . . Now, I know the routine. They saw my name and address and ran an FBI background check, 'cause it takes about four hours for that to go through. Then when they found nothing, they let me go with no paperwork or anything. Now, I'm a citizen here, and I'm usually very vocal. But I didn't say anything, because at the time they were detaining people like crazy because they passed that bill in Congress. . . . Now, I don't look Arab and I don't dress Arab. So for me, my problems are when they see my name and address. Those two things right there—especially being from Jersey City—that does it for me. . . . Now it's to the point where I don't even use my Jersey City ID. . . . It's just easier that way.

This man's experiences indicate that even the most Americanized Arab Muslims became targets of racial profiling because of their names and affiliation with Jersey City. In the wake of the Patriot Act and new federal initiatives and directives specifically singling out Arab nationals for scrutiny and legitimizing the racial profiling of Arabs, this man made the same decision that most Arab Muslims have made—not to make complaints or "cause trouble" about harassment or short detentions.

Discrimination by Landlords

Given the hostile climate toward Muslims and the monitoring of local mosques, the home became one of the few places where Muslim men and women could seek refuge. For Muslims in Jersey City, the significance of having a respectable home increased exponentially after 9/11 as public space became a dangerous site in which to foster community ties. However, according to Muslims I interviewed, after 9/11 landlords became more reluctant to do necessary repair work such as fixing leaks, painting, and keeping up with exterminator services. Since many Jersey City Muslims were not homeowners, this imposed a toll on Muslim women, who took great pride in being able to keep their apartments clean. Even more problematic, some landlords raised rents well above the allowable increases. Although a number of Muslim women I spoke with thought about challenging the rent increases, their husbands often insisted on paying the high rents because they did not want to "cause trouble," given their precarious status as Arab Muslim immigrants. This suggests that some landlords took advantage of Muslims' vulnerability as a way to obtain financial gain.

Feeling Cast Out of the Larger Community

After the World Trade Center attack, Arab Muslims in Jersey City were deeply upset by the loss of lives and the destruction of the twin towers. Quite a few wanted to participate in volunteer efforts in downtown Jersey City—that is, until it became clear that they were not welcome by the wider community in these volunteer activities. A young Pakistani Muslim woman explained:

I'll never forget that day as long as I live. I felt so bad for all the people, all the families. All the people looking for their sisters, brothers, fathers, mothers. It was horrible. Then I heard people were volunteering down-town. So I said, I have to do this. I was so determined. I got dressed, went downstairs, and told my father I was going to volunteer. For some reason, I wasn't even thinking about the hijab or being Muslim or any-thing. But when I saw my father's face, I realized what he already knew. He said: "I don't think that's a good idea right now." I felt so hurt. I really, really wanted to go. But I couldn't go. And that really hurt. I'm an American. I was raised in Jersey City. I went to Catholic school. But I couldn't go.

This woman was clearly upset that she was unwelcome in volunteer efforts. In her eyes, before 9/11 her Muslim background would not have prevented her from socializing and volunteering with those in the larger non-Muslim community. In fact, her parents had sent her to Catholic rather than public school because they believed she would receive a better education, learn man-ners and good behavior, avoid bad influences, and mingle with good students from different backgrounds. Thus, for this woman the realization that she, a Jersey City–raised Catholic schoolgirl, would not, as a Muslim, be welcome in local volunteer efforts was particularly hurtful. After 9/11, she said that she no longer knew how to act with her non-Muslim friends and often felt uncomfort-able. As a result, she began to associate more with Muslims and to gain a new sense of herself as a Muslim.

Hostility from Neighbors

One of the most bitter aftereffects of 9/11 that Muslims faced was hostility from their neighbors. To be sure, relationships between Muslims and other groups in Jersey City had been strained since the 1993 World Trade Center attack. But after 9/11, it seemed to become socially and politically acceptable for people to watch and be suspicious of their Muslim neighbors and to openly express and act on hostilities they had been harboring. One might say that 9/11 served to reopen the existing fault lines in Jersey City, making a Muslim background a more important marker of identity and difference.[5]

Just two weeks after the 9/11 attack, a group of white ethnic Catholics passed out flyers for an emergency community meeting to explain "How Ter-rorism *Lives* in Your Own Backyard!" The purpose of this meeting, as its flyer suggests, was to express collective outrage over what it meant to live in a place that the FBI and the media had labeled a "Terror Town." It was an emotional meeting with as much internal bickering as external "othering." Chief on the agenda was an urgent call to defend the neighborhood from terrorism by rooting out sleeper cells, which local media reported could be disguised as Muslim neighbors. With such images available and sanctioned, some residents used them to drum up support for a protest to close down a local mosque. One woman at the meeting said:

> I was here probably with many of you when we were here protesting that mosque being opened, about ten years ago. Maybe it was less than that. And their high priests or whatever were here with us, you might remember that. Now we fought back *then* for it not to be open for just these types of reasons—that Jersey City's being called Terrorist City. Why can't we *now* protest to have it closed down? Can we do that? Because I don't feel safe.

To some extent, the fear over what might be happening at the local mosque was understandable in light of the intense FBI investigations into and media coverage of Jersey City neighborhoods and mosques. During the initial weeks after 9/11, television crews lined up by the dozens to capture glimpses of FBI agents raiding Jersey City apartments, while journalists throughout the country and the world ran lead stories depicting Jersey City as a "Terror Town." In effect, this media campaign strengthened local residents' resolve to take personal responsibility for watching their Muslim neighbors and "doing something" to defend their neighborhoods. As one man warned:

> Here's really what you do, what I think every one of us has to do. We have to watch everything they [Muslims] do. We all have ears, and we're all pretty smart people. Nobody puts nothing over on us. . . . I'm a street guy. I walk these streets. Okay. . . . But when I walk around here . . . they don't like me. . . . They don't like any of us. They don't want to be here. Not all of them. Not everybody's bad. Most people are good. But let me tell you something. We got a problem here. You all know it. What I'm saying to do is WATCH. You see something, call the FBI. Don't call the Jersey City police; it's a waste of time. They got too many other things to do. Call the FBI. And guess what. Maybe they'll get three or four phone calls about the same house. And maybe, just maybe, they'll do something about it. But otherwise, it's up to us.

In some ways the phenomenon of neighbor turning against neighbor in Jersey City is similar to what has been observed in studies of the effects of "ethnic cleansing" in the former Yugoslavia, where the ideological movement to construct ethnic and religious categories as a way of promoting ethnic cleansing and nationalism had a traumatic impact on neighborly relations (Bringa 1995). The socially constructed image of Muslims in Jersey City as terrorists, though clearly working on a much lesser scale, nevertheless hampered trust and amicable relations among neighbors.[6] Indeed, as the Associated Press reported in November 2001, applications for gun permits in Jersey City increased 250 percent after the September 11 attacks, reflecting the heightened fear and panic.[7]

MUSLIM RESPONSES TO LIVING IN TERROR: EMPHASIZING "THE TRUE ISLAM"

Given the extreme hostility that Arab Muslims experienced in Jersey City, it would not have been surprising if they had lashed out against local Americans. It would also not have been surprising if many had tried to blend in or mask their Muslim-ness, especially in public. But these were not the reactions of many of the people I interviewed.[8] They did not, in most cases, press charges against authorities. And while some reacted by staying away from mosques and keeping a low profile, in general the response was to want to make the Muslim community stronger and show America "the true Islam." How each individual responded depended on a variety of factors, including citizenship status, socioeconomic position, ancestry, age, and the nature of his or her transnational and local ties. On the whole, however, there was a significant swing toward traditionalism in the city's Arab Muslim community.

The observation that most Arab Muslims in Jersey City did not attempt to blend in or downplay their Arab or Muslim appearance presents a challenge to the classic model of assimilation, which suggests that immigrants eventually lose their homeland culture and melt into the mainstream (see Gordon 1966). At the same time, this observation supports what sociologists noted many years ago: when an identity—ethnic, religious, or cultural—is used to discriminate against a group, this identity, paradoxically, becomes even more important for the group to defend and emphasize (see Becker 1963; Goffman 1963; Erikson 1966). Arab Muslims in Jersey City believed that it was the responsibility of every Muslim to correct perceived misrepresentations and to follow religious practices that honored their own sense of the true Islam. As an Egyptian American Muslim civic leader put it:

> I know there are some people who get the looks and the stares and the curses and the broken windows . . . and of course there are the people being detained. And this is terrible. But we all know this. Everybody knows this. I like to focus on the positive. It is a terrible situation, but I like to see the shining light. You see, the way I look at it, September

11 shook the Muslim community. It shook us to see who was weak and who was going to survive. And in this way, it made us stronger. . . . Now we have to make the American society see the *true* Muslim community.

The issue of determining what is the true Islam is of course open to interpretation by both leaders and followers. Interpreting the true Islam became a significant source of internal conflict between more progressive civic leaders like the one quoted here and more traditional or even fundamentalist imams in Jersey City. On the basis of my field observations, I would argue that the actual meaning of the true Islam was not as important to Muslims as the process of constructing the true Islam. It was through this construction that the process of learning, creating, and re-creating the true Islam took place.

In line with the comments of the Egyptian Muslim civic leader, many of the Arab Muslims I interviewed spoke of a responsibility to change the way Islam is represented and understood by the media, political leaders, and the larger society. They seemed to propose a collective ethos: if all Muslims would just practice the true Islam, its peace and simplicity would shine through so powerfully that it would not only make the in-group stronger but enable the rest of society to see the true Islam. In this sense, practicing the true Islam, it was believed, would alter the way Americans viewed Islam, garner popular support for opposition to the perceived war on Islam, and even recruit new Muslims in the process.

One way in which Jersey City Muslims attempted to emphasize the true Islam was through renewed and intensified interest in the Qur'an. Many Muslims began reading and discussing the Qur'an more closely. Given that many Arab Muslim immigrants had not learned to read Arabic in their native country, this was a time-consuming undertaking. A number of men began reading the Qur'an with an imam or a sheik, while others initiated small reading groups, which were separate for men and women. The collective nature of reading and discussing the Qur'an served as a community-building activity as well as a means of religious identity construction.

Another way in which Muslims in Jersey City emphasized the true Islam was by means of Islamic dress. Before September 11, a substantial number of Muslim women wore the hijab and dressed in covers with distinct Egyptian or Pakistani styles. For the most part, these styles persisted after the twin towers disaster, even though passages in the Qur'an state that it is acceptable for women to take off their covers (and for men to shave their beards) in hostile times. For many women, maintaining their covers was a way to counter what they saw as a misrepresentation of Muslim women as oppressed, docile victims who are forced to cover. These women emphasized that covering was something they sincerely wanted to do, that it empowered them and made them feel special.

To be sure, some Muslim women did stop wearing the hijab out of fear of losing their jobs, being beaten up, being targeted for questioning, or "causing trouble." This was especially true among some very poor women and recent immigrants who found it necessary to take off their covers to counteract employment discrimination related to their Arab Muslim appearance. Yet such actions did not undermine their commitment to construct identities and practices in line with the true Islam. These women took off their covers to support their families during difficult times, and as noted, the Qur'an states that women may do so if wearing a cover will harm them.

Arab Muslims also sought to honor a sense of the true Islam through traditional Islamic weddings in which men and women remain in separate rooms. Before September 11, weddings had become more Americanized, and couples were renting wedding halls with mixed-gender groups. After 9/11, lavish and mixed-gender weddings came to be considered haram (forbidden), especially in light of the poverty and suffering overseas. In addition, a renewed importance was placed on praying at the mosque beyond Friday prayers. The practice of Muslim men sleeping at the mosque also became more common. This was seen as a way to earn the highest level in Paradise; it also fostered ties among the men who prayed together.

Finally, in trying to practice the true Islam, some Muslims paid closer attention to Islamic rules governing social interactions. The interpretation of Islamic rules did of course vary among imams, leaders, and individual Muslims. Yet, because a significant number of Muslims in Jersey City embraced the more traditional reading of these rules, certain practices—listening to popular music, going to clubs, drinking alcohol, smoking, wearing nail polish, talking with non-Muslims—became problematic. Also, rules on gender interactions, such as avoiding shaking hands or making eye contact with members of the opposite sex, became important social markers for Muslims to identify and classify what they saw as the true Muslim in public places.

In addition, some in the Muslim community began to practice Islam for the first time after 9/11. Oral histories drawn from newly practicing Muslims suggest that this change was related to personal experiences of stigmatization by non-Muslims after 9/11. For those who began to practice after 9/11, the quest to be "the true" became all-consuming, perhaps in part to make up for years of not practicing. One Tunisian man who lost his job right after 9/11 told me:

Before September 11, I didn't know anything about Islam. I was drinking alcohol. I was smoking cigarettes. I was going to the discotheque. I was with too many girls. I was like ignorant, really. But after this happened, people started to call me terrorist, Osama bin Laden. And then these people on the TV are saying this is Islam, that is Islam. And this is *my* religion, *my* culture. And I don't know. So I had to find for myself what is Islam. Now Al Hamd li Allah, I feel so much good, so much peace to know "the true."

Frantz Fanon once described the search for cultural identity in postcolonial societies as "passionate research . . . directed by the secret hope of discovering beyond the misery of today, beyond self-contempt, resignation and abjuration, some very beautiful and splendid era whose existence rehabilitates us both in regard to ourselves and in regard to others" (cited in Hall 1997, 51). Fanon's words speak to the internal struggle for validation and recognition among Jersey City's Arab Muslims, whose cultural essence was challenged after 9/11. Many began searching history to resurrect an essential core of Islam that would "rehabilitate" their image in their own eyes and in the eyes of others. This search for authenticity and recognition seems to resemble the resurgence of ethnic identities in the former Yugoslavia and numerous other post-Communist countries (Anderson 1983).

Yet it is not only through a renewed interest in historic religious practice and prayer that Muslims worked to construct "true" Muslim identities. It is also important to recognize the constantly changing nature of what it means to construct true Muslim identities in the context of the present and the often hostile experiences of everyday life. In his work on identity, Stuart Hall (1997, 52) observes that, "instead of thinking of identity as an already accomplished fact, which the new cultural practices then represent, we should think . . . of identity as a 'production,' which is never complete, always in process, and always constituted within, not outside, representation."

Hall's insight into the interaction between identity and representation helps to illuminate the dynamics of identity construction among Arab Muslims in Jersey City after 9/11. Many resented that non-Muslim and non-Arab political leaders of the United States were describing the meaning of Islam. After 9/11, it became important for Muslims to take ownership of the representation of Islam. In a situation where they could not influence how Islam was portrayed by political leaders and media figures, it became important to control the representation of Islam among themselves.

COMMUNITY COHESION

On one level, the increased importance placed on religious identity and the desire to defend against threats from the FBI and non-Muslim community members led many Muslims to withdraw from the larger society and rely almost exclusively on other Muslims in Jersey City. In turn, this strengthened face-to-face interaction and community ties among them. Reflecting this trend, many Muslim women and men stated that after 9/11 they gained a renewed sense of purpose in their roles as strong sisters and brothers of Islam. As I noted earlier, some began organizing discussion groups to read the Qur'an more closely. Some also began hosting purely social gatherings in their homes or in quiet public sections of the park. In this way 9/11 served to foster stronger in-group cohesion. One woman told me:

> September 11 is terrible, terrible. But at the same time, now the sisters are becoming stronger. We watch out for each other before. But now especially, we get even closer. Like now, we go shopping together, we make parties together, we do everything together. We don't let any sister walk by herself. We take care of each other. This is the way of Islam.

At the same time, several factors threaten the strength and cohesion of Jersey City's Muslim community. One is the out-migration of Arab Muslims, a consequence of the heightened investigations and hostile climate in Jersey City. As one woman told me: "After September 11, a lot of people leave Jersey City because they are afraid for their lives." Or as another woman put it: "This place used to be so nice. We had too many Egyptians here; too many Muslims. Like whole community. Now everybody is leave."

Egyptian Muslims spoke of feeling hurt and snubbed by community members who left them behind. In fact, Egyptian Muslims who had lived in Jersey City for a long time felt as though they had been left behind twice, since a similar exodus is said to have occurred just after the 1993 World Trade Center bombing, when Muslims in Jersey City came under similar suspicions.

The new emphasis on practicing the true Islam exacerbated tensions in the Jersey City Arab Muslim community, since even the slightest deviation from the true Islam became more noticeable and salient among Muslims. Activities that previously had been given little attention, such as wearing nail polish or makeup, saving photographs and children's artwork, or talking across gender or religious group lines, came under close scrutiny as important symbolic markers of who was and who was not practicing the true Islam. As an Egyptian Muslim woman told me:

> Now I don't go to [the mosque] anymore. I pray at home. Because everybody likes to talk. They look at what you're wearing, how you pray, how your kids are acting, what you put in—how you say—collection. Now everybody wants to be "the true." But they don't know what is the true. Because if they know, they're going to know that in Islam what is most forbidden is backbiting. This is very important. So when you fast, you are not only supposed to fast from water and food. This is easy. But the most difficult is to fast from the backbiting.

As this comment suggests, the pressure to be "the true" resulted in a kind of internal "othering" in the form of "backbiting." It could be argued that gossip and backbiting help to maintain moral order, but gossip and the pressure to conform, if they become too intense, can threaten in-group community cohesion (Erikson 1976, 186–246). Indeed, intense pressure to be the most perfect practicing Muslim backfired in a few cases in that people were so put off by backbiting that they avoided the mosque altogether.

CONCLUSION

In the wake of September 11, many Muslims in Jersey City responded to public scrutiny by seeking to defend, preserve, and represent Islam as a peaceful way of life. Far from trying to blend into American life, many Muslims embraced a more traditional adherence to "true" Islamic religious practices and Muslim identities. These practices included covering for Muslim women; studying and closely following the Qur'an; limiting social interactions with non-Muslims; and in the case of local leaders, preaching a responsibility to represent the true Islam. Although some Muslims stopped wearing Islamic dress and going to the mosque, this reflected their precarious position as illegal immigrants rather than a rejection of Islam. In upholding their responsibility to be "the true," most Arab Muslims opted not to "cause trouble"; they often responded to state practices of racial profiling and detention, as well as social harassment and demoralization, not with confrontation but with adherence to practices and beliefs that reflected their sense of the true Islam.

The felt need to protect and defend themselves by being true Muslims led many to rely almost exclusively on each other, thereby strengthening in-group community cohesion. However, the effort to construct true Muslim identities created countervailing, divisive pressures in the form of backbiting and gossip about who was and who was not a good or true Muslim. These pressures in turn exacerbated an existing rift between more traditional and progressive Muslims.

Moreover, the highly publicized FBI investigations linking suspected terrorists to Jersey City had significant effects on intergroup relations. Although some close friendships and working relationships with non-Muslims in Jersey City that were formed before 9/11 remained more or less intact, the constant questions about Osama bin Laden, the Middle East, the FBI investigations, the war, and the "Jersey City connection" made many Muslims feel under the spotlight. This pressure led many to feel uncomfortable with non-Muslim friends. In the wake of FBI reports of "suspicious behavior," casual face-to-face interactions among neighbors often deteriorated into verbal or physical assaults, anthrax scares, or rumors. An even starker consequence was that the possibilities for developing friendships and political alliances with non-Muslims were significantly hampered by the polarized us-versus-them atmosphere as well as by the restrictions on interactions across gender and religious lines dictated by Islamic laws.

How relations between Muslims and non-Muslims will develop in Jersey City in the years to come is an open-ended question. Also in need of analysis in the future is how the experiences of Arab Muslims in Jersey City differed from the experiences of their counterparts in other cities with high concentrations of Arab Muslims, such as Dearborn, Michigan. What is clear from this account is that Arab Muslims in Jersey City have suffered a blow since September 11, and many have turned inward to their own community and their own religion as a response to being targeted and victimized in what have most definitely been hostile times for them.

I would like to thank the Russell Sage Foundation, the Institution for Social and Policy Studies at Yale University, and the Center for Urban Research and Policy at Columbia University for their generous support of this research at various stages. I am especially grateful to Nancy Foner for providing critical feedback on numerous drafts and shedding light on the big-picture findings. Comments by Kai Erikson, Vron Ware, Paul Gilroy, Chris Rhomberg, Josh Gamson, and Nicole Bryan were also instrumental to this research. I thank Jeff Wenger and Natalie Mancuso for producing demographic maps of Jersey City. Of course my greatest debt is to the people of Jersey City, who entrusted me with their deepest and most searing memories, experiences, and dreams. If this work captures one-tenth of their humanity, it is because they have shown me ten times that amount.

NOTES

1. "Terror Town" was the *New York Post* headline on September 23, 2001.
2. For a discussion of the impact of economic restructuring on poor and working-class people in Jersey City, see Michelle Fine and Lois Weis (1998).
3. The top five most densely populated cities are New York, New York; Paterson, New Jersey; San Francisco, California; Jersey City, New Jersey; and Cambridge, Massachusetts (U.S. Department of Commerce 2000b).
4. For a thorough discussion of the issues facing immigrants detained in the United States before and after 9/11, see Michael Welch (2002).
5. I am grateful to Kai Erikson for suggesting, in a personal communication (March 2003), the notion that 9/11 reopened the existing fault lines in Jersey City.

6. The topic of intergroup relations in Jersey City will be the subject of a future paper. For a discussion of neighborly relations between Muslims and Catholics in Bosnia after ethnic cleansing, see Tone Bringa (1995).
7. This percentage reflects a comparison of gun permit applications from September 11, 2000, to November 20, 2000, and from September 11, 2001, to November 20, 2001.
8. Over the course of my research I met a few Muslims whom others referred to as having "lost their way" or as downplaying their Muslim identities after 9/11. For the most part, these were high school and college students who were dressing in American-style clothes and listening to hip-hop music. The topic of young people negotiating Muslim identities will be the subject of a future paper.

REFERENCES

Amnesty International. 2002. "United States of America Amnesty International's Concerns Regarding Post–September 11 Detentions in the USA." AI INDEX: AMR 51/044/2002. *Amnesty International* (March 14).

Anderson, Benedict. 1983. *Imagined Communities: Reflections on the Origin and Spread of Nationalism.* London: Verso.

Becker, Howard Saul. 1963. *Outsiders: Studies in the Sociology of Deviance.* London: Free Press.

Bringa, Tone. 1995. *Being Muslim the Bosnian Way: Identity and Community in a Central Bosnian Village.* Princeton, N.J.: Princeton University Press.

Erikson, Kai. 1966. *Wayward Puritans: A Study in the Sociology of Deviance.* Boston: Allyn & Bacon.

———. 1976. *Everything in Its Path: Destruction of Community in the Buffalo Creek Flood.* New York: Simon & Schuster.

Filkins, Dexter. 2001. "A Nation Challenged: Rumors; As Thick as the Ash, Myths Are Swirling." *New York Times*, September 25, p. B–8.

Fine, Michelle, and Lois Weis. 1998. *The Unknown City: Lives of Poor and Working-Class Young Adults.* Boston: Beacon Press.

Goffman, Erving. 1963. *Stigma.* Englewood Cliffs, N.J.: Prentice-Hall.

Gordon, Milton M. 1964. *Assimilation in American Life: The Role of Race, Religion, and National Origins.* New York: Oxford University Press.

Hall, Stuart. 1997. "Cultural Identity and Diaspora." In *Identity and Difference*, edited by Kathryn Woodward. Thousand Oaks, Calif.: Sage Publications.

Kovaleski, Serge F., and Fredrick Kunkle. 2001. "Focus Continues on Two New Jersey Men; Longtime Friends Facing Charges of Falsifying Passports in Their Native India." *Washington Post*, September 28, n.p.

Morrill, J. 2001. "Autopsy: Heart Disease Toxicology Report Due on Prisoner." *Jersey Journal*, October 25, n.p.

U.S. Department of Commerce. Census Bureau. 2000a. *Census 2000 Redistricting Data (Public Law 94–171) Summary File.* Washington: U.S. Department of Commerce.

———. 2000b. *County and City Data Book.* Washington: U.S. Department of Commerce.

Available online at: www.census.gov/prod/www/ccdb.html (accessed November 16, 2004).

U.S. Department of Justice. Federal Bureau of Investigation. 2001. *Hate Crime Statistics.* Washington: U.S. Department of Justice.

Welch, Michael. 2002. *Detained: Immigration Laws and the Expanding INS Jail Complex.* Philadelphia: Temple University Press.

PART III

The Impact of 9/11 on
Occupational Groups

CHAPTER 6

The Impact of 9/11 on the New York City Airline Industry

William Kornblum and Steven Lang

THE TERRORIST attack on the World Trade Center had a far-reaching impact on New York's standing as a global port and dealt a devastating blow to New York's airline workers, the port's largest population of employees. For passenger and freight transport, contemporary globalization is associated with the replacement of maritime workers, longshoremen, and stevedores in particular by pilots and flight attendants, airplane mechanics, ticket agents and reservation clerks, baggage handlers, security and food service workers, and many other airport-based occupations. But while the government gave significant assistance to the airline corporations in their efforts to recover from the terrorist attack, there were few attempts, outside those of organized labor, to address the displacements suffered by the airlines' workers and their families.

The perceptions and personal accounts in this chapter are based on field research and interviews with displaced airline workers, union representatives, employment counselors, and industry officials over the course of six months beginning in the spring of 2002. Quantitative findings about airline workers' post-9/11 experiences are from a survey of displaced airline workers' post-9/11 experiences in the region that the authors conducted in cooperation with the International Association of Machinists and Aerospace Workers (IAMAW) in June 2002.[1]

The attacks of 9/11 brought on global economic impacts for air travel and all industries related to travel. Airports were immediately closed, flights were grounded, and thousands of workers were laid off. The economic impact on the major carriers was swift and severe. On September 15, Continental announced that it would cut 12,000 jobs. One by one, the other airlines followed suit: United and American, the two largest companies, announced approximately 20,000 layoffs each, Northwest 10,000, and U.S Airways 11,000. Delta forecast the elimination of 13,000 jobs. Less than three months after the attack—at the end of what we now know was merely the first wave of layoffs—approximately 140,000 airline workers had lost their jobs. Even as passengers resumed flying, the economic losses continued to climb, erasing any hopes for a quick recovery. Losses were especially severe for airline workers in the New York metropolitan area.

In the immediate aftermath of the terrorist attack, the airlines laid off 10,000 workers in the New York area. Losses in the air transport, hospitality, and related industries most heavily affected by the terror attack were two to three times as great as in the nation as a whole (Parrott 2002). The city's two airports experienced greater losses in passenger traffic and cargo movements than virtually any other major airport in the nation. A year later the air transportation sector had lost 16.5 percent of its jobs—a decline from 54,700 jobs in August 2001 to 45,700 in August 2002, by far the most of any city industry. The next highest percentage of job losses was the securities industry, with a loss of 9.0 percent (Bowles 2002). A year after the terrorist attack an estimated 54 percent of airline workers in the metropolitan New York area who had been displaced were still unemployed (Kornblum et al. 2002).

On September 21, 2001, President Bush and Congress reached agreement on a $15 billion emergency economic assistance package to stem the massive losses sustained by the nation's airlines. As enacted, the Air Transportation Safety and System Stabilization Act (ATSSA) would provide $10 billion in federal loan guarantees and credits as well as $5 billion in compensation for direct losses incurred, beginning on September 11, 2001, as a result of the terrorist attack and for the resulting losses that would be incurred through the end of the year. To monitor the disbursement and allocation of these funds and to oversee the loan guarantee program, the Air Transportation Stabilization Board (ATSB) was established, comprising the transportation secretary, treasury secretary, Federal Reserve Board chairman, and comptroller general. On November 11, 2001, President Bush signed the Aviation Transportation and Security Act (ATSA), which spawned the Transportation and Security Administration (TSA). With the passage of the act, the security workforce became federalized and was required to undergo training. Although some of the security workers who worked for private firms were able to switch over to the TSA, most lost their jobs.

The airlines received billions of dollars in federal aid, but displaced airline workers did not benefit from this assistance. In the wake of 9/11, Congress passed emergency legislation to extend unemployment benefits from twenty-six weeks to thirty-nine weeks. After that extension, and despite bipartisan support to extend unemployment another thirteen weeks, a measure to extend benefits again failed in Congress. Unemployment benefits for most of the airline workers displaced after 9/11 expired in July 2002. On October 22, 2002, an airline union official told the *New York Times*, "The crisis for New York's airline workers is about to get worse": many of the unemployed were about to lose their medical coverage because they could no longer afford the premiums. This warning was ignored by the Republican leadership. House majority leader Dick Armey said during debates on assistance to displaced airline employees that "the model of thought that says we need to go out and extend unemployment benefits and health insurance benefits and so forth is not, I think, one that is commensurate with the American spirit here" (Alvarez 2001, C6).

This chapter documents the experience of airline workers in the New York metropolitan region who lost their jobs in the aftermath of 9/11. It considers the human experiences behind the summary statistics—particularly those of the city's airport-based airline personnel who struggled to make ends meet and to cope with government indifference. The question of whether it would have violated the "American spirit" to extend assistance to these workers will have to be decided by individual readers, but three particularly revealing aspects of the displaced airline workers' experience after 9/11 have direct bearing on how one answers that question.

First, responses after 9/11 to sudden and catastrophic unemployment among the region's airline workers were complicated by the structural changes that were occurring among major carriers in the airline industry just at the time and shortly after the attacks. Although the 9/11 attack itself looms largest in the minds of displaced airline workers as the cause of their distress, their ability to adjust to sudden unemployment—and especially their ability to find new airline jobs—was made far more difficult than it might have been otherwise by the corporate reorganizations and downsizings in the airline industry before and after the attack.

Second, airline workers' material, social, and psychic losses were compounded by the inadequacies of the social safety net. The majority of airline workers with whom we spoke voiced strong feelings about having been abandoned by their companies and by the agencies of their government.

Third, efforts to assist displaced airline workers—motivated and conducted primarily by the relevant labor organizations—were confounded by limitations on airline workers' eligibility for assistance, their isolation from their former occupational communities after layoffs, and the government's refusal to assist labor unions in securing employment for displaced members after the attacks.

Each of these summary observations is based on firsthand accounts from the airline workers, union officials, and industry experts whom we have interviewed or spent time with in group discussions. These sessions took place in employment counseling and referral centers, union halls, and area airports. The interviews and ethnographic material on which the chapter is based are supplemented with results from a survey of 1,800 area airline workers who were members of different locals of the International Association of Machinists and Aerospace Workers, the largest union representing displaced airline personnel in the region. The IAMAW represents almost all the different occupations—with the exception of pilots and flight engineers—who make up the majority of airline personnel in the metropolitan region.

CATASTROPHIC UNEMPLOYMENT AND ITS IMMEDIATE CONSEQUENCES

Assessment of the impact of the terrorist attack on the World Trade Center on airline workers is complicated by the difficulty of separating structural and catastrophic unemployment effects. Major structural changes in the airline industry were causing a good deal of job insecurity and unemployment before 9/11, as were decreases in air travel due to economic recession. But the World Trade Center attack led to immediate and overwhelming job losses that can only be termed catastrophic unemployment, because airline workers' usual responses to periodic economic downturns in their industry were rendered ineffective.

In April 2001, American Airlines had announced that it would purchase the bankrupt Trans World Airlines and become the world's largest airline. This merger was by far the largest and most controversial structural change occurring in the industry at the time of the attack, but others were also in the works; reductions in the labor force were planned at United, Delta, and many other airlines. The rise of smaller and more cost-competitive air carriers, like Jet Blue and ATA, were expected, however, to offset some of the job losses. American Airlines had also announced its intention to rehire, with no job seniority, almost all of the TWA personnel, especially its highly skilled mechanics. Many TWA workers, however, were to be reassigned to jobs at major American Airlines hub airports in St. Louis or Kansas City.

The case of Mary, a former TWA ticket agent, is representative of airline employees' experience and perceptions of the situation they faced after the merger and the terrorist attack that followed quickly thereafter. A fifty-two-year-old African American woman, she was divorced with three grown children and had worked for the company for over eighteen years. She suffered badly from asthma. Mary took care of her ninety-one-year-old mother, so family obligations made it impossible for her to consider moving to another city.

I loved it at TWA and worked hard. This whole thing has put us in a bad way—I'm at loose ends. . . . They gave me seventy-two hours to make a decision about whether to move to Kansas City or St. Louis. I received a letter after September 11. Because of September 11, they had to change the original plan. I was laid off October 6. American was supposed to take all who were working for TWA. When September 11 happened, it was all down the drain.

Anyone over fifty-five or with sixteen years could take a retirement package. You wouldn't get any money, but you would get medical benefits. It was a one-time decision. I took the early retirement. But it isn't any money since I wasn't working for them. . . . I had to make a choice, and I chose medical because of my asthma. I need medical benefits. I could never do without them. It is very stressful.

Most of my friends at the airlines got laid off. Some went to Kansas City. But their situation was much different than mine. Everybody's situation was different in terms of going to work in another city. But I hear that some of the people who made the move aren't doing so well. I've even heard that their jobs aren't secure.

Versions of Mary's experience were repeated to us over and again. For example, a fifty-five-year-old woman who worked in TWA's purchasing department for twenty-nine years told us: "The merger and September 11 were intertwined. I was supposed to go over to Kennedy Airport because American was supposed to take all of the people who were working for TWA. I was laid off on October 6. They gave me seventy-two hours to make a decision about whether to move to Kansas City or St. Louis or to retire."

The perception that layoffs due to mergers and bankruptcies were "intertwined" with the terrorist attack was almost universal among airline workers in the New York area. The strength of this perception was reinforced in the metropolitan region by statements from political leaders, who claimed, in rousing speeches at Ground Zero, that help would be forthcoming for workers and their families who had suffered sudden unemployment as a result of the attacks.

Vague but encouraging promises of help, the uncertainties of moving to a new city in the hope of landing an airline job, and previous experiences with airline layoffs in which new airport jobs had soon materialized played a significant part in delaying workers' adjustments to the bleak future for airline employment. Recognition of these factors is of critical importance, because the length of unemployment and its consequences for families are directly related to how quickly the unemployed job seeker comes to a new understanding of the realities of the job market.

Unemployment and Adjustment to Changed Conditions

The classic finding in the literature on unemployment dates to the studies of Marie Jahoda, Paul Lazarsfeld, and Hans Zeisel (1921/1971) on the Austrian community of Marienthal, which experienced sudden and massive unemployment in the 1930s. This work was closely followed by the pioneering studies of E. W. Bakke (1934) and Mirra Komarovsky (1940) on unemployed workers and the families of the unemployed in the United States during the Great Depression. These studies all showed that in the face of structural and catastrophic unemployment, the longer workers hold on to the hope that they will find jobs of the same quality and remuneration as those they lost, the longer their spell of unemployment. The sooner they adjust their expectations to the new realities of the changed labor market, the more likely they are to be reemployed, usually with reduced pay and lower occupational prestige. These results have been replicated under many different conditions and apply best to situations of sudden job loss in which structural changes make it unlikely that the majority of displaced workers will find employment in the same industry (Blau 1999).

In recent decades the unemployment literature has more often explored issues of counseling and job training, but even with provisions like unemployment insurance and Social Security retirement benefits, instituted after the Great Depression, the earlier findings are especially relevant to the catastrophic unemployment that occurred among airline workers in the New York metropolitan region after 9/11 (Knapp and Harms 2002). The following observations from a union official who was engaged in counseling displaced ground crews confirm the relevance of the classic unemployment research for the situation faced by the region's airline workers. A year after the attack he told us:

> A lot of people are holding out. They are typical airline workers trying to tough it out. They are in denial. The airlines used to hire in summer and fire in the fall. It was common knowledge. People got furloughed and waited for their recall. But since 9/11, things are different. They might be waiting for a very long time. At least six years if they are lucky. They aren't seeing the big picture. They should get some retraining. A lot of workers think they are coming back, but they are kidding themselves.

A few months later this union official was hearing different stories from the airline workers. "People are getting less choosy as time goes by and their unemployment runs out. I spoke with a guy who turned down a Port Authority job for thirteen dollars an hour last January. He recently changed his mind and decided to take it. He called them up, but it was too late." Another respondent, a laid-off customer service agent to whom we spoke in the summer of 2002, told us that she would "jump at the chance to take a job she turned down in February. What looked like a lousy job back then looks good now. I didn't realize just how bad things were."

Mike, a ramp worker in his early forties with six years at United, was furloughed on October 6, 2001. Though essentially laid off, he was given hiring priority if the airline filled job openings in the future. Lacking seniority, he was one of the first to go when the massive layoffs came. He was not, in his words, "making top dollar for a ramp worker, but was on the way to decent money when the terrorists struck the World Trade towers." Although he was on a list to be called back, he did not hold out much hope. Like many of the displaced airline workers with whom we talked, Mike was keenly aware that decent-paying jobs with good benefits are very hard to come by. As an unskilled worker with only a high school degree, he spoke of having been on "easy street" in the airline industry. "In today's job market I'd be lucky to get eight or nine dollars an hour." He also mentioned that many other companies do not like furloughed airline workers because they are always waiting to get called back to the airline and therefore "lack commitment" to any other job.

Displacement and the Occupational
Ethos of the Mechanics

The greater the skills and seniority of displaced airline workers, the more likely they were to rely on unemployment benefits and seek interim work in the hope of an eventual callback at a wage and seniority level similar to what they had lost. The laid-off airplane mechanics with whom we spoke illustrate this point. For displaced mechanics, whose skills had always been in high demand after previous mergers, bankruptcies, and seasonal layoffs, the potential loss of seniority was an important determinant of income and job-search strategies. Moreover, because they are so highly skilled, many mechanics felt they were especially poorly treated by the airlines. One laid-off mechanic with twenty years at TWA recounted his "terrible experience" at a job fair in Manhattan's Madison Square Garden after 9/11. "I almost threw up. There were lines around the block. There must have been twenty thousand people there."

The mechanics seemed to have the hardest time adjusting to the grim reality of jobs at lower wages. Highly skilled and licensed workers, with extensive training backgrounds, mechanics often mentioned that their skills are not easily transferable outside the airline industry. According to a fifty-three-year-old mechanic who spent twenty-seven years at TWA and who, at the time of the interview, was going to school for medical billing, "My skills aren't that transferable because everybody is so specialized these days. My age makes it especially difficult."

The displaced mechanics were bitter and angry that industrywide downsizing had made many of them redundant. Mechanics who were still employed at the time of our interviews were worried about layoffs, concessions, and the outsourcing of their skilled jobs to companies with lower pay scales. Some were also extremely angry that, because of the way the airline industry unions are structured, mechanics are lumped together with and treated the same as the unskilled workers who make up the vast majority of airline employees. Mechanics often blamed these less-skilled workers for driving up the cost of labor. A former TWA mechanic told us that he "wasn't getting a square deal while the ramp rats were making out like bandits."

> What skills do they have? Anybody can stack bags. Why should a baggage handler get paid so much? Why should they be making twenty-three dollars an hour and get the same pay percentage increases as us? I try not to regret anyone getting paid more, but we are getting paid a pittance. For instance, auto mechanics make fifty dollars an hour. It is like comparing a sanitation worker with a fireman.

Another mechanic told us that although he thought Carl Ichan, a financier and the former owner of TWA, "was a butcher who destroyed TWA," he strongly agreed with him on one key issue. "It's like Ichan the Terrible used to say: 'I don't mind paying a mechanic whatever the going rate is, but why should I pay a janitor eighteen dollars an hour when the going rate is eight dollars outside the industry?' I don't think anybody can argue with that. A lot of the ramp rats are going back at twenty-three dollars and change. No wonder we're all going down."

The difficulties that mechanics were experiencing on the job market made some resentful and jealous of others, but even more worrisome for all the displaced airline workers was the realization that terrorism had changed their industry in ways that made them doubt their future in it. And for those still employed, who often brought back tales of what it was like to work for the airlines in the post-9/11 period, the catastrophe and its consequences sometimes made their job insecurity unbearable.

A Catastrophe That Would Not Go Away

On the job and off, the terrorist bombings had direct and persistent impacts on an industry that prior to the event had been symbolic of all the most dynamic aspects of globalization. For weeks and months after 9/11, fear of new attacks, rumors of security plans that would reduce union jobs, and grief over lost friends all added immensely to workers' perceptions that their troubles related directly to the terrorist attack. Their feeling that they were continuing to live through the consequences of the bombings contributed to their hopes for interventions that would ease their plight. Clinging to this essentially futile hope, flight crew personnel coped with the trauma of having had coworkers killed in the attacks and knowing that their occupational world was forever changed after 9/11.

The flight attendants whom we interviewed often spoke of extremely high levels of stress and anxiety after the attack. Many knew one or more of the flight attendants who died in the attack. Several expressed anxious thoughts about working on a flight crew again if they ever did get called back. One flight attendant who was still working told us that this is "a brave new world since 9/11, and we are on the front lines in the war on terror along with pilots and other cabin crew." Another abruptly unemployed flight attendant said:

This layoff has affected me as deeply as when my husband passed away ten years ago. I keep hoping to get the job back, but I must realize, as I did after my husband's passing, that it is never going to be the same again. The feelings are so similar it's eerie. A sense of dread, depression, worry, anxiety, etc. . . . I pray every night for strength and answers as to why this happened.

The vast majority of displaced airline workers reported that their family and marital lives had suffered since the layoffs. Sixty-eight percent of survey respondents said their family lives were worse since September 2001, and 51 percent said their marital or other significant relationships were weaker. Not surprisingly, large proportions of the displaced workers also reported experiencing a variety of physical and emotional conditions usually associated with increased stress and financial insecurity. Many complained of headaches, stress, sleeping problems, depression, fatigue, or stomach problems. Since being laid off, displaced airline workers in the survey said they experienced the following changes in their health status: high blood pressure (27 percent); chest or heart problems (17 percent); stomach or digestive problems (47 percent); sleep problems and insomnia (68 percent); other medical problems (30 percent) (Kornblum et al. 2002). A sixty-three-year-old Hispanic ramp worker who had spent most of his adult life working at TWA told us: "I have been sick. I don't know why—maybe it is because of losing my job. I don't know. Maybe it is going to my head. I would like to go back to work. I have diabetes, high blood pressure, since the layoff. It is the stress about paying bills. . . . I don't to want to live like this. I can't stand it."

Among the "other" medical problems reported, the most common was severe depression. Scores of written comments on the survey form attest to this finding. A former baggage handler wrote:

My wife and I don't even talk to one another sweet, gentle, or with kindness anymore. She calls me names (Loser!), and I am depressed and pretty much discouraged with myself. . . . When I'm alone in the house or in the car, I go into tears thinking how my life just went into shambles. My manhood, my fatherhood, my dignity was taken away from me all because of many reasons, like the 9/11 incident. . . . TWA couldn't keep up with competition and poor management for the last twenty years.

A flight attendant spoke about having similar symptoms:

My calm, ease, or sense of well-being is gone. . . . Since September 11, I've sought counseling. I've been diagnosed with post-traumatic stress, depression, panic disorder, and anxiety attacks. I've been prescribed anti-depressants, tranquilizers, sleeping pills, muscle relaxers, etc. On the drugs or off the drugs, I still don't sleep normally and continue to have panic attacks.

Flight attendants continually spoke of difficulties dealing with passengers due to increased levels of anxiety. Customer service workers, still on the job but fearing layoffs, described intensified human relations problems, stemming especially from the new stresses of dealing with anxious passengers and heightened security. For those still at work when we spoke to them, job security remained a foremost concern. All around them they saw friends and co-workers worrying about the imminent loss of medical benefits and even about the possible loss of their homes.

Loss of Medical Benefits

After loss of income, the most severe and immediate consequences of the sudden layoffs were workers' loss of medical benefits and health insurance and the threat of losing their homes. Forty-seven percent of the airline workers in the survey who lost their jobs after 9/11 kept their health insurance, largely because they paid into relatively expensive COBRA plans until they found other employment. But 27 percent had no health insurance for some months, and 26 percent remained without any health insurance for at least sixteen months after 9/11, when they responded to our survey. Workers of minority status were more likely than nonminority workers to be without health insurance. Twenty-one percent of white workers said they were still without health insurance a year after the tragedy, while 39 percent of African Americans and 37 percent of Latinos said they still did not have health coverage. Differences between men and women were negligible.

Self-reported stress levels among our respondents were extremely high, especially among older workers and family members, who talked of being overwhelmed and angry at being forced to worry about basic health care costs at a period in their life when medical concerns can loom large. A fifty-seven-year-old customer service agent, for example, spoke of how the shock of losing her health coverage made her extremely anxious and fearful about getting sick. "I'm terrified of getting sick or hurting myself. I can't really afford to pay for a simple visit to the doctor and prescription drugs. It is crazy—just thinking about it almost makes me sick and depressed. My whole attitude is down, and it makes it even harder to think about work and the future."

Several people, especially those over fifty, said they had been forced to take an early retirement package in order to hold on to necessary medical benefits. This is what happened to a fifty-two-year-old woman who had worked in shipping and receiving at TWA:

I had great benefits and a great health plan—full medical and dental. When American came in, I was forced to retire to hold on to my medical benefits. I was told I could relocate to Kansas City or stay here and take a chance. I couldn't move. I had family ties. A home. I couldn't do it. . . . I was told to buy COBRA or take the early retirement. . . . I have to pay for dental. I used to have it. It is unbelievable that dental isn't considered a medical necessity.

Shelter Insecurity

Severe disruption of family home lives was also a consequence of the terrorist attack and subsequent layoffs. Some unemployed airline workers had to move to less expensive apartments, and others, unable to keep up with mortgage payments, subsequently lost their homes. Respondents in the survey were asked: "Since the layoffs, have you had to move your home because of financial reasons?" Thirteen percent said they had been forced to give up their home, and 31 percent said they had not yet had to do so but feared they would soon be unable to meet mortgage payments or rent and be forced to move.

A jobless aviation crew chief who worked at TWA for twenty-seven years had to sell his house in Queens because he could no longer afford the monthly mortgage payment of $885. "It feels strange having to sell our house after living there for twenty-seven years." A former American Airlines employee wrote: "I had to move to a smaller and less expensive house. . . . With two kids in college, it has been a challenge. . . . I had to change my lifestyle drastically. Unemployment insurance helps, but it is not enough. All in all, I am anxiously awaiting my recall."

Employees who had been in less secure, less well paid airline occupations were most likely to have been forced to move after the layoffs. Twenty-one percent of reservations clerks and 21 percent of baggage handlers and workers in related occupations had to move, as opposed to 7 percent of airline mechanics. But mechanics, the most skilled among the union members in the sample, were more likely than the less skilled to fear losing their home in the near future.

As weeks and months passed after the attacks and extended unemployment benefits began reaching their end, workers and their families listened with increasing bitterness to debates in Congress, where pleas for assistance for workers were repeatedly rebuffed, while federal assistance to the companies they once worked for and served loyally appeared to be generous. Faced with the loss of medical insurance and their homes, and with their prospects for the future clouded by continuing structural unemployment in the airlines, displaced airline workers often turned to the only available means of assistance— union-sponsored job referral and counseling services.

OUTREACH AND ASSISTANCE TO DISPLACED AIRLINE WORKERS

Despite government promises of aid to those injured in the attacks, it soon became apparent that anyone who was not injured in the attack itself and any displaced workers who had worked outside what was considered the high-impact zone around Ground Zero would have a difficult time establishing a claim. Since the majority of airline workers resided in Queens, Brooklyn, and Long Island, they were not eligible for the emergency relief money that was restricted to lower Manhattan residents. A disaster relief coordinator whom we interviewed described a coordinated policy of "geographic exclusion" that especially hurt airline workers. "There is a straight-line connection to September 11, but many of the airline workers in New York City were categorically excluded because of artificial geographic boundaries that placed restrictions on who gets aid."

A coordinator from the Catholic Charities organization in Rockville Center, Long Island, told of helping displaced airline workers who were ineligible for economic assistance because of their place of residence.

Airline workers were out of the loop, like other residents of Long Island who didn't work in the towers or live near them. After the massive layoffs of October 6 and 7 of last year, we started seeing a lot of people who were in desperate need of financial assistance but weren't eligible because of the narrow geographic restrictions. So far we have seen approximately 1,300 people or 400 families. Over a third of them were airline workers.... It is about the same in Brooklyn and Queens.

An exception to the narrow geographic qualifications came with changes at the Federal Emergency Management Agency (FEMA) and its Mortgage and Rental Assistance (MRA) program in October 2002. Thanks largely to efforts spearheaded by the New York Labor Coalition, people who did not live in Manhattan but worked for a company that was economically injured by the World Trade Center attack became eligible for mortgage and rental assistance. (Unlike FEMA, the other major disaster relief agencies did not change their geographic requirement, thereby continuing to exclude the majority of airline workers.) To qualify they had to show proof of a 75 percent loss of household income since 9/11 or a late notice or eviction notice received from their landlord or mortgage company. Many displaced airline workers would have qualified for this assistance, but many did not know about it. A relief coordinator we spoke with in early November 2002 spoke of efforts to organize a press conference at JFK International Airport that would publicize the new rules and make people aware of the severity of the economic fallout for airline workers a year after the attacks.

The most active and well-organized efforts to address their needs were sponsored by the International Association of Machinists and Aerospace Workers and its partners in the metropolitan region through the Center for Administering Rehabilitation and Employment Services (IAM CARES). Its partners included other agencies in the private and public sectors, particularly the Consortium for Worker Education (CWE), the AFL-CIO labor councils, and various One-Stop Centers that were established throughout the country. After 9/11, the IAM set up an IAM CARES office in Manhattan and hired two recently displaced TWA workers to run its outreach program. They spent their days trying to make contact with displaced airline workers to see how they were holding up and to help them with retraining opportunities.

The IAM CARES program began sending displaced workers to the One-Stop Centers located throughout the metropolitan area for counseling and job referrals or retraining courses. The program worked especially closely with the One-Stop Center in Jamaica, Queens. Given its location near both JFK and LaGuardia Airports, that One-Stop Center saw the largest number of displaced airline workers. In the year following 9/11, two hundred people came through its doors seeking advice and help with retraining and job placement. One counselor at the One-Stop Center told us, "They [the airline workers] are good people, but it is very tough going for them. I really feel for them." She observed that "most of them, with the exception of the mechanics, lack skills and education, but they're used to great salaries. Even with training, they would be lucky to make the same money they made in the airlines. We are trying to help, but it is very hard."

Mary, the displaced ticket agent quoted earlier in the chapter, was typical of the displaced IAM workers who came to the One-Stop Center in Jamaica, Queens, for job counseling and employment advice. She had high hopes of finding some type of steady, "decent" work outside of the airline industry. Like many other displaced airline workers, she was forced to confront a harsh reality and make a very painful decision in the immediate aftermath of September 11. After concluding that the economic disaster unleashed by the terrorist attack was going to have a lasting impact on the airlines, she decided to jump ship and start over. She was planning to enroll in an intensive training program in medical billing that involved learning computer skills.

Mike, the ramp worker in his early forties with many years of productive work ahead of him, began training for the computer field. He had friends who were programmers and thought job opportunities were available. With only a GED and a semester at a CUNY community college, he had a long way to go in retraining but was fortunate because his wife's work as a nurse's assistant brought in medical benefits for the family. He was often discouraged, however, and wondered in his down moments whether retraining would do any good. He spoke of the uphill struggle to go to school and learn new skills, and he knew that he might not make as much as he did in his unskilled jobs at the airlines. Although such thoughts caused him constant stress and anxiety, it was "better than holding out for a nonexistent job at the airlines. Those days are over."

In the two years following the attack it was increasingly clear that Mike's perception was essential to his readjustment. Mike had once worked for United Airlines, but that company faced bankruptcy within a year after the attack. In a desperate attempt to remain solvent, it began to reduce its post-9/11 workforce of 83,000 (already pared down from 101,000 just prior to the September 11 attacks) to 74,000. And most analysts believed that even more jobs would have to be eliminated if the carrier was to meet the prerequisites for assistance from federal and private sources. A customer service agent who worked for thirty-five years at United spoke of "the years and years of struggles, givebacks, and the final gut-wrenching days before the final collapse."

> I'm definitely thinking of changing careers. I'm looking into being a nurse's assistant or a nursing technician. I've been looking into going to school at Queensborough Community College. I've had it with the airline industry. I'm finished. I'm very bitter and think we're getting a bad deal. I try to keep a positive outlook, but I'm bitter and disgusted. The fact that all these things happened right around 9/11 has made it worse for me.

Many worried that even after retraining they would have trouble getting jobs. An ex–customer service agent taking computer courses at Queens College spoke about her ambivalence about going back to school after working at the airlines for twenty-nine years. "Sometimes I wonder if retraining is the way to go. There is no sense in painting a rosy picture if there are no jobs out there." She also expressed a great deal of anxiety and fear about the "age thing."

I'm trying to be proactive about changing my life by going to school, but my big fear is my age. I think age really counts. That's what worries me about retraining and preparing for a whole new type of work. Are people going to look at your age? Someone told me that as soon as you get gray hair, then it is time to get out. But where am I supposed to go?

Another fifty-three-year-old woman expressed similar doubts:

If we keep talking, I'm going to get so angry. I wish I had more positive things to say to you, but I don't feel that way. I feel we were cheated, and it is so much worse for me at my age. It is hard for me to think about going to school at my age. I'm not sure it would do any good. People are being taken advantage of.

An ex–customer service worker summed up what many older displaced workers felt about their employment prospects: "Being fifty-eight years old does not help one to be a sellable commodity."

ISOLATION FROM OCCUPATIONAL COMMUNITIES AND THE ROLE OF UNIONS

Adding to their burdens, sudden displacement brought former airline workers a new sense of isolation. Most of the unemployed airline workers we interviewed spoke of feeling isolated and cut off from their friends at work. Some stayed connected with other airline workers by phone or e-mail, but social contacts with former coworkers diminished markedly when they were no longer seeing each other on the job.

Earlier in the twentieth century port workers lived in well-established neighborhoods near the docks and warehouse areas of the city. These neighborhoods were a vital part of the human ecology of the maritime port. Hoboken, Jersey City, and Perth Amboy on the New Jersey shore, Red Hook and Sunset Park in Brooklyn, Chelsea and Hell's Kitchen on the Manhattan side of the Hudson, and the dockside neighborhoods of Staten Island—these and many others were cohesive dockside communities with histories extending back into the nineteenth century. Families of workers who plied the maritime trades on the docks, barges, and tugs and in the warehouses were often part of extensive social networks that had their origins in these neighborhoods. Even if younger workers and their families were more dispersed throughout the city and suburbia, the old neighborhoods remained at the heart of their occupational and social networks. During hard times the local churches, political clubs, union halls, and taverns became centers for mutual support (Bell 1960/1988; DiFazio 1985).

In the modern global port, dominated by the technologies of jet transport, the workplaces are necessarily on the city's edges, connected to each other and to the major subregions of the metropolis by an ever-expanding system of expressways and interstate highways. Because airline workers tend to live within convenient commuting distance to the airports, some residential concentrations of airline personnel have formed in the city's outer boroughs and in suburban communities along the commuting routes. But these communities are far more heterogeneous than the old dockside neighborhoods, and the likelihood that one's neighbors are part of the airline world is quite small. When airline workers were displaced in large numbers and cut off from the occupational communities they had formed over years of work in the airports, they found little understanding or support for their plight in their residential communities. Their isolation made communicating with them about assistance difficult and increased their sense of anomie and distress. Many turned to their unions for support, but labor organizations were also fighting for their survival in an industry that was using every means possible to reduce the density of union representation among its employees.

Airline Unions Under Attack

Less than 15 percent of the American workforce is unionized, but 85 percent of workers in the airline industry are (or were until recently), making it one of the most highly unionized sectors of the American workforce (Cappelli 1995, 1). It is not difficult to explain why blue-collar and lower-skilled service workers in the industry seek the representation of unions and the benefits of collective bargaining. But why have unionization rates been extremely high among pilots, air traffic controllers, and other engineering-related professions? Indeed, unionization among high-level airline employees has set precedents for union representation in all other airline occupations (Jacobs 1962; Shostak and Skocik 1986). As in the case of the railroads, which created earlier precedents for transport worker unionization, scheduling issues and seniority were issues that provided a major impetus for unionization. No matter what their skill level, workers who are obliged to travel far from home in the service of trans-port companies are entirely at the mercy of management unless they are backed by strong unions. Like train crews before them, cockpit crews, before unionization, could be on a bad weather layover in a distant or foreign city only to be told by management that they were on personal time until they began their return trip. Although politically moderate or even conservative, airline pilots and flight engineers saw that only through collective agreements could they gain an effective voice in the complex scheduling issues that played so great a role in their working lives. As they formed strong labor associations, so in turn did flight attendants, whose history is an important example of women's labor militancy. In consequence, air transport was one of the few U.S. industries in which unionization increased in the 1980s. Today the majority of airline workers are affiliated with one of these national or international unions: the Airline Pilots Association (ALPA), the Association of Flight Attendants (AFA), the International Association of Machinists and Aerospace Workers (IAMAW), and the Transport Workers Union (TWU).

The airline industry has been a political bellwether for the state of the labor movement as a whole since President Ronald Reagan fired striking air traffic controllers in 1981 (Shostak and Skocik 1986; Nordlund 1998). But the airline unions are extremely balkanized (Ward 2002). For example, four smaller unions compete with the Association of Flight Attendants, and there is also considerable union rivalry and raiding in other occupations. The various unions and the occupational groups they represent do not always cooperate, and often they simply look out for their own interests. Differences in income distribu-tion, gender, and work status keep workers apart and prevent them from over-coming their conflicting interests (Sleigh 1995, 221).

Airline workers identify strongly with the carriers they work for and rarely view themselves as members of an industrywide workforce with common bonds across carriers. Several commentators have pointed out that this identi-fication with the airline has made it difficult to organize workers on an indus-trywide basis. After a merger or takeover, internal struggles within occupa-tional groups stem from the continued identification of employees with their previous airlines (Pollack 1995; Sleigh 1995; Walsh 2001).

In the present environment of neo-laissez-faire policies and government hostility to organized labor, airline unions are vulnerable to persistent carrier demands for concessions. Once one carrier wins concessions from its workers, other carriers demand similar treatment. The end result is leapfrogging up in prosperous times and leapfrogging down in bad times (Pollack 1995). Workers are also threatened by new business strategies, such as the formation of hold-ing companies, mergers, and the creation of non-union "alter ego" carriers (Walsh 2001, 5). The rise of new low-cost companies, which have no unions and no seniority policies, has led to major disparities among the airlines and intensified the downward spiral of givebacks and the relentless "race to the bottom."

Although they were responsive to the needs of unemployed members, the unions were limited in their ability to serve as communal centers and thus address problems of isolation. Some union locals provided places where the unemployed could congregate and sponsored get-togethers and job fairs, but they were also embroiled in the difficulties of adequately representing the needs of members who were still at work. At Delta, United, Air West, Continental, and American Airlines, to name only the most important companies, there were continual demands from management after September 2001 for employment cuts as the negative effects of the bombings on tourist air travel continued and were compounded by severe cuts in corporate travel budgets. Bush administration efforts to pass homeland security measures in Congress also figured prominently in the creation of an anti-union ethos in the airline industry. The legislation was stalled for weeks after 9/11 while the administration fought organized labor's attempts to ensure that newly federalized airport security workers would have the right to join unions. In consequence, the continuing search for jobs by displaced workers took place against a background of what they could not help but perceive as a widespread attack on their unions as well as on their occupational security.

Most displaced airline employees believed that the lower-cost, more flexible companies made profits by hiring low-wage, non-union labor (Doganis 2001). Displaced workers who used services at the Jamaica One-Stop Center, for example, reported that Jet Blue, one of the most highly publicized newcomers, was receptive to the idea of hiring experienced airline workers. According to an ex–TWA flight attendant who found part-time work for American: "They don't want older, experienced, seasoned people who have a lot of experience with union politics and issues. They want younger, inexperienced people who they can mold. Seasoned airline workers won't take nonsense from management."

A customer service agent expressed similar thoughts about her job potential at the smaller companies: "We know the game, and that makes us suspect. We are older, disgruntled employees. That is why they don't want us. We have been through the war." And according to a job counselor at the Jamaica One-Stop Center: "A lot of the people who come here from the airline industry aren't Jet Blue material. They want a non-union, lower-paid workforce who have that younger, groomed look." In a similar vein, a director of an aviation institute who is involved in creating a training program for the TSA security jobs mentioned that it was hard to place experienced airline workers in jobs at the smaller companies. "Many of these displaced workers with experience and union backgrounds are tainted."

CONCLUSION: DISPLACED WORKERS IN
THE CORPORATE WELFARE STATE

Tainted, isolated, shunted aside, superannuated, not eligible for emergency relief, not considered worthy of special consideration—these were the typical experiences and feelings of airline workers in the New York metropolitan region during the long months of their struggle to cope with the effects of 9/11 on their family lives, on their industry, and on their occupations. Compare this bitter experience with the accolades showered during the same weeks and months on firefighters, police officers, emergency workers, and demolition crews at Ground Zero and one gains an added understanding of the desolation and bitterness that can be heard in so many of the comments of displaced airline workers. They knew they were not heroes, but they were also unprepared for the level of neglect and hostility they would face from the nation's corporate and political leadership.

One can argue with some justification that the workers who speak on these pages were not victims of the terrorist attack alone, but of the broader problem of an economic recession, compounded by mergers and other structural changes in the airline industry. This was essentially the argument used by those Republican congressional leaders and members of the Bush administration who refused to seek anything beyond token measures—a paltry extension of unemployment benefits—for thousands of displaced airline workers after 9/11. But the same congressional leaders and members of the Bush administration then turned around and used the terrorist attack of 9/11 as the primary justification for a massive and highly public bailout of the airline corporations. They assured the displaced workers that the best way to get them back to work was by providing welfare for their companies.

The unemployed workers, who were losing their incomes, their medical benefits, and whatever security they had managed to gain over the years, experienced a far different reality. As they perceived it, the events of 9/11 had everything to do with their predicament. In past recessions and downturns in their industry, there had been a reasonable prospect of rehiring, and in the meantime there was temporary work and assistance from their government and their unions. A different reality prevailed in the crisis they experienced after 9/11, however, and it would take added months to adjust to it. Their industry was being financially supported by the government, but the only new hiring would be at new airline corporations with a far more laissez-faire approach to success in the global competition in jet transport. These companies wanted to avoid paying the sort of wages and benefits that the displaced workers had gained in their collective bargaining efforts over many decades. And as we have seen, many of the experienced airline workers seeking jobs after 9/11 believed they were discriminated against for their age, their former experience, and their union background. As the region's airlines have continued to face severe financial difficulties in the period since 9/11, the worst fears of displaced airline workers have been realized. As more airlines faced bankruptcy and continued to cut their job rolls, it remained extremely difficult for former mechanics, ticket agents, and other unemployed ground crew members to find airline employment. At this writing, those who were displaced and not rehired continue to seek retraining for new careers, and in this effort still there has not been much help extended to them beyond what their own unions have been able to develop.

NOTES

1. The survey was designed and administered by Dr. Steven Sleigh of the International Association of Machinists and Aerospace Workers and analyzed by William Kornblum. Survey forms were sent in June 2002 to the entire population of employees of United and TWA/American in the New York metropolitan region who lost their jobs after 9/11. The survey form was completed and returned by 609 displaced airline workers, resulting in a 34 percent sample of the approximately 1,800 IAMAW members who were known to have lost their jobs or were unable to be reassigned to new jobs as a consequence of the terrorist attack on New York City. At the end of the survey respondents were invited to write additional comments about how their lives had changed since 9/11, and over half the sample wrote such comments. Although not technically a random sample, the demographics of those who returned the survey forms correspond extremely well to the overall demographics of the universe sampled.

   The chapter also draws on longer, in-depth interviews conducted by Steven Lang from April through October 2002. Lang interviewed forty-five displaced airline workers at union meetings and at the Jamaica One-Stop Center. Respondents were asked about current employment status and the economic and psychosocial consequences of the layoffs and questioned about what, if any, assistance they had received since the layoffs. He also conducted interviews with union officials and job counselors and attended numerous meetings of displaced workers and their union representatives. All names of respondents have been changed to protect their privacy.

REFERENCES

Alvarez, Lizette. 2001. "A Nation Challenged: The Benefits; House Republican Leaders Balk at Help for Laid-off Workers." *New York Times*, September 26, p. C6.

Bakke, E. Wight. 1934. *The Unemployed Man: A Social Study*. New York: E. P. Dutton.

Bell, Daniel. 1960/1988. *The End of Ideology: On the Exhaustion of Political Ideas in the Fifties*. Cambridge, Mass.: Harvard University Press.

Blau, Joel. 1999. *Illusions of Prosperity: America's Working Families in an Age of Insecurity*. New York: Oxford University Press.

Bowles, Jonathan. 2002. "Bumpy Skies." New York: Center for an Urban Future.

Cappelli, Peter. 1995. *Airline Labor Relations in the Global Era*. Ithaca, N.Y.: Cornell University Press.

DiFazio, William. 1985. *Longshoremen: Community and Resistance on the Brooklyn Waterfront*. South Hadley, Mass.: Bergin & Garvey.

Doganis, Rigas. 2001. *The Airline Business in the Twenty-first Century*. London: Routledge.

Jacobs, Paul. 1962. "Dead Horse and the Featherbird." Report. Santa Barbara, Calif.: Center for the Study of Democratic Institutions.

Jahoda, Marie, Paul F. Lazarsfeld, and Hans Zeisel. 1921/1971. *Marienthal: The Sociography of an Unemployed Community*. Chicago: Aldine, Atherton.

Knapp, Tim, and John Harms. 2002. "When the Screen Goes Blank: A Television Plant Closing and Its Impacts on Workers." *Sociological Quarterly* 43(4): 607–26.

Komarovsky, Mirra. 1940. *The Unemployed Man and His Family: The Effect of Unemployment upon the Status of the Man in Fifty-nine Families*. New York: Dryden Press for the Institute of Social Research.

Kornblum, William, Rolf Meyerson, Steven Lang, and Steven Sleigh. 2002. "New York Airline Workers in the Aftermath of 9/11/01." New York: New York Fiscal Policy Institute.

Nordlund, Willis J. 1998. *Silent Skies: The Air Traffic Controllers' Strike*. Westport, Conn.: Praeger.

Parrott, James. 2002. "Update on New York City's Employment Situation: Monitoring the Recession and the Economic Aftermath of the World Trade Center Attack." New York: Fiscal Policy Institute.

Pollack, Andy. 1995. "The Airline Industry and Airline Unionism in the 1970s and 1980s." In *Trade Union Politics: American Unions and Economic Change, 1960s–1990s*, edited by Glenn Perusek and Kent Worcester. Atlantic Highlands, N.J.: Humanities Press.

Shostak, Arthur B., and David Skocik. 1986. *The Air Controllers' Controversy: Lessons from the PATCO Strike*. New York: Human Sciences Press.

Sleigh, Steven. 1995. "The Difficulty of Sticking Together in Tough Times." In *Airline Labor Relations in the Global Era*, edited by Peter Cappelli. Ithaca, N.Y.: Cornell University Press.

Walsh, David J. 2001. "Continuity and Change in the Structure of Union Representation in the U.S. Airline Industry, 1969–1999." *Industrial and Labor Relations Review* 56(October): 337–60.

Ward, Rodney. 2002. "September 11 and the Restructuring of the Airline Industry." *Dollars and Sense* 241(May–June): 15–25.

CHAPTER 7

Moving On: Chinese Garment Workers After 9/11

Margaret M. Chin

THE CHINESE garment workers of Chinatown in New York City experienced tremendous disruptions in the aftermath of the September 11 tragedy. Chinatown itself, located less than ten blocks from the twin towers site, suffered unprecedented economic losses. In the first eight days after the attack all vehicular and nonresidential pedestrian traffic was prohibited in the whole area south of Canal Street. In the first two weeks following the attacks the majority of garment workers could not get to work because subway stations and major roads in the community were closed or access was limited.[1] Within Chinatown, Bowery, Broadway, and Lafayette Streets were designated checkpoints because they were close to City Hall, the New York Police Department headquarters, and the courthouses. The N&R subway line did not service the Canal Street station for six weeks, and certain sections of Bowery, Henry, and Madison Streets were not open until January 2002. Phone service was disrupted in parts of Chinatown for up to three months.[2] As of this writing, Park Row remains closed. By the time travel and phone service were restored, much of the work that the garment workers expected to do had moved overseas.

Orders could not be placed, orders in the midst of production could not be completed, and finished orders could not be picked up. Many midtown garment manufacturers were in the midst of planning holiday production and could not phone or even go to see the garment shop proprietors to negotiate rates and delivery dates (Barry 2001; Greenhouse 2001; Murphy 2001). Without orders in September and uncertain about future orders, many shops closed their doors, filed for bankruptcy, and sent their workers to the unemployment lines (Curan 2001; Horyn 2001).

In the four months after September 11, many Chinatown garment shops closed their doors and laid off as many workers as they had done in each of the previous two years. By the one-year anniversary in 2002, Chinatown garment shops had closed at more than double the rate of the previous two years.[3] Why did the attack on the World Trade Center affect the garment industry so dramatically? And what are the consequences for Chinatown if its largest industry disappears?

In this chapter, I discuss the ways in which the September 11 tragedy accelerated trends in the garment industry as a whole and affected firms in China-town, as well as the implications of the loss of jobs for the community and for the workers. I am particularly concerned with looking at how the garment workers and their families managed during financial crises during the year after September 11, 2001. I draw upon interviews with Chinese garment workers and field observations made in summer and early fall 2002. The analysis offers an opportunity to critically evaluate the enclave model, which has been so prominent in scholarly discussion of Chinatown. This examination of the effects of 9/11 on Chinatown makes clear that the ethnic enclave can provide jobs for immigrants without English skills only in good economic times. When the Chinatown garment industry soured, Chinese immigrant workers who had always depended on Chinatown jobs were stranded and at a loss as to how to get other work.

NEW YORK CITY'S GARMENT INDUSTRY

Garment manufacturing is an important industry in New York City. Despite extensive job losses over the last two decades, apparel is one of the two largest manufacturing industries in the city, with annual revenues of $11 billion and 56,600 employees before 9/11 (Curan 2001; Horyn 2001; AAFNY 2002a). It is the city's fourth-largest export sector and a critical supplier of jobs, especially for immigrants, and of services to the city's designers and merchandisers. According to a recent Fiscal Policy Institute (FPI) (2003, 10) report, "Every million dollars of apparel production in New York State represents 16.2 jobs, 10.6 within the apparel and textile sector itself and another 5.6 jobs in other industries ranging from business services to banking to health care." The FPI estimates that for every garment worker job, another one and a half jobs are generated elsewhere in the state's economy. Similarly, every million dollars of apparel production in New York State results in a total increase in economic output in the state of $1.7 million. The FPI estimates that apparel workers earned $4.2 billion in 2000, which contributed to local taxes and supported a multitude of local industries and services in the workers' ethnic communities.

Since the garment industry's inception in the 1850s, it has been continuously remade by the movement of new groups of people into the industry, and the Chinese are the latest part of the story (Greene 1997; Aikman 2003). In recent years new immigration, co-ethnic recruiting, and the nurturing of innovative young designers have allowed the industry to retain sizable numbers of production and creative workers. New York City apparel firms have adjusted to the global market by creating their own niche production. Despite the availability of cheaper foreign-made goods, New York City production shops have been able to compete because of the quality of their handiwork, their quick delivery, and their close proximity to designers and manufacturers. Since the 1970s, garment shops have spread all over New York City. In fact, in 2001, 56 percent of all apparel and textile manufacturing employment was located in Manhattan, primarily in the midtown garment center and Chinatown; 22 percent of the rest of employment in the industry was located in Brooklyn and 20 percent in Queens (FPI 2003).

Before 9/11: A Manhattan Industry in Decline

The Manhattan sector of the garment industry, including garment producers in Chinatown, has a reputation for quick turnaround times on relatively small orders (usually runs with a few thousand pieces). With computerized operations, retail stores and designers can easily track inventory and forecast needs. When a store, distributor, or designer runs out of a popular item and needs quick replenishment, they call on Manhattan garment factories (including those in Chinatown). Proprietors of the Manhattan factories are able to assemble the workers, textiles, and supplies needed to produce select items in a timely manner.

Production executives have also found that working with Manhattan shops is especially efficient. Instead of making expensive and extended trips to Asia, they can easily go to Chinatown to monitor production. The close proximity of designers, manufacturers, suppliers, and garment shops allows for a production relationship that cannot be duplicated overseas.

This said, it is also true that the garment industry in New York City has been in decline and struggling with overseas competition for decades (Waldinger 1986; Bonacich and Appelbaum 2000). Wages in the United States are much higher than those paid to workers overseas in Asia, Mexico, and the Caribbean. Clothing prices have not risen in proportion to prices for other goods. As a result, over time, wages paid to U.S. workers have become a larger portion of manufacturers' expenses, especially compared to foreign-produced goods. To remain competitive and profitable, U.S. garment manufacturers and designers, even those committed to producing in this country, have diversified their production to include both foreign- and U.S.-made goods (Aikman 2003). As they have sent work overseas for foreign workers to sew, an increasing number of Manhattan-based production shops and suppliers have closed. Those production shops that are not yet ready to close have tried to reduce their costs by leaving Manhattan or by closing their Manhattan branch, moves that not only reduce (or consolidate) their rent but also allow them easier access to workers who would rather not join the Union of Needletrades, Industrial, and Textile Employees (UNITE). Although such moves reduce overall costs, these shops are also forgoing the opportunities that are so plentiful from working in Manhattan.

In Manhattan other pressures contributed to the decline of the garment industry, including the rapid spread of dot-com firms in the 1990s into spaces that had formerly housed garment factories (NYIRN 2001). Real estate holders and brokers catered to dot-comers, who were amenable to spaces in lofts above the hustle and bustle of Chinatown and in the garment district in midtown Manhattan. As the competition for space raised real estate prices, many apparel firms were pushed out of the city and others were forced out of business.

Finally a word about the highest-profile problem of the garment industry: illegal sweatshops and illegal immigrant workers. The industry has been depicted as a haven for illegal immigrants who are paid far less than the minimum wage and who work in unsafe and crowded conditions (Kwong 1997). These images are often the only ones that the general public has of the New York City garment industry. For those who blame undocumented immigrants for many societal ills, sweatshop conditions reinforce the negative image of the industry and limit sympathy for immigrant garment workers (Hum 2003). For others who want to improve the lives of low-wage immigrant workers, these conditions are a rallying point and engender compassion for these workers.

Many shops hire illegal immigrants, and many proprietors pay less than the minimum wage, but most shops, especially in Manhattan, employ thousands of legal immigrant women and pay them the minimum wage (Chin, forthcoming). In Chinatown before September 11, 86 percent (12,000) of the 14,000 workers in the 250 shops were members of UNITE (AAFNY 2002a; Greenhouse 2001). The implication from these union membership numbers is that far fewer than 2,000 garment workers in Chinatown were illegal. And many of the 2,000 workers who were not union members might not have joined because they already had health coverage, they did not work the requisite number of hours, they made under the threshold, or they were being paid cash off the books. According to the Asian American Federation of New York (2000a), there were only thirty-five non-unionized shops that might have hired only non-unionized workers (of which some would have been undocumented workers). The fact is that, unbeknownst to many, Chinatown garment work has been a very desirable job for legal immigrants who do not speak English. But by 2004, conditions in the garment factories were deteriorating and membership in UNITE was falling—not because of an increase in the number of illegal immigrants who wanted to work in the garment industry, but because of a decrease in the number of jobs available in the industry.

Since 9/11: From Bad to Worse

If the garment industry was already in trouble before September 11, afterward things got much worse. Now, on top of overseas competition, the garment industry suddenly had to contend with delivery delays caused by the increase in bridge and tunnel security, the rerouting of traffic, and the closing of Park Row (AAFNY 2002a). A massive number of orders were canceled throughout the year (Curan 2001; 2002). Six weeks after the attack every factory that had contact with UNITE had laid off workers or reduced work hours (Horyn 2001). Ann Taylor, Brooks Brothers, Talbots, Neiman Marcus, Donna Karan, Prada, and Bergdorf Goodman were just some of the stores and designers who watched customers retreat from buying their products and shopping in their stores. In turn, they decreased or canceled orders from New York City producers (Horyn 2001).

Garments and Chinatown

The post–September 11 losses sustained by Chinatown's garment industry were devastating to the entire Chinatown community. While Chinatown is home to only 56,000 Asian residents, before September 11 it housed close to 250 garment factories that employed 14,000 Chinese workers (AAFNY 2002a). A conservative estimate of the total weekly wages of the 14,000 garment workers in Chinatown before 9/11 is $3.5 million.[4] A year after September 11, with 75 shops closed and 3,500 garment workers out of work, the total weekly wages had dropped to an estimated $2.51 million.[5] Even this figure may be too high because most garment workers were working only a fraction of their normal hours. Before September 11, approximately half of the 14,000 garment workers lived outside of Chinatown; they came to the neighborhood five days a week, earning about $1.75 million of weekly wages, some of which they spent in the community.[6]

Given these numbers, the garment workers' loss of income and the resultant decrease in spending sent a huge ripple through Chinatown. The garment workers are tied in myriad ways to the local Chinatown economy. Not only do they shop there and buy food in the restaurants, but they use a variety of services in the community, from banks, hair salons, travel agencies, and video

FIGURE 7.1   CHINATOWN

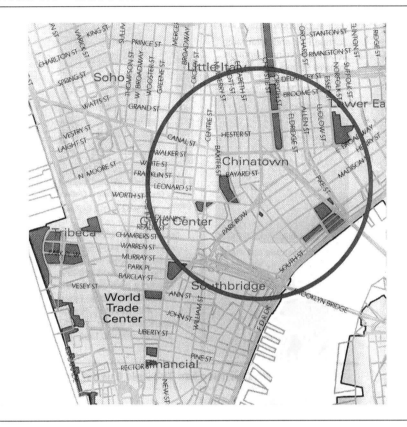

Source: Kay (2003, 16).

and clothing stores to physicians and dentists. Each garment worker may spend only a small amount at various shops, but multiply this spending by 7,000 and the amounts are significant indeed.[7] The net effect is a Chinatown ethnic enclave where stores are kept stocked and pockets are full. When stores lose customers, such as the garment workers, there is a domino effect: stores stock fewer items, and regular customers who do not live in the vicinity be- come discouraged because they cannot find necessary items. If they have other options, they do not return to Chinatown.

Chinatown also lost income because, in the wake of the World Trade Cen- ter attack, many tourists and shoppers found it difficult to get there.[8] China- town and the garment shops are in close proximity to the area known as

Manhattan's civic center: City Hall, police headquarters, and downtown municipal and federal buildings. The increasing concern about terrorism and public safety caused not only short-term disruptions in garment manufacturing but long-term changes in the neighborhood. Extra security and police vehicles were deployed to patrol Chinatown and the surrounding areas to protect the civic center. As of the spring of 2004, Park Row, a wide street that had been used by tour buses, remained closed to vehicles. Congestion in the Chinatown area continued to be worse than before September 11 because cars and trucks were often redirected (Wyatt 2002). In addition, many on-street parking spaces used by Chinatown businesses, shoppers, and visitors were eliminated to accommodate the extra police and security vehicles. The public municipal parking garage adjacent to One Police Plaza, with four hundred spots, remained closed for security purposes. With fewer on-street parking spaces and a major public parking garage closed, many would-be tourists and shoppers have gone elsewhere. In short, the combination of a reduction in the garment workers' buying power and the decrease in the number of other shoppers and tourists has caused major upheaval in the enclave.

At the same time, in the first six to nine months after September 11 economic aid from the government was, in general, not forthcoming. Canal Street, which runs right through the center of Chinatown, was the northern border used to define the "disaster zone." For at least six months those who worked or lived north of Canal Street were ineligible for government aid (AAFNY 2002a; Chen 2002a; 2002b; Henriques and Barstow 2002; Lee 2002). Eighty percent of Chinatown's garment shops were located north of the disaster zone. A sizable proportion of the owners and workers in these shops received no federal aid even when the artificial designation of Canal Street as the boundary was removed in April 2002. Many who were rejected were leery of applying again, and many others were disqualified because they could not produce the formal paperwork required by the federal regulators (AAFNY 2002a; Chen 2002a, 2002b).

September 11 has affected Chinatown in yet another way—the real estate market. Before September 11, real estate owners were unwilling to renew garment factory leases and in fact were waiting for factory leases to expire to acquire the spaces for more lucrative rentals. Until the economic recession and the new media and dot-com bust, real estate holders in Chinatown were ready to remodel and refurbish their lofts for these new companies. The recent economic downturn in Chinatown after September 11—and in the garment industry in particular—turned the tables. Real estate holders, late in 2002, wanted to renew those leases—many had expired or would expire by 2004—but Chinatown garment factory owners were unwilling because they were not even sure they could remain in business.

NEW YORK CITY'S CHINATOWN
AND THE ENCLAVE MODEL

Before September 11, 2001, New York's Chinatown was the largest Chinese neighborhood in the United States. It was depicted by scholars as a classic immigrant ethnic enclave (Wilson and Portes 1980; Portes and Bach 1985; Zhou 1992). An ethnic enclave is an alternative economic system. It is similar to the larger economic system but specifically supports ethnic businesses and co-ethnic employees. Immigrant ethnics can achieve upward mobility in an ethnic enclave economy by using their own ethnic resources to find work that is equal to or better than the jobs they could find in the secondary labor market. Moreover, they can do this without learning English and "American ways."

Chinatown has also been described as a mobility trap, a place where workers are exploited on a daily basis (Kwong 1997; Nee and Sanders 1987). According to Peter Kwong (1997), wages are driven lower and conditions made worse by the arrival of illegal immigrants. All who work in Chinatown face deteriorating conditions because the undocumented are so much more compliant as employees. Legal immigrants have no recourse when the employers have easy access to a cheaper and more vulnerable labor force. If they have nowhere else to go, these legal immigrants are exploited along with the undocumented. Kwong also argues that both legal and illegal immigrants stay in the enclave and never have a chance to learn English, thus limiting their ability to leave. Thus, Kwong disagrees with his academic predecessors (for example, Wilson and Portes 1980; Portes and Bach 1985; and Zhou 1992), who have viewed the absence of a need to learn English as an amenity that benefits immigrants in enclaves. Conceding that this is a benefit to immigrants who might otherwise remain unemployed, Kwong nevertheless sees the enclave as undermining immigrants' ability to obtain the language skills that are crucial to their ability to work outside of the enclave. In this sense, he views the enclave as a trap rather than a refuge. Thus, as with the traditional ethnic enclave model, Chinese immigrants do not learn English, but for different reasons. In the ethnic enclave model, they never need to because they can achieve mobility without using English. In Kwong's model, they are trapped in low-paying jobs without access to opportunities to learn English.

Victor Nee and Jimy Sanders (1987) would argue that Chinatown is also a mobility trap because so few have a real chance at socioeconomic mobility. Only those with human capital are able to work in their own businesses as entrepreneurs. The entrepreneurs, not the workers, are the only ones who can move up the economic ladder. Nee and Sanders would blame the low wages not on the illegal immigrants but instead on the exploitative nature of co-ethnic relationships between entrepreneurs and workers. Disputing the rosier picture of Chinatown found by Min Zhou (1992), they would argue that only a small number can attain mobility and the rest are trapped.

My own study reveals that Chinatown provided jobs and promoted the mobility of both the garment workers and the garment shop entrepreneurs before September 11. The workers I interviewed did not characterize their pre-September 11 jobs as mobility traps, even though they never learned English. Moreover, in the Chinatown garment industry there were far fewer undocumented workers than suspected both before and after September 11. The high rate of unionization in the industry, the low percentages of undocumented female workers, and the increase in the number of legal Fujianese immigrants refute the idea that illegal immigrants are the cause of low wages in the garment industry.

Both the economic enclave and the co-ethnic hiring and recruiting practiced there were particularly important for these immigrant workers. Immigrants who come to New York with little money or education have only family and friends to help them adjust to their new home. Friends and family or their social networks lead these new immigrants to the neighborhoods where they will live and the jobs they will take. And most often they will live and work with others just like themselves.

The community's economic activity and vitality are connected to ethnic entrepreneurs who have access to ethnic creditors and to ethnic wholesalers who can sell them equipment and supplies that can be used by their co-ethnic employees to create products. If these products are sold in the ethnic markets, their own co-ethnic employees are consumers (Foner 2001). Those who bring wealth with them from their home country are also avid consumers and investors in Chinatown (Lin 1998). Those with more human capital can frequently become entrepreneurs, often making links to non-co-ethnics, and earn higher returns than they would if they joined the secondary labor market. Immigrants with few skills rely on family members and friends in their social networks to help them find jobs in the enclave (Zhou 1992).

In Chinatown the ethnic enclave offers a venue for economic mobility that does not require interacting with or depending on the larger population outside of the ethnic community (Portes and Jensen 1989; Zhou 1992). For example, without ever becoming fluent in English, many of the Chinese who have worked in Chinatown have been able to save money and purchase homes in Brooklyn and Queens. Purchasing a home is considered a major achievement, a symbol of success in life and of upward mobility (Zhou 2001).

After September 11, however, Chinatown's ethnic enclave economy suffered severe blows. As Chinatown garment shops closed or relocated, immigrant workers were less attracted to the neighborhood as a source of jobs. Neighborhood businesses that depended on garment workers' patronage, like hair salons, banks, travel agencies, and groceries, found their customer base dwindling. In 2003, the ethnic enclave was still in trouble.

The vulnerability of the ethnic enclave to a disaster like the collapse of the World Trade Center raises questions about the positive gloss so frequently painted in the literature. The impact of 9/11 dramatically highlights the limits of ethnic enclaves. Chinatown was able to provide jobs to low-skilled, non-English-speaking immigrants before September 11, but afterward the very dependence on co-ethnic social networks that the ethnic enclave nurtured turned into a liability.

Garment workers' networks are still strong, but they carry information that is no longer useful. Most displaced Chinese garment workers get information about jobs from other family members. The problem is that this information mostly pertains to industries hurt by the September 11 attacks and to Chinese neighborhoods in the New York area (Sunset Park, Brooklyn; Flushing and Jackson Heights in Queens; the growing community in Bensonhurst, Brooklyn) that no longer have the capacity to absorb new workers. All of the Chinese neighborhoods have been hurt by the trickle-down effect of the disaster. Over half of the displaced garment workers live outside of Manhattan, and many live in the Chinese neighborhoods in Queens and Brooklyn. The majority of these workers have not worked full-time since before September 11. With less income, they have chosen to spend less in their own Chinese neighborhoods. Although many of the garment factories in these outer-borough neighborhoods did not close, they also have not been able to provide full-time work. In addition, car services, van services to Chinatown, restaurants, and grocery stores have all been affected by the garment workers' loss of income.

Members of these displaced workers' social networks have few, if any, leads to work opportunities outside of their own Chinese neighborhood. Not only did the enclave limit workers' social networks, but enclave workers were not exposed to opportunities to acquire the skills necessary to find jobs outside of the enclave. My interviews revealed that these workers did not speak fluent English. Although many had taken English as a Second Language (ESL) classes, few had become fluent because everyday life did not require them to converse or read in English.

Before the tragedy this lack of fluency in English was not a barrier to employment. As a result, many of the Chinese workers in this study had never filled out a job application form or interviewed for a job, and most had relied on word-of-mouth recruiting and hiring. Hardly any were aware of the skills required for jobs in non-enclave industries such as home healthcare, hotels, or offices. During good economic times the enclave provided many benefits for Chinese workers and entrepreneurs, but when disaster hit, the features that had not mattered in a segregated enclave became vulnerabilities and weaknesses that hampered the Chinese workers' ability to recover by finding jobs outside of the enclave.

THE EXPERIENCES OF IMMIGRANT GARMENT WORKERS

The liabilities of the ethnic enclave in the wake of the September 11 attack become clearer when we examine more closely the experiences of the garment workers interviewed for this study in the summer and fall of 2002. The displaced garment workers were recruited from three sites that conducted ESL and retraining classes in Chinatown.[9] When interviewed, 64 percent of the sixty-one respondents were unemployed, 26 percent were working part-time in garment shops, and 10 percent were retired or had become home health aides. The interviews also provide insight into how these workers coped after September 11 with the difficulties of working in an already declining industry that had now suffered a series of blows.

Garment Work Before September 11

Before September 11, the garment workers we interviewed had steady manufacturing jobs in unionized shops. (The majority of garment shops in Chinatown, as detailed earlier in the chapter, are unionized.) Although their wages averaged only $250 to $350 a week, the jobs gave them health benefits for their family, and the money made a significant contribution to the household economy. Many of the women contributed $15,000 to an annual household income of $35,000. The two men interviewed contributed significantly more, between $400 and $450 a week. Between their wages and low rents, many had been able to save enough for down payments on homes in Brooklyn or Queens.

In addition to the money and health benefits, the women appreciated the flexible hours in garment factories, where work was paid by the piece. It was not unheard of to come in at 9:30 A.M. after dropping off the children at school, skip lunch, and then leave by 2:00 or 3:00 P.M. to pick up the children at school. Many women with young children worked only twenty to twenty-five hours a week. Even those who worked full-time often arrived at 9:30 A.M., took time off during the day to shuttle their children between school, babysitters, and/or after-school programs and to do errands and shop, and then worked until 7:30 P.M. As one garment worker noted, "This job is for mommies." The women did not have to worry about missing hours at work during school holidays or when their children were sick—there were no penalties for taking time off. Those with older children were able to work more hours, but they too took advantage of lunchtime to run errands.

The camaraderie on the job was also important to the garment workers.

Sharing an immigrant background and a common language, many coworkers became good friends from spending hours on the job together.[10]

The workers said that by the summer of 2002, for the first time, they missed the jobs they once held. They had never considered the possibility that they would long for the job that they used to complain about so bitterly. This was true for young and old alike, and for workers who were long-term immigrants as well as those who had just arrived.

The Immediate Impact of September 11

The day of September 11 was traumatic for many of the workers. Most were on their way to work when the planes hit the towers, having just dropped off their children at school. Some saw the burning towers as their subway crossed the Williamsburg Bridge. Others got off the subway in Chinatown and smelled the smoke on Canal Street. Still others witnessed the burning towers from the street as they walked to work.

Once at work, the workers and owners listened to the radio to get updates on what was happening right down the street from them. Those with views of the towers watched with horror. When the first tower collapsed, most decided to leave and, most important, to get their children home. "Our window [at work] faces it [the World Trade Center]," said one woman. "I saw a lot of fire, heard explosion sounds. I saw it and everyone was scared. I was worried about my daughters. I didn't know whether their schools might close. I ran and ran. While going down the stairs, I got all banged up and my legs were all bruised. Everything, my watch, everything broke when I fell."

Immediately after the collapse of the towers, phone service to Chinatown was cut, and it was unclear when it would be restored. Streets south of Fourteenth Street were declared a disaster area and a "frozen zone," off limits to non-official cars and nonresidents. By Wednesday, September 12, the major streets in Chinatown were almost completely blocked by National Guard troops, who were stationed at, among other places, both ends of Canal Street and on the border of Chinatown by the city and federal buildings. Residents without identification had trouble getting to their homes in the disaster area. On September 14 the northern boundary of the frozen zone was moved south to Canal Street—right in the middle of Chinatown.

Although many workers were asked back to work by employers a few days after the attack—orders had to be completed—those who came from Brooklyn and Queens had a hard time getting into the frozen zone. Those lucky enough to have kept an old pay stub with the factory address were allowed in; others had to walk around the perimeter until they found a breach in security.

Getting to work turned out to be the least of their problems. The only work available was work left over from before September 11. At many factories no additional work was available because no new work orders were coming in: the phones at the factories were out of order, and roadblocks in the area made it hard for trucks to pick up clothing and deliver orders. The women saw the work they would have done shipped out of state or out of the country. One worker explained that her factory had produced clothing for the Jones New York label from goods that were flown in from China. When the planes could not enter New York, Jones New York negotiated an arrangement to keep all of the production in China. By November 2001, this worker's factory had closed.

No new work came into the majority of factories until January 2002. Even then, factories slowly continued to shut their doors as orders failed to materialize. Those without work in the fall of 2002 were on the verge of bankruptcy a few months later. Some ended up closing their doors permanently. Some other factories used another strategy, they reopened under a different name early in 2002, having declared bankruptcy (to save what little they could) and trying again. Many workers were unable to get any work at all; others managed to find only part-time work in the factories.

Getting Benefits

After September 11, an array of benefits was available for displaced workers, including unemployment benefits, specific moneys for those living and employed near the trade center site, and special health insurance packages. Those workers who lost their jobs were able to collect unemployment benefits when they were laid off. This was not a new experience for them. Because garment work in New York is seasonal, short layoffs are common, and many of the women interviewed had collected unemployment benefits in the past, usually for eight to ten weeks a year. The women knew where to apply for unemployment benefits, and they generally knew how much money they would receive and how long the payments would last. Generally, unemployment benefits can be received for six months, as long as the recipient can show that he or she is looking for work, and compensation is based on a percentage of the last paycheck. After the tragedy of September 11, an extra thirteen weeks were made available to those unemployed because of the attack, and most garment workers took advantage of this benefit. The few unable to get unemployment benefits—or any of the special September 11 benefits—had been working for cash right before September 11 and could not prove they had been employed.[11] On average, most of those interviewed received $100 to $150 a week for thirty-nine weeks—about half of what they would have earned had they been able to work.

It was much more difficult for the women to gain access to September 11 relief funds. Organizations such as the Federal Emergency Management Agency (FEMA) and the American Red Cross provided a variety of subsidies. There was cash assistance for buying food and utilities, rent relief, and wage assis-tance. The Tzu Chi Buddhist Foundation, the World Vision Fund, and Catho-lic Charities provided additional cash grants.[12] For garment shop owners, loans were available from the Small Business Administration (SBA), and loans and grants were also being distributed by the Office of the Manhattan Borough President, the Renaissance Economic Development Corporation, and Asian Americans For Equality (AAFE). Yet only thirty of the sixty-one workers inter-viewed received any specific September 11 aid. Of these thirty, ten received less than $1,000, fourteen between $2,000 and $3,000, and six over $4,000.

One problem that workers had in getting September 11 relief aid was that most of the agencies followed guidelines that originally delineated the disaster area as south of Canal Street. (One exception was the World Trade Center Business Recovery Grant and Loan Program, which was designated for the area south of Houston Street.) This designation effectively eliminated 80 percent of the garment shops and their owners and employees from aid during the first nine months after September 11 (AAFNY 2002a, 2002b). Workers who lived in the designated areas received residential aid money, although they did not qualify for work relief.

Complicated rules and procedures were also a problem. Although most of the major agencies had Chinese translators and people capable of answering questions, workers were often unsure about where to go to apply for aid or whether they were eligible. One woman said that she and her friends spent an entire day at one location only to find out that they did not qualify for the aid being offered there. There was no single place or source to go to for informa-tion on all the aid available. In addition, eligibility requirements kept changing. So many workers were turned down for aid before the disaster zone was ex-panded in April 2002 to include areas north of Canal Street that quite a num-ber never reapplied, even though they had become eligible for assistance.[13]

Garment shop owners, it should be noted, also had difficulty getting access to September 11 aid in the first crucial months after the attack because most shops were located north of Canal Street. This lack of aid was no doubt a critical reason why so many factories folded: some were sold to new owners, some later reopened under a different name when orders increased, and some disappeared from the scene altogether. Some of the owners consolidated their shops, especially those who owned shops in both Sunset Park and Chinatown. Owners often closed the Chinatown shop, which cost more to run, and kept open the Sunset Park shop, which had easier access to roads and supplies.

A final—and critical—benefit for the women workers and their children was health benefits, which, remarkably, most were able to retain after Septem-ber 11, even when they were not working. Three-quarters of the workers (and all of their school-age children) were covered by health benefits at the time of the interviews in the summer of 2002. Workers who went back to the factories recovered their health benefits, and this was a major reason why they returned, even though they could not get full-time work; they might in fact have received more money by applying for unemployment benefits. If they earned $7,000 a year, or $1,750 a quarter, they could maintain family coverage under the union-negotiated health plan. Fortunately, since the required income was low, some of the workers had earned enough by September 11 to keep their health coverage for the rest of the year. And others who needed to make the required threshold were able to do it on part-time work.

Those who did not return to work and no longer qualified for the union health insurance package enrolled their children in Child Health Plus, a New York State government plan that provides health coverage to children in families with incomes up to two and a half times the poverty-level income. (In 2003 the monthly income of a family of four could not exceed $3,834. Families with higher incomes who had no other options could also buy coverage for $45 per month per child.) As for workers themselves and their spouses, many without health insurance took advantage of the September 11 Disaster Medicaid or enrolled in the Family Health Plus program, which is for families with incomes up to one and a half times the poverty level. (In 2003 the monthly income of a family of four could not exceed $2,300.) Many community groups, including Chinatown Manpower and UNITE's Union Health Center, publicized these various health programs and helped Chinese families apply for them. It is hoped that when the September 11 Disaster Medicaid program runs out for many workers, these groups will assist them in getting access to other benefits.

Making Ends Meet

Chinatown garment workers made ends meet, for the most part by marshaling resources from able-bodied adults in their households. Not surprisingly, those who did the best had older children and/or spouses who worked steadily, and they were living in government-subsidized housing, where rent fluctuates with income. Although it was difficult to find jobs in the New York economy of 2002, all household members who could do so found work, including occasional babysitting, construction jobs, and even extra work in garment shops on weekends.

On average, after September 11 the annual household income of those interviewed was reduced by almost half, to $16,000. Over half of the husbands also worked in industries that were hard hit by the September 11 tragedy, most commonly the restaurant industry.

In some months these garment workers and their families had to borrow from relatives or use savings to make ends meet. College-age children or those who had moved out of the family home were often a significant source of help.

In one family a college-age student paid half of his parents' monthly mortgage payment. In another a working-age child rented a floor of his house to his parents for only $200 a month. In addition to helping with rent, working children often paid their parents' gas and electricity or telephone bills. Other children helped parents by buying them groceries.

Those who did not live in subsidized housing and had no older children to help or other family members to loan them money found it hard to pay bills and were contemplating drastic measures. One garment worker and his wife were considering selling their house. When interviewed, this worker was earning $400 to $500 a week, and his wife was making $250. Like most others interviewed, he and his wife did not qualify for food stamps or Medicaid because their income and savings were too high. Even if they had met income requirements, a few of the people we interviewed were ineligible for food stamps or Temporary Aid for Needy Families (TANF) because they immigrated after August 22, 1996, when new citizenship rules began to regulate access to public assistance.

One woman was particularly desperate. She had given up subsidized housing several years earlier to buy a house, and if the mortgage payment could not be made, her family would have nowhere to go. "Right now every mortgage payment I've made is through borrowed money," she said. "All that I've saved I've already spent. Since July, for every payment I've made I've borrowed money. 'Just return it when you have a job' is what they are saying. But I have to pay them back, right?" She was one of the few people interviewed who reported seeing a psychologist as a result of the events of September 11; she said that she was having anxiety attacks that caused her body to cramp up.

Four other workers were also having trouble making their mortgage payments. Their homes were supposed to be their nest eggs and their security. When interviewed, these four were working part-time in the garment industry, waiting it out until there was more work. When I asked about retraining, they were not interested; they felt that they needed a check now and could not invest the time to look for a new job.

Remain Underemployed or Retrain?

To retrain or not retrain—this was a dilemma faced by the workers we interviewed. Whether they chose to be underemployed garment workers (often taking ESL classes that met twice a week) or to take intensive, fee-based retraining classes (including English and work-related classes) largely depended on their financial situation. Two of the workers had already received retraining to become home health attendants; four older displaced workers had decided to retire.

If money was tight, they usually chose to go back to work, even for a few hours a day. Most of these women garment workers had young children, and the flexible hours in garment work were important to them. They feared that jobs outside the garment industry would be less accommodating. They also wanted to continue to be able to participate in the UNITE health insurance program. Many believed that if factories remained in Chinatown, eventually they would be able to get better garment jobs.

Unfortunately, the garment industry has become more competitive since September 11, and many factories no longer can afford flexible hours. One woman said: "I do what the boss wants. When he calls and asks me to do a rush order, I come in early and leave late. I tell my mother-in-law I have to do this to keep my job (and that is why I need her babysitting help). Others who can't keep up with what the boss wants are told to leave." Moreover, many of the factories that are still open are contemplating a move outside of Manhattan to avoid the union and lower costs.

Those garment workers in a better financial position—their families had no immediate need for their wages—were likely to choose retraining in the hope of obtaining a better job. Also among those seeking training were women who tried to return to the garment shops but found that they were no longer welcome—or who feared they would no longer be welcome. One forty-five-year-old worker with two high school–age children and a mortgage payment was afraid that her boss's warning of an impending shutdown would come true. She enrolled herself in a retraining class in November 2001. Even if workers had reservations about whether retraining would in fact lead to a job—and they knew that the retraining centers had not placed many people in jobs—they felt that knowing English would be a help. They hoped that they would hear about job openings in other fields by going to the community centers where the classes were held. In other words, they were trying to broaden their networks, since, as discussed later, their existing social networks had not led them to new job opportunities.

The Liabilities of the Ethnic Enclave

Many workers were retraining for other jobs, but their networks were not much help. Chinatown's enclave had provided them with jobs that required little English and few skills and that offered flexible hours, camaraderie, and health benefits. Once garment work became less available—and the conditions less desirable—and they looked for work elsewhere, they found that their resources were limited.

A major problem was their lack of networks to other jobs. Hardly any of the women interviewed for this study knew someone in another field. Most of them had heard about other women who successfully made the transition from garment worker to manicurist, home health aide, or hotel worker, but they did not know anyone personally who worked in these fields.

The interviews revealed that a high proportion of the displaced garment workers' family members worked in various jobs in New York City's Chinese communities. Of the fifty-nine women interviewed, forty-seven had husbands who worked in a Chinese-owned restaurant, the vast majority in Chinatown. The people they knew and could count on for assistance in their job hunt worked in Chinese-owned firms and lived in Chinese communities. All of the family members who worked outside of a Chinese neighborhood were men. This helps explain why so many of the women knew so little about other jobs for women outside of the Chinese communities. The only job information they had led them to industries in the enclave that were already hurting from the aftereffects of the tragedy.

Take the case of a thirty-eight-year-old woman who had been living in the United States for sixteen years. She and most members of her family lived in Flushing, Queens, and most of her family members worked in Manhattan's Chinatown or in one of the Chinese communities in Brooklyn or Queens: a sister, two cousins, and three sisters-in-law worked in the garment industry; her husband, three cousins, two brothers-in-law, and a sister-in-law worked in restaurants; and her husband's uncle and wife worked in Chinatown as a doctor and pharmacist, respectively. Those in her family who were in New York City but not working in a Chinese community included her sister, a pattern maker, and her brother-in-law, who was an electrician in a hotel; both worked in midtown Manhattan. These two members of her family who did not work in a Chinese community had jobs for which the old word-of-mouth referral method had not been acceptable. Given her family job network, it is not surprising that she knew few people who could introduce her to jobs outside of the Chinese neighborhood.

Or consider another longtime immigrant worker whose family members also were concentrated in New York's Chinese communities. Even the professionals in her family—an accountant, a nurse, and a bank supervisor—worked in the city's Chinese communities. For the most part, her relatives who had left the Chinese communities had left New York altogether, so they were not of much help. She had never learned to speak English because she had always worked in the enclave, and all of her contacts led her back to nonexistent enclave jobs.

Newer immigrants also ran into the same problem, although their connections tended to be to lower-skilled jobs. Thus, one forty-four-year-old woman who had been in the United States for nine years lived, like most of her family, in Sunset Park. Her family job network, however, kept her in Manhattan's Chinatown—in the garment and restaurant industries and jewelry peddling.

The workers' limited networks may also explain why they knew so little about other kinds of jobs. When I asked the women about the kinds of jobs they were interested in, they gave me hardly any answers. Few knew how to find a human resources office. Nor were they sure if they could fill out a job application by themselves. A few workers who had gone that far and filled out job applications mentioned how humiliating it was to write down that they had only a grade school or eighth-grade education. They felt that their educational level and previous experience as garment workers led others to view them in a negative way and prevented them from getting the jobs they wanted. It should be noted that the women were also concerned about having to work less flexible hours in other lines of work such as home health care—which employs a growing number of Chinese women—and not being able, as in the garment shops, to bring children to work in emergencies. Many, especially those with young children, worried about being assigned to the night shift.

Yet even those who wanted jobs in other fields like home health care were having trouble getting them. As I have emphasized, they lacked networks that would steer them toward these jobs. And they also lacked fluency in English. English was not needed in the factories, so they had not been very motivated to learn it when working there. After leaving the factories and garment shops, however, knowing English became important. This was yet another way in which being submerged in the enclave—living in Chinese neighborhoods, shopping at Chinese stores, using the services of Chinese professionals, working in Chinese firms—hindered the women in their search for work after September 11.

CONCLUSION

The attack on the World Trade Center on September 11 was a onetime event, but the effects on Chinatown will be long-lasting. The consequences for the community have not been fully determined yet. The number of workers who go daily to Chinatown has decreased dramatically. The number of tourists and workers from the twin towers and surrounding areas who eat and shop in Chinatown has also decreased. Meanwhile, there has been no increase in Chinatown-based jobs for the displaced non-English-speaking worker. This is especially true in the garment industry. Since September 11, about 100 Chinatown garment shops have closed their doors, eliminating 8,000 Chinese garment worker jobs. This leaves only 150 garment shops employing no more than 6,000 workers (Phillips Preiss, Shapiro Associates, and AAFE 2004).

In exploring the effects of September 11 on Chinatown garment workers, this chapter has shown that even though the benefits of Chinatown's enclave once outweighed the drawbacks for the workers, at this moment the reverse seems to be true. Before September 11, women worked in Chinatown because the jobs accommodated their personal needs in many ways (Bao 2001; Zhou 2001; Chin, forthcoming). They were mothers who needed flexible hours, and they needed to work in a non-English-speaking environment. Their social networks took them to a place where work and living meshed together. These networks are still strong. The current problem, as I have pointed out, is that these social networks have not been as successful in helping them obtain jobs outside of the enclave since September 11 as they were in helping them find enclave jobs before September 11.

At present, the workers are in the midst of producing their own sea change in the industry and community by changing the way they look for work. Chinese garment workers have found that the old methods of finding jobs through family networks are no longer effective. As the interviews indicate, these workers are not sure how to move on. They do not have the right connections to others to help them find jobs outside of the community, and the connections they do have led them to jobs that are no longer secure. Even though the first few months of 2004 showed an upturn in garment work in Chinatown (because of the recovering economy), workers were not returning to sew. Workers fear returning to an unstable industry, even though they have the most personal contacts in that industry. Owners report that they are short of workers to produce necessary items. What is clear is that the workers have learned that they cannot rely on co-ethnic ties alone anymore or on resources that connect them only to the ethnic community. These workers have realized that these methods succeeded during prosperous times but are less useful when the industries in the community are having difficulty.

Second, English-language skills seem all the more important when it comes to finding a job outside of the ethnic community. Before September 11, it was a benefit when a job did not require learning English, but it now seems that their lack of English skills is preventing a huge number of garment workers from looking for a job outside of Chinatown. We have yet to see whether lack of education or skills also prevents these workers from getting jobs.

There is also the question of how Chinatown itself will change if the community cannot produce jobs. If there are no new jobs in Chinatown and job losses continue, few former workers will go there just to shop and use services. It was the thousands of Chinese workers who shopped and used local services that made the ethnic economy hum. Tourists alone cannot fuel the economy of Chinatown. Moreover, job losses in Chinatown may reverberate throughout the other Chinese communities in the city where some interviewees lived. With their lower incomes, they have less to spend in stores and services there as well. Less business for the other communities, in turn, hurts other family members who may have jobs or live in these other Chinese communities.

It is an insecure time for the New York Chinese community, especially for workers without jobs. They want to work, but they are not sure where they should turn for help. Chinese immigrant workers want to continue the strides they have made toward financial independence and upward mobility, especially in terms of homeownership. Clearly September 11 and its aftereffects have had a dramatic effect on Chinatown and its residents and workers, and how they move on from these dire times is one of many questions for their future.

Research for this chapter was supported by grants from the Russell Sage Foundation, Professional Staff Congress–CUNY (PSC-CUNY) grants, and the CUNY Asian/Asian American Research Institute. Many thanks to Karen Lam and Boon Ngeo, who conducted most of the garment worker interviews. I would like to also thank the employees of UNITE, Garment Industry Development Corporation (GIDC), and Chinatown Manpower, who allowed us into their offices and gave us access to the garment workers. I am grateful to all the individuals in Chinatown and at the September 11 Fund, Asian American Federation of New York, the Fiscal Policy Institute, GIDC, and UNITE who have shared their thoughts on the New York City garment industry with me. I especially want to thank Nancy Foner, Kathy Kaufman, and Deborah Gardner for their thoughtful comments on earlier versions of this chapter.

NOTES

1. Subway service was not fully operational in Chinatown (specifically the Canal Street station) for six weeks. Canal Street, which cuts across the middle of Chinatown and connects the Holland Tunnel (leading to New Jersey) to the Manhattan Bridge (leading to Brooklyn), was closed initially for three days, but later it became a "border crossing"—any vehicle entering Manhattan and the downtown area had to pass through National Guard checkpoints there. National Guard troops were stationed on Canal Street until the end of 2001.
2. Two Asian American Federation of New York (2002a; 2002b) reports state that phone service was interrupted for up to two months. However, interviewees have told me that phone service was not dependable until January 2002. There were phone outages throughout the fall of 2001.
3. This is similar to the rate of job loss in the New York City garment industry as a whole. According to a New York State Department of Labor report (Curan 2002), garment industry jobs tumbled 13.4 percent to 49,000 in 2001 from 56,600 in 2000—more than double the decline from 1999 to 2000.
4. This figure is based on an average weekly wage of $250, multiplied by 14,000 to get $3.5 million.
5. The total income figure assumes that all of the remaining workers worked full-time and earned $250 a week.

6. Based on my interviews with UNITE officials, garment shop owners, and garment workers, I estimated that 50 percent of garment workers lived in Manhattan. For this study, a higher proportion of workers interviewed lived outside of Manhattan.
7. Seven thousand is the number of Chinatown workers who did not live in Manhattan (half of fourteen thousand).
8. A 2002 report by the Rebuild Chinatown Initiative (AAFE 2002) found that a high proportion of visitors to the area were tourists and shoppers. Parking, traffic, and transportation to the area were important issues.
9. The sixty-one workers were between the ages of thirty-five and sixty-five. All had lived in the United States for at least five years (62 percent had lived here more than ten years); none were undocumented (74 percent were citizens); and most lived in Brooklyn (61 percent) or Manhattan (26 percent), with the rest living in Queens, the Bronx, and Staten Island. The interviewees were contacted through the ESL or retraining classes they were taking in the summer of 2002. Between July and November 2002, I conducted fifteen of the interviews, and the rest were done by my research assistants, Karen Lam and Boon Ngeo. I also conducted interviews with UNITE officials, other Chinatown agency officials, garment industry specialists, and garment shop owners.
10. As discussed later in the chapter, the majority of the friends and relatives of these garment workers also worked in Chinatown or one of the other satellite Chinese communities.
11. Two of the six workers who did not qualify for September 11 benefits because they were taking cash wages on September 11 are still looking for jobs. The other four are working fewer hours in the garment industry. Those who are underemployed have younger children (elementary or junior high age) and worry about keeping their health insurance through UNITE.
12. The Greater Blouse Association helped to distribute some of the World Vision Fund money, and Catholic Charities, administered through the Chinese Staff Workers Association (CSWA), distributed cash grants directly to the Chinese who worked north of Canal Street. The average World Vision grant was $7,000, distributed to 430 workers. Catholic Charities and the CSWA distributed $300,000 to 100 individuals (AAFNY 2002a).
13. This change was partly the result of widespread publicity generated by the Asian American Federation of New York (2002a) report on the economic impact of the 9/11 disaster on Chinatown.

REFERENCES

Aikman, Becky. 2003. "Changing Patterns: New York's Shrinking Garment Industry Keeps Redesigning Itself, with an Increased Focus on High Fashion and New Fads." *Newsday*, August 18, p. A29.
Asian American Federation of New York (AAFNY). 2002a. "Chinatown After September 11: An Economic Impact Study—An Interim Report." New York: AAFNY.
———. 2002b. "Chinatown One Year After September 11: An Economic Impact Study." New York: AAFNY.

Asian Americans for Equality (AAFE). 2002. "Rebuild Chinatown Initiative: The Community Speaks—One Year After September 11, 2001." New York: AAFE.

Bao, Xiao Lan. 2001. Holding Up More Than Half the Sky: Chinese Women Garment Workers in New York City, 1948–1992. Urbana: University of Illinois Press.

Barry, Dan. 2001. "After the Attacks: The Scene: Normality Proves Elusive Amid Bomb Scares and Transit Woes." New York Times, September 14, p. A12.

Bonacich, Edna, and Richard Appelbaum. 2000. Behind the Label: Inequality in the Los Angeles Apparel Industry. Berkeley: University of California Press.

Chen, David W. 2002a. "After Criticism, U.S. Broadens 9/11 Aid Pool." New York Times, June 29, p. A1.

———. 2002b. "More Get 9/11 Aid, but Distrust of U.S. Effort Lingers." New York Times, August 27, p. B1.

Chin, Margaret M. Forthcoming. Sewing Women: Immigrants and the New York City Garment Industry. New York: Columbia University Press.

Curan, Catherine. 2001. "Garment Makers Are Falling Apart at the Seams; Job Cuts Unending Since September 11 Attack." Crain's New York Business, November 12.

———. 2002. "Garment Firms Are Torn Apart; Attack Puts Ailing Industry in Dire Straits; 13 Percent Drop in Apparel Jobs." Crain's New York Business, March 4.

Fiscal Policy Institute (FPI). 2003. "New York City's Garment Industry: A New Look?" New York: FPI.

Foner, Nancy. 2001. New Immigrants in New York. New York: Columbia University Press.

Greene, Nancy. 1997. Ready to Wear and Ready to Work: A Century of Industry and Immigrants in Paris and New York. Durham, N.C.: Duke University Press.

Greenhouse, Steven. 2001. "A Nation Challenged: Notebooks; A City on Your Sleeve." New York Times, October 13, p. B11.

Henriques, Diana B., and David Barstow. 2002. "Change in Rules Barred Many from September 11 Disaster Relief." New York Times, April 26, p. A1.

Horyn, Cathy. 2001. "Ripple Effect from Attack: Suppliers Have No Demand." New York Times, October 23, p. A20.

Hum, Tarry. 2003. "Mapping Global Production in New York City's Garment Industry: The Role of Sunset Park, Brooklyn's Immigrant Economy." Economic Development Quarterly 17(3, August): 294–309.

Kay, Elizabeth. 2003. New York Chinatown Travel Guide. New York: Asian American Business Development Center (AABDC).

Kwong, Peter. 1997. Forbidden Workers: Illegal Chinese Immigrants and American Labor. New York: New Press.

Lee, Jennifer 8. 2002. "Report Says 10 Percent of Jobs Lost Post September 11 Were in Chinatown." New York Times, April 5, p. B3.

Lin, Jan. 1998. Reconstructing Chinatown: Ethnic Enclave, Global Change. Minneapolis: University of Minnesota Press.

Murphy, Dean E. 2001. "A Nation Challenged: Chinatown, Its Streets Empty, Quietly Begins to Take Action." New York Times, October 4, p. B1.

Nee, Victor, and Jimy Sanders. 1987. "Limits of Ethnic Solidarity in the Enclave Economy." American Sociological Review 52(6): 745–73.

New York Industrial Retention Network (NYIRN). 2001. The Garment Center: Still in Fashion. New York: NYIRN.

Phillips Preiss, Shapiro Associates, and Asian Americans For Equality (AAFE). 2004. *America's Chinatown: A Community Plan.* New York: AAFE.

Portes, Alejandro, and Robert L. Bach. 1985. *The Latin Journey: Cuban and Mexican Immigrants in the United States.* Berkeley: University of California Press.

Portes, Alejandro, and Leif Jensen. 1989. "The Enclave and the Entrants: Patterns of Ethnic Enterprise in Miami Before and After Mariel." *American Sociological Review* 57(3): 929–49.

Waldinger, Roger. 1986. *Through the Eye of the Needle: Immigrants and Enterprise in New York's Garment Trades.* New York: New York University Press.

Wilson, Kenneth, and Alejandro Portes. 1980. "Immigrant Enclaves: An Analysis of the Labor Market Experiences of Cubans in Miami." *American Journal of Sociology* 86(2, September): 295–319.

Wyatt, Edward. 2002. "At Ground Zero, a New Divide; Some of 9/11's Neediest Get the Least Government Aid." *New York Times,* June 5, p. B1.

Zhou, Min. 1992. *Chinatown: The Socioeconomic Potential of an Urban Enclave.* Philadelphia: Temple University Press.

———. 2001. *Chinese: Divergent Destinies in Immigrant New York.* In *New Immigrants in New York,* edited by Nancy Foner. New York: Columbia University Press.

CHAPTER 8

Of Hardship and Hostility: The Impact of 9/11 on New York City Taxi Drivers

Monisha Das Gupta

WHEN I asked New York City yellow cab drivers to describe how their business had changed since the September 11, 2001, attack on the World Trade Center (WTC), a Bangladeshi driver expressed a sentiment shared by many of the drivers: "Before 9/11, it was beautiful. We enjoyed our job. We made some money. I would help my parents financially. I couldn't complain. Everything was fine. Now the job, people in the street, customers, neighbors—all the people have changed." As a researcher who has been studying New York City's taxi industry since 1996 (Das Gupta 2001; forthcoming), I was jolted by the contrast the drivers drew between pre- and post-9/11 conditions. After all, before 9/11 drivers worked long hours for poor pay in an occupation with one of the highest rates of homicide and a high incidence of police brutality (see Advani 1997; Davar 1995; Esser et al. 1999; Zia 2000, 195–223).[1] As a veteran driver observed about 9/11, "Good conditions in this industry are bad, and then it goes from bad to worse."

After 9/11, drivers reported a severe drop in income, increased financial worries, a sharp rise in hostility from passengers, and a resulting decrease in the pleasure they got out of their work. All of these factors increased their levels of tension about work, money, and personal safety. Drivers also worried about their families' economic security and safety in South Asia and the Middle East. In addition to these emotional costs, quantitative and qualitative data collected for this study show that drivers had not recovered the initial loss in income even a year after the disaster. To make matters worse, yellow cab drivers, like other low-income workers (see Chin, this volume), have had difficulty in qualifying and applying for relief (AAFNY 2002).

Despite these acute difficulties, 9/11 did not induce an entirely new crisis. Rather, it brought to a head preexisting problems in the taxi industry. This chapter links drivers' 9/11-related woes to the anti-immigrant and anti-labor policies and anti-Muslim rhetoric of New York City government agencies. Moving away from treating discrimination as a matter of backward attitudes or overtly bigoted acts, this analysis draws on frameworks that treat race, class, ethnicity, and citizenship as organizing principles, and inequalities based on these categories as institutional (Glenn 2002; Omi and Winant 1994; Wellman 1993). I argue that the rise in the levels of violence[2] that drivers experienced and their economic losses derived in large part from two developments: the industry's transition to leasing in the 1970s and punitive policies in the 1990s that promoted negative images of an increasingly immigrant and predominantly Muslim workforce. By the late 1990s the workforce was estimated to be 60 percent South Asian, 85 percent Muslim, and 95 percent immigrant.

The sociologist Kai Erikson (1994) argues that both disaster and trauma can be better understood by blurring the line between chronic conditions and acute events. Studies in this volume suggest, as I do, that 9/11 exacerbated already existing trends. Although drivers experienced 9/11 as a crisis, they also understood that the magnitude of its impact was related to city policies and public perceptions of taxi workers that predated the event itself. Policies regulating drivers in the 1990s, for instance, depicted them as putting public safety at risk. These representations inflected post-9/11 violence. South Asian and Middle Eastern[3] drivers, already under duress from police brutality and muggings, faced an anti-immigrant and anti-Muslim backlash from passengers, people on the streets, and neighbors, many of whom conflated Muslims and immigrants with terrorists. To make sense of the violence and the economic crisis, this chapter examines the ways in which structural inequalities configured the experiences of taxi drivers after 9/11.

Seen through the eyes of yellow cab drivers, 9/11 produced neither a monolithic nor a newly unified community of survivors, and this perspective calls into question the dominant narrative of solidarity that followed the event. Class, national, and racial divisions were not leveled by the disaster. Instead, they structured post-disaster solidarity and community formation. Some disaster theorists complicate models of post-disaster solidarity as a phase of recovery (for solidarity models, see Barton 1969; Fritz 1961; Hoffman 1999; Pennebaker and Harber 1993; Wolfenstein 1957). They either insist that responses to disasters are culturally specific and local (Oliver-Smith 1999; Stein 2002) or reject the idea of a "city of comrades" by tracing the fault lines that divide those affected from those spared, or those harmed from those responsible for the harm (Erikson 1994). These critiques, however, take a behavioral rather than a structural approach (for trauma studies' neglect of race until recently, see Cvetkovich 2003, 119). Thus, they have largely neglected the systemic hierarchies that shape precrisis conditions and in turn inform survivors' experiences of and responses to disasters at every stage. As the feminist scholar Elaine Enarson (1998) has argued in the case for gendering disasters, structural locations inform not only the degree to which certain social groups are vulnerable but also how they respond to disaster.

METHOD

The chapter draws on a survey of forty-five drivers and semistructured interviews with twenty more. The post-9/11 quantitative and qualitative data pertain to the first year of the disaster. All participants in the study were male. The survey was designed in collaboration with the New York Taxi Workers Alliance (NYTWA), which organizes yellow cab drivers and currently has five thousand members.[4] Four NYTWA driver-members and two members of the staff administered the survey face to face with participants between July and November 2002. Since the drivers did not have a fixed workplace, participants were recruited at South Asian restaurants on Lexington Avenue in Manhattan and at the LaGuardia and JFK Airport holding lots, where taxis wait to get in line to pick up passengers. Thirty-nine drivers were recruited at these locations; the remaining six were members of the NYTWA. The nonrandom sample resulting from locational constraints led to the oversampling of South Asians, who make up 60 percent of the workforce but were 77 percent of those surveyed. The 25 to 30 percent of this workforce (depending on its size) who own their cabs was undersampled: only four agreed to participate in the survey. Sixty-three percent of those surveyed were lease drivers. Thirty-three (73 percent) were Muslim. Unfortunately, there were no Middle Eastern drivers among those surveyed (for the breakdown of drivers by nationality and religion, see tables 8.1 and 8.2). Survey participants had driven for an average of eight and a half years.

The survey asked questions about the economics of the industry, safety issues, emergency relief, and demographics. The economics section was designed to compile data between September 2000 and March 2002 on operating costs, meter bookings (total fares on the meter at the end of a shift), daily trips with passengers, weekly trips to the airport and lower Manhattan, hours worked, methods of lease payment, and leasing or ownership arrangements. For each year data were collected under three time periods—spring, summer, and fall. To capture the immediate impact of the September 11 attacks, week-by-week data were collected for the period between September 11 and October

TABLE 8.1   NATIONAL ORIGIN OF DRIVERS (SELF-REPORTED)

Country of Origin	Surveys	Interviews
Afghanistan	1	1
Bangladesh	9	4
Egypt	1	1
Ghana	1	
Guinea	1	
Haiti	3	1
India	6	1
Nigeria	1	
Pakistan	19	5
Palestine		1
Puerto Rico	1	
United States	2	2
West Africa		4

Source: Author's compilation.

10, 2001. Operating costs and meter bookings were collected for drivers' last full shift.

The qualitative data were collected through semistructured interviews I conducted in August 2002. Participants had taken part in my pilot studies, were referred to me by the NYTWA, or had agreed to talk to me when I met them riding cabs in the city. Half of my interviewees were NYTWA members. I asked drivers about pre- and post-9/11 conditions at work and about emergency relief, and I asked for their thoughts on how the industry might recover

TABLE 8.2   RELIGION OF DRIVERS (SELF-REPORTED)

Religion	Surveys
Buddhist	1
Catholic	2
Christian	2
Hindu	2
Muslim	33
None	2
Sikh	3

Source: Author's compilation.

from the crisis. The drivers were eager to tell their stories and met me at the end of twelve-hour day shifts or before their night shifts. Still others took time in the middle of the workday to talk with me. All of them wanted the research to yield concrete outcomes that would improve their conditions at work.

INDUSTRY AND POLICY BACKGROUND

Yellow taxicabs, livery (or car service) cabs, and black cars (or limos) are all part of the taxi industry. To become a commercially operable vehicle, a taxi must have a medallion license, which ranged in price from $220,000 (for an individual license) to $253,000 (for a corporate license) in early 2003 (Schaller Consulting 2003, 2). Until recently, the city restricted the number of medallions to 12,187. Starting in 2004, the industry's regulatory body, the Taxi and Limousine Commission (TLC 2002c), was allowed for the first time since 1997 to issue 300 new medallions each year for three years in order to generate revenue for the city and respond to the increase in taxi ridership. The prices of medallions auctioned in 2004 increased to $292,600 for individual licenses and $344,000 for corporate ones (Lipton 2003; Schaller Consulting 2003, 25–26; 2004, 1–2).

The current structure of the taxi industry emerged in 1971 when the TLC was established as a mayoral agency in charge of licensing drivers and regulating all components of the industry. As part of its regulatory functions, the commission enforces rules and adjudicates violations. In 1995 the city, under then-mayor Rudolph Giuliani, transferred the enforcement of rules to a new taxi unit within the New York Police Department (NYPD). This transfer was accompanied by increased reports of police brutality against drivers (CAAAV 1996, 3).

Between 1971 and 1979, the city reorganized the taxi industry by converting taxi drivers from unionized workers who earned a commission on fares to independent contractors who lost such workers' benefits as health insurance, unemployment and disability insurance, and pension. In 1979, leasing, which had been outlawed in 1937, was legalized (Schaller Consulting 2003, 25). Garages and brokers began buying up medallions to lease them for a fee. The number of owner-driven cabs consequently dropped. In 2003, there were only 3,400 owner-drivers (Schaller Consulting 2003, 33). Since there are over 40,000 licensed drivers, of whom 18,000 to 20,000 are on the road (Strozier 1998a; Desai 2002), most drivers leased medallions or medallions and cabs from garage owners or brokers. Lease drivers lease cabs and medallions daily, weekly, or monthly. Forty-four percent of cabs are leased weekly or monthly, and 27 percent daily (Schaller Consulting 2003, 2). The fees that drivers pay to garages or brokers for medallions and cabs are called "leases" in industry jargon. Some lease drivers lease only the medallion, paying monthly installments on their car if they do not already own it. The leasing system has in effect transferred the risks of the business to drivers. Whether business is bad or not, garages and brokers are assured of their income because drivers have to pay their lease in advance. The driver-to-medallion ratio has also led to the organization of work into two twelve-hour shifts so that the same medallion cab can be leased out twice in twenty-four hours.

The work conditions accompanying the lease system have deteriorated as drivers work longer hours, earn poorer returns, and receive no benefits. Worsening conditions have led in turn to a demographic shift in the workforce since the 1980s. Taxi driving has become an "immigrant" job: 95 percent of yellow cab drivers are first-generation immigrants from countries in South Asia, East Asia, the Middle East, the Caribbean, West and East Africa, and Eastern Europe. Increased reliance on immigrants to fill low-paying jobs in the expanding service sectors is part of the large-scale deindustrialization and economic restructuring in the United States (López-Garza and Diaz 2001; Sassen 1998). The shift from U.S.-born whites and African Americans to immigrants in the taxi industry was accompanied by the TLC's hyperregulation of immigrant drivers in the 1990s on the premise that they had little skill, did not know the city, and had little respect for traffic rules. The intensity of ticketing by the NYPD increased during the 1990s. For most TLC violations, drivers are summoned to a mandatory hearing in the TLC's taxi court system. Along with stepped-up enforcement, rules and fines have become more elaborate since the mid-1990s.

Understanding the significance of the industry's restructuring is critical in contextualizing the hardships that drivers faced after 9/11. First, under the leasing system, most drivers had to make their payments even though their fares plummeted in the first five weeks of the disaster. Second, because drivers were no longer technically workers but independent contractors, those who could not work in the wake of 9/11 were ineligible for unemployment insurance, even if they were documented or citizens. Third, the post-9/11 abuse that drivers encountered was reinforced by the harmful images that the TLC policies had painted of the workforce.

"BUSINESS IS BAD": SHORT-TERM LOSSES, LONG-TERM EFFECTS

After 9/11, drivers' earnings dropped both in the short and long run. More than half of the drivers surveyed and all of the drivers interviewed said that their savings had dwindled or disappeared and their personal debts had escalated as a result. These drivers fell behind not only in lease, car, and medallion payments but also in rent, other bills, and remittances to families abroad. Even a year after the disaster, drivers had not recovered from the initial losses. The

TABLE 8.3   ECONOMIC IMPACT OF 9/11 ON NEW YORK CITY TAXI DRIVERS

Per Shift	Pre-9/11 Average	Disaster Month 2001 Average	October to December 2001 Average	January to March 2002 Average	Last Full Shift 2002 Average
Income	$88.75	$1.05	$29.16	$40.56	$62.03
Operating costs	105.44	98.42	103.41	101.58	112.05
Meter bookings	194.19	99.47	132.57	142.14	174.08
Number of hours worked	9.42	8.06	8.65	9.20	9.30
Number of trips with passengers	27.00	14.31	17.51	19.65	n.a.[a]
Number of airport trips	9.87	1.33	3.00	4.00	n.a.

Source: Author's survey conducted between July and November 2002.
Note: n.a. = not applicable.
[a]No data were collected on trips for the last full shift.

first few weeks of reduced or deficit income, in other words, had long-term consequences.

Drivers surveyed between July and November 2002 reported a 30 percent reduction in their income from pre-9/11 averages. On average, they were making $62.03 per shift compared with $88.75 before 9/11. Average incomes, meter bookings, and number of trips with passengers slowly increased between October 2001 and November 2002, but they were far from climbing back to pre-9/11 levels (see table 8.3). Even though most drivers had returned to working the same number of hours per shift by October 2001, and some worked more shifts than usual, they were making less money.

For drivers, losses during the week of 9/11 and the three weeks that followed were the most severe (see table 8.4). The losses resulted from a combination of the drastic drop in fares, shorter hours of work, and fewer shifts worked during this period. Drivers making weekly and monthly lease payments needed to meet costs even though they lost days at work. Their negative income in the week of 9/11 is attributable to their operating costs surpassing what they earned.

Bridge and Tunnel Closings

In the three days after 9/11, most drivers could not go to work because of bridge and tunnel closings. Drivers who were out on the street when the WTC was hit described being trapped in the city as all arteries connecting Manhat-

TABLE 8.4   IMMEDIATE ECONOMIC IMPACT OF 9/11 ON NEW YORK CITY TAXI DRIVERS: SEPTEMBER 4 TO OCTOBER 10, 2001

Per Shift	Pre-9/11 Week (9/4 to 9/10) Average	9/11 Week (9/11 to 9/17) Average	9/18 to 9/24 Average	9/25 to 10/2 Average	10/3 to 10/10 Average
Income	$83.67	–$17.01	$2.89	$8.83	$9.49
Operating costs	103.08	89.58	95.05	101.54	107.52
Meter bookings	186.75	72.57	97.94	110.37	117.01
Number of hours worked	9.40	6.16	8.29	8.69	9.09
Number of trips with passengers	27.43	10.14	14.00	15.86	17.26
Number of airport passengers	8.82	0.11	1.48	1.19	2.52

Source: Author's survey conducted between July and November 2002.

tan to the outer boroughs and New Jersey were ordered closed. They recounted difficulties in returning their cars to their garages or night-shift partners. Drivers who lived outside Manhattan or whose garages or partners were in the outer boroughs had no option but to park their cabs in safe neighborhoods and find their way home. Drivers in the outer boroughs could not get to Manhattan because the Brooklyn, Manhattan, and Williamsburg Bridges and the Holland Tunnel were closed (Kennedy 2001a; Barry 2001). A September 13, 2001, *New York Times* story reported that taxis "were still extremely sparse for a weekday" and that the bridge and tunnel closings had prevented many taxis from coming into Manhattan (Kennedy 2001a). Since drivers with weekly or monthly schedules had paid their leases in advance, they lost money on the days they could not work.

Fear of Reprisal

The fear of reprisal for the deaths at the WTC discouraged South Asian and Middle Eastern Muslims and Sikhs in the study from going to work in the first week of the disaster. Reports of anti-Muslim and anti-immigrant violence made many drivers fear for their bodily safety. Most drivers, however, returned to work out of necessity after the first week, although a few drivers stayed away for two weeks to as long as two months.

South Asian drivers were persuaded not to go to work by fearful family members in the United States and abroad, as well as by coworkers, friends, and even dispatchers at the garages where they leased their cars. In her ethnography of South Asian Muslims in New York, Aminah Mohammed-Arif (2002) notes the immediate panic and fear that spread in the Muslim, Arab Christian, and South Asian Hindu and Sikh communities following the attack. Drivers in this study said they heard that coworkers were beaten in Manhattan the day after the WTC collapsed, and friends told of unpleasant encounters with passengers. News of a Sikh man being beaten with a baseball bat in Richmond Hill, Queens, along with stories of South Asian and Middle Eastern civilians being profiled, mistreated, and detained, terrified the South Asian drivers (see Idupuganti 2001; Singh 2002; on post-9/11 hate crimes, see Lee 2002). A Bangladeshi night driver who decided to go to work on 9/11 described how a passenger flagged him down, but on seeing his name on the hack license flew out of the taxi saying, "You Muslims did this." Such public conflation of Muslims with terrorists and media reports about the involvement of Afghanistan and Pakistan in the WTC attacks filled South Asian drivers with apprehension.

From the moment the second WTC tower was hit, the South Asian and Middle Eastern drivers interviewed said they anticipated a backlash. A Bangladeshi driver working downtown the morning of 9/11 said, "When the second plane hit, I clearly understood it was planned and predetermined.... I was very afraid. I started to think that we come from another country. When the Middle East started coming on the news, I knew that we looked alike and would be targeted." Thus, South Asian and Middle Eastern drivers felt vulnerable—an emotional state they shared with people across the nation (Ellis 2002), but for different reasons. The fear of being targeted kept the South Asian drivers from venturing out, even into their own neighborhoods. Another Bangladeshi driver likened those days of being confined in his apartment to "house arrest."

Traffic

When drivers returned to work, they contended with street closings, time-limited openings of certain thoroughfares, reroutings, and security checks. Gridlock and extraordinary traffic delays were widely reported as one of the many 9/11-related woes with which New Yorkers struggled (Barry 2001; Kennedy 2001b; 2002a; 2002b; Hanley 2001). Those drivers in the survey who reported working shorter hours in the four weeks after the disaster cited bad traffic as one reason. Traffic-related challenges continued to plague drivers in the long term. In the year following the attacks, sudden street closings and reroutings continued to choke the roads in a city where even before 9/11 congestion in the central business district had been estimated to cost the city $1 billion annually (Kennedy 2002a; 2002c).

For drivers, the phrase "time is money" is more than just an aphorism. Drivers explained that their business depended on being able to move through the city as quickly as possible, picking up as many fares as they could. In the first month after 9/11, drivers lost income negotiating bumper-to-bumper traffic when taking passengers downtown or to the outer boroughs. They reported inordinate delays on the Manhattan, Brooklyn, and Williamsburg Bridges. Yet they could not refuse passengers going to these congested areas without risking being fined and having their licenses revoked under TLC regulations. Drivers took the risk of wasting their shift sitting in traffic rather than being put out of work for violating the rules.

No Breaks in Payments

Despite the difficult conditions drivers faced when they returned to work, many garages and brokers did not reduce payments on leases or cars, thereby compounding the drivers' financial hardship. Eighteen out of twenty drivers interviewed said they got no breaks from their garage or broker on payments. Among the forty-five surveyed, twenty-two out of the thirty-eight who worked the week after 9/11 got small breaks. This form of aid dropped sharply the next week, when only four drivers received a break. Thus, the discounts that drivers got were partial and small. They still had to make the bulk of their payments at a time when they were losing money because they were not going to work and the number of their fares was sharply reduced. This dimension of their economic hardship was directly related to the restructuring of the taxi industry in the 1970s. As independent contractors, drivers had to meet the cost of being in business, no matter what.

Drivers who were working during the day on 9/11 had to pay their full lease even though a number of drivers asked their garages for a reduction. Most received no more than two or three paid fares that day, amounting to twenty-five to thirty dollars. Many drivers stopped their meters and gave free rides to pedestrians and emergency workers. Drivers who paid their leases daily and could not return their vehicles to garages at the end of their shift because of bridge and tunnel closings were charged for the next shift. One African driver who was forced to abandon his taxi in the Bronx, on realizing that he would be charged for another shift, spent the entire day on September 12 getting the car back to the garage in Queens.

Weekly lessees had already put their money down for the week and in most cases did not get a discount. Unable to do business, those drivers who were making monthly car and medallion lease payments and owner-drivers who were buying their medallions in installments were similarly affected. Because drivers depend on their meter bookings to make their payments, having no income spells economic disaster. Many withdrew money from their meager savings accounts or charged their credit cards to make their payments. Some drivers were forced to borrow money from friends or family.

Decreased Fares

To explain their drop in income, drivers repeatedly said, "Business after 9/11 is bad." By this they meant that fewer New Yorkers were riding taxis. There were fewer tourists in town, and trips to the airports declined sharply (see table 8.3). The WTC disaster struck at a time when drivers were entering a busy season after slow summer months. The summer of 2001 had been slower than usual because of the economic recession that had started in January (Parrott and Cooke 2002). Drivers went into September hoping that business would pick up. Instead, they were faced with a recession that worsened as air transport and tourism—sectors that drivers depended on for business—were hard hit. It is also worth noting that fares, which are regulated by the TLC, remained at 1996 levels (Cuza 2002), despite higher leases and gas costs.

Drivers said that they depended on New Yorkers for about 80 percent of their fares and that most fares travel in Manhattan between Fifty-fourth Street and Battery Park. On a daily average before 9/11, a driver picked up one or two fares worth ten to twelve dollars from the Upper East Side to the WTC. That business disappeared in the first month after the disaster. Even as some semblance of normalcy was restored downtown, traffic on parts of Canal Street and West Street and in the Battery Tunnel continued to be restricted (Hanley 2001; Kennedy 2002b), making it difficult for drivers to get back the lower Manhattan share of their fares.

Describing the pace of business before 9/11, cab drivers talked about rushed New Yorkers who had their arms raised to hail a taxi even before stepping out of the revolving doors of skyscrapers and onto the sidewalks. How much money drivers made thus depended on moving quickly through Manhattan to get passengers to their destinations on time and then picking up new customers right away. Most drivers in the study had experienced the financial boom on Wall Street, which was the city's fastest-growing sector during the economic expansion of the 1990s (Parrott and Cooke 2002, 7). A night driver recalled a "let the good times roll" attitude among his Wall Street passengers, who were willing to "throw money around." Overflowing bars and restaurants and a high volume of nighttime passengers marked those days. After 9/11, Wall Street, on which the city increasingly depended for its economic well-being, was especially affected.

Drivers had started noticing the effects of the economic recession that had set in by January 2001, and the accompanying drop in spending power. But after the disaster it was much worse; drivers spoke of a far more sober and thrifty New York. They attributed the decline in business to job losses in the wake of 9/11. New York City lost 131,300 jobs altogether in 2001, and 73,900 of those jobs disappeared in the fourth quarter of that year. The fourth-quarter losses were related directly to the WTC attack (Parrott and Cooke 2002, 13).

Night drivers, who were used to Manhattan and parts of Brooklyn never going to sleep, described New York as a dead city after midnight in the months that followed the attacks. With too few fares, many night drivers reported returning their taxis by 2:00 A.M. instead of 5:00 A.M. Day drivers made similar observations. In the words of one driver, "People are losing jobs. When you know that your job can be gone, you will hold on to your savings. You'll travel by train rather than by taxi." Passengers who did ride taxis were tipping less. This reported austerity on the part of New Yorkers is consistent with the finding that consumer spending in New York City dropped sharply after 9/11 (Parrott and Cooke 2002, 13).

Both day and night drivers depend on tourists, particularly during the summer months, when business from New Yorkers, many of whom go away on vacation, drops. Day drivers rely more heavily on tourists than night drivers, and they complained bitterly about the hit that tourism had taken. In 2001 the city, which generates more national tourism revenue than any other metropolitan area, lost $1.6 billion in this sector (DRI-WEFA 2002). Both domestic and international tourism suffered. Furthermore, New York City was projected to suffer the worst decline in absolute terms in international travel and spending receipts between 2000 and 2002. Veteran drivers, referring to the summer of 2002, said they had not seen a leaner season since 1991, also a recession year. Drivers attributed their dismal summer earnings in 2002 to the fear of terrorism that kept tourists away. A day driver noted that the initial swell of patriotism and support for New York that brought people from other parts of the country to the city had subsided by the summer of 2002, and he could no longer count on tourists for a portion of his income.

Though most drivers usually make a few trips a week to one of the area's three major airports—Kennedy, LaGuardia, and Newark—some do the bulk of their business out of the airports. Survey data show a dramatic drop in airport passengers during the month that followed 9/11 (see table 8.4). The WTC attack shut down the airports for three days. Even after the airports reopened, domestic travel was severely affected (Sharkey 2001; Barry 2001). In September 2001, domestic and international travel fell by 30 percent nationwide (*Honolulu Advertiser* 2002). Although some recovery was seen by June 2002, domestic and international travel was 11.4 percent below June 2001 levels (*Honolulu Advertiser* 2002). Given these circumstances and the long waits for passengers at airports, it is not surprising that many drivers reported avoiding trips to the airports or returning to the city empty after dropping off a passenger.

Tickets

Since the 1990s, tickets for traffic, service, and equipment violations have become a constant feature of drivers' lives. Tickets hurt drivers not only because they are hefty and numerous, but also because most TLC violations require drivers to take time off from work to make a mandatory appearance in court for a hearing. While drivers received considerable relief from ticketing in the first three months after the disaster—a period when police were engaged with security and cleanup—they reported that enforcement was stepped up after January 2002.

Drivers gave me detailed accounts of the increase in unfair ticketing in 2002. For example, they said they dreaded dropping off passengers at Grand Central Terminal, which was heavily monitored by NYPD's taxi unit after 9/11. A number of drivers interviewed complained that they got a $250 ticket if they were caught dropping off passengers at the terminal in what the officer on duty marked as the "wrong" lane. Even veteran drivers who prided themselves on avoiding frequent ticketing said that however careful they were driving in the city, they were often ticketed. When asked what was different about post-9/11 ticketing, many said that they could no longer ask the ticketing officer for clemency or a reduction in fines. They felt that they were being heavily ticketed to make up for the loss in fines between September 2001 and January

2002 and to reduce the city's budget deficit, which was projected to be between $3 billion and $4 billion in 2002 to 2003 (Parrott 2001).

Dwindling Savings, Escalating Debt, and Unmet Responsibilities

Over the long term, drivers reported depleting their savings and spiraling into
debt. The statement, "I simply didn't take home anything [in the first month]
and I haven't gotten anywhere near caught up," illustrates how drivers related
their longer-term difficulties to the immediate crisis. In the first months more
than half the drivers surveyed went into debt hoping to make up for their
losses with the return of normalcy. By the end of 2002, however, business still
had not normalized.

Survey data show a marked shift in sources of payment for leases from
meter bookings in the week before 9/11 to savings, credit cards, and personal
loans in the weeks that followed. Forty out of forty-five drivers paid their
leases out of meter bookings in the week before the disaster struck, but only
twenty-two did so during the disaster week and twenty-eight in the following
week. By the time the survey was completed in November 2002, 55 percent of
the drivers surveyed reported having fallen behind on credit card bills.

Drivers whose savings were depleted kept borrowing money to cover unanticipated costs or temporary unemployment. Sudden costs from tickets, car
repairs, or temporary disability from work-related injuries and assault, which
had been a part of their jobs before 9/11, further strained drivers' incomes after
the disaster. After 9/11, according to the survey, 52 percent of the drivers lost
time because of backlash-related injuries or damage to their cabs, and 26 percent had to pay for damages to their taxis. A Bangladeshi driver who suffered
eye and head injuries after being punched and beaten by passengers in July
2002 had not been able to go back to work. He pointed to a pile of unpaid
bills when I met him in August 2002, and he worried about not being able to
afford groceries that week. Already in debt because he could not meet his car
payments after 9/11, this driver felt that he had no option but to borrow more
money from his relatives until he could claim his meager workers' compensation.

Despite working additional shifts in the year following the disaster, drivers
found that most days they had little left after covering their operating costs.
With their debt accumulating, their earnings depressed, and no hope of improved business in sight, many drivers questioned how long they would last
in the industry. Since lease drivers cannot work unless they make their payments, many of them failed to meet other financial responsibilities such as
rent, utility bills, and remittances to families abroad. As one North African
driver put it, "The fight is now between paying lease and paying living ex-

penses." Thirty-three percent of the drivers surveyed were behind on rent. Two drivers could not keep their interview appointments with me because they were being evicted. Some drivers found themselves responsible for more than their share of rent because their roommates had lost their jobs and moved out in the wake of 9/11. Drivers were uniformly worried about how to keep a roof over their heads with their reduced incomes.

As immigrant workers, drivers support family members left behind in their home countries. After 9/11, they found it difficult to keep up with these remittances, which are essential for their families' daily survival and go toward paying for siblings' education, births, marriages, funerals, and medical treatment. Among the drivers surveyed, 22 percent said they were behind in sending money home. Being unable to meet these obligations was particularly painful to the drivers because they had immigrated to the United States in the hope of being better able to support their families. One West African driver told me with much anguish that he was responsible for twenty family members back home and had not been able to send any money after 9/11. Drivers reported sleeplessness from constant anxiety about money. While many drivers wanted to leave the taxi business, they felt trapped because they had few viable alternatives for employment. One driver said, "I think every day that I have to change my job. But I don't know how I will survive if I leave driving."

The Need for Structural Change in the Taxi Industry

Even though the disaster has caused drivers to despair, it has also mobilized them to become their own advocates, which is a common and constructive post-disaster response that researchers encourage institutions to utilize (Oliver-Smith 1999). The economic crisis that the majority of drivers in the industry have faced since 9/11 has catalyzed long-standing demands that the NYTWA has made on the TLC to increase fares and lower lease payments in order to increase the margin of drivers' take-home income. In 2003, the NYTWA's lease-fare campaign gathered momentum and support, with its membership rising to 5,000 from 3,700 in 2001. Responding to drivers' demand for a living wage, the TLC approved a 26 percent fare increase in May 2004 and increased the lease cap only by 8 percent (Luo 2004; Schaller Consulting 2004, 16).[5]

The direct and immediate impact of 9/11 on drivers' livelihoods can be traced to road closings for security reasons and emergency work, increased congestion, loss of business in lower Manhattan, the downturn in the air transport and tourism sectors, and the fear of reprisals that kept some drivers home. But these reasons do not explain why drivers had not recovered from their losses a year later. Preexisting conditions in the industry related to leasing as well as the continued recession have made it hard for drivers to recover. The current recession, though not as severe as the 1989 to 1992 downturn in some respects, has been characterized by a higher rate of job loss and a flimsier safety net for unemployed workers (Parrott and Cooke 2002). This has increased the vulnerability of all workers. However, workers' ability to cope with these developments depends on how their occupation is structured and how they are positioned in the labor market. Taxi drivers work in an industry in which leases are high and fares artificially depressed—conditions the city has begun to address only recently. In order to work, drivers have to pay their operating costs up front without the assurance of earning back what they have paid. After 9/11, these conditions magnified drivers' economic insecurity. Short-term losses, long-term income reduction, and accumulating debts further marginalized these immigrants who work in the lower rungs of the service sector and have few economic alternatives.

Relief

Drivers have had problems gaining access to federal and private disaster assistance, despite their 9/11-related economic hardship. The initially narrow delineation of the geographical area affected by the attack posed obstacles. So did the exclusion of permanent residents from certain forms of public assistance and the formal status of taxi drivers as self-employed independent contractors.[6] The U.S. Department of Labor excluded New York City and Washington, D.C., cab drivers from disaster unemployment insurance on the grounds that they were not technically workers; many other agencies followed suit. Additionally, the Federal Emergency Management Agency (FEMA) initially denied direct monetary relief to yellow cab drivers because their income was not solely dependent on the delineated disaster area—lower Manhattan. These restrictions deprived thousands of small business owners and workers in Chinatown of FEMA assistance (AAFNY 2002). Criticism from labor advocates, including the NYTWA, lawmakers, and community organizations, led FEMA to alter its guidelines and expand the area covered in June 2002 (Chen 2002a).[7]

These new guidelines, however, did not lead to a significant increase in applications from drivers, many of whom were demoralized by the initial denial of assistance. Even after FEMA expanded its geographical definition of the affected area, assistance was limited to citizens, permanent residents, or those who had U.S.-born children, and assistance could only be used toward rent or mortgage. Eligible drivers found the paperwork overwhelming. Of forty-five drivers surveyed, only seventeen (38 percent) had applied for relief. Among the twenty drivers interviewed, four had applied for FEMA assistance before June 2002. Three of these drivers were rejected for assistance; two reapplied after the guidelines were revised. Those who did not apply for relief cited the initial ineligibility of yellow cab drivers for assistance. Unlike black car drivers who served Wall Street, yellow cab drivers could not meet the "Fourteenth Street and below" criterion for their business.

The exclusion of drivers from much-needed assistance needs to be placed in the context of their efforts to provide relief to others after 9/11. According to the TLC, for three months after the disaster yellow cab drivers gave five thousand free rides to grieving family members of victims, rescue workers, and other volunteers at Ground Zero (Desai 2002). When talking about their offers of free rides, drivers proudly identified themselves as New Yorkers who needed to rise to the occasion and support those who were suffering. Yet, other than certificates from the TLC, they received little public recognition for their efforts, which would have countered the all-too-frequent image of drivers as callous and reckless foreigners.[8]

South Asian, Middle Eastern, and West African drivers who ferried relief workers from point to point, sometimes through bad traffic, spoke of their efforts as an obvious human response to the crisis they were witnessing. "For us," said a West African driver, "that was the only way to help. We were not doing well, but we did our best by giving people free rides." Another West African driver, who was unemployed when I interviewed him and in ill health from respiratory problems that had worsened from the air pollution produced by the WTC collapse, said:

I stood in line to pick up volunteers for 9/11. A *lot* of drivers picked up people. They put signs on their windows. That means we care about the community. Anything New York City faces, we face. We picked up people: ten-dollar rides for free; fifteen-dollar rides for free. We did this for not one week but a long time. Lease drivers volunteered their time! We talked to the rescue workers nice. We gave them more courage telling them they were doing a great job.

Drivers had served the city at a time when they were financially hurting. To be turned away from assistance on the grounds that they were yellow cab drivers disillusioned them. The majority of drivers interviewed said that they were discouraged by the lack of reciprocity, which was a factor in their reluctance to apply for aid. Initial denials of assistance on the part of relief agencies damaged what Erikson (1994, 232, 239) calls "the texture of community" woven "at least in part of trust and respect and decency, and in moments of crisis, of charity and concern."

Since June 2002, the chances of drivers applying for and being approved under FEMA's Mortgage and Rental Assistance (MRA) program have increased. Although drivers would have preferred general cash assistance—not just help with rent and mortgage—as self-employed independent contractors, they were disqualified from receiving many types of assistance that those who are technically workers can receive. The MRA program helped eligible drivers who were on the verge of eviction. But because relief was restricted to rental assistance, those drivers who met FEMA's 25 percent income reduction criterion but had avoided falling behind on rent received no help.

Citizenship or legal residency requirements for FEMA assistance deterred many drivers from applying even after the relaxation of FEMA's criteria. FEMA guidelines state that only U.S. citizens and permanent residents are eligible for any cash assistance (FEMA 2002b). Nonqualified persons whose children were U.S. citizens could seek cash and noncash assistance provided that they met other application requirements. At a time when immigrants, including South Asian Muslims, have been detained and deported, even legal immigrants and naturalized citizens have felt apprehensive about inviting any scrutiny of their status. Citizenship and residency requirements have left out those who are undocumented, a particularly vulnerable group of people who have almost no access to disaster-related federal assistance (Navarro 2002). Pressures to exclude undocumented immigrants from federal disaster relief and private donations are not new (Chavez 1997, 63, 64). After 9/11, only through advocacy have the families of undocumented workers who died in the WTC been recognized as valid recipients of aid from the federal September 11 Victims Fund if they can provide evidence that their family member worked there, a difficult enough task (Henriques and Barstow 2001). Beyond making an exception for undocumented victims, no steps have been taken to address the economic distress of those undocumented workers—among them taxi drivers—who form the backbone of many businesses and services in New York City.

Even after the revisions, FEMA's evidentiary requirements for establishing a drop in income and an inability to pay rent or mortgage were exceedingly narrow and required considerable paperwork. Each of the four FEMA application forms for MRA had to be submitted with supporting documents. Under the new guidelines, a driver needed to establish a 25 percent decline in income by providing pre- and post-9/11 trip sheets. Along with such proof, drivers had to produce an eviction notice or proof of late payment or delinquency on rent or mortgage. Rent payment made with credit cards or loans also needed to be documented. Drivers found the paperwork overwhelming. Many did not have the type of documentation needed. A South Asian driver who paid his rent on time from his savings and a West African driver who was uncomfortable asking his friends to document the rent money they had loaned him felt that these practices disqualified them. The mismatch between drivers' needs and FEMA's evidentiary requirements continues to leave the neediest people without support. Disheartened and frustrated, most drivers have decided that the only way to recoup their losses is to work a full shift every day of the week, regardless of the toll such a grueling routine takes on their bodies.

"GO BACK WHERE YOU CAME FROM": ANTI-IMMIGRANT AND ANTI-MUSLIM HOSTILITY

After 9/11, taxi drivers from South Asia and the Middle East were confronted with an anti-immigrant and anti-Muslim backlash before they could recover from their own shock and grief. The fact that they were a part of a majority-Muslim, majority-immigrant workforce and earned a living by traversing public space made them particularly visible and vulnerable. Nationally, gas stations, convenience or grocery stores, and restaurants—workplaces where South Asian and Middle Eastern Americans are concentrated—were targets of 9/11-related violence (Singh 2002, 14; Lee 2002).[9] As an occupation with one of the highest homicide rates, the taxi business has never offered a safe workplace. Before 9/11, taxi drivers routinely protested police brutality and lack of protection from muggings. After 9/11, they complained more about the violence that South Asian and Middle Eastern drivers faced from passengers who expressed their anger against Muslims and immigrants and associated them with terrorism. As elaborated in this section, while African and Anglo-American drivers remembered sympathetic passengers, South Asian and Middle Eastern drivers recalled few such instances because the overt hostility of some passengers left them too afraid to discuss 9/11 even with those who were friendly. Taking into account the extent of the abuse that drivers faced well into 2002 requires reassessing claims (see Mohammed-Arif 2002, 269) that 9/11-related incidents were low in the city, particularly in Manhattan, in comparison with the rest of the country.

The exposure of New York City taxi drivers to violence in the year that followed 9/11 was facilitated by public policies governing the taxi industry in the 1990s. These policies sent out an anti-immigrant message by criminalizing drivers and representing them as threats to public safety. The policies empowered passengers at the expense of drivers. It was in this preexisting environment that post-9/11 hostility erupted.

Drivers faced a range of hostile acts. They were verbally harassed, assaulted, and cheated out of fares. Some passengers boycotted South Asian or Middle Eastern drivers, refusing to ride with them in order to protest terrorism. Even when dealing with polite passengers, drivers observed a new vigilance on the part of these riders, who took note of their names and appearance. People on the street yelled at drivers, threw trash at their vehicles, spit at them or their taxis, broke windshields and mirrors, and slashed tires. All these acts taken together inflicted physical injury; incurred economic loss as a result of damage to property and time lost from work; and were psychologically damaging to drivers, who felt betrayed, fearful, and humiliated.

Of the forty-five drivers surveyed, 60 percent reported experiencing some form of backlash. Verbal harassment was the most commonly reported form of abuse (51 percent). Thirty-one percent said they were physically threatened; 26 percent said that people threatened to damage their cabs; 22 percent said that their cabs were indeed damaged; and 11 percent said that they were physically harmed. The violence fell along national and religious lines. Muslims were disproportionately targeted, and among those who participated in the study, Pakistanis and Bangladeshis bore the brunt of the violence. All of the South Asian Muslims we interviewed reported several incidents over the span of a year.

Interestingly, West African Muslim drivers said that they were spared because they are racialized as black in the United States. A few drivers said that they tried to hide their affiliation with Islam. Two drivers, a Palestinian and a Pakistani, passed themselves off as Greek, while an Afghan said he avoided telling his passengers where he was from. "If I tell them I'm from Afghanistan, [I fear] they will kill me right away without any judgment," he said. "But I am not a criminal or terrorist. I know the consequences. I try not to answer the question." This driver's fears are particularly poignant because he lost family members in the Taliban's purges. A Pakistani driver said that many of his compatriots were passing as Indian, partly because American media coverage cast India as a willing partner in the "war against terrorism," making it a safer country to cite.

In the face of the WTC deaths and destruction, New York resident and Arab American scholar Moustafa Bayoumi (2002, 83) notes, "for a moment, it felt that the trauma of suffering—not the exercise of reason, not the belief in any God, not the universal consumption of a fizzy drink, but the simple and tragic reality that it hurts when we feel pain—was understood as the thread that connects all of humanity." Such a shared experience of trauma can form new, if temporary, communities in which previous divisions disappear (Erikson 1994, 230–32; Hoffman 1999; Oliver-Smith 1999). But South Asian and Middle Eastern drivers, traumatized like other New Yorkers and determined to battle with the magnitude of the disaster, found their membership in these communities to be short-lived. On 9/11, a Pakistani driver who gave free rides all day was abused in his neighborhood when he returned home late that night. A group of young men threw eggs at him and called him a "terrorist." As the days went on, drivers were troubled by the discrepancy between their volunteer efforts and their treatment as enemies of the nation by suspicious passengers and neighbors. In Coney Island, which has a large Pakistani community, drivers reported seeing posters that spread hatred against "Arabs" and "Muslims" within days of the disaster, as well as a drive-by shooting at a row of Pakistani-owned restaurants (Mohammed-Arif 2002, 269).

In this volume, Irwin Garfinkel and his colleagues, in their analysis of the differential impact of 9/11 on New Yorkers, show that Muslims and immigrants felt particularly vulnerable. This was certainly the case among the taxi drivers we interviewed; those who were likely to be targeted as Muslims felt deeply insecure. Describing his first few days at work, a Bangladeshi driver said, "I was scared to pick up passengers; I was scared to ask anything; I was scared. It felt very difficult; I was always anticipating problems." This apprehension came from not being able to predict how a passenger would react. While West African drivers said that they and their passengers often relived the day when the towers collapsed, South Asian and Middle Eastern drivers did not share such talk with their passengers. Their own caution and reticence about referring to the WTC attack could have discouraged such exchanges. South Asian drivers risked talking about the attacks with their passengers only when they sensed that the passenger was genuinely interested in knowing more about Afghanistan, Pakistan, Bangladesh, or the Middle East. They would use these moments as opportunities to educate their customers, often stopping their meters to finish the conversation.

Punitive Regulations and Consumer Entitlement

The association of Muslims with terrorism that was resuscitated in the wake of 9/11 and the public support for profiling that arose at that time (Kang 2002; Zia 2002) were responsible for much of the backlash that drivers faced. But the level and extent of the violence they encountered can be traced to preexisting public perceptions of yellow cab drivers perpetuated by city policies in the 1990s. Tougher rules and standards issued by the city coincided with the entry of recent immigrants into the taxi industry to replace native-born drivers who left as work conditions deteriorated.

New entrants in the yellow cab industry were predominantly immigrant. For example, between 1992 and 1996, the estimated percentage of South Asians—whose numbers were being tracked by the New York City–based Lease Drivers' Coalition—rose from forty-three to sixty. In response to studies reporting a 40 percent increase in the number of accidents involving yellow cabs, livery cars, and passenger vans between 1990 and 1996, the TLC adopted several policies directed at yellow cab drivers, many of whom were new to the industry and were from "Third World" countries. In the TLC's view, yellow cabs imperiled public safety and civility (Strozier 1998a). Although other factors contributed to these accidents—such as congestion, the hectic pace of the city, passengers' impatience, and drivers' exhaustion from long hours of work—policy decisions focused on monitoring drivers who were seen as accident-prone, lax, and incompetent to drive in a city like New York. A veteran white driver observed, "Cab drivers are demonized supposedly because they are bad drivers but really because they are immigrant, particularly Muslim." In other words, concerns about bad driving revolved around those who drove the cabs.

A passengers' bill of rights, instituted by the TLC in the mid-1990s, entitles riders to a "courteous English-speaking driver who knows Manhattan and the way to major destinations in other boroughs," a radio-free, smoke-free, and incense-free environment, and a scrupulously clean cab (TLC 2002b). If a passenger complains to the TLC and it upholds the complaint—which it frequently does (Barnes 2001)—then the driver pays a fine. Through this seemingly neutral process, a driver's lack of fluency in English, for example, becomes a punishable offense. That the TLC codified courtesy, knowledge of the city, a "silent ride," air quality, and cleanliness as conditions of service at a time when the workforce turned overwhelmingly immigrant evoked and cemented racist and nativist perceptions that immigrant drivers are rude, dirty, noisy, and disrespectful of rules. The bill validates passenger perceptions, circulated through oft-told "taxis from hell" stories, that the industry is dominated by "rude, manic drivers who don't know the city; don't speak English, or equally irritating, speak English with an accent; [and] drive funky-smelling cabs" (Zia 2000, 210). The TLC's rules enact what the critical legal theorist Robert Chang (1999) calls "nativistic racism," a term he uses to capture the specific ways in which immigrants are racialized. Foreign bodies, like bodies perceived as racially different, become potent sites of meaning production. These meanings, then, render foreigners intelligible.

Although drivers in the study supported passengers' right to be protected from unsafe, dishonest, or discourteous cab drivers, they saw the bill as punishing them economically for not speaking good English, not coming across as polite, listening to the radio, or eating "smelly" food in their taxis because they had no time to stop. Explaining the harassment and financial loss that comes with passenger complaints even before the case goes to court, one driver said, "Customers spend half an hour by sitting in the cab . . . to call TLC to complain. . . . They use curse words. . . . We don't fight them. . . . We forget about our rights in order to work! Even a five-minute loss is hard because the lease is hard." The TLC's efforts to publicize its complaint procedure and its hotline number have familiarized passengers with technicalities such as a cab's medallion number, which now appears on the roof as well as on the sides of a cab, and a driver's hack license, which has the driver's name and must be displayed in the top left corner of the partition separating the driver from the passenger in the backseat (TLC 2002a). The increased surveillance and the passage of a passengers' bill of rights without a corresponding one for drivers rendered drivers vulnerable before 9/11 and fed into post-9/11 violence.

In May 1998 the TLC passed fifteen rules out of seventeen proposed by then-mayor Rudolph Giuliani holding drivers to a far higher standard than private operators. The criminalizing spirit and language of the rules represented drivers as immigrants who threaten civility and order in the city. For instance, the first rule increased the fine for discourteous behavior from $25 to $125. Rule 8 was promulgated "to protect the riding public from drivers who operate their vehicles in an unsafe manner." Drivers stood to have their licenses suspended for two traffic violations in eighteen months, a stringent requirement in a city like New York. They were required to pay out of pocket for defensive driving classes and a drug test. Faced with these policies made for the entire industry when, by the TLC's own admission, only a minority provided bad service, drivers were mobilized to strike.

When drivers followed up a work stoppage with plans for a demonstration against these rules, the city responded by continuing to promote xenophobic and racialized images of the workforce. Announcing plans to deploy the police in full force in reaction to some flyers announcing a motorcade by drivers to City Hall on May 21, 1998, Giuliani declared that "if a similar document had been found in the hands of a terrorist group, 'then everybody would understand that you cannot allow that to happen'" (Barry 1998, A1). Reinforcing this statement, then–police commissioner Howard Safir said, "It's no different than if we discovered a terrorist threat and we moved to stop the terrorists from carrying out their act" (Strozier 1998b, 22). The two public officials, in making these public statements, constructed the demonstration—later upheld in federal court as within drivers' First Amendment right (Weiser 1998)—as a terrorist act meriting a public safety response that involved suspending a constitutional right. By equating a largely nonwhite, Muslim, and immigrant workforce with terrorists, the city officials publicly profiled taxi drivers and presented such profiling as common sense. The statements racialized drivers' brown and black foreign bodies as posing a particular kind of danger: terrorism. Decrying the strengthening and popularizing of the image of drivers as terrorists three years before the 9/11 attacks, a Middle Eastern driver said, "We taxi drivers were asking for our rights, and we were being called terrorist for asking them!" The obstruction of the drivers' demonstration is hardly the first time that their civil rights have been violated. The TLC routinely holds its hearings in closed courts and frequently denies due process to drivers. As a result of legal pressures from the NYTWA, the New York City Office of Administrative Trials and Hearings and federal court rulings have begun to recognize that certain city and TLC measures have disregarded drivers' civil and human rights.

Post-9/11 Implications of Taxi Industry Policies

The TLC's policies heightened drivers' concerns about their safety after 9/11. South Asian and Middle Eastern drivers felt unsafe because passengers could guess their ethnicity by looking at their hack license. Drivers' efforts to protest mistreatment were likely to lead to fines and possible license suspensions. Although drivers were accustomed to being ordered around and treated as temporary residents before 9/11, they experienced the overt hostility directed at them by some passengers as new.

Many New Yorkers refused to ride with South Asian or Middle Eastern drivers upon catching their names on the hack licenses. Among those who did use taxis, the driver's identity took on a new significance. The South Asian and Palestinian drivers I interviewed consistently mentioned passengers' eyes seeking out the name on the hack license. Drivers with common Muslim names like "Mohammed" and "Ahmed" said that some passengers reacted with comments such as, "You're Mohammed. You know who bombed the WTC?" or, "You're a Mohammed; why did you come to this country?" A Bangladeshi American driver whose first name provoked a series of abusive encounters in the first three months after 9/11 reported two separate incidents in which a passenger lumped together all Muslims as terrorists. In one incident the passenger said, "You Muslims are oppressing us. You should all leave." These passengers refused to pay their fare. In another incident the passenger paid the fare but insisted, "All you Muslims are the same. You're terrorists." In this instance, the driver confronted his passenger by asserting, "I am a citizen. Not all Muslims are responsible. Why are you abusing me?"

In the face of such xenophobic and anti-Muslim treatment, South Asian and Middle Eastern drivers found the attention paid to the hack licenses frightening. As one driver put it: "Most customers look for the name. When they see a Muslim or Asian name, they are not friendly. They ask unacceptable questions such as: Where are you from? Why are you here? When will you go back?" Passengers' ability to feel free to tell their drivers to "go home," regardless of their citizenship status, demonstrates the perception that immigrants are perpetual outsiders.[10]

Noting the difference between pre- and post-9/11 responses from passengers to their country of origin, drivers said that the previously casual tenor of their exchanges with passengers had become charged with the politics of war and terror. After the WTC attacks, when Bangladeshi, Pakistani, and Indian drivers, on being asked, told their passengers where they were from, they were sometimes greeted with remarks like, "Oh, that's a dangerous place," or, "Muslim people killed us." Before the attacks, drivers found their interactions with passengers to be "frank and easy." Explaining one of the major attractions of his job, a Bangladeshi driver said, "It is a public service. I can talk to people. I can know more. This is how I enjoy the job. So many diverse people get in my cab." Other drivers echoed this sentiment. But after 9/11, the pleasure of meeting different people and getting the chance to talk about their home country and family evaporated. In the words of an Egyptian driver, drivers and passengers now approached each other with some "trepidation." But while passengers were formally and discursively empowered to act on their fears about terrorism, drivers were not.

Some drivers tried to cover their names on the hack license with their rate card or even placed the license out of the passenger's view. By taking these makeshift measures to feel safe, drivers were risking violation of TLC standards. As one South Asian driver said, "If they are caught, they will get a ticket. But it is worth it. Hurt [physical injury] from the passenger is worse than the police giving you a ticket."

Drivers also reported being targeted on the basis of their appearance. Writing about this form of exposure to hatred, as well as about unsolicited sympathy, Bayoumi (2002, 82) reflects: "Now it has become not just a question of whether we—New Yorkers—are so vulnerable as a city but whether we—in the Arab and Muslim communities—are so vulnerable by our appearance." A Pakistani driver recounted being called a "fucking terrorist" by a person who had pulled up next to his taxi a week before I interviewed him in August 2002. He said:

If we are terrorists, why are we working so hard? Working twelve hours? If we didn't work like this, the taxi business will not survive. The taxi industry is on our shoulders. They don't think a taxi driver is a human being; just a driver; just an animal. . . . Everybody said there are human rights over there [in the United States], but for immigrants there are no human rights.

For this driver, as for others who had been subjected to similar insults on the basis of their appearance, the idea that ordinary working people could be treated this way was inseparable from public perceptions that immigrants had no rights.

When drivers talked about their powerlessness in the industry, they repeatedly pointed out that taxi driving has become an "immigrant" job and that they are expected to be deferential, indeed servile, to (white and minority) customers. These expectations, according to drivers, come from a perception that immigrants should be grateful to be allowed to enter the United States and work. Since 9/11, routine demands from rushed passengers that drivers run lights and stop signs, make illegal turns, speed, and drop them off in zones where cabs are not allowed to stop have often been accompanied by anti-Muslim rhetoric and threats of deportation. A Pakistani driver described the attitude of some passengers: "'You should be happy you are here; you don't show me the law. . . . You should be happy that you are not put into detention.'" These threats of detention and deportation add yet another layer to the anti-immigrant abuse that drivers have long faced.[11]

But the cost of complying with passenger requests is heavy. The fine for any traffic violation is $250, and the fine for discourteous behavior is $125.

Either way, along with lawyers' fees and time spent in court, a driver stands to lose more than a week's earnings in a time of economic hardship. Since drivers rarely win cases against customers unless the customer fails to appear in court, the pressure to avoid passenger complaints, and unnecessary tickets, is great.

After 9/11, drivers were caught between serving two masters at the same time. Refusing to comply with passengers could lead to violence and fines. Pleasing them could mean tickets and further loss of income. The TLC's harsh penalty system, the passengers' bill of rights, and consumers' right to complain to the TLC at the slightest dissatisfaction reinforced the fragility of drivers' rights in the weeks and months after 9/11.

Drivers have faced post-9/11 hostility as first-generation Muslim immigrant workers. After 9/11, abusive passengers felt that they could take the law into their own hands and justifiably mistreat drivers, whose very identity and presence such passengers saw as a threat to national security. Drivers resisted the prevalent images by talking about their pride in their work, the responsibility they felt to help keep the city running, the efforts they made to alleviate the sufferings of fellow New Yorkers in a disaster-torn city, and the belief that they too had rights and needed to be able to work in a safe environment with dignity.

CONCLUSION

The accounts of yellow cab drivers reveal that structural hierarchies of class, race, immigration status, national origin, and religious identity mediated their experiences of economic hardship and hostility after the terrorist attack of September 11. By illuminating the specific impacts of 9/11 on drivers, their responses to the disaster, and their recovery from it, this chapter demonstrates that disasters do not temporarily sweep away differences. Thus, this study takes up the call of theorists to account for the intersecting social relations of power that constitute the very "terrain" of disaster (Enarson 1998). In keeping with some other analyses of 9/11 (Cvetkovich 2002; Ellis 2002; Low 2004; Sturken 2002; White 2004), my attention to difference destabilizes metanarratives of 9/11 that seek to fix the meaning of the disaster. It captures what the anthropologist Setha Low (2004) calls the "vernaculars" of disaster and recovery: local voices telling their own situated stories about what 9/11 and its aftermath meant to them.

Centering what drivers had to say about their economic predicament gives us a sense of how 9/11 affected them as immigrant workers who routinely lack economic security, labor protections, and social services. This vernacular, instead of being limiting in its grammar, opens up comparisons with other disaster-hit workers in low-paying, immigrant-reliant sectors. Like taxi drivers, they too are casualties of late-twentieth-century economic restructuring accompanied by deunionization, cutbacks in spending on public programs for the poor, and the exclusion of immigrants from many types of public assistance. Thus, 9/11 provides scholars with an opportunity to document and compare the effects of these long-term developments on poor working-class immigrants at a moment when vulnerable workers most need a social safety net to recover. In this sense, the testimonies of drivers hold important lessons. They highlight how the aftershocks of a disaster can dislodge those who are precariously positioned in society. And they demonstrate that demands for economic rights to a living wage and public assistance are just as urgent as those for civil liberties and due process. Drivers' experiences call on us as scholars to put economic justice on the post-9/11 immigrant rights agenda.

Driver testimonies also compel us to challenge the dominant interpretations of 9/11. Given that 9/11 did not have the same impact on all those affected (see Garfinkel et al., this volume), nor did it hold the same meanings for them, how can we as ethnographers of the disaster move away from state, corporate, and mass mediated public representations that focus on a highly emotive "human" face of sufferers and convey a singular significance of the event itself? Anthropologists studying disasters have made a case for the cultural specificity of disaster responses (Oliver-Smith 1999) and reminded us that disasters are narrated through socially shared meanings about who can be considered heroes and victims, what can count as trauma, and what sorts of responses and crisis management can be seen as appropriate (Stein 2002). Whose sufferings, then, do these narrative modes overlook, and whose do they privilege? By calling into question the official processes of memorializing 9/11, scholars like Setha Low (2004), Geoffrey White (2004), and Marita Sturken (2002) ask exactly these crucial questions about whose experiences, whose needs, and whose histories are being showcased—and in the process, what is being occluded.

In contrast to the players in hegemonic narratives of a nation united, South Asian and Muslim drivers did not feel drawn into the community of sufferers, even though they responded with a sense of unity, purpose, and service, as survivors of disasters often do. In fact, they were retraumatized by the violence directed at them. The 9/11 attacks, seen from the drivers' perspective, solidified rather than dissolved the lines drawn along ethnic, religious, national, and racial difference. Social solidarity coalesced within hours around those who were represented as legitimate sufferers—those members of the nation deemed worthy of protection in the face of the sudden and brutal shattering of their security. In those same hours an impermeable line was drawn to separate this emergent community from those represented as its enemies on account of their religion and national origin.

In rendering visible the particular sufferings of one group of low-income immigrant workers, my ethnographic practice has required asking what is disastrous for whom and why. At the same time, I have had to keep in sight the grief, loss, insecurity, and resilience that drivers shared with other New Yorkers. I have done this in the hope that we do not have to wait for years to retrieve too easily silenced voices, or "for history to someday open its mouth and speak," to use the words of a Bangladeshi driver reflecting on the invisibility of taxi drivers' hardships. A survivor of the 1971 war of independence that created Bangladesh, he had witnessed how official versions of the war jostled lived experience out of the way. He was only too aware of which histories get told and which ones remain obscured. With the history of 9/11 far from completely told, it is my hope that, through further studies such as this one, the experiences of marginalized groups become part of our collective memory and understanding of the wounded city.

Some of the material in this chapter appeared in a different form as "A View of Post-9/11 Justice from Below" in *Peace Review* 16(2, June 2004): 141–48. My heartfelt thanks to the drivers who made this study possible. I want to thank the Russell Sage Foundation for funding the final research project; the New York Taxi Workers Alliance for its collaboration and partial funding of the database; the Global Affairs Institute at Syracuse University for funding the pilot study; Himanee Gupta for her superb research assistance; and Payal Banerjee and Mohua Das for their time and valuable suggestions during the early stages of this project. Thanks also to Kalpana Nitzsche, Leslie McLees, and Jessica Schmidt for their work on the database. Nancy Foner's staunch encouragement on the qualitative part of this study has lent it its richness. The chapter has greatly benefited from discussions with my colleagues Cynthia Franklin, Linda Lierheimer, Robert Perkinson, Richard Rath, Naoko Shibusawa, and Geoffrey White, who carefully commented on several drafts. The Committee on Human Subjects of the University of Hawaii at Manoa approved the research.

NOTES

1. According to the U.S. Department of Labor's (2002) Occupational Safety and Health Administration (OSHA), taxi drivers face the highest risk of fatal injuries, along with police, private guards, and food service managers. Taxi drivers are thirty-six times more likely to be killed on the job than the national average for job safety.
2. The term "violence" as used in this chapter encompasses physical, verbal, and mental abuse as well as economic exploitation, in keeping with the extensive body of literature produced by feminist and Asian American academics and activists in

the last two decades. For exemplary works, see R. Emerson Dobash and Russell P. Dobash (1992; 1998), Catharine MacKinnon (1993), and Patricia Wong Hall and Victor M. Hwang (2001).

3. For the purposes of this chapter, I do not include Israelis in my definition of "Middle Eastern."

4. I designed the survey in close consultation with the NYTWA, which approached me in November 2001 to help it document the impact of 9/11 on yellow cab drivers. Those who administered the surveys were trained by me in several sessions. Since I was not based in New York, I did not administer any of the surveys.

5. The *New York Times* reports the fare increase to be 26 percent based on an average trip of 2.6 miles (Luo 2004), and Schaller Consulting (2004) calculates the increase to be 28 percent based on an average trip of 2.8 miles.

6. The 1996 Personal Responsibility and Work Opportunity Reconciliation Act (PRWORA) bars even permanent residents from most federal means-tested assistance, including food stamps and supplemental security income (SSI).

7. Between October 2001 and June 2002, FEMA's delineation of the affected area never spread beyond Fourteenth Street. As the *New York Times* reporter David Chen (2002a) points out, this criterion departed from FEMA's usual practice of not requiring applicants to prove that they were directly affected by a disaster. The geographic restriction led to an astounding number of rejections. FEMA rejected seven out of every ten applications between September 2001 and June 2002 (Chen 2002a). As a result, only $20.6 million was distributed to 3,583 households during that period (Chen 2002b). Even after a review of 7,200 wrongly rejected applications, only eighty-five were approved (Chen 2002a). During this period FEMA had barely touched the $255 million in aid it had earmarked for individuals and families (FEMA 2002a). Within two months of the revision of the guidelines, FEMA granted another 3,053 households $25.3 million in assistance (Chen 2002b).

8. See, for example, the litany of complaints about cheating, violent, lewd, and lying drivers that appeared in a May 2002 *Daily News* article (Donohue 2002). The drivers mentioned by name are South Asian, African, and Latino. Even though the article quotes the TLC commissioner as saying that the vast majority of the drivers are "honest and hardworking," it does not cite a single example of such common acts of honesty and courtesy as drivers returning wallets and expensive equipment left in their cabs by passengers or helping elderly passengers.

9. The media reported violence against Arabs, Sikhs, and Muslims, many of whom worked in or owned gas stations, small businesses, or fast-food restaurants or were students or professionals (Tamar and Niebuhr 2001; Sherwood 2001; Fries 2001; Singh 2002; Lee 2002). Racial profiling of airline passengers also received a fair amount of media attention (Singh 2002, 15; Goodstein 2001). However, the violence directed at taxi drivers in New York City was underreported. This is borne out by drivers in the study who said that the police often failed to record their charges of 9/11-related acts of vandalism and assault as hate crimes. The only story I found in the media about post-9/11 abuse of a New York taxi driver featured twenty-year-old Parwinder Singh, who was beaten up in Brooklyn by a group of young men who said, "There's Osama's relative, let's do the job now" (Jacinto 2001, n.p.).

10. The persistent placing of Asian Americans outside the national body politic and national culture has profoundly shaped the history of Asian Americans in the United States (Chan 1991; Lowe 1996; Chang 1999).

11. The fear of deportation has haunted drivers since the 1996 Anti-Terrorism and Effective Death Penalty Act and Illegal Immigration Reform and Responsibility Act. The acts were used to deport undocumented immigrants with criminal charges against them, however minor (*News India-Times* 1997; Williams 1996). Within two months of September 11, 2001, immigration laws were used to detain an estimated 1,200 people, mostly South Asian and Middle Eastern, for questioning, and 762 of them were arrested on criminal charges or for violating immigration law (U.S. Department of Justice 2003).

REFERENCES

Advani, Anuradha. 1997. "Against the Tide: Reflections on Organizing New York City's South Asian Taxicab Drivers." In *Making More Waves: New Writing by Asian American Women*, edited by Elaine H. Kim, Lilia V. Villanueva, and Asian Women United of California. Boston: Beacon Press.

Asian American Federation New York (AAFNY). 2002. "Chinatown After September 11: An Economic Impact Study." New York: AAFNY.

Barnes, Brooks. 2001. "Fear of a Fare Fight: Taxi Drivers Dread Their Day in Court." *Wall Street Journal*, July 5, pp. 1, 7.

Barry, Dan. 1998. "Show of Force Checks Protest by Cabdrivers." *New York Times*, May 22, p. A1.

———. 2001. "After the Attacks: The Scene; Normality Proves Elusive Amid Bomb Scares and Transit Woes." *New York Times*, September 14, p. A12.

Barton, Allen H. 1969. *Communities in Disaster*. New York: Doubleday.

Bayoumi, Moustafa. 2002. "How Does It Feel to Be a Problem?" In *Asian Americans on War and Peace*, edited by Russell C. Leong and Don T. Nakanishi. Los Angeles: UCLA Asian American Studies Center Press.

Chan, Sucheng. 1991. *Asian Americans: An Interpretive History*. Boston: Twayne.

Chang, Robert S. 1999. *Disoriented: Asian Americans, Law, and the Nation-State*. New York: New York University Press.

Chavez, Leo R. 1997. "Immigration Reform and Nativism: The Nationalist Response to the Transnationalist Challenge." In *Immigrants Out! The New Nativism and the Anti-immigrant Impulse in the United States*, edited by Juan F. Perea. New York: New York University Press.

Chen, David W. 2002a. "After Criticism, U.S. Broadens 9/11 Aid Pool." *New York Times*, June 29, pp. A1, B3.

———. 2002b. "More Get 9/11 Aid, but Distrust of U.S. Effort Lingers." *New York Times*, August 27, pp. B1, B6.

Coalition Against Anti-Asian Violence (CAAAV). 1996. "Police Brutality in Asian Communities." *CAAAV Voice* 8(1): 3–4.

Cuza, Bobby. 2002. "Getting a Fair Hike." *New York Newsday*, February 25, p. A4.

Cvetkovich, Ann. 2002. "9-11 Everyday." *Signs* 22(1): 471–73.

———. 2003. *An Archive of Feelings: Trauma, Sexuality, and Lesbian Cultures.* Durham, N.C.: Duke University Press.

Das Gupta, Monisha. 2001. "Emerging Tactics: Organizing South Asians in the New York Taxi Industry." Paper presented to the meeting of the Association of Asian American Studies, Toronto (March 28).

———. Forthcoming. *Unruly Immigrants: Post-1965 South Asian Activism in the United States.* Durham, N.C.: Duke University Press.

Davar, Tamina. 1995. "What Is the Lease Drivers Coalition?" *Peela Paiya* (Summer): 10–13.

Desai, Bhairavi. 2002. "New York Taxi Drivers Need Disaster Relief." *New York Times,* March 2, p. A15.

Dobash, R. Emerson, and Russell P. Dobash. 1992. *Women, Violence, Social Change.* London: Routledge.

———, eds. 1998. *Rethinking Violence Against Women.* Thousand Oaks, Calif.: Sage Publications.

Donohue, Pete. 2002. "Cabbies from Hell Get the Heave Ho; Insulted, Assaulted, and Cheated Riders." *New York Daily News,* May 19, p. 8.

DRI-WEFA. 2002. "The Role of Travel and Tourism in America's Top 100 Metropolitan Areas." Report prepared for the United States Conference of Mayors. Lexington, Mass.: DRI-WEFA.

Ellis, Carolyn. 2002. "Shattered Lives: Making Sense of September 11 and Its Aftermath." *Journal of Contemporary Ethnography* 31(4): 375–410.

Enarson, Elaine. 1998. "Through Women's Eyes: A Gendered Research Agenda for Disaster Social Science." *Disasters* 22(2): 157–73.

Erikson, Kai. 1994. *A New Species of Trouble: Explorations in Disaster, Trauma, and Community.* New York: W. W. Norton.

Esser, Dominique, Kevin Fitzpatrick, Mohammed Kazem, Biju Mathew, and Rizwan Raja. 1999. "Reorganizing Organizing: Immigrant Labor in North America: Interview with New York Taxi Workers' Alliance." *Amerasia Journal* 25(3): 171–81.

Federal Emergency Management Agency (FEMA). 2002a. "September 11—A Nation Recovers: Charts and Summaries." Available at: http://www.fema.org/remember911/911_charts.shtm (accessed November 9, 2004).

———. 2002b. "What Is Mortgage and Rental Assistance?" Available at: http://www.fema.org/remember911/911_place.shtm (accessed November 9, 2004).

Fries, Jacob. 2001. "Complaints of Anti-Arab Bias Dip, but Concerns Linger." *New York Times,* December 22, p. B8.

Fritz, Charles E. 1961. "Disaster." In *Contemporary Social Problems,* edited by Robert A. Merton and Robert K. Nisbet. New York: Harcourt Brace.

Glenn, Evelyn Nakano. 2002. *Unequal Freedom: How Race and Gender Shaped American Citizenship and Labor.* Cambridge, Mass.: Harvard University Press.

Goodstein, Laurie. 2001. "American Sikhs Contend They Have Become a Focus of Profiling at Airports." *New York Times,* November 10, p. B6.

Hall, Patricia Wong, and Victor M. Hwang, eds. 2001. *Anti-Asian Violence in North America: Asian American and Asian Canadian Reflections on Hate, Healing, and Resistance.* Walnut Creek, Calif.: Altamira Press.

Hanley, Robert. 2001. "Officials Pleased by Morning Traffic with Car-Pooling Rule." *New York Times,* October 2, p. D2.

Henriques, Diana B., and David Barstow. 2001. "A Nation Challenged: Compensation: Victims' Fund Likely to Pay Average of $1.6 Million Each." *New York Times*, December 21, p. A1.

Hoffman, Susanna M. 1999. "The Worst of Times, the Best of Times: Toward a Model of Cultural Response to Disaster." In *The Angry Earth: Disaster in Anthropological Perspective*, edited by Anthony Oliver-Smith and Susanna M. Hoffman. New York: Routledge.

Honolulu Advertiser. 2002. "One Year, One Nation: Attacks Crippled Travel and Tourism Industry, Multiplied Security Costs." *Honolulu Advertiser*, September 8, p. D6.

Idupuganti, Anura. 2001. "List of Publicly Reported U.S. Hate Crimes Against Arabs, Muslims, and Other South Asians from September 11 Through September 26, 2001." Educators for Social Responsibility. Available at: www.esrnational.org/discrimincidents200109.htm (accessed November 9, 2004).

Jacinto, Leela. 2001. "Bias Fallout: How One Sikh-American Learned a Hard Lesson in Identity Politics." abcNEWS.com (October 30).

Kang, Jerry. 2002. "Thinking Through Internment: 12/7 and 9/11." In *Asian Americans on War and Peace*, edited by Russell C. Leong and Don T. Nakanishi. Los Angeles: UCLA Asian American Studies Center Press.

Kennedy, Randy. 2001a. "After the Attacks: Transit: Part of Subway Tunnel May Have Collapsed Under Weight of Debris, Officials Fear." *New York Times*, September 13, p. A13.

————. 2001b. "Ban on Lone Drivers at Some New York Gates." *New York Times*, September 26, p. A1.

————. 2002a. "It's All Aboard, If They'll Fit, as September 11 Jolts Mass Transit." *New York Times*, January 3, p. A1.

————. 2002b. "Car Restrictions in Manhattan Are Extended." *New York Times*, February 6, p. B3.

————. 2002c. "Study Says Single-Rider Ban Hurts Economy." *New York Times*, February 11, p. B3.

Lee, Stephen. 2002. "A Chronology of the 'War on Terror' and Domestic Hate Crimes." In *Asian Americans on War and Peace*, edited by Russell C. Leong and Don T. Nakanishi. Los Angeles: UCLA Asian American Studies Center Press.

Lipton, Eric. 2003. "Finding the Intersection of Supply and Demand: Already Facing Demand for Higher Pay, City Considers Adding 900 Taxis." *New York Times*, November 21, p. A31.

López-Garza, Marta, and David R. Diaz, eds. 2001. *Asian and Latino Immigrants in a Restructuring Economy: The Metamorphosis of Southern California*. Stanford, Calif.: Stanford University Press.

Low, Setha M. 2004. "The Memorialization of 9/11: Dominant and Local Discourses on the Rebuilding of the World Trade Center Site." *American Ethnologist* 31(3): 326–39.

Lowe, Lisa. 1996. *Immigrant Acts: On Asian American Cultural Politics*. Durham, N.C.: Duke University Press.

Luo, Michael. 2004. "Taxi Commission Backs 26 Percent Rise for Fares in City." *New York Times*, March 31, p. A1.

MacKinnon, Catharine A. 1993. *Only Words*. Cambridge, Mass.: Harvard University Press.

Mohammed-Arif, Aminah. 2002. *Salaam America: South Asian Muslims in New York*. London: Anthem Press.

Navarro, Mireya. 2002. "For Illegal Workers' Kin, No Paper Trail and Less 9/11 Aid." *New York Times*, May 6, p. B1.

News India-Times. 1997. "Raids on Illegal Aliens Rise as New Law Takes Effect." *News India-Times*, November 11, p. 1.

Oliver-Smith, Anthony. 1999. "The Brotherhood of Pain: Theoretical and Applied Perspectives on Postdisaster Solidarity." In *The Angry Earth: Disaster in Anthropological Perspective*, edited by Anthony Oliver-Smith and Susanna M. Hoffman. New York: Routledge.

Omi, Michael, and Howard Winant. 1994. *Racial Formation in the United States: From the 1960s to the 1980s*. 2nd ed. New York: Routledge.

Parrott, James. 2001. "Economic Impact of the September 11 Terrorist Attacks and Strategies for Economic Rebirth and Resurgence." Fiscal Policy Institute, www.fiscalpolicy. org (December 6).

Parrott, James, and Oliver Cooke. 2002. "Tale of Two Recessions: The Current Slowdown in New York City Compared to the Early 1990s." Fiscal Policy Institute, www. fiscalpolicy.org (December 3).

Pennebaker, James W., and Kent D. Harber. 1993. "A Social Stage Model of Collective Coping: The Loma Prieta Earthquake and the Persian Gulf War." *Journal of Social Issues* 49(4): 125–46.

Sassen, Saskia. 1998. *Globalization and Its Discontents: Essays on the Mobility of People and Money*. New York: New Press.

Schaller Consulting. 2003. *The New York City Taxicab Fact Book*. Available at: http://www. schallerconsult.com/taxi/taxifb.pdf (accessed December 3, 2003).

———. 2004. *The New York City Taxicab Fact Book*. Available at: http://www.schallerconsult. com/taxi/taxifb.pdf (accessed November 9, 2004).

Sharkey, Joe. 2001. "After the Attacks: The Travelers; Tighter Airport Security Will Slow Business Fliers." *New York Times*, September 13, n.p.

Sherwood, Robbie. 2001. "Valley Rally Condemns Hate: Slain Sikh's Relatives Honor Him." *Arizona Republic*, September 20, n.p. Available at: www.arizonarepublic.com/ special44/articles/0920attackshatecrimes20.html (accessed September 29, 2001).

Singh, Amardeep. 2002. "'We Are Not the Enemy': Hate Crimes Against Arabs, Muslims, and Those Perceived as Arab or Muslim After September 11." *Human Rights Watch* 14(6): 3–40.

Stein, Howard. 2002. "Toward an Applied Anthropology of Disaster: Learning from Disasters—Experience, Method, and Theory." *Illness, Crisis, and Loss* 10(2): 154–63.

Strozier, Matthew. 1998a. "Manhattan's Streets Strangely Empty as Taxis Went on Strike over New Rules." *India in New York*, May 22, p. 20.

———. 1998b. "Blocked on Bridge, Yellow Cab Drivers Protest on Foot." *India in New York*, May 29, p. 22.

Sturken, Marita. 2002. "Memorializing Absence." In *Understanding September 11: Perspectives from the Social Sciences*, edited by Craig Calhoun, Paul Price, and Ashley Timmers. New York: New Press.

Tamar, Lewin, and Gustav Niebuhr. 2001. "Attacks and Harassment Continue on Middle Eastern People and Mosques." *New York Times*, September 18, p. B5.

Taxi and Limousine Commission (TLC). 2002a. "Complainant Hearing Guide." Available at: http://www.nyc.gov/html/tlc/html/passenger/file_complaint_guide.shtml (accessed November 9, 2004).

———. 2002b. "Taxicab Rider Bill of Rights." Available at: http://www.nyc.gov/html/tlc/html/passenger/taxicab_rights.shtml (accessed November 9, 2004).

———. 2002c. "What Is the New York City Taxi and Limousine Commission?" Available at: http://www.nyc.gov/html/tlc/html/about/about.shtml (accessed November 9, 2004).

U.S. Department of Justice. Office of the Inspector General. 2003. "The September 11 Detainees: A Review of the Treatment of Aliens Held on Immigration Charges in Connection with the Investigation of September 11 Attacks." Available at: http://www.usdoj.gov/oig/special/0306/chapter1.htm (accessed November 9, 2004).

U.S. Department of Labor. Occupational Safety and Health Administration (OSHA). 2002. "Workplace Violence." Available at: http://www.osha.gov/oshinfo/priorities/violence.html (accessed September 21, 2002).

Weiser, Benjamin. 1998. "Cabbies Denied Free Speech, a Judge Rules." *New York Times*, May 27, p. B1.

Wellman, David T. 1993. *Portraits of White Racism*. 2nd ed. New York: Cambridge University Press.

White, Geoffrey M. 2004. "National Subjects: September 11 and Pearl Harbor." *American Ethnologist* 31(3): 293–310.

Williams, Lena. 1996. "Week in Review Desk. July 14–20; Pulling in the Welcome Mat." *New York Times*, July 21, sec. 4, p. 2.

Wolfenstein, Martha. 1957. *Disaster: A Psychological Essay*. Glencoe, Ill.: Free Press.

Zia, Helen. 2000. *Asian American Dreams: The Emergence of an American People*. New York: Farrar, Straus & Giroux.

———. 2002. "Oh, Say, Can You See? Post September 11." In *Asian Americans on War and Peace*, edited by Russell C. Leong and Don T. Nakanishi. Los Angeles: UCLA Asian American Studies Center Press

CHAPTER 9

New York's Visual Art World After 9/11

Julia Rothenberg and William Kornblum

IN THE weeks and months following 9/11, New Yorkers crowded art and photo exhibits that touched on the devastating events. Their keen interest in graphic representations of the horror and heroism was a vivid reminder of the importance of the visual arts in the cultural and economic life of the city. But as this chapter documents, the attack on the World Trade Center damaged some important neighborhoods of the arts community. Depending on their proximity to the twin towers, artists and gallery owners experienced shocks and challenges to their livelihoods and to their ability to contribute to the city's recovery. Those in the arts community who fared the worst were the younger, less-established artists on whom the future of the arts in New York depends. Somewhat surprisingly, however, the higher end of the market for visual art experienced only temporary disruption, and the importance of art and artists was quickly recognized in planning for the rebuilding of lower Manhattan.

The visual arts—including galleries, museums, and artists working in every medium imaginable—are a vital growth sector in the city and the region's economy (for a general background discussion of the economics of art, see Caves 2000). The international visibility of the New York art scene has helped to foster the image of the United States as the global leader not only of finance and politics but of culture as well. Striving artists, like aspiring actors and other creative but impoverished young professionals, also provide energetic and relatively low-paid labor for the city's building, design, and service industries. Lower-income neighborhoods of the deindustrialized central city, where less-established artists find studio space in old warehouses and lofts, have become trendy destinations for innovative galleries and restaurants. Once a fledgling art scene takes root, it attracts the more affluent young, who drive up rents and property values, forcing more experimental, and thus less commercially stable, artists and galleries into an endless pursuit of affordable space in untried neighborhoods. In this way artists have contributed, unwillingly perhaps, to the redevelopment of Greenwich Village, SoHo, Tribeca, Chelsea, and Williamsburg, among other thriving communities in the city. This dynamic has persisted since New York City became the center of modern art movements after the Second World War, but it presents severe problems for the continuity of an arts community in the city in the post-9/11 period (Deutsche and Ryan 1984; Zukin 1982; Smith and DeFilippis 1999; Hackworth 2002). In this chapter, we show that while established galleries and their artists rebounded quickly from the terrorist attack and its aftermath, more vulnerable galleries and less-established artists did so less easily.

As New Yorkers in and outside the visual arts community looked to artists for representations of the terror of 9/11 and its causes, the city's artists struggled to come to terms with how their individual work would or would not respond to the new world situation. Historically, artists in New York have been an important cultural and political presence. Often oriented toward the political and cultural left, they have spoken out through their work against war, racism, sexism, homophobia, totalitarianism, and capitalism. Although recent movements in art have centered more on aesthetic than political issues, prominent exceptions can be found, especially among feminist and Third World artists and among many artists who use video and other media in their work. Faced with the artistic and intellectual challenges of 9/11, the question of the place of art in a world of global crisis is of special importance for understanding the possible future of the arts community in the city.

More definitive answers to questions about how artists adjusted in the post-9/11 city and how their work responded to the events of 9/11 must await, in part, more insight into the roles given to artists and their organizations in the cultural life of a rebuilt lower Manhattan. For years before the bombings, civic and cultural leaders in lower Manhattan—and particularly in Tribeca and Battery Park City—had been developing a lively calendar of art exhibits, concerts, and other cultural events. They were seeking to attract museums, galleries, and other cultural institutions to the West Side of lower Manhattan, hoping to enliven communities in the financial district, which, after the bustling nine-to-five weekdays, was often dark and distant from the cultural excitement of Manhattan to the north. In addition to the scattered but thriving galleries of Tribeca, the Winter Garden of Battery Park City had become an exciting exposition and performance space. Plans to develop, restore, or enhance the Holocaust Museum, the Irish Famine Memorial, Battery Park itself, and other cultural venues in the area were well under way at the time of the attack.

After 9/11, lower Manhattan became the focus of even more intense artistic attention. With the creativity of internationally known architects and artists brought to bear on the design of new buildings and memorial sites, the importance of the rebuilt area as a cultural as well as a commercial center was further signaled. Vast new spaces in the rebuilt transit hub and in rebuilt office and public buildings will invite artistic embellishment and provide new venues for expositions. Inevitably, these spaces will present shows that help the public come to terms with the tragic events of 9/11 and the way they changed America's global presence. In consequence, when we analyze the negative impacts of the attack on the city's arts community, we need to keep in mind as well the opportunities and challenges that lower Manhattan's rebuilt and reinvigorated cultural landscape will present for New York's visual arts community.

NEW YORK'S VISUAL ARTS COMMUNITY

The city's contemporary art community includes artists at all levels of achievement and reputation, some of whom live and work in studios in established art communities like Williamsburg and DUMBO (Down Under the Manhattan Bridge Overpass) in Brooklyn and Long Island City in Queens. The majority of artists, however, are dispersed throughout the city and region but think of the city as the center of their arts world. The visual arts community, and those who rely on this community for their livelihood, numbers in the thousands and includes those who work in the galleries and museums on which the artists depend (or hope to someday); art buyers and interior decorators who select art for private and corporate patrons; art supply stores where amateur and professional artists purchase their supplies; and art transporters, framers, appraisers, auctioneers, and employees in a myriad of nonprofit arts organizations. Although all these play important roles in the arts community, with which they readily identify, the most important actors are the artists who strive to make a difference by breaking new ground in artistic expression.

New York's visual arts community has undergone considerable change in the last half-century. The city attained global dominance as a visual arts center following World War II with the emergence of abstract expressionism. Though the work of the abstract expressionists, it has been argued, was used to promote U.S. hegemony during the Cold War (Guilbaut 1983; Crockoft 1974), all of the artists themselves lived most of their lives in relative poverty, with strong ties to one another but outside of mainstream society (Shapiro and Shapiro 1990; Greenberg 1961; Ashton 1973). By the 1960s much of the city's art scene had relocated downtown to SoHo from the Upper East Side's 57th Street and Madison and farther north (an area that is still home to several well-established blue-chip galleries and auction houses). By the early 1960s, the work of pop artists like Roy Lichtenstein and Andy Warhol was selling for exorbitant prices, and social contact with the art world had become a mark of distinction for New York's elite. By the 1970s, the recession and a general lack of confidence in the political and economic status quo in the United States had begun to affect the art world. Many artists began nonprofit collectives and experimented with alternative modes of expression, such as body art, environmental art, and conceptual art. These strategies of opposition called into question art's status as a commodity and resulted in work that temporarily evaded the market. Later, however, photo and video documentation of ephemeral or site-specific artworks (such as Robert Smithson's *Spiral Jetty*) became objects of conventional modes of exhibition and sale in New York galleries.

By the end of the 1970s, the rising predominance of master of fine arts (M.F.A.) programs had led the New York art world to become increasingly professionalized. This was also the period when the artists' role in initiating the processes of urban gentrification intensified. With the revival of the city's economy in the 1980s, the art world also experienced an unprecedented boom, and the market increasingly became the arbiter of artistic value. The surge in sales collapsed at the beginning of the 1990s, and at the same time the art world became more politicized. Artwork and exhibitions addressing the AIDS epidemic, marginalized sexualities, racial and ethnic identity, and censorship flooded the market.

As the economy revived later in the 1990s, collectors picked up the pace of buying and art world actors once again adopted an attitude of ambition and professionalism. By the end of the decade, the art market was booming and there were several notable sales, such as the $55 million sale at Christie's of Picasso's *Woman with Crossed Arms* and the $1.8 million paid for Jeff Koons's *Pink Panther* (Szanto 2003). The number of galleries in New York City increased by 15 percent between 1990 and 1996 (to 366), and several of the city's museums and exhibition spaces, the Museum of Modern Art (MOMA) most notably, made ambitious plans for expansion. The city's art community of the 1990s remained dominated by a business model, which equated success with commercial sales.

By the turn of the twenty-first century, the central gallery district for contemporary artists had relocated from SoHo, which had essentially become a boutique shopping area, to the far western reaches of Chelsea. In a familiar pattern, galleries in Chelsea snatched up large and (relative to SoHo) inexpensive space. Chelsea real estate prices rapidly escalated, and galleries that came in after the first wave were forced to pay exorbitant prices in order to be in the trendiest gallery area. The area became home to "high-end" contemporary art galleries featuring already well-known artists. With a few exceptions, artists could not afford to live there, and in consequence Chelsea remains an exception to the pattern of artist-initiated gentrification that has characterized development in Williamsburg, Long Island City, and the DUMBO area, where artists live as well as exhibit. At this writing, artists in search of affordable space in which to live and work are moving to neighborhoods as far from the commercial and exhibition art center as the South Bronx, the Rockaways, and even Bridgeport, Connecticut.

In the wake of the World Trade Center attack, the separate but interwoven worlds of visual art, the media, fashion, and glamour were joined by the world of finance. Successful figures in these worlds often met for entertainment at Chelsea's 150 galleries and restaurants in the neighboring meatpacking district, just south of Fourteenth Street and west of Ninth Avenue. Their spending helped transform both neighborhoods from seedy marginality, especially the old meatpacking district, into ultra-chic restaurant and bar districts where cobbled streets and antique signs provided the backdrop for Wall Street's young financial elite. In an era of global technological interconnectedness, when physical proximity to an industry hub is no longer economically essential, artists and other cultural actors helped create the ambiance that continues to attract and hold other elites in the central city. After 9/11, young and cosmopolitan elites in finance, law, banking, and other financial services still wanted to remain close to the city's most exciting cultural institutions—the restaurants, theaters, clubs, galleries, and museums that serve as important status markers and sites of a "common elite culture" (Castells 1996; Grabher 2002).

THE ECONOMIC IMPACT OF 9/11
ON ARTISTS AND GALLERIES

The economic connections between the city's corporations, real estate markets, and artists and galleries are quite direct. The economic recession that gripped New York during the months before the suicide bombings had already begun to weaken the art market, but 9/11 had immediate effects that worsened the situation. Galleries in the vicinity of the attacks that were out of commission for critical months experienced dire losses. Financial and other corporate institutions were regular buyers of contemporary art, and some galleries and their artists located near the twin towers depended on their patronage. Not surprisingly, the attack on September 11 had an especially significant effect on these galleries and artists. Over the larger metropolitan region, more-established artists and galleries were negatively affected by the recession and the terrorist attacks but were able to rebound as the market for their work improved. Younger artists were most directly affected by the recession and decline of the art market, and perhaps even more so by the loss of employment opportunities in other sectors of the city's economy. Functioning as a "semi-ethnic" group in the real estate market, visual artists have made formerly undesirable neighborhoods safe for middle-class consumption (Zukin 1982). In addition, artists bring their relatively high educational levels, middle-class backgrounds, and high degree of cultural capital to their search for flexible but not intellectually demanding sources of income, thus providing a ready labor force for the city's high-end service industry. As managers and servers, they mediate between restaurant and bar owners and their patrons (successful members of the bourgeoisie and the financial elite) and the less-educated immigrant workers who usually make up the rest of the service staff. Artists also often serve as a cheap, non-union source of labor for the carpentry, renovation, and graphics trades, working at low wages for the very class from which they originated. In any recession the demand for their services in these economic sectors is reduced, but it was no ordinary recession that followed 9/11.

The City's Artists

It is difficult to estimate just how many artists live and work in New York City. However, New York is the city to which aspiring visual artists have been flocking at least since the 1920s, a pattern that has also held true for actors, dancers, musicians, and those in many other areas of artistic expression. This population, though significant in numbers, remains highly vulnerable economically for the most part. Most visual artists lack (often by choice) full-time work and have no health insurance or other benefits. Although many artists are middle-class in origin and hence do not risk homelessness or complete destitution, their existence in New York City is often precarious. The attack on September 11, in combination with the recession, has made things much worse for them. One year after the World Trade Center attack a survey conducted by DowntownNYC! on behalf of the New York Foundation for the Arts in conjunction with the Consortium for Worker Education (CWE) (FPI 2002) provides a portrait of the declining fortunes of city artists since the attack. The survey, which included 705 respondents, revealed that since September 11, 22 percent of the respondents had become unemployed, 66 percent had lost sales or income, and 69 percent had lost business opportunities or independent contractor jobs. A year after the attack 75 percent of the respondents reported income loss, with the average loss in income over 46 percent. The survey notes that prior to the attack only one in five artists reported income losses as a result of a weak economy and that no other industry in New York City reported 9/11-related income losses this great.

Given their financial straits, it is no wonder that many artists had housing difficulties. Seventy percent of the artists surveyed did their work at home.

Thirteen percent of the artists who rented their homes faced eviction or had been evicted, and 16 percent of the artists who rented their workspaces faced eviction or had been evicted. Although one-third of the respondents had applied for some kind of disaster aid, many were frustrated that they did not meet the requirements for aid because of the kind of unpaid work they did or because they did not live in direct proximity to the World Trade Center site.

In all likelihood, these survey results underestimate the event's economic impact on the city's artists because the survey focused on only certain sectors of the arts community. Artists were identified for the survey if they were members of trade unions and artists' associations or had applied for grants through the New York Foundation for the Arts. This sampling strategy weighed the sample toward more economically stable artists who may well have been more successful than the average artist living and working in New York. Though three-quarters of the artists in the survey had health insurance, for example, most artists interviewed for this chapter did not. For them, not only did work sources dry up (graphics, web design, and construction are all industries that have been severely crippled by the recession), but because they lacked health insurance, they lived in constant fear of sickness or accident. In addition, while work was scarce, rents continued to escalate, causing additional strain to members of the arts community; artists who could get commercial work took on more hours, thus leaving themselves less time to produce their art.

Many artists interviewed for this chapter were reluctant to discuss their financial situations, but those who were willing described a bleak picture. Not atypical is the situation of an artist who lived and worked in a small studio with only a skylight (no windows facing outdoors) in Williamsburg for which she paid $650 a month. The space had no kitchen or bathroom, which were located down a long hallway on the floor and were shared communally with other residents living in similar spaces. The property was zoned only for commercial use, so the residents did not qualify for rent stabilization. Artist-residents rented out the spaces from others who actually held the lease on the floor. This sort of "cockroach pyramid" scheme was popular in Williamsburg before it became gentrified, and apparently it still goes on. Not surprisingly, this artist said she would like to move, but she doubted that she could find anything less expensive in the New York area. She had originally moved there because "I thought I would benefit from the artists' community, but with the rents having gotten so high, it's mostly European club kids."

This artist also noted that her economic situation had steadily deteriorated since 9/11. Adjunct teaching provided her main source of income, but a number of her courses had been canceled, especially during the summer, because of lack of enrollment. During the summer of 2003 she had no work at all for the first time in eight years. She did not have health insurance. She explained:

Work, rent, etc., in New York is so difficult, you find yourself living in your thirties like you did in your twenties. A day doesn't go by when I don't say, "I'd like to get out of here." [But] I've been in New York for ten years, and it's taken me this long to feel a sense of community.... To get up and go somewhere else—then you have to start all over.

Arts Institutions and the Art Market

Despite forecasts of doom and gloom after the terrorist suicide bombing, major commercial art dealers and auction houses were soon reporting business as usual. By the late fall of 2001, several established New York art dealers told a *New York Times* reporter that not only had business picked up where it left off before 9/11, but people were "buying more than ever." However, the reporter pointed out, only established, "blue-chip" artists were selling well. Rather than risking their money on emerging or experimental artists, collectors were looking for already famous ones, particularly Americans like Roy Lichtenstein, Jasper Johns, and Andy Warhol. At Sotheby's 2001 (post-9/11) auction, these artists sold right in the middle of the estimated $36 million to $50 million (Vogel 2001). In fact, art critics speculated that the attacks may have strengthened the market for postwar American artists.

Why was the high end of the art market still healthy despite dire economic times? The sociologist Andras Szanto, an expert on art markets, noted that after the stock market crash of 1987, the art market held up until 1990. "When the stock market crashed," he said in an interview (fall 2002), "lots of people found a haven in art (it had been doing well since 1982). The two markets go hand and hand, but art responds much more slowly. It's not like stocks. People hold on to it." He also claims that "the art market has independent determinants besides the larger economy.... The market has some autonomy." Such "independent determinants" may also have been at play in the art market's belated response to the recession combined with the devastating economic effects of September 11. For example, some collectors may have viewed investment in postwar American art as a patriotic response to an attack on American culture and values.

The Impact on Selected Galleries

Julia Rothenberg's field research from September through November 2002 further demonstrates that the economic impact of 9/11 was not felt, in the short run, across the board by all sectors of the art market.[1] The case studies discussed later also indicate that a variety of circumstances, including geography and adherence to mainstream artistic standards, affected the degree to which various galleries were affected by both 9/11 and the recession.

Rothenberg, who lives next to New York's most active commercial art district, West Chelsea, visited the area about a week after the attack. Deep gloom pervaded the gallery area: the galleries and streets were sparsely populated, and people spoke in hushed tones. However, just a couple of weeks later she observed that the same gallery district was back in full swing. More recent interviews corroborated her observation that the Chelsea slump was short-lived. A staff member at Mary Boone, one of the most successful galleries for contemporary art, explained that "our shows always sell out before or a couple of days after the opening. In the few weeks immediately following September 11 there was definitely less street traffic—fewer people were making the rounds in Chelsea. But our sales did not really suffer. We are continuing to do very well." Indeed, all of the works in the exhibition featured at the time of the interview—the work of a figurative painter named Will Cotton—had red dots next to them, indicating that they had already been sold.

An informant from Gagosian, a gallery with branches in Chelsea and up-town as well as in Europe and Japan and a full staff of salespeople occupying a row of desks in a separate room in the back of the gallery, told Rothenberg that "just after 9/11 the place was empty, but then, all of a sudden, everyone came to see the [Richard] Serra show. It was like the floodgates had opened and everyone wanted to come and see art again. No, our sales haven't really suffered as a result of 9/11. People continued to buy. Of course, because of the stock market people are buying smaller things now. But they're still buying."

Commercial galleries further downtown—for example, in Tribeca—and those with a more specialized or "riskier" roster of artists experienced far more negative effects. The experience of one dealer, Sherry French, underlines the precariousness of less conservative entrepreneurial enterprises in a weak economy. Her gallery, which specializes in the relatively marginal market (by Chelsea standards) for realism, shares a building space with FBI headquarters on Twenty-sixth Street between Eleventh and Twelfth Avenues. Because of street closings and the priority given to FBI activity in her building (in terms of phone lines, for example), French's business practically closed down for over a month after 9/11. However, since she was not located within the official boundaries of Ground Zero, she did not receive any compensation from the city for financial loss and damage. As she put it: "I was devastated after twenty years in the business." The stress of her financial losses from 9/11, combined with the increased financial burden of having twin infants who required full-time care, clearly left their mark. She could no longer afford a nanny and was forced to bring the twins with her to work, where she had converted a corner of the gallery into a nursery, with two cribs and neatly stored toys. French expressed grave doubts about the future and talked of shutting down her gallery and operating solely through the Internet.

The gallery owner Cheryl Pelavin also indicated that innovators who departed from mainstream offerings were particularly vulnerable after 9/11. Her gallery is another example of the economic and cultural connections between the office space market, particularly in lower Manhattan, and the world of artists and their galleries. Originally trained as a printmaker, Pelavin purchased her Tribeca space in 1981 to use as a print shop. At that time Tribeca was still a food market district, with an emerging residential neighborhood ecologically related to the World Trade Center.

Pelavin decided to expand her business to include a gallery in 1997, when the market picked up in the years following the crash of 1990. Geographically her gallery was on the margins of the previous art center (SoHo) and far from Chelsea. She chose to represent unknown, midcareer women, artists who typically have the hardest time achieving commercial success. She pointed out that, unlike the star artists and dealers in the business, she was "totally dependent on the economy." Also, since she could not afford expensive, full-page magazine ads, her business depended on word of mouth. In the early 1980s her most important clients were corporations such as Chemical Bank and Pfizer, which bought through consultants. She explained that corporations had been relying on the advice of full-time professional "art consultants" since the early 1980s as they spent large amounts of money on contemporary art; such acquisitions created cultural legitimacy for these corporations, first for banks and later for other kinds of corporations. With the crash in the late 1980s, however, many corporate buyers "grew to hate their collections, so they dumped them. People became hostile—they blamed art."

Given her gallery's location, Pelavin continued to be dependent on the sales generated through corporate consultants. "There are no walk-ins in Tribeca," she said. "If the market crashes, you lose everything. I'm a sensitive barometer [to the market] because I'm so small [and] I have no alternative market [because my work is] totally contemporary. I'm in the moment." By this she meant that she had no spare Jasper Johns or Lichtensteins that she could sell if times were tough. Only her low overhead enabled her to weather bad times. Nonetheless, "everything stopped when the dot-coms crashed. Business had been very good. I was selling everything. January 2001, it all stopped."

She was sure, however, that by September 2001 she would have had a winner—the landscape painter Daisy Craddock's show was scheduled to open on September 13, and Craddock had previously been able to sell very well with Pelavin. On September 11, Tribeca closed down completely, postponing the opening for two weeks. Even then, only a handful of people attended. Pelavin sold a couple of paintings and a few drawings, but Craddock was an artist who usually sold 70 percent of her show. This time, "nobody looked. Nobody came." Soon after, Pelavin started writing grants for artists and for herself to scrape together enough money to remain open.

Pelavin's next show after 9/11 featured an artist whose works on paper were usually all sold before her show even opened. This time, when the show opened, the gallery had not sold even one monotype. In fact, nothing in this show sold. And since Pelavin liked to give her artists a long run, this meant that there were no sales between November 2001 and January 2002. By then, the gallery was 70 percent behind in its projected sales for the season.

It was around this time that the viewing platform for the disaster site opened. Although Pelavin expressed some bitterness that the distribution of tickets only in the South Street Seaport area was bringing all the tourist dollars to that part of lower Manhattan and none to Tribeca, in the long run opening up the disaster site to viewing had a positive effect on Tribeca. Now everyone was talking about downtown. Pelavin and other Tribeca business owners formed an organization devoted to renewal in the area. Pelavin's next show opened in January 2002. Unlike the previous two shows, this one did very well. Pelavin attributed its success to a combination of timely subject matter and something new for the gallery—sales from walk-ins. Ground Zero, in its role as a tourist destination, had attracted many more people to the area.

She claimed that "we have had fabulous luck since January 2002." However, despite better sales than she would have anticipated considering the devastation of September 11 and the market failures, the gallery was still in dire financial straits. "If we don't get those corporations back," she said, "I don't know what we'll do." She added, "Even if we had the buyers all of a sudden, many of the artists have been forced by the economy to take full-time jobs and don't even have the time to take advantage of opportunities that present themselves."

Michael Richards and the Lower Manhattan Cultural Council

One of the most profound effects of September 11 was felt—physically, emotionally, and financially—by the Lower Manhattan Cultural Council (LMCC), a nonprofit organization founded alongside the development of Battery Park City. The LMCC advocates and organizes a number of downtown cultural events and opportunities for artists. Prior to 9/11, the LMCC's offices were located in the World Trade Center, where it also ran the Worldviews studio program. Worldviews funded a small group of young artists whose work had some relationship to New York City to work for a nine-month period in studio spaces on the ninety-second floor of Tower One. These studio spaces were located in unused office space donated to the program by leaseholders.

Michael Richards, one of the artists in residence on the ninety-second floor, was killed during the attack. In addition, the artwork in the rest of the studios was destroyed, as were all of the records, equipment, and physical home of the LMCC. Mouchtar Kocache, the LMCC's director of media, said the losses for his organization were not just monetary but profoundly emotional, especially with the death of a promising young artist. Perhaps because of its relationship with the fallen towers, at first the LMCC received an outpouring of support in the form of contributions. However, as months passed and the city's economy continued to suffer, organizations like this one experienced a steady decrease in donations.

Nonprofit Arts Organizations: The Vital Intermediaries

Nonprofit arts organizations like the LMCC advocate for the arts and serve as intermediaries between artists and institutions that may provide studio space, markets for artistic production, museum shows, arts fellowships, and much more. Most of these organizations have experienced a significant loss of economic resources, in both private donations and government subsidies, since 9/11.

Nonprofit cultural organizations and the visitors they attract to the city create over $5.7 billion annually in economic benefits for New York City, and they were linked to an additional $12 billion in commercial activity in 2001 (Alliance for the Arts 2002). In addition, the cultural sector generates more than twice as much in tax revenues than it receives in support from the city (Alliance for the Arts 2002). In 2001 New York City's nonprofit cultural sector generated 54,000 jobs. Approximately 20,000 of those jobs were provided directly by nonprofit cultural organizations (Alliance for the Arts 2002).

Unfortunately, the economic news from the 2,000 museums and other nonprofit arts organizations in the New York metropolitan area in the months following 9/11 was largely negative. These museums and organizations—including well-funded cultural institutions such as the Metropolitan Museum, the Lyric Opera, and the Museum of Modern Art, as well as community arts centers like the Jamaica Center for Arts and Learning and the countless theater companies, not-for-profit gallery and performance spaces, and arts advocacy organizations such as the LMCC—typically raise funds from a combination of government grants, private contributions, tickets, recording and gift sales, and rehearsal space rental. The dramatic downturn in foreign and domestic tourism to the city appears to have been the primary explanation for the decline in visits to cultural institutions.

The Center for an Urban Future's (CUF) November 2001 survey of the economic situation of nonprofit arts organizations revealed that all such organizations have been badly hurt since 9/11. Aside from the job losses in the form of layoffs following the recession and loss of tourist revenue to the city after 9/11, which primarily affect individuals, the organizations have seen cuts in all of their funding sources. It is difficult to gauge the impact of decreased exhibition attendance because museum entrance fees often vary from day to day and are sometimes based on a "pay what you will" system. It is possible to report high attendance but still experience considerable loss in revenue if visitors come on the free days or choose to pay one dollar instead of seven. Gift shop sales, a mainstay of many cultural institutions' budgets, have dropped significantly. The CUF survey found that 90 percent of arts organization fund-raisers raised significantly less money than they had anticipated in the months following 9/11. In addition, 50 percent of the organizations surveyed reported that major gifts and donations were canceled or postponed. Government cutbacks by the end of 2001 included a 15 percent cut at the city's Department of Cultural Affairs, a 10 percent cut in the state cultural budget, and the elimination of state line-item grants.

Nonprofit organization staff were understandably anxious about their own futures and the future of their organizations. When interviewed nine months after the CUF survey, their situation had only worsened. For example, Alexander Campos, director of the Jamaica Center for Arts and Learning, said that cultural institutions like his experienced a 15 percent cut in state and city funding in the months following 9/11, a 5 percent cut in July 2002, and a 7.5 percent cut in September 2002. He explained that while these cuts affected cultural organizations throughout the five boroughs, larger institutions, like the Metropolitan Museum of Art, had other strong sources of funding and were thus not as severely affected as smaller, community-based organizations such as his.

In sum, while the most well established artists, galleries, museums, and nonprofit organizations suffered negative economic impacts after 9/11, more innovative galleries, museums, and nonprofits, and the artists who depend on them, fared far worse. One result is increasing polarization and stratification in the city's visual arts community. What will be the impact of the rebuilding of lower Manhattan and the eventual revival of the city's corporate economy on the region's art market and visual arts community? In part, the answer to this question hinges on how artists themselves address the issues raised by 9/11 in their work.

ART FOR A WOUNDED CITY: IMPACTS OF 9/11 ON ARTISTS' WORK

The terrorist attack on New York City generated an almost insatiable demand for visual representation. Most New Yorkers' first experiences of 9/11 were visual, and the ghastly images of the collapsing towers were repeated in a seemingly endless televised loop. Still, the public craved more images and created them everywhere in the ensuing weeks, in the form of mental pictures of Ground Zero, photographs of the missing, homemade shrines and memorials, and countless art and photography shows curated and sponsored by members of the city's visual arts community. A public that had, for the most part, come to expect controversy and outrage from art during the Giuliani mayoralty began to talk about art's "healing power," and attendance at cultural events became an act of patriotism and hope.

Public discourse in the city turned to discussion and debates about commemorative architecture, memorials, and the uses of aesthetics in the built environment. Debate over the censoring of Eric Fishl's sculpture *Tumbling Woman* in Rockefeller Center, for example, led residents of New York City to contemplate the healing aspects of art in a traumatized social environment. But as pundits called for art to be put to what they judged to be socially constructive uses, many artists interviewed for this study reported a "chill effect" of the bombings and the extreme nationalism they evoked. Other artists asserted that unbridled creative production was the best way to affirm free speech and expression and the "Western" way of life.

The city's arts community responded to the new demands and issues with an outpouring of artwork that dealt specifically or indirectly with 9/11. This art covered a wide range of responses and approaches. The first impulse of many artists interviewed was to document the events themselves, and even painters and sculptors reached for their cameras and video recorders to fix images that would help make sense of the disaster. All the artists interviewed claimed that they were profoundly affected by the events, as the work we discuss later documents. With few exceptions, they tended to represent the tragedy as directly involved New Yorkers who wished to convey their experiences and feelings to the outside world rather than as Americans who wished to express their patriotism or their wounded sense of national pride.

New York Artists as Cultural Ambassadors

Nonetheless, some artists who had never before contemplated their identity as Americans found themselves doing so in their post-9/11 work. Their intent was not to promote or represent a particularly U.S.-centered patriotism or ideology, but rather, in their attempts to engage the interpretations and assumptions of the European and non-Western world, to explore their position, in the eyes of a global audience, as representatives of an American culture. This was not always a comfortable position for artists who had long considered themselves outsiders in or critics of their own culture.

Lee Songee, who works with video, created *WTC RIP*, a videotape she submitted successfully to the 2001 Venice Biennale. It describes the intersection of the artist's personal feelings and desire to address the rest of the world. In the days following the attacks Songee randomly filmed images of the city and its shaken residents. She explained that the attack, particularly the loss of the buildings, had left her stunned and saddened. "When I first came here [from

Taiwan] is when construction began. It was my birth in America. I identified New York with the twin towers. Now, a year later, I can talk about it more easily. But when I was editing, I tried to do it during the day because at night I would feel chills."

Shortly after 9/11 Songee spoke with a friend who reported the anti-American sentiments he had recently heard on vacation in Italy: "[He] came back from Venice saying that the Italians said Americans deserve this." It was then that she decided to use the footage she had collected after the attack to make a short video and enter it in the Venice Biennale competition. "I made this focusing on Venice," she explained. "I wanted to show them that nobody deserves this."

The video explores questions of community, nationalism, and loss. Songee explicitly set out *not* to make "a political tract" but rather to present a "tribute or portrait ... not sensationalistic. Just showing, not shaping—it is a personal tribute. It humanizes. It's a personal piece to represent New Yorkers. I try to capture the moment and how New Yorkers felt, as a New Yorker." Songee conceived her video as an attempt to communicate to the European world in particular that regardless of the foreign policies of the U.S. government or the evils of U.S. imperialism, no human beings, including Americans, "deserve" this sort of catastrophe. She also suspected that part of the reason her film was chosen for the Biennale was that she had listed her birthplace as Taipei, although she considered herself Chinese American. It was possible, she conjectured, that the judges saw her as an "outsider" in American culture and thus thought she would be more objective.

For Songee, the creation of the video was more than an aesthetic and commemorative exercise. While thinking through the ideas that motivated its production, she wrestled with important ethical and sociological questions concerning nationalism, racism, and her own experience as a young child in Taiwan and as a Chinese American. At first, she admitted, the attack made her hate and fear Arabs and Muslims. But then it occurred to her that

being a minority myself, I wondered how it would be if a Chinese person had done it. I thought about the Japanese encampments—a lot of Chinese people were afraid. I had that constantly in my mind. As a Chinese/Taiwanese person, I was raised to hate Japanese ... and I began to try and understand why Arabs hate us. So I went to myself and asked why I hate Japanese. Well, it's just something they are raised with. If you are raised hating a nationality that you have nothing to do with, you are impressionable. You can hate a state without hating each individual. But there are deep feelings, like Jews about Germans.

Another artist, Tina Laporta, had similar experiences creating artwork in a post-9/11 world. Reflecting on events through her preferred media of photography, video, and the computer, she addressed issues of national identity and the role of culture in shaping the way the world is interpreted. Like Lee Songee, Laporta was deeply troubled by the image of Americans abroad and profoundly affected by the collapse of the towers. While in a state of inertia and shock, she wondered what the role of artists should be. Like Songee and many of the other artists interviewed for this study, Laporta first responded by taking pictures. In line with themes from her previous work concerning communication and technology, she photographed images from television: "Then the weather got colder, and I'm glued to the TV for the first time in my life. Finally, all the channels came back (I don't have cable). I was getting channel 25 with news broadcasts from all over the world. I started to take Polaroids from the TV."

Laporta was not yet thinking about what she would do with these images, many of which were of veiled or masked Middle Eastern men and women. Then she was invited to take part in an artist-in-residence program in Istanbul. She decided to use the time there to create an installation, which she called *Total Screen*. Based on the Polaroid photos she had taken from TV news images after 9/11 of events and people in Afghanistan and the Middle East, the work pays special attention to representations of gender via the veil, hijab, burka, or chador. "The gender differences between the veiled woman and the masked man are of particular interest to a Western audience just becoming exposed to Eastern practices of covering," she explained.

In line with the nature of the media with which they work (film, video, computer, Internet) and their previous preoccupations (communications, documentation, architecture), Songee's and Laporta's artistic responses to the events of 9/11 were particularly relevant and accessible to a large public. As Laporta explained, "I am like a sponge. I just absorb and respond to the things that happen around me." Like journalists, they provided images, or representations, of the event and its context. But as artists, they had license to create images from a particular, sometimes personal perspective. This perspective, they came to realize, was informed by their particular experience as Americans and as New Yorkers, but also by their more universal experience as human beings. Thus, as "cultural ambassadors," they were able to provide a unique and nuanced perspective on the situation.

Addressing the Political

Other artists created images that addressed the causes and effects of the attack more directly. Jean Michel Ulriqu Desert's *Burqua Project*, consisting of four Western flags (the United States, France, Germany, and England) made into full-body Islamic veils, was exhibited in the front windows of the Lower East Side Tenement Museum. The artist's statement explained his intentions:

This project is an opportunity for meditation on themes we cannot grasp easily. Ordinary and familiar signs (the flag, the veil, praying beads) are merged in a simple direct manner that fills a gap where we struggle for words. What is nationalism? What is colonialism? Faith? Belief? What do we fear? What do others fear? This artwork intends to activate and liberate the viewer's process of interpretation or personal exploration of the many fluid and shifting emotions and memories the project evokes.

Some of the noncommercial galleries visited for this study managed to re-main within the mainstream of art-world discourse while encouraging work that would not fit the conventionally commercial bill. The work they featured reflected in a directly political manner on issues of U.S. foreign and domestic policy, censorship, patriotism, racial profiling, and the post-9/11 loss of civil liberties. Juan Puntes, who directs White Box, an alternative exhibition space in Chelsea that tends to feature the work of politically engaged artists, took a more direct approach to politics. In May 2002 White Box hosted "The Blame Show," curated by the critic Eleanor Heartney and the video artist Larry Litt. The exhibition included a video by Litt entitled *The Blame Video* in which close to one hundred "ordinary people" are asked to comment on "who or what is to blame for the current homeland situation." Litt created this video by setting up his camera at White Box and inviting pedestrians in Chelsea to participate. He claimed that the line went around the block, thereby demonstrating the desire of citizens to have a political voice.

The White Box exhibition also included works by Dan Perkins (aka Tom Tomorrow), the Artists Network of Refuse & Resist, the Independent Media Center, and Political Artists Open Media Lab, as well as documentation by artists who worked for the free-speech watchdogs, the American Civil Liber-ties Union (ACLU) and the National Coalition Against Censorship (NCAC). Svetlana Mintcheva of the NCAC created a "Censorship Timeline" document-ing selected acts of censorship since 1989. Heartney and Litt also organized "Art Now: Polite, Politic, or Political?"—a public forum that focused on dis-senting political art since 9/11. During the forum discussion, Mintcheva pro-vided specific examples of censorship in art since 9/11. For example, the Federal Bureau of Investigation (FBI) searched a Houston art gallery looking for "ter-roristic" artwork, and the Armory Show in New York pulled a work because it incorporated the World Trade Center and attacking airplanes in a video-game-style presentation. Mintcheva also described the broadened powers of surveillance granted by the passing of the Patriot Act, which, for example, allows investigators to obtain court orders to compel libraries and booksellers to turn over private information about their patrons and customers (AufBau 2002). This act could have repercussions for the art world as well if the U.S. government were to feel threatened by works of art that it deemed too critical.

The Power of Stepping Back

The artists mentioned here addressed the events of 9/11, and the larger political situation surrounding them, in a directly sociological or journalistic manner. While the work of Songee, Laporta, and Desert is personal, poetic, and evocative, it is also explicitly concerned with representing social and political meaning. Other artists we interviewed incorporated the events—in terms of both the imagery and the emotional climate following the attack—in a much less explicit and more aesthetically formal fashion. Susanna Heller, for example, is a Greenpoint-based painter whose work reflects a preoccupation with the ephemeral nature of urban space and motion in New York City. Much of the work on view in her Greenpoint studio hinged on the theme of the World Trade Center. She had been one of the original recipients of the CityScape residencies organized by the LMCC. From her studio high atop Tower Two, she had a helicopter's-eye view of the island of Manhattan, and the strange, distorted perspective seen from the top of Tower One is the theme of a recent piece, *Tower One*. After September 11, Heller almost immediately returned to the site and began making drawings of the rubble, which were pinned to the wall of her studio.[2] From these drawings she was beginning to put together a new series of paintings and a companion piece to *Tower One*—a portrait of Tower Two in ruins. She had already shown a number of these paintings in group shows in New York and from her gallery in Ottawa, Canada, when we interviewed her in November 2001. *Tower One*, in fact, was purchased by a Canadian museum, and at the time of the interview she was preparing to travel to Shanghai to take part in a major museum exhibit there. "I'm not addressing it [the attacks] in a political way," she said. "It's about the power of stepping back and looking. If you take time to step back and look, you might see that something is going wrong."

Winners and Skeptics

Some of the artists and gallery representatives we interviewed were wary and even disgusted by what they considered "9/11 sensationalism." Several were openly skeptical of the buzz created around "9/11 art" and felt that artists and galleries had capitalized on the visibility and newsworthiness of the tragedy to promote their own work. One gallery director said, "I refuse to deal with the towers. I've been through the 9/11 things. The press has done this—thinkers, writers, have already approached it. What is an artist going to add?" Another gallery director echoed this sentiment with even less charity. Speaking of works like Max Protech and Exit Art, he said: "Personally, I think it's a cheap shot. Okay. It's good for funding, etc. We accept politics in the debacle of art. We could benefit because it touches a nerve, but you need ambiguity. I don't spend my time on shows that are just for the moment."

The attitude of some representatives of the more established Chelsea galleries, such as Mary Boone, Luhring Augustine, and Gagosian, was equally dismissive of "9/11 art," but for slightly different reasons. One dealer said that he represented "established artists. They're not going to change their work just because of 9/11." The implication seemed to be that artists whose careers were not yet in full swing might find it efficacious to exploit popular interest in the terrorist attack to gain notice, but legitimate artists—or, to put it another way, artists showing at legitimate galleries—had no need to respond to current events because their work was already a valued commodity. Visits to Chelsea galleries in the year following 9/11 confirmed this dealer's statement. The most "important" galleries continued to exhibit high-profile artists like Richard Serra, Rebecca Horn, and Mike Kelley, whose work seemed to remain untouched by world events. Exhibitions of works by emerging artists in these blue-chip galleries featured more "eye candy" (paintings, generally, that are particularly "pretty" and "fun") than usual. However, galleries in Western Europe, like the prestigious Fondation Cartier in Paris, sponsored highly successful shows, largely by New York and other American artists, that focused explicitly on the social and political issues raised by the attacks on the World Trade Center.

CONCLUSION: REBUILDING LOWER MANHATTAN AND THE NEW YORK ART WORLD

The impacts of the terrorist suicide attacks of 9/11 ranged from the immediate destruction of galleries and studios in the vicinity of the World Trade Center towers to the varied influences of the events on the work of artists themselves. We have seen that younger artists and galleries that depended on sales of art to decorators and others in the commercial office sector suffered the greatest economic losses. More established artists with national and international reputations and the galleries that represented them soon rebounded from the attacks.

Another important impact of the attack was the effect it had on the creative work of artists in the metropolitan region. As we have seen, the tragic events had a profound influence on some artists' work, while other artists, especially those with established followings, were more likely to stay with the styles and concepts that had made their art successful. For younger artists, the creation of new exposition spaces and galleries in lower Manhattan offers—but does not guarantee—exciting possibilities for shows and expositions that showcase their work, especially work that reflects on the meanings and consequences of changed post-9/11 realities. More established artists, like Jennifer Bartlett and Andy Goldsworthy, have already created excitement in the art world with their installations in the vicinity of Ground Zero, although their work does not reflect directly on 9/11 and its consequences. The extent to which arts organizations in lower Manhattan will also engage the talents of younger artists whose work challenges received wisdoms in art and politics remains to be seen.

The rebuilding of lower Manhattan presents unprecedented opportunities for the city's visual arts community. When 15.5 million square feet of prime office space was completely destroyed on 9/11, and another 15.5 million square feet severely damaged, the city lost the equivalent in office space of fifteen Empire State buildings, or the entire downtown of a moderate-sized city, like Louisville, Kentucky (*Real Estate Marketplace* 2001, 5). But the re-creation of so much commercial space and the aesthetic care being lavished on the planning and architectural designs offer the hope, if not the promise, that artists and galleries will make contributions on many fronts to lower Manhattan's cultural and aesthetic renaissance.

Artists themselves are unlikely to be key players in the politics of their own participation in this rebuilding. Nor is their most innovative or daring work likely to adorn the walls or the public spaces of new corporate lobbies and reception areas in the rebuilt downtown. Fiercely independent and understandably wary of the aesthetic costs of political or corporate patronage, the city's artists will depend on the curatorial efforts of the arts organizations that represent their interests and can work with the corporations and other groups that control exhibition space. With so much new potential exposition space, and with art events assuming such a central role in attracting nonbusiness trips to New York and other world cities, it is likely that lower Manhattan's competitive efforts to rise as a cultural center will add a good deal of unexpected artistic excitement to the city's art scene in the post-9/11 environment.

NOTES

1. Between October 2001 and December 2002, Rothenberg conducted some twenty formal interviews with established artists and members of the far larger group of artists struggling to achieve critical and financial success, as well as with critics, collectors, art dealers, and nonprofit arts organization personnel. In addition, she engaged in participant observation in the art world, which included attending gallery openings and other art world events and engaging in informal discussions with artists and other residents of artists' neighborhoods.

2. Heller had been a recipient of the LMCC residency prior to the attack. By the time of the attacks, her residence in the World Trade Center was already over. She was working in her Greenpoint studio at the time of the attack.

REFERENCES

Alliance for the Arts. 2002. "New York City Culture Facts." *Alliance for the Arts Newsletter* (November).

Ashton, Dore. 1973. *The New York School: A Cultural Reckoning*. New York: Viking Press.

AufBau, Sara Ogger. 2002. "Fifteen Minutes of Blame—The Blame Show: A Forum for Political Art." *The Arts* 10. Available at: http://www.artistsnetwork.org/news4/news171.html (accessed August 10, 2002).

Castells, Manuel. 1996. *The Rise of the Network Society*. Cambridge, Mass.: Blackwell Publishers.

Caves, Richard. 2000. *Creative Industries: Contacts Between Art and Commerce*. Cambridge, Mass.: Harvard University Press.

Crockoft, Eva. 1974. "Abstract Expressionism: Weapon of the Cold War." *Artforum* 12(10): 39–41.

Deutsche, Rosalyn, and Cara Gendel Ryan. 1984. "The Fine Art of Gentrification." *October* (31, Winter): 91–102.

Fiscal Policy Institute (FPI). 2002. "The Impact of September 11 on the New York City Arts Community." New York: Consortium for Worker Education and New York Foundation for the Arts.

Grabher, Gernot. 2002. "The Project Ecology of Advertising: Tasks, Talents, and Teams." *Regional Studies* 36(3, (May): 245–62.

Greenberg, Clement. 1961. *Art and Culture: Critical Essays*. Boston: Beacon Press.

Guilbaut, Serge. 1983. *How New York Stole the Idea of Modern Art: Abstract Expressionism, Freedom, and the Cold War*. Chicago: University of Chicago Press.

Hackworth, Jason. 2002. "Postrecession Gentrification in New York City." *Urban Affairs Review* 37(July): 15–44.

Real Estate Marketplace. 2001. "Real Estate Update." *Real Estate Marketplace*, September 19.

Shapiro, David, and Cecile Shapiro, eds. 1990. *Abstract Expressionism: A Critical Record*. New York: Cambridge University Press.

Smith, Neil, and James DeFilippis. 1999. "The Reassertion of Economics: 1990s Gentrification in the Lower East Side." *International Journal of Urban and Region Research* (December): 638–54.

Szanto, Andras. 2003. "Hot and Cold: Some Contrasts Between the Visual Arts Worlds of New York and Los Angeles." In *New York and Los Angeles: Politics, Society, and Culture: A Comparative Approach*, edited by David Halle. Chicago: University of Chicago Press.

Vogel, Carol. 2001. "High Energy and Prices at Contemporary Art Sale." *New York Times*, November 15.

Zukin, Sharon. 1982. *Loft Living: Culture and Capital in Urban Change*. Baltimore: Johns Hopkins University Press.

CHAPTER 10

The Psychological Treatment of Trauma and the Trauma of Psychological Treatment: Talking to Psychotherapists About 9/11

Karen Seeley

IN THE hours after the 2001 terrorist attack on the World Trade Center, New York City hospitals prepared to receive the wounded. At St. Vincent's Hospital in Greenwich Village, gurneys dressed in clean white linens were neatly arrayed along Seventh Avenue, awaiting a deluge of injured survivors. But the hospital beds remained empty; the physically wounded did not materialize. In lieu of bodily injuries, many of those who survived the attack suffered wounds that were psychological. As the loss of life, the property damage, and the terrorist threat were measured, and as the shock and fear set in, attention turned to psychological injuries and to the public's mental health.

Disasters are known to cause extensive psychological harm (Vlahov 2002). Disasters that involve acts of mass violence, that are humanly caused and intentional, and that damage property and the economy have been found to produce especially severe and widespread distress (Norris 2002). Following the deadliest terrorist attack ever to take place on American ground, experts in public health anticipated unusually high rates of psychological disturbance. Though the unprecedented nature of the attack made it impossible to estimate accurately how many persons would develop psychological injuries, these experts generated a range of predictions. Some public health officials foresaw mental health problems not only for the 12.7 million residents of New York City and its surrounding counties, but for every resident of New York State

(Jack and Glied 2002). Others estimated the attack's psychological effects by extrapolating from the rates of mental disorder produced by the 1995 Oklahoma City bombing. They predicted that 34 percent of those who were "most exposed"—including those injured in the attack, families of the injured and the deceased, rescue workers and their families, and World Trade Center employees and their families, or approximately 528,000 persons—would develop post-traumatic stress disorder (PTSD) (Herman, Felton, and Susser 2002a). Further, they predicted that an additional 3 million New York metropolitan area residents would experience other kinds of psychological distress, such as anxiety or depression (Herman, Felton, and Susser 2002b).

Early studies of the mental health consequences of September 11 supported predictions of elevated rates of distress. In a survey conducted a week after the attack, 61 percent of those who lived within one hundred miles of the World Trade Center reported experiencing traumatic stress (Schuster et al. 2001). Studies in the first few months after the attack found a higher incidence of psychological symptoms after 9/11 (Galea et al. 2002), as well as greater consumption of alcohol, cigarettes, and marijuana (Vlahov et al. 2002) among New York City residents. Increased distress was not limited to adults: tens of thousands of New York City children developed a range of psychological symptoms, including nightmares, anxiety, and agoraphobia (Goodnough 2002), in reaction to the attack. A more recent survey found that nearly half of the New Yorkers interviewed had had difficulty sleeping or concentrating since 9/11 (Garfinkel et al., this volume).

To address this pervasive distress, the New York State Office of Mental Health designed Project Liberty, a disaster mental health program strikingly different from its previous initiatives. Promised more than $150 million in federal funding, Project Liberty was soon up and running. Within a month and a half of the attack it had hired new counseling staff; trained thousands of mental health professionals in disaster mental health and community outreach; designated hundreds of existing social service agencies as program sites; created television and print publicity campaigns to educate the public about traumatic stress; and extended free counseling to anyone affected by the attack (Felton 2002). Not only were free mental health services made available to the public, but they were aggressively marketed. Project Liberty's services were advertised on buses and subways, on radio and television, and on postcards and paper cups (Wunsch-Hitzig et al. 2002). Celebrities were hired as spokespersons to reduce the stigma of seeking mental health treatment in response to the attack (Jack and Glied 2002).

New York State's mental health programs were in place within weeks of September 11, 2001, but New York City psychotherapists responded to the attack within hours. Following the attack, approximately nine thousand therapists (HoffSommers and Satel 2005) contacted disaster relief organizations and their professional associations to learn how they might help. Beginning that day, and continuing for the next several months, therapists volunteered their services. They worked in the Armory, comforting persons who were searching for the missing; on telephone hotlines, speaking with callers who could not locate their relatives; at the Pier, consoling the families of the deceased; at family assistance centers, helping the newly displaced and unemployed; and at Ground Zero, supporting rescue and recovery workers. In firehouses, community centers, city schools, and corporate boardrooms, as well as in their private offices, they listened as evacuees, witnesses, and relatives of the deceased told their stories. Although there is no precise count of the number of psychotherapists who delivered mental health services to individuals who suffered psychological harm as a result of the attack, in the weeks and months after September 11 therapists seemed to be everywhere. If there are indeed "eight million 9/11 stories" in New York City (Rich 2002), then there are untold numbers of therapists who have listened to thousands of them.

This chapter explores the impact of the events of September 11, 2001, on New York City mental health professionals who treated the emotionally injured in the days, weeks, and months after the attack on the twin towers. It examines how psychotherapists—few of whom had been formally trained in community mental health, disaster mental health, trauma, or public health—responded professionally to an unprecedented act of mass violence. In addition, this chapter investigates the emotional costs of providing psychological care. How were therapists personally affected by spending month after month listening closely and repeatedly to patients' horrific accounts of 9/11? This question is of particular significance given the fact that after the attack, therapists found themselves in the novel clinical situation of treating individuals suffering from a catastrophic event that they too had experienced. Further, by presenting therapists' reports of their patients' reactions to the events of September 11, this chapter provides a window into the psychological consequences of acts of mass violence. Because therapists hear patients' most private thoughts and fears, and because they notice signs of distress and behavioral change that patients themselves may not be aware of, New York City mental health professionals had information on individuals' responses to the attack that was not available from any other source.

From September to December 2002, I interviewed twenty-nine psychotherapists. Fifteen were psychologists, and fourteen were social workers; half of them had additional training in psychoanalysis. Twenty-five participants had private practices, and all of them worked in New York City. To discover the widest range of personal and professional consequences of 9/11, I interviewed therapists who delivered brief crisis treatments to survivors and to victims' families immediately after the attack, as well as therapists who were still working with them over a year later, at the time of this research. Owing to the study's time constraints, I did not control for participants' training, theoretical orientation, or any other variables, and I selected as participants therapists who could be interviewed immediately rather than those working in hospital or agency settings where outside research projects are subject to lengthy reviews. Though this sample is not representative, participants' unique vantage points provide new kinds of data on the impact of September 11 on psychotherapists and suggest directions for future research. To maintain participants' confidentiality, I do not distinguish between social workers, psychologists, and psychoanalysts but refer to all of them using the broader categories of "therapists," "psychotherapists," and "mental health professionals." All other identifying information pertaining to participants and their patients also has been changed.

TREATING THE UNNAMABLE

In a profession that places the highest value on saying the unsayable, after September 11 psychotherapists, uncharacteristically, were at a loss for words. Confronted with an inconceivable act of violence that, to this day, is primarily referred to by numbers, therapists acknowledged the difficulty of naming "our loss, the attack, the disaster, the catastrophe, the act of war, what should we call it?" (Dimen 2002, 451).

Because the events of September 11 proved so difficult to name, many therapists who were eager to help after the attack were unsure of the kinds of aid to provide. How could they provide psychological help to persons suffering from overwhelmingly painful events that resisted classification? And how should they identify the sufferers? To some of the therapists in the study, they were survivors of a disaster, like people who had lost everything to hurricanes or floods. To others, they were families of crime victims, like those who had lost loved ones to murder. Although some therapists thought that the mental health sequelae of September 11 defied psychiatric categorization, others diagnosed individuals who had been experiencing flashbacks, intrusive memories, and recurrent nightmares since the attack with post-traumatic stress disorder.

"Trauma" is the term that mental health professionals most frequently have used to refer to the psychological consequences of September 11. Some of the therapists in the study considered "trauma" the appropriate term because it describes responses to events that are horrific, inconceivable, and psychologically overwhelming—events that, as one participant said, "should never happen to you." "Trauma" may also have become the accepted term because it has colloquial as well as medical meanings. It is possible to describe someone as "traumatized" without invoking the severe symptomatology that is specific to PTSD (APA 2000). Yet even when participants agreed that many who survived the World Trade Center attack were suffering from PTSD, they did not agree on its treatment. Because many basic principles of trauma treatment contradict those of traditional therapeutic approaches, the various kinds of mental health professionals disagree as to the most effective clinical interventions for PTSD (Ballenger et al. 2000) and for other trauma-related disorders. Moreover, although the field of mental health has shown a renewed interest in trauma in the past twenty years (Herman 1997), several participants who were professionally trained before the early 1980s said that they had never been trained in trauma. Therapists who are otherwise highly trained and experienced may be unfamiliar with, and dismissive of, specialized treatments for trauma, while trauma specialists often claim that traditional therapeutic approaches can exacerbate the symptoms of PTSD.

Though many of the therapists in the study felt their lack of training very keenly after September 11, they did not let it interfere with their wish to help. Several described themselves as "tough" or "levelheaded" or "effective in crisis," suggesting that even if they were untrained in trauma, their personal characteristics qualified them to intervene. Other participants sought to acquire new clinical skills as quickly as possible. They surfed the Internet for information on treating survivors of disasters, exchanged articles with peers on the Oklahoma City bombing, and took crash courses in trauma. Still, after the attack many of them found themselves delivering mental health services they had never been formally trained to provide, to populations they had never been trained to treat, in a catastrophic situation for which they had never been prepared.

Even participants who did have related clinical training and experience felt unprepared to treat those persons who were deeply wounded by September 11. Therapists who were experienced in providing relief after earthquakes, hurricanes, and airplane crashes were unsure how to help victims of a terrifying and incomprehensible act of mass violence. Those who had worked intensively with individuals with histories of trauma, including Vietnam veterans, victims of torture, and survivors of abuse, had little idea how to treat persons suffering from a current traumatic event. Those who specialized in bereavement had not been trained to help persons whose relatives had been killed by terrorists, those who had to mourn in public, those whose losses could be counted in dozens, or those who had lost their "whole peer group." One participant described a patient who "lost sixty-one of his colleagues and his best friend." Another spoke of working with firefighters who "knew a hundred people who were dead."

Struggling to comfort the terrorized, the disoriented, the numbed, and the bereaved, many of these therapists had little sense of what to do; instead, "we made it up as we went along," said one. "None of the old models worked," another noted. "We were just going by the seat of our pants."

PSYCHOLOGICAL FIRST AID

The need to "make it up as we went along" was especially common among therapists who volunteered their services in the first hours and days after the attack. As the magnitude of the destruction became clearer, many participants, desperate to help, contacted the Red Cross. But New York City airports, bridges, and tunnels were closed on September 11. National Red Cross leaders and their most experienced disaster responders could not get into town for days. Numerous participants who went to the New York City chapter of the Red Cross to volunteer described the local office as "disorganized" and "chaotic." One remarked that "they had far too many therapists, and they didn't have a clue how to use them." Another participant said that he and his colleagues were told by the Red Cross to "figure it out for ourselves."

In the absence of a coordinated mental health response after the attack, many therapists improvised. Rather than waiting for the wounded to come to them, they searched for people in need of psychological first aid. A psychoanalytic institute in Greenwich Village opened its doors to the public, offering free group treatment. A few therapists set up tables in their Brooklyn neighborhood, handing out literature on trauma and referrals for psychotherapy. Some of them enjoyed the freedom of reaching out to their communities in unconventional ways—it took them back to their professional roots. One said that she felt as if "it was 1890, and you were a charitable organization social worker, and you had to go door to door . . . we were out there."

Other participants found being "out there" less gratifying. Though hundreds of thousands of people were believed to be in distress, therapists could not always find them. One therapist recalled that he and his colleagues had gone from one location to another on September 11, frantically searching for people to help. Having walked to the Red Cross right after the attack, they were put on a bus to the World Trade Center. When access to the site was restricted, the Red Cross redirected the bus to Penn Station, expecting to find commuters who were injured or in shock and trying to get home. This participant learned to identify World Trade Center survivors by looking down at their feet: those who had escaped the area had white dust on their shoes. But Penn Station was virtually empty; those who had survived the attack fled immediately, walking over bridges or hopping on trucks and ferries, doing "whatever they could to get out. No one relied on traditional transportation." Frustrated that the Red Cross had failed to connect them with the wounded, he and his colleagues decided that they would no longer take its direction. "We lost all contact with them. So we're acting like we're under the auspices of the Red Cross, but frankly, it just gained us admittance." After an unsuccessful attempt "to wrestle down an ambulance to bring us to the Trade Center," they walked from hospital to hospital offering their services. They finally found a small hospital whose emergency medical workers had been wounded at the twin towers and whose director asked them to work with his staff.

When therapists did find people to help, their interventions were not always appreciated. One participant told of walking into her neighborhood fire department, which had been among the first responders to the attack, and offering her services. "We sat down and literally ran a group with a lot of guys that were in shock, a lot of PTSD . . . they were crying, they were numb, they were flashing back."

In this participant's professional assessment, the firefighters were unfit for active duty—as she put it, "I wouldn't want them responding to my fire"—and she counseled them to take time off to recover. Her advice was rejected by the firehouse lieutenant, who told her, "You don't understand. We can't put them on leave . . . we don't have anybody here. They have to go back."

Many therapists who volunteered their services had little idea how to deliver them. Sent to work at various relief sites set up throughout the city, they found themselves amid human misery and devastation on an unimaginable scale. There were "thousands and thousands of people with thousands of needs"; the poor and the wealthy stood on line together for hours, often in great anger and distress, to tell relief workers,

> I'm living on the streets, I'm stuck. I have lost all of my papers, I have lost everything, all of my identity in the World Trade Center. Or I was stuck in an elevator. Or I got down the stairs, and now I can't breathe. . . . Can you give me $500? Can you get me a hotel room? Can you help me with my creditors? I have no apartment, I can't get into my apartment in Battery Park City.

Therapists quickly learned that they could not practice in the usual ways under these circumstances. As one participant remarked: "You suspend all that you've ever learned about how to be in the perfect setting with the two chairs properly placed and the pristine office with the box of tissues available." Another participant recalled trying to figure out how she could help people waiting on line in a family assistance center, and how she should approach them. She decided

> that you should just work the room, which is not what any of us are trained to do. . . . In this case, I just worked the waiting room. I just went from one person to another to another to another to another to another to another to another, and I would talk to thirty people in the course of four hours. And if anybody was really breaking down, or saying things that were too much for other people to handle, or talking too loud . . . you would pull them aside.

Others who volunteered their services were sent to settings at Ground Zero below military checkpoints that felt like war zones and "looked like the embodiment of anguish." Although they were there to help rescue and recovery workers, many therapists were themselves disoriented, dazed, and "couldn't take it in; it was in some ways like watching a movie." One participant described working eight-hour shifts, from four in the afternoon until midnight, in a respite center set up in a condemned hotel, where "everything was covered with plastic—the walls, the floors, everything." The overpowering "smell of death" gave her the sense of "being in this biological stew," and her shifts were punctuated by "Catholic priests rushing in and throwing on Red Cross jackets and rushing out, so you'd know they'd found a body or body parts."

Therapists were asked "to just sit down and talk" with workers, and they stationed themselves in the dining areas where rescue workers took their breaks. Several participants noticed that many of the workers, whose twelve-hour shifts involved not only clearing debris but locating the bodies of colleagues and friends, were "losing it": they were sobbing, looking glazed and unresponsive, and "self-medicating like nobody's business." Yet these therapists, who knew that their overtures might not be wanted, were uncertain how to intervene "so you didn't become a pain in the neck, on the one hand, [and] on the other hand, you were available if somebody needed you." They also realized that workers could not afford to connect with them on an emotional level during their breaks because "they all had to go back to work. . . . They had to go back out onto the pile or into the pit. They were really in shock, and they were just going, going, going, driving themselves."

When their shifts were over, after walking through the "absolute muck" of the site, therapists would arrive at the washing point, where their shoes were washed off with water. "I'm thinking, I've just walked through toxic material. Are we both going to participate in this fiction that my shoes have just been made clean with water from a hose?"

After washing the dust off their shoes, therapists returned to the rest of their lives. They tried, with mixed results, to get the dust and the smell of Ground Zero off their bodies, out of their clothes, and out of their apartments. They also tried to erase the scenes of Ground Zero from their memories, but at unexpected moments "those guys would pop into my mind." The faces of the recovery workers and of the injured, the displaced, and the bereaved, as well as images of the Armory, the family service centers, and Ground Zero and fragments of conversations, remained with them. At the time of the interviews some participants—especially those who usually worked with patients for months or years at a time—still worried about the people they had spoken with for a few minutes, in a state of profound emergency, desperation, grief, and fatigue, and then had never seen again.

"GET ME COUNSELORS!"

As psychotherapists confronted a variety of unfamiliar, urgent, and extreme situations in the wake of the attack on the World Trade Center—situations to which standard clinical models did not readily apply—the demand for mental health services grew. The state and federal governments stoked this demand. Indeed, in the eyes of many New York psychotherapists, another unusual consequence of September 11 was government endorsement of mental health services as legitimate and effective remedies for the suffering produced by an act of mass violence. Government officials publicly recognized mental illnesses such as post-traumatic stress disorder and depression, provided moneys to educate the public about them, and supplied an array of psychological services to treat them. Mental health was firmly identified as a key component of public health. For psychotherapists, this was a rare validation of their services and skills. Following many discouraging years in which psychotherapy had been deprived of insurance coverage, displaced by psychopharmacology, and generally derided, after September 11 New Yorkers in distress were advised to get themselves to a therapist.

Several factors supported the influx of new psychotherapy patients. Project Liberty provided mental health services free of charge to anyone who felt upset by the terrorist attack. In addition, those who had been employed in the World Trade Center and its vicinity had had relatively high rates of insurance coverage for mental health treatment. In cases where the primary policyholder had died in the attack, many insurance companies agreed to continue covering family members (Jack and Glied 2002). Though many therapists suffered financial losses after the attack—because they could not get to their offices in the "frozen zone" below Fourteenth Street, they scaled down their practices to volunteer their services, or their patients from other boroughs and the suburbs stopped coming into Manhattan for therapy—several participants said that after 9/11 their telephones "never stopped ringing." As one therapist asked, "Was there ever a time when everyone in New York City wanted treatment?"

The demand for mental health services came not only from individuals but from all kinds of organizations. Participants who worked in educational settings and had been providing psychological treatment to students were suddenly asked to help faculty and staff. Employees of many downtown firms had watched the towers fall, had seen people jumping from windows, had climbed over bodies as they fled, had been trapped in clouds of dust, had been stuck in elevators, had walked miles in states of terror, had been displaced from their homes or offices, or had lost close colleagues and friends. These firms hired therapists to help those who were too numb, too preoccupied, or too terrified to come back downtown or to go back to work. One participant estimated that a large corporation that had lost hundreds of employees "had three thousand people in acute stress disorder." Human resource managers' concerns for their employees' well-being were equaled by their need to get them back to work quickly so that their businesses would survive. Therapists were expected to be available immediately, sometimes without pay, and to provide large-scale relief instantaneously. All over town managers were shouting, "Get me counselors!"

To meet the urgent demand for psychological treatment, mental health organizations and psychoanalytic institutes acted as clearinghouses, compiling lists of therapists who wished to donate their services and matching them with sites requesting help. Therapists trained other therapists to work with survivors—one participant trained sixty therapists in trauma the week after 9/11. Some mental health agencies hired additional therapists; others brought in experts from Oklahoma City or Israel to teach their staffs about the psychological consequences of terrorism.

Although these strategies often worked smoothly, they sometimes caused resentment. Therapists who gave up private practice income to volunteer their services, as well as therapists who were paid their usual wages in extraordinarily demanding situations, found themselves working next to newly hired and highly paid mental health consultants. Some participants felt that their employers had pressured them into providing pro bono services when they could not afford it. They also felt pressured into providing services they were not trained to deliver, to one traumatized group after another. "It was 'You're doing debriefing on Monday, and you're doing debriefing on Wednesday . . . and can you also do debriefing here, and can you do debriefing there?'" Service delivery could be disorganized, with "too many therapists" competing to provide help at the same location. Moreover, some therapists were perceived as "ready to move in with their own agenda" rather than respecting the needs of the communities they volunteered to serve.

Because of the spike in demand for mental health services, many therapists were also working overtime. A participant who had worked three hours a week in an educational setting before September 11 was suddenly working thirty. In the fall of 2001 some volunteers worked long shifts at Ground Zero at night, then returned to their regular jobs during the day. One participant who shuttled between the World Trade Center site and her private office uptown said that if she planned it right, "I could get back here and get a couple of hours of sleep before I sort of tumbled into the next day." After just "throw[ing] water on my face," she hoped that she did "not look, or smell, like I had just come from there."

Therapists who specialized in trauma or bereavement were flooded with new patients. Some enlarged their practices and offered free therapy to those who could not afford it. In explaining their availability, many participants mentioned a sense of duty "to be available after 9/11 for whomever I needed to be available for." Others simply saw themselves as the best qualified for the task at hand. As one participant said, "This is my specialty. If I don't do this, who's gonna do it?"

EMOTIONAL CONTAGION

Psychotherapists struggled with a variety of professional challenges in the post-9/11 clinical landscape, but the majority of the participants in this study found the emotional aspects of their work the most burdensome. Many participants who made themselves available to survivors of the attack and to families of victims did so at their own expense, as their deep, empathic, and intimate connections with these patients made them unusually emotionally vulnerable. One participant explained that doing psychotherapy requires therapists to enter every patient's subjective world. "I was really taught . . . that you can't really understand what your patient is feeling unless you allow yourself to be drawn into that subjectivity. And then the work of the therapy is really to pull yourself back and to come out and look at it in a much more objective way."

But many participants experienced a new inability to pull themselves out of their patients' subjective worlds, so that they lived in the throes of their anguish. Moreover, although those who specialized in working with the traumatized and the bereaved were aware that their own emotional stability depended on limiting the number of severely distressed patients they treated, they abandoned such considerations after September 11. Since the attack, they had filled their practices with greater numbers of "horror cases"—persons profoundly devastated by an unthinkably violent act. In consequence, as one participant said, "almost every day is death and destruction and grief and abject pain."

Many participants, uncertain how much tragedy they could cope with, felt pushed beyond their capacities. Unable to take refuge in the "protective coma" (Didion 2003, 54) that shielded so many others, they struggled to remain emotionally present several hours a day, for weeks and months on end, to patients whose stories were among the most painful and gruesome they had ever heard. They spoke of being dazed, exhausted, and numb; after spending several hours a day in their offices listening to patients tell their stories, many spent their nights at home in tears.

Although several therapists said that after 9/11 they had wept in front of patients for the first time, others emphasized how important it was for them to maintain their composure—"to look somebody right in the eye and let them tell you about the atrocities and the devastation and not flinch." One participant told of a patient's reaction when a Red Cross worker broke down after hearing his story. "All he kept saying [was], 'I made the Red Cross lady cry, I made the Red Cross lady cry. I must be really bad because I made the Red Cross lady cry.' I wanted to find this Red Cross lady . . . her crying traumatized this guy."

The most wrenching clinical situations that psychotherapists faced after 9/11 involved the uncertainties and confusions surrounding the missing and the deceased. Some participants described the conflicts they felt in offering hope to persons who were searching local hospitals for relatives and friends, even after they themselves had concluded that no one had survived the towers' collapse. Others had shared with the families of the missing inaccurate lists of the dead they had been given, so that they had unwittingly misinformed some family members. Two participants lost patients in the attack. One who worked with uniformed services personnel at Ground Zero recalled looking down into the site and wondering, "Is my patient down in there? Are they going to find him?" Another reported that a patient who lost dozens of friends in the attack phoned her one morning to say that he was about to jump onto the subway tracks and to ask her to tell him why he should not.

Some participants suffered from their new acquaintance with the dead. One who worked with numerous families of the deceased said that the dead had begun to "inhabit" her.

I'm getting to know the people who died extremely well through the people who are talking about them. . . . I find myself looking at the pictures [in the newspaper] of the people that I know through the people I'm working with and saying, Oh, so that's what you look like. . . . And I find myself wondering the kind of things that their grievers are wondering. Did you suffer? Were you panicking? What was it like for you in the last few minutes?

Several participants described the anguish of lacking the usual proofs of demise, so that the deaths of particular individuals in the mass slaughter could not always be ascertained. Even when a death was established or accepted, family members could not grieve in conventional ways because there was often no body to bury. Many families had received fragments of bodies and been told that more pieces would follow. "And the families say, 'What are we going to do? Have another memorial service? Are we going to dig up what we buried?'"

Therapists who had listened to their patients' graphic descriptions of people on fire, of bodies falling from windows, of various body parts, or of tissue fragments in the debris spoke of feeling emotionally battered by their mental "videotapes" of these accounts. "I'm a very visual person. So I am knocked to the fucking floor. And I am stuck in the elevator, and I am choking down the stairs and tripping over something and losing my briefcase . . . it's all very vivid . . . and it was a lot to carry around."

Though many therapists tried to manage their anxieties by shutting out the media, their patients brought them daily information and rumor, along with their idiosyncratic terrors. Listening to patients' stories, participants absorbed their fears as well as their anguish.

I found myself becoming much more anxious when I had certain patients coming in talking about their theories, and talking about how they would only ride in the front of the train or the back of the train, because a bomber wouldn't go to those cars. Or how they would kill themselves if a nuclear blast went off, 'cause they didn't want to die of radiation poisoning.

Many participants noted that they had never before been so affected by their patients' emotional experiences and psychological symptoms. One re-marked, "If I'm treating an alcoholic, I'm not going to start drinking." But 9/11 was different. As another participant said, "There wasn't one of us there that wasn't hearing it and taking it on."

SIMULTANEOUS TRAUMA

The communal nature of the catastrophic attack on the World Trade Center heightened the transmission of emotional distress from patient to therapist. Contrary to conventional conceptualizations of mental disturbance as individ-ually located and owned, the attack's psychological repercussions were shared both within and across communities and spread as if contagious. September 11 was a collective trauma not only in the sense that it damaged the bonds of community (Erikson 1995), but also in the sense that it was experienced communally. In the words of one participant, "The experience, the visceral, psychic, mind-heart continuum experience, was a collective experience. We all reacted out of a collective archetypal knowledge of survival and dread. . . . That level of communal experience outweighed the personal story." Another spoke about the collective nervous system that was damaged by the attack. "Every-body's trauma was so raw. . . . It didn't matter who you were talking to—relief worker, direct victim, other therapists—you were all the same body in some ways."

This injured social body inhabited the clinical consulting room. In the wake of the attack, patients' individual identities and idiosyncratic body languages seemed to have been erased. "The first week or so, people just sat. They just sat. I had somebody who always sits like this, with her feet in the chair, and she was just sitting [slumps]. For the first week or two, somatically, people were just here."

Not only was this trauma collective, but therapists and their patients had experienced it simultaneously. Some of the therapists in the study had family members who were injured or personal property that was damaged in the attack. Others had witnessed the attack from their offices, walked with throngs of stunned evacuees over bridges to Brooklyn and Queens, rushed to retrieve their children from school, or spent hours in a state of panic because they had not heard from friends or relatives who worked in the towers. Several participants said that they thought they were going to die.

This simultaneous trauma produced an extremely rare clinical situation: therapists were shaken and hurt by the same catastrophic event that had shaken and hurt the patients they were treating. For some participants, this meant that "we all kind of were in the same world in a way that we hadn't been. . . . When a patient would say to me, 'That smoke, the smell of that smoke,' I smelled it, it was in my lungs. We couldn't pretend that she had to tell me what that was." This simultaneous trauma also produced a clinical situation in which the therapists, who in theory had worked through their psychological conflicts and anxieties, were trying to help patients while their own wounds and fears were still raw. Some participants saw themselves in their patients' devastation and seemed comforted by patients who voiced feelings that they shared. One participant said, "So many times I've been in session and I want to say, 'Me too! Me too!'"

Indeed, the events of 9/11 blurred therapeutic boundaries in several ways. For some participants, the fact that they and their patients were stricken by the same attack eliminated the usual distinction between therapist and patient—perhaps the most important distinction in psychological treatment. As one participant said, "If you're my patient, and you've been through this, and I've been through it, and I'm calling you sick, then I'm sick too." Many participants found it more difficult than usual to separate their lives from their patients' lives. They continually had to remind themselves, "This is your life. Your husband isn't dead, your kids aren't dead. You're okay." One participant said that after working for several months with families who had lost children and had told her of their last words to them, whenever she saw her son, "if he said good-bye in a particular way . . . I'd be going, 'Oh jeez, the way he said that, something is surely going to happen. That was significant, that was different than the way he usually says that.'"

Many participants noted the irony of providing mental health treatment to others when they felt sorely in need of it themselves. Some returned to treatment, while others imagined giving up their professional role. "You don't want to be the therapist . . . the one who couldn't cry, who had to know what to do. . . . What happens if I couldn't cope? . . . I didn't want everybody depending on me."

TRAUMATIC MEMORIES

Many participants in this research had a psychodynamic orientation to clinical material: they tended to interpret their patients' responses to the terrorist attack in light of their distinctive psychological histories. They anticipated that the attack would have aroused patients' most disturbing feelings and memories and retraumatized those with prior experiences of violence or abuse. As one participant explained, external events resonate internally with each person in particular ways. In treating patients after the attack, she tried to understand "how the reality of what we all know is going on dredged up old feelings of being unsafe, or old feelings of being vulnerable."

Although participants expected the attack to trigger disturbing feelings and memories in their patients, many were unprepared for their own traumatic memories awakened by the event. Several participants said they were caught off guard when they began to reexperience agonizing pieces of their personal histories after September 11. Like their patients, participants found themselves upended not only by the violent assault on their city and by the continuing climate of danger, but by vivid and intrusive memories of degradation and despair. One participant saw clear visual images of a traumatic injury he had sustained as a one-and-a-half-year-old child, memories that had not surfaced during his lengthy psychoanalysis. When another remembered forgotten aspects of his deceased mother, he had to mourn her again. A third therapist, who stood on the sidewalk watching the towers burn and collapse, recalled watching her "whole city" burn in Japan during World War II. A fourth, who noticed that Project Liberty staff members had excluded mental health professionals of color from positions of responsibility, relived prior experiences of racism. In the weeks after 9/11, when newly installed security guards asked her for identification, she wondered, "Do you do this to other people? Or is it just because I'm a black African American woman?"

CULTURAL TRANSFERENCES

While some participants confronted historically devalued racial identities after September 11, others contended with newly problematic cultural identities. Heightened public suspicions of Arabs and Muslims extended to psychotherapists. Therapists of color, therapists who were not American, and therapists who spoke English as a second language were suddenly located and named. The two participants from the Middle East and South Asia noticed that some patients began to mistrust them. "People can suspect . . . that I could be from some other part of the world. . . . Could I be like these hated fanatics? . . . Am I one of them? And am I safe? Who am I?" The suspicions of newly fearful patients materialized in the stories they told their therapists.

> The patient started to talk about the fact that the other day some U-Haul trucks were stolen by some unknown Arabs, and they were danger-ously running around the country with explosives, and there might be attacks. And I could see that in many ways there are concerns about me—can I be trusted, or am I one of these dangerous Arabs with power-ful explosives running around in the street?

Though participants worried that this cultural stigma would intensify, rather than taking patients' mistrust at face value, they analyzed its psycholog-ical meanings. In almost all cases, even patients who had grown more wary of their therapists chose to stay in treatment.

THE UNDERSERVED

Unlike participants whose cultural identities became highly visible after the attack, many minority groups remained invisible. Though Project Liberty's men-tal health programs were meant to reach "non-white, non-English-speaking groups at rates proportional to their representation in the general population of the disaster area" (Felton 2002, 432), in the view of some participants, these programs were neither available to nor culturally appropriate for various communities. As a result, after September 11 the most vulnerable New Yorkers, who often were severely affected by the attack (Garfinkel et al., this volume), did not receive sufficient help. According to participants, underserved groups included the elderly, some of whom were afraid to come out of their apart-ments; illegal immigrants and undocumented workers, who worried that they would be deported if they sought relief; Latinos, some of whose responses to the attack were exacerbated by poverty, discrimination, and the crash in No-vember of American Airlines flight 587, whose passengers were on their way to the Dominican Republic; Muslims, who became targets of hate crimes and arrests; and African Americans, who did not want to be seen as "want[ing] handouts." A participant who worked with the gay community said that al-though gay firefighters and police officers were among the rescue and recovery workers, their contributions were not publicly acknowledged, nor were surviv-ing partners in gay relationships eligible for many government benefits. After running a group for the partners of gay men and lesbians who died in the attack, this participant had a heightened sense of this community's invisibility. She recalled a session in which the group read the New York Times "Portraits of Grief" obituary of the partner of one of its members; the couple had been together for twenty years. As the obituary was read aloud, "we all thought we would die, 'cause ... it said something to the effect of, he was so busy with his work he wasn't interested in having a relationship."

Several participants noted that the social hierarchy was reproduced after the attack on the World Trade Center, complete with its glaring disparities. Some experienced these disparities firsthand. One participant of color said that her supervisors sent her "very affluent" colleagues to debrief employees of prestigious corporations and sent her to help the poor. Moreover, although these supervisors expected her to volunteer after September 11, they asked her to stop her volunteer work with the Dominican community after the crash of flight 587. Other participants confronted these disparities through their patients' reactions to the attack. Some described patients who resided in neighborhoods filled with violence and ruin or who had lengthy histories of trauma—these patients who had been "living in hell" prior to the 9/11 attack were unmoved by it and deeply resented the outpouring of money and support for its victims. Participants treating persons who were socially disenfranchised said that because some of them viewed the attack on the World Trade Center as a well-deserved assault on the structures of American power, they had little sympathy for the injured.

Many participants worked overtime to reach out to underserved communities after September 11. In addition to their usual professional responsibilities and volunteer clinical work, they made efforts to locate bilingual therapists, design culturally appropriate services, establish social supports for illegal immigrants, and obtain legal aid for undocumented workers and detainees.

THE FLORENCE NIGHTINGALES OF THE WORLD

As therapists served the wounded and the bereaved, they themselves had little relief. At the time of the interviews, which were conducted more than a year after September 11, 2001, many participants said they had not yet had time to process the attack or to mourn. One participant who worked closely with a particularly devastated population said that in the first few days following the attack, "the rest of the country was gathering with family and friends and going to vigils and grieving this whole thing, and we were just here working." One evening, still at work, she and a coworker heard noise from the street below their office. They looked out the window, "and the whole street was filled with people holding candles. ... And it was like, it's nice that everybody's doing this, but we have a department to take care of. ... You worry about yourself later."

Although many participants received comfort and support from their colleagues, or professional supervision, others did not. Having chosen not to expose others to the horrific stories they heard at work every day, they had no one with whom to discuss their work. Therapists were taking care of the city, but no one was taking care of therapists. As one participant said, "It was almost like we didn't count. We were just the Florence Nightingales of the world."

Without proper care, many therapists suffered. Several participants reported being unable to eat or sleep or having nightmares and flashbacks. Others became so numb and depressed, or so irritable and withdrawn, that their suffering affected their work. Some grew frustrated with patients who were wounded on 9/11 and showed no signs of recovery. Others were intolerant of patients who were not disturbed by the attack and whose usual psychological complaints suddenly seemed trivial and self-centered. Almost all of them had difficulty leaving their work behind when they went home. After spending the day with patients, said one therapist, "I couldn't listen to anything else. I didn't want anybody else stressing me out. I could not listen to other people's problems. I just wanted to do my patients and listen to the families who were going through this trauma. And that's what I did for a year."

Some participants wondered whether they had pushed themselves to work overtime with victims of the attack in order to avoid facing their own emotional responses to 9/11. One feared that he had become like "the firemen who won't quit digging, because if you quit then you've got to deal with what's going on." A participant who was pregnant on September 11 worried that her constant crying would harm her baby. Another was concerned about the long-term psychological consequences of her intensive clinical work with scores of emotionally ravaged firefighters; she imagined herself "curled up in a ball somewhere, unable to go to work."

Lacking preexisting systems of support, participants found various ways to care for themselves. Some went into psychotherapy to understand how the attack had affected them as individuals and as mental health providers; others sought refuge in spiritual practices or in their art. They cooked for themselves, cut back their schedules, and met with fewer patients in a day. Some conducted private rituals to cleanse themselves of the toxins they felt themselves absorbing as they listened to their patients. Others took every course they could find in trauma and catastrophe. One therapist focused on putting her financial affairs in order and made plans for herself and her family to escape the country together in the event of another attack.

PARADIGM SHIFTS

If the attack on the World Trade Center signified a piercing of national boundaries, for many therapists it signified a rupture of clinical boundaries as well. In response, they modified their usual modes of practice, abandoning the orthodoxies of their training. Inspired by the unconventional therapies they delivered as volunteers, some resolved to continue "to do anything and every-thing, in any way you can," in the name of mental health.

One clinical boundary that was broken on September 11 was the boundary between therapist and patient. As one participant said, "We crossed a line, because there was no line anymore. We were in it with everyone else." While some felt uncomfortable without the line and sought to reinscribe it as quickly as possible, several participants welcomed the lack of distance and separation between themselves and their patients, saying that it made them more emo-tionally present and honest.

Other participants noted that the attack on the World Trade Center had ruptured the usual clinical boundary between the world outside the consulting room and the world within it. The therapeutic space had been breached and no longer could be seen as protective or safe. Some felt a new need to keep "an eye toward the outside all the time." The noises of airplanes and sirens were not taken as routine; one participant recalled interrupting sessions to turn on the radio or look out the window to make sure that the world was intact.

Similarly, some participants whose prior clinical work had focused on pa-tients' intrapsychic life felt that the attack forced them to move "out of the safety of the symbolic world [and] into the real." But after the attack on the twin towers, who was to say what was real? Having experienced an event that brought their patients' most violent fantasies to life, an event that numerous participants described as cinematic and surreal—it was as if "we're all living in a dream," said one therapist—many of them no longer felt qualified to speak on behalf of either reality or rationality. They could no longer assure patients that the world was safe, nor could they always distinguish patients' paranoid anxieties from logical thinking. In the eyes of some participants, patients who lived with constant fears of violence and assault suddenly seemed to have a realistic appreciation of life's brutish possibilities.

In another clinical shift, many participants who previously had focused their clinical work on patients' personal histories now emphasized more cur-rent events. After September 11, they were likely to see patients who spoke about their past as avoiding their feelings about the attack and about the newly menacing present. With the future now in question, some participants approached their work with a new sense of urgency. One said that since the attack, she had begun to be more directive with her patients, so that they might more quickly make changes in their lives.

More importantly, as the first year after September 11 wore on, several par-ticipants began to reevaluate the fundamental nature and purpose of their work. Some began to view patients' responses to the attack not as symptoms of mental disorder but as elements of the human condition. They questioned both the utility of psychological analysis and their ability to help patients recover. As one participated stated, "I'm much more inclined now . . . to see the kinds of human suffering that life contains as part of what life contains. . . . Life is filled with suffering. . . . Ultimately, life cannot be fixed."

It is impossible to say whether such paradigmatic shifts will endure. Yet at the time of these interviews, many participants expressed little interest in returning to the traditional therapist's role or to conventional modes of practice.

LONG-DISTANCE RUNNERS

In the first fourteen months after 9/11, participants observed a broad range of psychological responses in their patients. Some who were psychologically injured in the attack had fully recovered, while others had become self-destructive. Some patients, paradoxically, felt healed by an act of horror that normalized a personal history of violence or trivialized a private misery. Some who only recently had realized the depths of their wounds finally had been able to tell their stories; others still were unable to speak of what they had experienced on September 11.

While there is little information on the long-term psychological consequences of terrorism, this research suggests that for many, its impact is enduring. At the time of this research, many survivors of the attack, as well as many family members of the deceased, remained in its grip. As one participant noted, "Each landmark brings another ripple. Each holiday brings up more memories and more side effects." For many patients, especially those who lost family members in the attack, it was as if September 11 was yesterday. One participant said, "I have people who come into my office and sit down, and I say, 'How are you doing?' And they say, 'Well, you asked me that on November 1, [2001], and that's how I'm doing. . . . I'm still right there where I was. I'm still watching the plane on television hit my son.'"

This research also suggests that the impact of terrorism may widen over time. A year after the attack many participants began to see a "second tier" of patients composed of victims' and survivors' distant relatives and acquaintances. This second tier also included the families of recovery workers, some of whom feared that the toxic elements unleashed by the disaster would spread, contaminating their homes. One spouse worried that her husband's work clothes would bring "all the chemicals and the poisons and the jet fuel fumes in the house to poison the baby."

Even participants who recognized that traumatic experiences cause enduring and recurrent distress were surprised to find that after more than a year, the attack on the World Trade Center remained the focus of their work with both new and existing patients. Participants were also surprised that their clinical work had acquired an intermittent quality. Treatments seemed endless as patients returned to therapy again and again for more help.

Some participants reported that after a year their work with relatives of the deceased had become even more difficult. Rather than beginning to recover, they had begun to experience "the real suffering part." One said, "People are really starting to feel their sadness. They're really processing that he's not coming back, or she's not coming back, or I'm never gonna see him again."

If the report of a participant who treated a woman injured in the 1993 bombing of the twin towers is any indication, their suffering will continue for years to come. Like many 2001 World Trade Center survivors, this patient found that her psychological trauma was exacerbated by the physical harm she suffered while escaping from the towers. During seven years of psychotherapy, the therapist witnessed her patient's life "disintegrate." Too traumatized to return to work at the World Trade Center—indeed, too physically injured to return to work at all—her personal identity was shattered. Her marriage deteriorated, and "her husband became an old man." The patient's psychotherapy, which began shortly after the bombing, ended with her death from complications of her injuries.

Anticipating agonizing and protracted psychotherapies with patients profoundly damaged on September 11, some participants tried to pace themselves. "I feel like I've got to be a long-distance runner here. . . . I feel like I'm going to be best for them if I can be the slow and steady and predictable and permanent presence for as long as they choose to be here." In the face of such daunting work, one participant renewed her commitment to the mental health profession. In her view, it was the only way she could be of service in a time of national crisis. "All I can do is keep doing what I'm doing. I can't go dig, I have a bad back. I don't know how to fly a plane, I don't know how to carry a gun. [But] I can talk to people. I can try to help them. I can cheer them up. I can help them cry. I can hold their hands."

PSYCHOLOGICAL HEALING

So far I have detailed the numerous difficulties that participants encountered as they delivered mental health services in situations of unprecedented professional challenge following the terrorist attack on the World Trade Center. Yet some participants thought that New York City "pulled off an amazing job" in providing mental health services to thousands and thousands of persons in distress after September 11, and they reported a variety of clinical successes. In the attack's immediate aftermath, some participants found value in unconventional, and sometimes nonverbal, therapeutic interventions. According to one participant, the most effective relief workers were those "giving out the cookies and the coffee. They're the ones who are truly touching people. They create an environment where people will talk." Two participants were struck by the "therapy dogs" stationed at sites for the families of the deceased. Unlike their human counterparts, the dogs were available for physical contact and did not ask intrusive questions. As one participant noted, although people might not want to talk to a therapist, "you can pet a dog, and you're relating."

A number of participants swore by their traditional clinical skills. Psychoanalysts found that because traumatic experiences frequently resurface in disguised forms, patients benefited most from long-term depth treatments involving interpretations of their dreams, unconscious fantasies, and key personal symbols. Participants who worked with groups or in institutional settings found it helpful to teach people the physiology of traumatic stress reactions, normalize their emotional responses to the attack, and provide them with a supportive community. One participant who worked in a school felt he had successfully mobilized his "seriously traumatized" community's resources and skills, so that its members were able to "round up the wagons, pull together, and take care of ourselves." Many other participants found that after September 11, as in all other therapeutic encounters, psychological healing occurred primarily by virtue of therapists "being there with another person and helping them to understand their experience and reframe their experience, hopefully, in some way that moves them forward."

Several participants found that September 11 changed their understanding of therapeutic encounters and of the psychotherapist's role. They no longer viewed psychological healing as contingent upon a therapist spending a specified amount of time alone with a person identified as a patient, in a particular kind of office, enacting a certain kind of professional expertise and relationship, and implementing a body of clinical theory. Instead, they came to believe that healing takes place in the context of humane interactions. Recalling her work with rescue workers at Ground Zero after 9/11, one participant compared herself to other healers who minister to the suffering: "I wanted to use whatever spiritual capacities I have to connect in a real, authentic, humane way, in a present way, with other human beings, for even that five minutes, for even that one minute, for even that glance.... Because it seemed to me that humanity is what mattered more than anything."

RESEARCH IMPLICATIONS

After the terrorist attack on the World Trade Center, New York–area psychotherapists frequently found themselves in uncharted terrain. Seeking to help a large urban community of persons injured by an act of mass violence, they worked under great pressure, in scenes of unspeakable destruction, chaos, and horror where their standard clinical methods were often inadequate or inappropriate. Confronting a kind of human tragedy for which their discipline had no category and an inadequate knowledge base, and for which it had insufficiently prepared them, they alternately faced outsized demands for help and found that their presence was unwanted. Transforming their usual professional models and roles to alleviate the suffering of others, their own suffering often went untreated and grew worse after extended contact with patients. Recognizing that those deeply hurt by the attack would not soon recover and might need psychological treatment indefinitely, therapists resigned themselves to the fact that they would be reliving September 11 for years. In light of such significant challenges to therapists' usual modes of practice, I consider various implications of the attack for New York City mental health professionals.

Mental Health Preparedness

This research suggests that if psychotherapists are to be on the front lines in the event of another terrorist attack, and if mental health services are to be less disorganized, improvised, and redundant than they were after September 11, it is of vital importance to increase mental health preparedness. Above all, mental health preparedness requires removing mental health care from the margins to which it has often been consigned, identifying mental health treatment as a social priority, and generating clear conceptions of public mental health. Mental health preparedness in New York City also depends on establishing a permanent mental health infrastructure. Instead of assembling new mental health services on an ad hoc basis in the wake of a catastrophe, or waiting for out-of-town relief experts to get into Manhattan, this infrastructure could be mobilized immediately after an attack. Ideally, such an infrastructure would streamline the delivery of mental health services, deploy mental health professionals to sites requiring relief, develop systems of continuing psychological care, create centralized databases of survivors and of the deceased, and supply therapists with up-to-date information on all relevant aspects of the catastrophe. It would also provide services that are culturally informed and that reach out to minorities, immigrants, undocumented workers, the elderly, the young, and other vulnerable groups.

Further, mental health preparedness requires reconfiguring mental health training and research. If terrorism is now viewed as inevitable, then mental health programs must equip therapists to treat those who are injured by it. To ensure that mental health professionals are properly trained, courses in the skills, models, and perspectives that psychotherapists found most useful after the 9/11 attack, including crisis intervention, group treatment, disaster mental health, trauma, and bereavement, must become basic components of clinical education. There is also a clear need for intensive research investigating the range of immediate and ongoing psychological consequences of terrorism.

Treatment approaches that have been developed for previous terrorist acts and disasters, both in this country and abroad, deserve critical examination.

Finally, mental health preparedness is contingent upon maintaining an adequate supply of psychotherapists. Although thousands of New York–area therapists generously donated their time after September 11, it is uncertain whether an equal number would volunteer in the event of another attack. A permanent mental health infrastructure must guarantee the availability of mental health professionals following large-scale catastrophes and compensate them for their services. It must also protect their psychological safety. This research suggests that mental health professionals are more vulnerable than previously believed—their immersion in the anguish of others puts them at psychological risk. The risk intensifies in situations of simultaneous trauma, and it might also intensify if new terrorist acts retraumatize city inhabitants. Consequently, we must develop protections and supports for psychotherapists who may be emotionally harmed by providing mental health services to terrorized populations.

Expanding the Frame of Psychotherapy

In addition to pointing to necessary improvements in mental health preparedness, this research suggests that treating the suffering caused by acts of mass violence requires expanding the frame of psychotherapy. As September 11 made clear, the mental health field does not offer adequate models for treating trauma and bereavement. Existing models provide little guidance in treating trauma and bereavement that co-occur; that are deepened by multiple losses; that are worsened by physical injury; that are heightened by exposure to environmental toxins; that are complicated by losses of housing or employment; that are produced by incomprehensible terrorist acts; or that are experienced in a climate of unrelenting threat. Nor does this field currently offer adequate models for the treatment of trauma and bereavement that occur on a massive scale; that afflict communities as well as individuals; that are contagious rather than contained; or that require alleviation at both the social and individual levels.

These limitations might be addressed by expanding the mental health paradigm, which could incorporate psychologies of terrorism and war and generate a variety of disaster-specific diagnostic categories and models of treatment. Through interdisciplinary collaborations, it also could be informed by new research on culture, political violence, memory, neurobiology, and epidemiology so that it might provide deeper understandings of collective psychopathology, emotional contagion, political action, social bodies, and public mental health. Such complex conceptions of individual and social behavior not only would allow therapists to deliver more effective treatments but might lead to the development of new clinical strategies that combine psychological healing with political action.

The Limits of Psychotherapy

Alternatively, the findings of this research may suggest that mental health preparedness is impossible, that the mental health paradigm cannot be expanded, and that the events of September 11, by proving its theories and practices inadequate, expose the limits of this professional discourse. If human suffering cannot be verbalized, analyzed, interpreted, or eased, if it cannot be assimilated to a person's life history, if it cannot be individualized or contained—in other words, if it cannot be made sense of in psychological terms—then frameworks other than those of psychotherapy may be required. In this view, if therapists have been injured by their clinical work since September 11, it is because they have been out of their depth as they handle materials with professional tools that are ill-suited to the task. Further, if the psychological consequences of terrorism are contagious, then therapists and patients may continually reinjure each other, and therapists who turn to colleagues for support may spread emotional suffering throughout their professional community. In other words, the strategies that have been designed to reduce psychological harm may actually transmit it. If this is the case, then no type of clinical training will sufficiently prepare therapists to treat persons devastated by a terrorist attack, nor will any amount of protection fully shield them from the emotional risks of their work.

CONCLUSION

More than three years after September 11, 2001, the long-term effects of the terrorist attack on psychotherapists and on the field of mental health remain uncertain. There are preliminary indications, however, that in its wake some mental health professionals have begun to reconceptualize the scope and implications of both the therapeutic and social roles of psychotherapists. The attack has stimulated broader and more urgent clinical interest in the treatment of trauma and traumatic loss, in the psychological consequences of terrorism for individuals and collectivities, in the contributions of specific social and political events to emotional distress, and in trauma's transmission and containment. Further, the attack has precipitated a new sense of community awareness and social responsibility among psychotherapists. Some have organized politically and now seek public forums in which to discuss the emotional consequences of traumatic events and the psychological implications of government policies. Others have focused on improving psychological services and their delivery, either by developing community approaches to trauma or by promoting public mental health preparedness, in order to ensure an adequate therapeutic response in the event of future catastrophes.

Would a new mental health infrastructure respond effectively to the individual and collective consequences of terrorism? Can the mental health paradigm be expanded beyond its present limits? Do psychotherapeutic perspectives adequately address acts of mass violence? These are questions that cannot be definitively answered here, yet they require consideration. If psychotherapists are to be on the front lines in future disasters and acts of terrorism, they must candidly address the new challenges to their profession as well as the limitations of their field. This research suggests, however, that many therapists are less interested in grappling with such questions than in alleviating the immediate suffering of individuals. Even as they struggled to make sense of an act of mass violence, many renewed their commitment to helping those who had been harmed by it. As one therapist stated, "There is great suffering. And the only meaning one can make out of suffering is in some way to be in opposition to it."

REFERENCES

Altman, Neil. 1995. *The Analyst in the Inner City: Race, Class, and Culture Through a Psychoanalytic Lens.* Hillsdale, N.J.: Analytic Press.

American Psychiatric Association (APA). 2000. *Diagnostic and Statistical Manual of Mental Disorders.* 4th ed. Washington, D.C.: American Psychiatric Association.

Ballenger, James C., Jonathan R. T. Davidson, Yves Lecrubier, David J. Nutt, Edna B. Foa, Ronald C. Kessler, Alexander C. McFarlane, and Arieh Y. Shalev. 2000. "Consensus Statement of Post-traumatic Stress Disorder from the International Consensus Group on Depression and Anxiety." *Journal of Clinical Psychiatry* 61(suppl. 5): 60–66.

Didion, Joan. 2003. "Fixed Ideas Since September 11." *New York Review of Books* (January 16): 54–59.

Dimen, Muriel. 2002. "Day 2/Month 2: Wordless/The Words to Say It." *Psychoanalytic Dialogues* 12(3): 451–55.

Erikson, Kai. 1995. "Notes on Trauma and Community." In *Trauma: Explorations in Memory*, edited by Cathy Caruth. Baltimore: Johns Hopkins University Press.

Felton, Chip J. 2002. "Project Liberty: A Public Health Response to New Yorkers' Mental Health Needs Arising from the World Trade Center Terrorist Attacks." *Journal of Urban Health* 79(3): 429–33.

Galea, Sandro, Jennifer Ahern, Heidi Resnick, Dean Kilpatrick, Michael Bucuvalas, Joel Gold, and David Vlahov. 2002. "Psychological Sequelae of the September 11 Terrorist Attacks in New York City." *New England Journal of Medicine* 346(13): 982–87.

Goodnough, Abby. 2002. "Post 9–11 Pain Is Found to Linger in Young Minds." *New York Times*, May 2, p. A1.

Herman, Daniel, Chip J. Felton, and Ezra Susser. 2002a. "Mental Health Needs in New

York State Following the September 11 Attacks." *Journal of Urban Health* 79(3): 322–31.

———. 2002b. *Rates and Treatment Costs of Mental Disorders Stemming from the World Trade Center Terrorist Attacks: An Initial Needs Assessment.* Albany: New York State Office of Mental Health.

Herman, Judith Lewis. 1997. *Trauma and Recovery.* New York: Basic Books.

HoffSommers, Christina, and Sally Satel. 2005. *One Nation Under Therapy: Why Self-absorption Is Eroding Self-reliance.* New York: St. Martin's.

Jack, Kathrine, and Sherry Glied. 2002. "The Public Costs of Mental Health Response: Lessons from the New York City Post-9/11 Needs Assessment." *Journal of Urban Health* 79(3): 332–39.

Norris, Fran H. 2002. "Disasters in Urban Context." *Journal of Urban Health* 79(3): 308–14.

Rich, Frank. 2002. "Slouching Towards 9/11." *New York Times*, August 31, p. A15.

Roland, Alan. 1988. *In Search of Self in India and Japan: Toward a Cross-cultural Psychology.* Princeton, N.J.: Princeton University Press.

Schuster, Mark A., Bradley D. Stein, Lisa H. Jaycox, Rebecca L. Collins, Grant N. Marshall, Marc N. Elliot, Annie J. Zhou, David E. Kanouse, Janina L. Morrison, and Sandra H. Berry. 2001. "A National Survey of Stress Reactions After the September 11, 2001, Terrorist Attacks." *New England Journal of Medicine* 345(20): 1507–12.

Vlahov, David. 2002. "Urban Disaster: A Population Perspective." *Journal of Urban Health* 79(3): 295.

Vlahov, David, Sandro Galea, Heidi Resnick, Jennifer Ahern, Joseph A. Boscarino, Michael Bucuvalas, Joel Gold, and Dean Kilpatrick. 2002. "Increased Use of Cigarettes, Alcohol, and Marijuana Among Manhattan New York Residents After the 9/11 Terrorist Attacks." *American Journal of Epidemiology* 155(11): 988–96.

Wunsch-Hitzig, Robin, Jane Plapinger, John Draper, and Elsie del Campo. 2002. "Calls for Help After September 11: A Community Mental Health Hotline." *Journal of Urban Health* 79(3): 417–28.

PART IV

The Impact of 9/11
on Organizations

CHAPTER 11

Resolving Identities: Successive Crises in a Trading Room After 9/11

Daniel Beunza and David Stark

SO ACCUSTOMED have we grown to the image of the facades of the World Trade Center (WTC)—two tall rectangles cut against the skyline of Manhattan—that we seldom give any thought to what went on inside the towers. Although we have seen photographs of the victims of the 9/11 terrorist attack and learned about their personal lives, even now we rarely hear about the work that was done behind that curtain wall of concrete and tinted glass.

The World Trade Center was above all a place of finance—not retail banking, but types of financial activity that involved trading. If, before September 11, you had chosen a floor at random for exploration, you would more likely than not have ended up in a trading room, one of those vast open spaces where traders, salespeople, and analysts buy and sell stocks and bonds. Cantor Fitzgerald, for example, the bond trading company that suffered most in the attack, was a trading room. Morgan Stanley, the largest tenant of the towers with twenty-three floors, had several trading rooms.

In this chapter, we examine one such trading room and the experiences of its occupants by studying traders at a large investment bank located in the World Financial Center directly adjacent to the WTC. The collapse of the twin towers destroyed the trading room of the pseudonymous International Securities, along with its computers, connections, facilities, and data. The traders survived, but the attack forced them to relocate to a makeshift trading room in New Jersey. There they spent six long months exiled from the city. During that time they confronted anxieties and uncertainties that they had never faced in their typically young lifetimes: an inescapable sense of vulnerability, the difficulties of trading securities outside of Wall Street, and dramatic lines of fissure in their organization. One year later, however, the bank had restored its trading technology and returned to its original Wall Street office, and all of the original traders who relocated to New Jersey had remained in the company. The case of International Securities thus provides a privileged entry point into an understanding of organizational resilience. In this chapter, we document the unfolding processes of organizational sensemaking that let the traders cope with extreme uncertainty and allowed the organization to survive.

Confronting uncertainty, even extraordinary uncertainty, was not at all unusual for the traders at International Securities. Prior to September 11, the company's bread and butter was its demonstrable ability not simply to cope with but quite literally to thrive on volatility. Finding profit opportunities in an informationally efficient market such as Wall Street required that the bank specialize in complex and ambiguous cases and generate innovative interpretations of the economic environment. We elaborate later on how the trading room was organized to exploit market uncertainty. Briefly here, a trading desk is like a well-trained submarine crew, with finely tuned instrumentation and intricate patterns of interaction to execute complex maneuvers within rapidly changing markets. Traders sit in front of Bloomberg screens with their colorful waterfalls of data. The screens may be flat, but the informational world is rich and deep, and the actual experience is more like flying through the data than simply sitting in front of it. The speed is tremendous. At the extreme, the future is only two seconds away, and traders refer to price information that is fifteen minutes old as "historical data." To navigate successfully is to recognize patterns in the data, patterns remarkable for their complexity and elegance. The biggest challenge and the biggest money lie in successfully exploring uncharted territory—recognizing patterns in the terra incognita.

The terrorist attack destroyed the pillars of this delicate organization, posing a fundamental threat to its continuity. In the traders' journey of exploration, September 11 was like a terrible shipwreck. The story we tell here is less about the destruction of the vessel, for that is well known (see, for example, Salgado 2002; Wrzesniewski 2002; Bartel 2002; Kendra and Wachtendorf 2003), than about the six-month-long journey of recovery afterward. The 160 traders at International Securities were a surviving crew. The question was whether they could navigate their life rafts to safe harbor. To do so, they would need to define themselves not simply as survivors but as sailors who could apply their collective seafaring skills to a primitive technology. Some familiar routines could be modified, but the crippled equipment would require a restructuring of roles. And the intensity of the social life on the life raft would bring new uncertainties, new threats to the organization, and new challenges for leadership. Would their chances be improved by letting the separate life rafts take different courses, or should they navigate the life rafts in a coordinated manner so that the entire crew would arrive safely all together?

We are fortunate that we can approach this question on the basis of close familiarity with International Securities. Two years before September 11, we began ethnographic field research to study the social organization of trading. We benefited from the bank's generosity in providing us with a trader's pass to the World Financial Center, a desk, a computer terminal, a telephone extension, and, most importantly, the opportunity to interact with the traders and observe them directly at work. As a result of this rapport and trust, six days after the attack, amid chaos and confusion, the traders invited us to continue our fieldwork in their makeshift trading room in New Jersey. This is, to our knowledge, the only ethnographic study of an organization directly affected by September 11 that benefited from the presence of the researchers at the firm prior to the attack.

To understand how the traders at International Securities navigated the uncertainties of the post-9/11 crisis, we first sketch the organizational context of the trading room prior to the attack. We summarize the organization of trading at the bank, the bank's social character, and the ways in which it exploited financial uncertainty by developing multiple and rivalrous systems of interpreting markets. After sketching our orienting framework about sensemaking in times of crisis, we describe the devastating blow to the firm of September 11 and follow the traders across the Hudson River in their escape from Wall Street to New Jersey. We introduce the successive crises that flooded the lives of the traders: existential anxiety, questions of professional identity, uncertainty about the future of the firm, and ambiguities about the future location of the trading room. The trading room faced not one crisis—the immediate aftermath of September 11—but many. As we shall see, a given crisis was resolved by restoring identities, but identities, once restored, redefined the situation and led to new crises. That is, the successive waves of crisis were produced by each success in managing crisis.

THE TRADING ROOM BEFORE SEPTEMBER 11

(Pseudonymous) International Securities is a global, non-American investment bank with 128 offices in 26 countries across the United States, Europe, and Asia. Its American headquarters occupied some of the most prestigious real estate in New York—the gleaming, irregular postmodern towers of the World Financial Center, located between the World Trade Center and the Hudson River in lower Manhattan.

One cannot understand the chaos that September 11 brought to International Securities without appreciating just how close the bank was to the World Trade Center. The World Trade Center and World Financial Center complexes could almost be thought of as one and the same thing—in their daily commutes, the traders at International Securities entered the lobby of the Trade Center, walked through the boutiques and coffee shops below the twin towers, crossed West Street through an elevated corridor, and finally entered the Financial Center. On rainy days the traders stepped out of the subway and walked into their trading room without a drop of rain ever dampening their carefully chosen business-casual outfits.

For our ethnographic study we made sixty half-day visits over the course of three years (between November 1999 and September 2002). During those thirty-four months we undertook detailed observation at several trading desks, sitting in the tight space between traders, following trades as they unfolded, and sharing lunch and jokes with the traders. We did this with three of the ten teams in the trading room. We complemented the resulting data with in-depth interviews of traders in a more private setting, typically in a small conference room just off the trading room.[1] Our research produced important findings on the strategy and organization of International Securities that help explain the events after September 11.

The trading strategy of choice of quantitative traders at International Securities is arbitrage in its different blends and styles (for a detailed treatment of valuation and arbitrage, see Beunza and Stark 2004). The arbitrageurs at International Securities represent a far cry from the traditional traders of Wall Street of the 1980s, aptly described by Tom Wolfe (1987) as Masters of the Universe. Whereas the latter were characterized by their riches, bravado, and disdain for small investors, modern arbitrageurs have M.B.A.s, degrees in finance, and Ph.D.s in physics and statistics, and they are more appropriately thought of as engineers. None of them wear suspenders. This change in the outlook and personality of traders is part of a silent technological revolution that swept over Wall Street in the last two decades. This revolution—the quantitative revolution in finance—was ignited by the rise of derivatives such as futures and options, of mathematical formulas such as Black-Scholes, of network connectivity to electronic markets such as the NASDAQ, and by high-powered computers.

Arbitrage is a creative trading strategy that hinges on the possibility of interpreting securities in multiple ways and produces profits by associating previously disparate markets. For example, arbitrageurs associate the markets for the stocks of two merging companies when the merger makes their value momentarily comparable. Or they associate the stocks of two companies that are in the same index and hence move similarly, or a stock and a bond of the same company, whose value is linked by a legal clause that makes the bond convertible into stock. The point in every case is to avoid the conventional route of valuing a company by its intrinsic value or by how hot it is with market speculators and to choose instead a lens that produces an opportunity—a new, original valuation that differs from the value that the market assigns to a company. Thus, like a striking literary metaphor, an arbitrage trade reaches out and associates the value of a stock to some other, previously unidentified security. The two securities used for arbitrage have to be similar enough so as to hedge exposure, but different enough so that other traders have not seen the resemblance and realized the opportunity before. No trade, then, is ever exactly like the previous one. Alternative trading strategies such as value investing or momentum trading emphasize early access to information, but arbitrage draws on novel interpretation. Thus, whereas value trading is essentialist and momentum trading is extrinsic, arbitrage is associational (Beunza and Stark 2004).

The trading room at International Securities was purposely built to manage financial uncertainty. In its teams, its layout, its furnishings, and its technology, it was equipped to meet the challenge of recognizing opportunities and especially of making innovative associations. Each desk (merger arbitrage, index arbitrage, and so on) was organized around a distinctive evaluative principle and its corresponding cognitive frames—metrics, "optics," and other specialized instrumentation for pattern recognition. That is, the trading room was the site of diverse, indeed rivalrous, principles of valuation. And it was the interaction across this heterogeneity that generated innovation. The trading room was greater than the sum of the desks because the co-location of diverse arbitrage strategies in the same room created a powerful synergy among them. Traders acquired information from their Bloomberg screens, but the tacit knowledge to interpret this information and carry out complex calculations for recognizing opportunities was acquired through spontaneous social interaction with proximate desks in the trading room (Beunza and Stark 2004). For example, merger arbitrage traders would draw on the specialized knowledge of the nearby convertible bond traders or of those at the stock loan desk as they assessed features of a complex trade. Frequently, as the traders explained, they were not simply requesting particular information but rather learning about what they did not even know they should know.[2] That is, their judgments were often calibrated less by specifically directed questions than by unanticipated interactions and overheard communications.

The manager of the trading room promoted these crucial synergies by developing trust and risk-taking among the traders through a set of human resource policies that put people first. He replaced the subjective annual bonus, an infamous Wall Street tradition, with an objective bonus system to prevent traders from feeling personally undervalued when profits decreased for reasons beyond their control, such as the economic cycle. He made subtle changes in the seating arrangements in the room so that traders would not always be sitting next to the same people but would get to know others. The manager himself sat near the middle of the room, rather than in a closed office, to reduce status differences and promote the notion of open communication. A wall-less, table-less corner of the room surrounded by whiteboard served as a fast-turnover conference room where traders from different desks could exchange their perspectives without risk of being trapped in an interminable, corporate-style meeting.

Rather than being bureaucratically hierarchical, the trading room was heterarchical (Stark 2001; Girard and Stark 2002). In place of hierarchical, vertical ties, we found horizontal ties of lateral, distributed cognition; in place of a single metric of valuation, we found multiple metrics of value; and in place of designed and managed R&D, innovations were combinatorics (Kogut and Zander 1992) that emerged from the interaction across these coexisting principles and instruments. The trading room distributed intelligence and organized diversity. The workplace culture that resulted from this highly localized proximity was a resource with which the traders not only faced but in fact profitably exploited the uncertainties that the market threw at them day by day, minute by minute. This heterarchical organizational form proved to be a resource to cope with the more difficult uncertainties created by the attack on the World Trade Center.

SENSEMAKING IN A CRISIS

How do organizations cope with crisis? In his book *Cognition in the Wild*, Edwin Hutchins (1995) presents a fascinating account of organizational behavior in a time of crisis. While Hutchins was doing ethnographic research on a U.S. Navy vessel, the electrical power failed just as the large destroyer was entering San Diego Harbor. Reversing the engines would not take effect before the initial speed and the weight of the vessel carried it on a calamitous course of collision with other ships anchored at bay. The destroyer had to be navigated to safety, yet all of its sophisticated navigational instrumentation had been rendered inoperative. There was no time to issue orders down a chain of command. Hutchins documents, in a literally second-by-second account, the safe navigation of the vessel in a process of self-organized, laterally coordinated, and socially distributed cognition. Uncertainty was confronted by decisionmaking that was socially distributed across both people and artifacts.

With Hutchins's insights in mind, an observer would conclude that International Securities was particularly well prepared to withstand a shock. With its sociotechnical network of instrumentation and interacting desks, the trading room at International Securities relied extensively on distributed cognition to profit from market uncertainty on a daily basis. The company had succeeded in a highly competitive industry through a heterarchical organizational struc-ture with a flat hierarchy and competing subgroups that made sense of the environment in rivalrous ways (Girard and Stark 2002).

The experience of the World Financial Center traders after 9/11, however, differed in several fundamental ways from that of the sailors navigating San Diego Harbor. Whereas the sailors navigated through a crisis and thereby nar-rowly avoided a catastrophe, the traders were working in crisis following a disaster. The combined effect of the 9/11 attack, other terror threats, the an-thrax deaths and subsequent fear, war, and displacement led to a cognitive shock that is well captured by Karl Weick's (1993) notion of a "cosmological event" after which the universe no longer appears to make sense. For instance, the destruction of the twin towers precipitated an ontological crisis in which the basic laws of matter that one had learned as a child now seemed to be violated: chairs could tip over, and trees could fall down, but buildings of that size and scale were not supposed to so quickly vanish.

Unlike technological change, a financial crisis, or navigational failure at sea, a cosmological event is not fully captured by the notion of uncertainty, even in its extreme form. The remedies to it are accordingly different. The pressing anxiety about safety, career, and well-being that characterized the environment in the wake of September 11 did not need to be brought into the trading room in New Jersey—it was all too present, in the form of mourning for deceased friends, repeated images of a disaster site that was their former workplace, and worrying news of anthrax from the CNN monitors. If anything, the traders needed some isolation, at least emotionally, from these concerns.

The social-psychological contours of the September 11 crisis called instead for limiting the organization's exposure to environmental uncertainty and pro-moting within it the conditions that would enable the firm to overcome the crisis. For example, in a discussion of leadership, Weick (1995, 54) retells an extraordinary story about a military unit in crisis that survived thanks to the unwarranted resolve produced by a map that did not correspond to the actual territory they faced:

> The incident happened during military maneuvers in Switzerland. The young lieutenant of a small Hungarian detachment in the Alps sent a reconnaissance unit into the icy wilderness. It began to snow immedi-ately, snowed for two days, and the unit did not return. The lieutenant suffered, fearing that he had dispatched his own people to death. But on the third day the unit came back. Where had they been? How had they made their way? Yes, they said, we considered ourselves lost and waited for the end. And then one of us found a map in his pocket. That calmed us down. We pitched camp, lasted out the snowstorm, and then with the map we discovered our bearings. And here we are. The lieutenant

borrowed this remarkable map and had a good look at it. He discovered to his astonishment that it was not the map of the Alps, but the map of the Pyrenees.

The false map, then, saved the organization by preventing paralysis in the face of dissent, fear, and doubt. Weick (1995, 55) ends this account about sensemaking by referring to one business leader's comment on it: "Now, that story would have been really neat if the leader out with the lost troops had known it was the wrong map and still been able to lead them back." Weick regards this comment as very interesting, since it describes a situation that many leaders often face: the followers are lost and even the leader is not sure where to go.

We find the Hungarian soldiers' story apt for thinking not only about the problems at International Securities in particular but more generally about leadership in nonhierarchical organizations. Heterarchies are predicated on the belief that superiors do not have more or better information than other members of the organization. Indeed, in heterarchies solutions typically emerge from interactions within the organization instead of from its top. Knowledge flows not merely up and down along the lines of command but laterally across social networks. This view of organizations raises an important question about the actors formally charged with responsibility for the company: if leadership is not about being the repository of knowledge or the information hub of the organization, what does it mean to lead in a heterarchy?

EXPLODING UNCERTAINTY: THE 9/11 TERRORIST ATTACK

On September 11, 2001, the work of the arbitrageurs at International Securities was interrupted by a sudden explosion in the building adjacent to it, the World Trade Center. As they rushed to the windows of their trading room, the traders saw Tower One of the Trade Center go up in flames. From that vantage point, some saw the frightful approach of the second plane. That crash brought terror to the trading room and a tumultuous escape to the Hudson River. By the time the towers fell, many of the traders were on boats to New Jersey. Fortunately, none of them were harmed.

Like most other New Yorkers, the traders were thrown into a state of unprecedented confusion and equivocality by the attack. Is this real? Is it a nightmare? Consider, for example, the case of Ray, a senior trader at the customer sales desk. He was the first one to escape from the trading room on September 11. He left the building as soon as the first plane hit, took the ferry, and drove home to New Jersey, where on his living room television he watched the towers collapse. Even to someone like Ray who was at the World Financial

Center at the time of the attack, the collapse of the towers on TV had a sense
of unreality. He recalls that "watching [the towers fall], it was very easy to be
in denial. You are looking at the tower and wondering, how did they manage
to make this movie look so real?"

The unreality of the TV images stemmed from their abrupt departure from
the traders' established mental schemata. The images forced Ray, for instance,
to radically update his belief system: the twin towers were no longer there,
lower Manhattan was fractured at its core, and America suddenly was a vulnerable place. What did all that mean?

Like Ray, the rest of the traders at the bank desperately needed to make
sense of events. This process rapidly took on a social nature. On the night of
September 11, the manager of the trading room met with other senior traders
and technical staff to discuss the disastrous situation of the bank. The World
Trade Center had collapsed at its doorstep. The building was badly damaged.
As a result, the lively trading room that had once supported the innovative
work of arbitrage had become a dark hole with no electricity, no connectivity,
and no assurance of safety from toxic chemicals. The bank did have another
available facility, a back office in (pseudonymous) Escapaway, a small suburban town in New Jersey. But the only resource that the traders could count
on there was spare space in a basement where the firm stored corporate-style
minicomputers for processing payroll data. That basement had no workstations, no desks, and no connectivity. Nevertheless, the manager and the others
decided to do everything possible to continue International Securities' operations in equity arbitrage. They estimated that it would take them three weeks
to three months to begin trading again.

Like the group of traders who met with the manager, the rest of the employees in the trading room also needed to rein in the ambiguities of their situation.
Unlike the trading room managers and the technical staff, they did not have
the chance to meet face to face and decide on the trading room's future. They
resorted to phoning each other. As Ray says:

> The first two days it was talking to the people I'm most close to. We
> did not know what the hell was gonna happen. We didn't even know
> that place [the warehouse in Escapaway] existed. I was phoning from
> home, getting ahold of everybody, making sure they were okay. The next
> three days [I was] talking to others less close.

Some employees, especially those who did not have the home phone numbers of others, began to interact through the Internet. That interaction was
facilitated by the bank when it created, in the first days after the attack, a
website of "accounted-for" traders. On the site traders could post the news

that they had survived and could also indicate that they had been in contact with others who had managed to get home unharmed. Once the site was up, however, they began to use it as a means for sensemaking: sharing their puzzlement, asking questions of each other, and so on. The "accounted-for" website, according to an executive, had postings such as:

"No one has called me."

"I don't know if I still have a job."

"Can someone tell me what's going on?"

Hence, the traders' bricolage had turned an official list of survivors into a chat room of sorts. But this interactivity posed a problem: the medium gave every employee a view of everyone else's confusion. Instead of structuring the ways in which the employees made meaning of the tragedy in a way that gave reassurance, the website was promoting anxiety. Greg, an executive at the bank, was sensitive to the problem. Although it took only a matter of days, the bank's delay in answering those postings, he felt, was "eternal." On his own initiative, he posted a note saying, "We are trying to reestablish the systems and contact you." The point, he explained, was to send a deeper message to the employees: "It was basically so that they would see that someone was looking at this website and that someone cared. The message really was, 'Be patient. You are valued employees.'"

Beyond the confines of International Securities, a symbolic attack called for a symbolic response. On September 14 the chairman of the New York Stock Exchange (NYSE) vowed to reopen the stock market on September 17 to move the United States toward normality. Underscoring the dramaturgical character of the early market opening, the Exchange and the NASDAQ undertook a full-scale test of their communication, computer, and power systems three days before reopening—the financial equivalent of a dress rehearsal in theater. Emphasizing the message of the markets, President Bush tied the reopening of the market to the country's recovery, declaring that "the markets open tomorrow, people go back to work, and we'll show the world." Vice President Cheney went further, urging investors to buy and demonstrate "confidence in the country, confidence in our economy" (quoted in Stevenson and Fuerbringer 2001, A1). Selling was deemed unpatriotic. The neutral, impartial activity of capturing bits of financial value through arbitrage suddenly became laden with ethical and national value.

The management at International Securities also understood the importance of a symbolic response. It decided to reopen as soon as the markets did, not only for the sake of its customers but in particular to reassure its employees.

Despite the lack of facilities, computers, and connections, and even though they estimated it would take them at least three weeks to trade again, barely six days after September 11—by the time the New York Stock Exchange re-opened on September 17—the traders at International Securities were trading again.

We were privileged to witness how this was accomplished. Days after the attack we sent an email to the bank to ask whether everyone had escaped unharmed. To our relief, we learned that no one was injured. To our surprise, the return email also invited us to come over to New Jersey—indeed, insisted that we do so—to witness the recovery process. "It is chaotic," wrote the manager of the trading room, "but also very inspiring." Our presence would be "a reminder of normal times." As ethnographers, we felt enormously honored to be welcomed to document these extraordinary efforts.

MANAGING FEAR: HIGH-TOUCH, LOW-TECH

Thus, two days after the market reopened, we were back among the traders in our new role of conspicuous observers, this time in an improvised trading room in a converted warehouse in Escapaway, New Jersey. The trading room was located in the basement of the building. To reach it we had to cross through several rows of corporate cubicles and interminable corridors of beige carpet. And after the cubicles, there was a truly unexpected sight—the trading room. It was a cavernous, open-plan space, complete with traders, desks, computers, outsized TV screens, and multi-time zone clocks. The room had a makeshift feel to it: there were no windows, a low ceiling, and walls painted in industrial yellow, more fitting for a storage space than a trading room. Correspondingly, the dress code had shifted from business-casual to jeans and boots. The room was noisy, but the sound, as one trader put it, was "a wonderful sound of life."

Prominent—indeed, omnipresent—in the room were American flags. A huge American flag hung in the middle of one wall, and small flags were on nearly every trader's desk or attached to monitors. In these first days after the attack, to the question "Who am I?" the answer was, "An American." The task of reopening the securities exchanges in which the traders were participating was cast as an act of patriotism.

What was happening in those first days? Each trader was dealing with his own fear and grief in a situation in which all of his colleagues were also afraid and grieving. As one executive of a World Trade Center firm told us:

This was not a fire in a building which just destroyed two floors.... Most everybody lost people they knew. They were traumatized, there was fear of war. Nobody knew if the next day there was going to be more. I had a guy walking around with a picture of his wife and kids in his pocket and looking at it every two minutes because he was afraid he was never going to get home again. (quoted in Beunza and Stark 2003, 151)

The tragedy had affected the traders' moods, creating an understandable increase in their anxiety level. "I'm so stressed I almost stop by a drugstore and buy all the pills there," said one trader at International Securities. Cell phones, the tiniest ones imaginable and many purchased after September 11, were not placed within arm's reach on desks but kept in pockets or attached to belts so that in another evacuation this lifeline to family could not be forgotten. Such an evacuation in New Jersey was improbable, but the traders were anxious enough to take the precaution.

Bob, the trading room manager, understood the threat that the traders' uncertainties posed to the organization if they went unattended.[3] "Everything okay?" he asked, stopping by each trader's desk on his regular rounds through the trading room. At some point he came close to the desk that we were observing. "Everything fine" went the unanimous answer. But as he stayed two more minutes making small talk, one of the traders took him aside and said: "Actually, Bob, I wanted to ask you something. I'm buying a house, and the closing is in three weeks. I did it with the previous trading room in mind, but now I don't know where we'll be." The manager then spent some additional time chatting with the trader, aware that what had seemed like a question was also a request for more conversation.

By walking the room, Bob was gaining an appreciation from the traders of the different issues that affected their lives and the continuity of the organization. Before September 11, he used to walk the room for the purpose of "risk management," that is, to identify sources of market uncertainty unforeseen by mathematical risk models. Now he did so to gain a grip on the personal uncertainty of the traders.

As we moved to the statistical arbitrage desk, we found Todd assuring his administrative assistant—a middle-aged woman of Asian origin with a moderate command of English—that the risks of smallpox were low and detailing for her the difference between smallpox and chicken pox. A few feet away from them, Stan, a customer sales trader, was talking to a client on the phone, apparently explaining to him how to adapt his financial strategy to the new political context but ultimately just giving reassurance: "I just don't see this market going anywhere, and with any scare story, it might do something. . . . Are you nervous about it? Don't be nervous, man. I've got you covered."

As soon as Stan retreated from his front-stage role, however, he showed us a very different face. "We're nutty since the attack," he confessed. "Whenever I go home and drive near Newark Airport and see the planes fly so low. . . ."

One level up the command chain, Stan's boss, Ray, took up the task of reassuring Stan. After hearing Stan discuss the probabilities of a real biological threat, Ray replied, "I don't think they have the technology to do that." "If you say so," Stan conceded, though, unpersuaded, he then added, "but they had the technology to do something much worse!" Ray later told us that he saw his role as "reassuring people." Meanwhile, Ray's boss, the manager of the trading room, put on the same facade of reassurance toward the rest of the employees in the form of general assembly–like speeches. Thus, junior traders appeared calm and assured to clients but disclosed their fears to their senior counterparts. Senior traders, in turn, reassured junior traders and administrative assistants, despite being privately skeptical about the future. And in turn, the manager reassured the whole trading room and showed no cracks in public (though he voiced them to us in private). In this circumstance, "what made the difference," as one manager noted, "for every company that came back successfully [was] that kind of touch, high-touch, low-tech solution" (quoted in Kelly and Stark 2002, 1527; for another case history, see Freeman, Hirschhorn, and Maltz 2002).

IDENTITIES IN PRACTICE

After the attack, the traders were left wondering whether their firm would continue to exist, whether the trading room would operate again, what they should do, and even what they were. The basement turned those survivors back into traders. The layout of the room had been creatively inscribed to restore meaning and order to the traders. They were in New Jersey, unquestionably in a basement storage room in New Jersey. But a sign taped prominently on the wall gave different bearings: 20TH FLOOR, EQUITIES. In other corners of the same enormous room one could read: 21ST FLOOR, FIXED INCOME and 19TH FLOOR, RISK MANAGEMENT. Our traders were still between the nineteenth and twenty-first floors, but now horizontally rather than vertically. Moreover, within the constraints of those temporary quarters, they had arranged their desks to reproduce the layout of the Financial Center trading room. For example, every trader in the agency trading desk remained together, sitting on the same desk. In New Jersey they camped on a table partly occupied by two photocopiers and three fax machines in what used to be the fax station of the data center. They camped, but they stayed together.

To the question of "Who am I?" the computers, desks, and open-plan space answered, "A trader." The 20TH FLOOR sign not only reminded traders that the equities trading room was located between risk management and fixed income but also led employees back to their jobs as traders. To the question of "What should I do?" the 20TH FLOOR sign answered: "The same things you would be doing in the Financial Center trading room."

The Escapaway trading room offers a striking contrast to a crisis analyzed by Karl Weick—the Mann Gulch disaster in which fifteen firefighters perished. As part of a more general argument that identity is vital for sensemaking, Weick (1993, 637) carefully reconstructs how the firefighters became disoriented:

> The critical threat to the firefighters' role identities came when the leader told the retreating crew "throw away your tools!" A fire crew that retreats from a fire should find its identity and morale strained. If the retreating people are then also told to discard the very things that are their reason for being there in the first place, then the moment quickly turns existential. If I am no longer a firefighter, then who am I? With the fire bearing down, the only possible answer becomes, An endangered person in a world where it is every man for himself.

In the trading room, by contrast, the traders were told, in effect, "Pick up your tools"—begin the process of sensemaking and orienting yourself in the world by affirming your identity as a trader through the act of trading.[4]

If the traders were to confirm their identities through the actual practice of trading, the rudimentary technologies and limited bandwidth of the makeshift trading room required considerable improvisation on their part. In the face of damaged technologies and missing tools, the traders recombined old and new tools to be able to trade again. In the agency trading desk, for example, junior traders manually performed operations that had previously been automated by the trading engine, such as booking trades, registering them, breaking them up, and so on, effectively taking the bank back to the trading technology that it had used five years before. Lacking seats, they stood behind the lucky senior traders who had seats and computers, ready to help. When, in the middle of a phone conversation, a senior trader suddenly needed to record a transaction, at the shout of, "Gimme a ticket, somebody gimme a ticket!" three junior traders scrambled to offer tickets, paper, and whatever else he might need. Another junior was sent to "help with the tickets" and "relieve others" in a different desk. But he was told that with a sensitivity to the situation characteristic of International Securities: the senior trader who gave these directions added, "Oh, and this isn't permanent, by the way." So unusual was manual bookkeeping for the junior traders—the bricolage that it entailed was so radical—that some of them did not even know how to do it, or whether it was appropriate for them to do it.

What is the lesson from the makeshift trading room for the organization of responsiveness? Responsiveness, the experience of these traders suggests, is a combination of anticipation and improvisation (Tierney 2002; Beunza and Stark 2003; Kendra and Wachtendorf 2003; Perrow 2002). The bank had a space, but it was far from a perfect replica of the trading room at the Financial Center. Yet the traders managed to be trading in it from day one. How? By engaging in bricolage. The bank had a warehouse, with square feet and little else. In that square footage the traders saw a resource and used it to arrange the desks in almost the same configuration as in their former trading room. The tools the traders had at their disposal were rudimentary in comparison with the precision instruments they were accustomed to. In New Jersey they had only single-line phones, home laptops, reduced connectivity, and single-screen terminals. But the traders made them work: they managed to talk to other banks, enter orders, and connect to the market. Like good bricoleurs, the traders did not let imperfection stand in the way of accomplishing tasks. Instead of waiting for the trading engine to be restored or for new servers to be delivered, the traders readily recombined old and new technologies. They matched their do-it-yourself outfits—jeans and boots—with a corresponding willingness to solve problems. In this process, some traders became clerks, others manual operators, and still others roommates of bandwidth, sharing cable to the NYSE. These changes in role status did not detract from their status as traders; in fact, the changes reaffirmed their status as traders. Sometimes things have to change to remain the same. Their identities as traders were inscribed on their business cards. But what do traders do? They trade. By repositioning themselves in the damaged sociotechnical networks, the traders found ways to trade. Innovation is not having new resources to accomplish new tasks but recognizing configurations that others would not see as resources. Responsiveness is grounded in this resourceful recognition (Beunza and Stark 2003).

In contrast to the Mann Gulch firefighters, the traders at International Securities were told to "pick up your tools." Weick is correct. But to his insight we add another: success in restoring an identity can lead to new crises. Restoring the trading capability of the organization did not put an end to International Securities' problems. The repercussions of September 11 were far more complex than a single crisis of identity. As we shall see, the very fact of buying and selling securities affirmed the employees' identities as traders, but eventually it also affirmed their identities as particular types of traders, thereby leading to new crises of identity.

NO ESCAPE

Whereas trading resolved fundamental uncertainties by restoring basic identities, the particular circumstances of the fall of 2001 brought new uncertainties directly into the very practice of trading. On October 7, the anticipated war broke out between the United States and Afghanistan. "Investors," the *New York Times* wrote the following day, "will enter unfamiliar territory as stock markets in the United States and around the world open this morning for trading" (Berenson and Brick 2001, B13). Unfamiliar indeed: traders who had transformed financial uncertainty into probabilities and scenarios, facts and figures, now had to introduce the political logic of war-related news into their economic calculations. Even worse, those political developments were not unrelated to their own personal security and now threatened them directly. The emotional detachment that had served traders so effectively during peacetime was now much more difficult to re-create.

Because the war affected stock prices, traders at International Securities had to dissect incoming news from the war. Despite being arbitrageurs—in principle unconcerned by market direction—they could easily "get hooked" from a sudden fall in the market: they might be unable to find a counterpart for a trade in a sharply falling market and thus be stuck in the middle of a trade. The result would be precisely the sort of dangerous exposure to the ups and downs in the price of a stock that arbitrageurs try to avoid. War affected them in other ways as well. At the statistical arbitrage desk, Todd found that the conflict had altered the historical correlations of some stocks. For example, the price of Boeing and Northrop Grumman had traditionally moved in parallel, since the market valued both as aviation stocks. But with the rise of political uncertainty, the value of military stocks went up, while the value of stocks related to tourist travel decreased.

As market-driving events shifted from economic to political ones, the traders had to develop new mental frameworks to interpret developments. At the customer sales desk, for example, traders quickly learned that the market had knee-jerk negative reactions to news of American casualties from the war, as well as to news of accidents anywhere in the world, even before these could be confirmed as terrorist acts. Consider the following discussion between Josh, a senior trader at the customer trading desk, and Stan, a more junior one, about how to avoid being hooked (unable to complete an arbitrage hedge). Josh recommended trading following the advances of the American army:

> JOSH: You have to wait until they give more war news, something good, like they took another airport. You should short everything until the rangers get to Afghanistan.
> STAN: Is that good news?
> JOSH: I guess.

The traders modified their information channels to complement the switch to politics. The television screens in the trading room, normally tuned to the financial news channel CNBC, were tuned to CNN. And in their spare time, and without pausing for explicit direction from management, the traders discussed the war. According to Bob, the manager:

This is an information assessment room, and what they do is what they have always been doing all the time: incorporating all the information they receive. The problem is that now they do it with news of political uncertainty, and so, for example, do you know of daisy cutters? No? Well, let me tell you, they are the latest bomb. We're learning everything about that, and I can tell you all you want to know. We had been focused on anthrax, then moved on to smallpox, then strategies for war in Afghanistan...the whole thing. People compare notes, talk to each other.

Adaptation to wartime trading was not without cost. The traders were in a difficult bind. To trade they needed to be monitoring political developments minute by minute, but the more closely they followed the news about anthrax, biological weapons, war, and terrorism, the more they dwelled on matters of their own and their families' insecurity. They had narrowly escaped the immediate tragedy of the September 11 attack, but they could not escape the consequences of its aftermath. Trading, which had offered a momentary reprieve from the original trauma, was now a source of new anxieties. Although the economic uncertainty that traders characteristically transformed into risk could be boiled down to depersonalized numbers and dealt with in a detached manner, the continuous transformation of political news into risk had unintended effects: it exaggerated the traders' fears. As a consequence, the atmosphere in the trading room, Bob said, became "very depressing."

Technology also had an effect in this process. In the former room at the Financial Center, traders could choose whether or not to listen to the news, thanks to small individual speakers at every trader's desk. Indeed, most of the time many chose not to. In the trading room at Escapaway, however, there was only one large speaker, always turned on. Although obviously not as trapped in the war as American soldiers on Afghan soil, from a cognitive standpoint the traders in that Escapaway trading room were also trapped in the war.

WALL STREET TRADERS . . . IN NEW JERSEY

As the initial burst of patriotic fervor and the exhilaration of meeting the challenges of rebuilding gave way to the realities of long commutes and continued anxieties, Escapaway became increasingly burdensome for the traders. The temporary trading room was barely an hour's drive from Manhattan, but it felt a universe away from the excitement and activity of Wall Street. Located in a suburban corporate park, the building was surrounded by similar low-rise corporate offices of manufacturing companies such as Colgate-Palmolive and AT&T.

Just around the corner a farm announced HAY FOR SALE, and the surroundings offered an endless succession of indistinguishable shopping malls. The remote back office of International Securities had, in effect, become its front office too. The traders, in short, were Wall Street traders in New Jersey.

International Securities' move to an all-inclusive trading room in Escapaway had confirmed their identities as traders, but their occupational identities were not confined to such a simple construct. Over time, the circumstances in New Jersey began to threaten their identities as sophisticated Manhattanite professionals. As affluent Wall Streeters, the traders were recipients of the glamour and cachet bestowed upon them by countless artifacts of modern global culture, from Oliver Stone's *Wall Street* to Tom Wolfe's *Bonfire of the Vanities*. But once the landmark skyscrapers, the amenities of the financial district, and the fat bonuses were stripped away from trading, what did buying and selling stocks for a living mean? Indeed, to judge from the traders' appearance—from their improvised jeans-and-boots dress code to the cramped facilities and outmoded computers—they suddenly looked more like the working-class, rent-a-seat day traders whom one of us studied during the early months of the NASDAQ boom (Beunza 1999). September 11 had given a blue-collar appearance to a work environment that used to be highly refined even among the affluent white-collar professionals.

The grim suburban reality of Escapaway had no amenities for the traders to escape the pressure of their trading room. According to one trader: "Being in Escapaway was horrible. You were stuck. What could you do? You could drive to Wal-Mart, you could drive to Home Depot. One thing about Escapaway is, people who never lived in the suburbs were able to test it out. . . . Being there taught more than one that they did not want to live there."

The traders' new hometown quickly became a lightning rod for jokes. During one of our visits an excited junior trader announced to the rest of the desk that he had managed to download from the Web the streets of Escapaway so that "you can find all the fast-food restaurants." To this a senior trader replied in jest, "Why do you need a map for that? There's so many Dunkin' Donuts here, someone told me once to turn right on the Dunkin' Donuts, and I turned on the wrong one." Another trader described being in Escapaway as, "like, you know, when you go to Mexico, they say the locals can drink the water and not get sick. Well, the people in Escapaway can eat from McDonald's every day and not get sick."

The firm had put in place a makeshift cafeteria service, but like college cafeterias during exam periods, the food took up more than its share of blame for the anxiety of the customers. According to one executive:

> In the trading room of the Financial Center we had sushi Tuesdays and Thursdays. The food was pretty decent down there, steak, all that jazz.

Now we're eating junk. Deli food. There's enough for everyone. But because it's a buffet line, people unconsciously think there's gonna be shortage, so they eat more. People smoke a lot more, and some went back to smoking. So people either ate more, drank more, or smoked more.

The problem, of course, was not the food. Escapaway, as another trader put it, was "not consistent" with his choice of occupation. His most acute memory of those months was having to use backup chemical toilets, something "unheard of for someone working in the securities industry."

As we saw, traders frequently used humor, sometimes self-deprecating, sometimes cynical, to create psychological distance from Escapaway. But there were other ways of expressing their lack of identification with the locale. In one of the very frequent conversations about the commute, a trader commented: "Traffic moves now twenty miles an hour faster than before all this happened. If everyone is doing eighty-five, I'm doing ninety-five. I've got a sports car." This trader effectively ended up defying the law—traffic regulations—for reasons not unlike those of teenagers whether urban or suburban: to manifest his identity by stating that he was different from the locals and their rules did not apply to him.

As frustration mounted, some traders began to contemplate alternative jobs at rival banks in the city. "At least two I know were really ready to throw in the towel," a senior trader recalled. To the many questions that traders were asking themselves, now there was one more to add: do I want to work here? Ray, the senior trader at the merger arbitrage desk, told those who were considering switching jobs: "Now is not the time. Everything's changed so much, it's not time to change anything else. The job is at least something you can hold on to."

A THREAT TO THE FIRM: THE BREAKUP
OF THE TRADING ROOM

In December 2001 the bank's steady path to recovery suffered a sudden blow: a group of traders decided to leave the premises at Escapaway and establish themselves in a temporary trading room in midtown Manhattan. The heads of the merger, options, and convertible bond arbitrage desks, responsible for twenty-four traders in total, rented office space in midtown and began to trade from there. They were not changing jobs, but they were changing locales. The bank accepted their relocation. But it was widely felt that the move could jeopardize the unity of the trading room and ultimately the existence of the firm.

Bob, the trading room manager, explained the move as a solution to acute differences in preferences among traders about the desirable location for the trading room. The traders who lived in Manhattan did not want to work in New Jersey because they did not want to be outside the city in case of an attack while their families remained there. On the other hand, the traders who lived and had their families outside Manhattan did not want to risk their lives by going to work in Manhattan. "Manhattan traders," the manager explained, justifying his decision to give the departing traders the green light to go, "didn't *ever* sign up for a job in New Jersey. Some of the people [who chose to go] are really crucial." Thus, he concluded, the bank had to accept their conditions.

The departing traders, however, justified their move in a different way. They emphasized the networking and informational advantages of midtown Manhattan.[5] According to Max Sharper, head of the merger arbitrage desk, "The difference between midtown and Escapaway is like between being in the solar system or outside." Merger arbitrage, as noted earlier, is the practice of valuing firms based on the price of their merger partners. When two firms announce a merger, Max added, "we typically want to know their commitment" to the merger. Midtown Manhattan was particularly good for this purpose because companies announce mergers in presentations at midtown hotels. Being close to them enabled traders to attend those presentations, and doing so in person gave arbitrageurs an advantage over listening to them webcast over the Internet. "Perhaps," Max said, "there is something that you miss in the digital transmission; perhaps they show charts and graphs that are not on the website." Furthermore, webcasts of the analyst meetings "do not capture the reactions of the people in the room or in the corridors after the meeting." Midtown gave traders yet another advantage: improved networking possibilities with members of the arbitrage community. In this sense, Max observed, "Being in midtown allows you to have the occasional lunch or the drink after work. We are five people on the desk, and each week I'd say we do one or two lunches and one or two research meetings. This increases if there are earnings announcements."

The departing traders thus appeared to place greater importance on the external networks and communities of practice than on their intra-organizational ties.

Despite the many advantages of the midtown trading room for the departing traders, it had strong negative political and structural repercussions on the rest of the organization. For the traders who remained in Escapaway, the move felt like special treatment for a few, an unusual practice in a bank that minimized status differences. One of them noted that it "might have created jealousy even if, for some, being there [in Escapaway] was not more desirable."

The new trading room revealed the extent to which the firm based its knowledge-sharing on co-location of the traders. The desks that left the main trading room for the midtown trading room included merger arbitrage, options arbitrage, and convertible bond arbitrage. These desks had crucial information about the details of mergers and the volatility of stocks. Their departure cut off the rest of the desks at Escapaway—customer sales, long-short, stock loan, index arbitrage, and statistical arbitrage—from the vital circulation of knowledge. Commenting on the move, a senior trader who remained at Escapaway noted: "Before, it was like, they're the audience, we're the show, or the other way around, we're the audience, they're the show. But the truth is, they have the information we need." The midtown trading room thus began to threaten the continuity of the bank itself. The manager shared with us his concern about this issue in one of those moments when ethnographers become privy to worries that the confidant does not share with his or her colleagues. "Would you mind closing the door?" he asked in the middle of one of our conversations. (By December 2001 our meetings with the manager were no longer taking place on the open trading floor but in a windowless conference room.) Exhausted, peering up to the ceiling and speaking in hushed tones, Bob continued: "In the past what kept us all in International Securities was that the Financial Center was a very good compromise for everybody—for those of us who lived in Manhattan as well as those who lived in New Jersey." With the destruction at the Financial Center, Bob said, that truce was unsealed. The move of the traders to midtown "introduces personal economic uncertainty . . . for me too." Suppose, he said, that the departing desks did well in their new location. This, he thought, could mean the end of the trading room, for "if it becomes clear that we can trade separately, you wonder what's keeping us together, what's preventing some of us from starting an independent hedge fund."

Thus, the manager, along with his traders, faced a new question: what, after all, was the point of having all the desks together? What exactly were the synergies that made the trading room more than the sum of its desks? Before the attack, nobody questioned the advantages of being together, and no one considered leaving the bank. By December 2001, however, not even the integrity of the firm was taken for granted.

ENACTING BACK-TO-BUSINESS-AS-USUAL

Like the Hungarian detachment discussed by Weick (1995), the trading room at International Securities was an organization in crisis, and one whose leadership was similarly in the dark. What they could do was display confidence that the organization would hold together. They too had a kind of map—one that pointed to the return to the World Financial Center. The defection of the traders to midtown could be presented as "temporary" because the arrows from Escapaway and from midtown both pointed to the former trading room.

Aware of the need to reduce uncertainty, management presented the mid-town trading room as a short-term policy. Officially, the firm was committed to returning to the building it had left, the World Financial Center, as soon as it reopened. But the manager lacked crucial knowledge about the possibilities for returning. When we privately asked him for a tentative return date, Bob laid his doubts open:

> We don't know when it's going to open up, and indeed, whether it's going to open up at all. Well, of course time is the issue here, because it will likely open up at some point. But it may not be relevant for us, because people don't want to stay here, and the longer we stay the worse the danger of attrition.

The manager, in other words, did not know. But in every interaction that we observed or heard about, he conveyed the confident posture, "We will return." His commitment to returning to the Financial Center—a commitment to a future that resembled the past of the firm—was part of his broader program of publicly interpreting the situation as "on cruise to normality" in the hope of bringing about that very outcome: Bob the manager was enacting back-to-business (Weick 1979).

This strategy faced two difficulties. First, as Bob's remarks indicated, there was a real possibility that the trading room in the World Financial Center would not be reopened. What if the "bathtub," the infrastructure that supported the building against the Hudson River, was found to be structurally compromised? What if a mysterious mold was found, as happened in the Bankers' Trust building also adjacent to the World Trade Center? What if the dust absorbed by the air conditioning system, at first declared to be harmless, later turned out to be carcinogenic?

Second, as Bob's remarks also indicated, the strategy faced a ticking clock. When International Securities' fiscal year ended March 31, bonuses would be determined. As the executive in charge of relocation put it:

> We knew that people would start quitting after six months. The key thing to avoid that was to get back to Manhattan before then, to be back by the beginning of the new fiscal year. You see, the year ends on March 31, and bonuses are paid in the last week of April. If they were going to receive a disappointing bonus, we wanted them to feel they were already making a new start. Also, usually if people want to quit, they wait until having their bonus. No one threatened explicitly to quit, but I think there was a commonly understood agreement.

Informally among themselves, the traders had constructed a deadline. The construction became real in its consequences, forcing the bank to hedge against the possibility that the Financial Center would be declared structurally unstable or environmentally unsafe and not ready by April.

As with any sophisticated hedging strategy, betting that the Financial Center would be ready in time required a counterbalancing bet in the opposite direction—but a relatively low-cost one. The bank reacted to such uncertainty by searching for an alternative trading room that, contingent on events that had yet to unfold, could end up as an interim trading room, a permanent trading room, or a backup trading room.

The search for an alternative site took the traders far beyond merely functional considerations, forcing them to take into account issues as varied as international politics, structural safety, and the width of a building's stairways. The traders first considered a high floor in a landmark midtown skyscraper, the Citicorp Building. But further research on the tower revealed that, as the executive in charge of relocation put it, the building was "about the fifth most important terrorist target" in New York, because 5 percent of it was owned by a Saudi prince. In addition, one of the four external columns of the building was exposed (it has since been covered), and the traders feared that terrorists could bring down the building by taking out the column.

After considering but rejecting a building in Jersey City as too large and too costly, the bank finally chose a building in Hoboken, a recently gentrified New Jersey city across from the western shore of lower Manhattan with convenient access by mass transportation. The office was five minutes away from the World Financial Center by ferryboat, very close to midtown Manhattan by PATH train, and adjacent to the New Jersey Amtrak train station. Seen from the Hudson River as the ferry approaches the New Jersey shore, the area does not appear distinguished. Just beyond the waterfront, however, it offers an up-and-coming neighborhood of young professionals who work in New York City.

The traders' remaining fear of terrorism made some other features of the building particularly attractive. As one put it: "It is nice that we were able to secure a second floor. A first floor would have been ridiculous, but we wanted to be able to go down the stairs and leave the building fast if we needed to. The stairwells were wide enough. We measured them." From height to politics, from the width of stairwells to ferryboats, the traders' relocation criteria reflected the wide web of concerns, issues, and constraints that they experienced.

Thus, for several months the "map" portrayed two sets of arrows, one set pointing to the World Financial Center, another pointing to the Hoboken facility (which was rapidly being converted into a trading room). Although there was uncertainty about which of the trading rooms they would be moving to, that very ambiguity was a means to reinforce the certainty that all the desks would be reunited into one trading room in either case and thus prevent the organization from sliding into a dangerous free fall.

RETURN TO THE WORLD FINANCIAL CENTER

THANKS—WELCOME BACK read a huge sign next to an enormous American flag over the entrance to the World Financial Center as the traders returned to their old trading room in March 2002. In the end the World Financial Center had reopened, and the hedging renovation of the Hoboken facility was justified as a recovery site that would be maintained in the event of any future disaster.[6] All the desks were once again together. In fact, despite the six-month displacement to New Jersey, the extra commute, the potential for serious conflicts around the midtown move, the low bonuses, and many other difficulties, not a single trader had left the trading room. International Securities had retained its most precious assets.

Although the return was marked by a strong sense of accomplishment, it was also accompanied by a renewed experience of loss. Some traders chose not to look down from the twentieth floor to the hollow immediately below where workers were still removing debris, but none of them could entirely avoid the broad windows and the extraordinary emptiness where the towers had once stood. The trading room was familiar, uncannily so, but the daily journey there was now disconcerting. The World Trade Center subway stop had been destroyed, and the traders had to get off at other stations and walk around or alongside the WTC site. Instead of walking past the specialty shops in the old Trade Center, now along this ten-minute detour the traders passed numerous impromptu memorials. One, for example, displayed plastic-covered color photos of deceased police officers, firefighters, and Trade Center employees, with their names and a sign, REMEMBER ME, below each. As the trader walked, he or she confronted a succession of signs: REMEMBER ME, REMEMBER ME, REMEMBER ME. Different, but equally upsetting, were the tourists with their camcorders and gaudy clothes; the vendors selling memorabilia; the constant presence of so many police officers, both regular and plainclothes; the construction workers with their noise, trucks, diesel fumes, and dust. If getting back to work was a way to put closure on the trauma, the process of just getting to the workplace could be emotionally exhausting.

CONCLUSION

In this chapter, we set out to address the following question: how does an organization cope with a sudden and radical change in the world around it?

A long tradition of organizational literature dating back to the open systems school argues that organizations deal best with environmental uncertainty by reproducing it within the organization (Katz and Kahn 1961; Burns and Stalker 1961; Hedberg, Nystrom, and Starbuck 1976). In contrast, the sensemaking literature contends that in situations that challenge all prior mental schemata, the emphasis should be on protecting and preserving the organization—the team, the firm, the factory, the sociotechnical unit—even at the cost of misalignment with the environment. The case of International Securities, an investment bank severely damaged as a result of the terrorist attack on September 11, 2001, speaks to this debate.

The particularities of International Securities prompt another important question: what role should be taken by leaders—and in particular leaders of nonhierarchical organizations—in situations of extreme crisis? Exceptional circumstances seem to call for strong leadership. But heterarchical organizations eschew hierarchy as an organizing principle. Instead, they exploit day-to-day uncertainty by fostering lateral accountability and emergent initiative (Lane and Maxfield 1996; Stark 1999; Neff and Stark 2003). Should the leader of a heterarchy take absolute control of events, or should he or she resist the pressure and preserve the nonhierarchical character of the organization?

Our findings suggest that in conditions of extreme crisis, organizations should indeed favor internal stability. The makeshift trading room, as we saw, began to reduce uncertainty as it provided the means to reenact identities, first as patriots and then as traders. This finding is consistent with the sensemaking literature. For instance, in the case of the Hungarian detachment described by Weick (1995), the faux map was effective not because its leader had superior knowledge or a higher, more privileged, and more encompassing vantage point, but because the map was a device that could help hold the organization together. The "map" of their return to the World Financial Center filled a similar function for the traders at International Securities.

On the other hand, our study warns against the difficulties of simple recipes. As we also saw, the trading room could not entirely buffer the traders from the environment. To be a wartime trader required exposure. To take positions, to be exposed to risk, meant being exposed to the news of war. That news, as well as the continued perception of terrorist threat, interacted with other identities—for example, as spouses and parents whose loved ones were or might be (depending on the location of the trading room) across a river separated by bridges and tunnels that would surely be closed in another attack. These identities provoked differences between traders who lived in Manhattan and those who lived in New Jersey and opened up the black box of the truce in which the trading room's location had been taken for granted. Moreover, as we also saw, by providing the conditions for realizing their professional skills, the Escapaway trading room reinstilled more nuanced identities. How could one be not simply a trader but specifically a practicing merger arbitrageur if one could not have easy access to the midtown meetings where merger deals were announced? In sum, unlike the sailors studied by Hutchins (1995), the Escapaway traders were not all in one boat.

In such contexts, the function of leaders is to manage the employees' interpretations of the environment in ways that downplay conflict and uncertainty. Leaders do not need to abandon their nonhierarchical style and say to their employees, "I know more than you do." But they can hold the organization together to increase the chances that solutions will emerge through the interaction of the skills and knowledge of the members of the organization.

Our case suggests that this low-profile leadership style can be extremely effective. The traders at International Securities managed to navigate six months of exile successfully without losing a single trader. They could do so because their leadership provided some basic conditions—reducing uncertainty on some dimensions while allowing considerable freedom of action along others—that made it possible for the traders to avoid frames that would pull them apart. The organization held together through a leadership style that managed ambiguities, rebuilt identities, assuaged fears, and restored the initiative of organizational actors, creating the conditions for new solutions to emerge.

Research for this chapter was supported by grants from the Russell Sage Foundation and the National Science Foundation (IIS-02-33489). It was written while David Stark was a visiting scholar at the Russell Sage Foundation.

NOTES

1. All names of interviewees reported throughout the chapter are pseudonyms.
2. We think of this as a search process in which you do not know what you are looking for but will recognize it when you find it (see Beunza and Stark 2004).
3. Siegal Barsade (2002, 644), for example, refers to "emotional contagion"—the "transfer of mood among people in a group, and subsequent effect on group dynamics."
4. Identities are made through social interaction: "The characteristic features of the actor arise in the interaction with the context and, in that sense, the actor is made, just as he helps to make the other actors in the network.... Identities (the reproduction of actors) thus cannot be taken for granted. If the conditions are not met, identities will not be sustained" (White 1995, 81). The social character of identities is also sociotechnical (Callon 1998, 15): it includes interactions with things as well as with people. That is, among the "conditions to be met" are the tools with which people can enact their identities.

5. Elsewhere (Beunza and Stark 2003) we discuss the changing urban geography of finance in the context of debates about the future of lower Manhattan. For overviews on the geography of finance, see the papers in Stuart Corbridge and Nigel Thrift (1994), Andrew Leyshon and Nigel Thrift (1997), Ron Martin (1999), and Gordon Clark, Maryann Feldman, and Meric Gertler (2000).

6. Across the Hudson River from the World Financial Center, the Hoboken disaster recovery room can be reached by ferry. Tests confirm that it can be fully operative within thirty minutes after an evacuation from the Manhattan site. Replete with backed-up data and up-to-date computers—one for each trader, with the trader's name marked on top—it is an eerie, unoccupied space.

REFERENCES

Barsade, Siegal. 2002. "The Ripple Effect: Emotional Contagion in Groups." *Administrative Science Quarterly* 47(4): 644.

Bartel, Caroline. 2002. "'I Love New York, More Than Ever': Changes in the People's Identities as New Yorkers Following the World Trade Center Terrorist Attacks." *Journal of Management Inquiry* 11(3): 240–48.

Berenson, Alex, and Michael Brick. 2001. "Investors Expected to Take Raids in Stride." *New York Times*, October 8, p. B13.

Beunza, Daniel. 1999. "New Cognitive Practices in the Trading Rooms of Wall Street." Unpublished paper. New York University, Leonard N. Stern School of Business, New York.

Beunza, Daniel, and David Stark. 2003. "The Organization of Responsiveness: Innovation and Recovery in the Trading Rooms of Lower Manhattan." *Socioeconomic Review* 1(2): 135–64.

———. 2004. "Tools of the Trade: The Sociotechnology of Arbitrage in a Wall Street Trading Room." *Industrial and Corporate Change* 13(2): 369–400.

Burns, Tom, and G. M. Stalker. 1961. *The Management of Innovation.* London: Tavistock.

Callon, Michel. 1998. "Introduction: Embeddedness of Economic Markets in Economics." In *The Laws of the Markets*, edited by Michel Callon. Oxford: Blackwell.

Clark, Gordon L., Maryann P. Feldman, and Meric S. Gertler. 2000. *The Oxford Handbook of Economic Geography.* Oxford: Oxford University Press.

Corbridge, Stuart, and Nigel Thrift, eds. 1994. *Money, Power, and Space.* London: Blackwell.

Freeman, Steven F., Larry Hirschhorn, and Marc Maltz. 2002. "Moral Purpose and Organizational Resilience: Sandler, O'Neill & Partners in the Aftermath of September 11, 2001." Working paper. Cambridge, Mass.: Massachusetts Institute of Technology.

Girard, Monique, and David Stark. 2002. "Distributing Intelligence and Organizing Diversity in New Media Projects." *Environment and Planning* A34(11, November): 1927–49.

Hedberg, Robert, Paul C. Nystrom, and William H. Starbuck. 1976. "Camping on Seesaws: Prescriptions for a Self-designing Organization." *Administrative Science Quarterly* 12(1): 41–65.

Hutchins, Edwin. 1995. *Cognition in the Wild.* Cambridge, Mass.: MIT Press.

Katz, Daniel, and Robert L. Kahn. 1961. *The Social Psychology of Organizations*. New York: John Wiley.

Kelly, John, and David Stark. 2002. "Crisis, Recovery, Innovation: Learning from 9/11." *Environment and Planning* A34(9, September): 1523–33.

Kendra, James M., and Tricia Wachtendorf. 2003. "Elements of Resilience After the World Trade Center Disaster: Reconstituting New York City's Emergency Operations Center." *Disasters* 27(1): 37–53.

Kogut, Bruce, and Udo Zander. 1992. "Knowledge of the Firm, Combinative Capabilities, and the Replication of Technology." *Organization Science* 3(3): 383–97.

Lane, David, and Robert Maxfield. 1996. "Strategy Under Complexity: Fostering Generative Relationships." *Long Range Planning* 29(2): 215–31.

Leyshon, Andrew, and Nigel Thrift. 1997. *Money/Space: Geographies of Monetary Transformation*. London: Routledge.

Martin, Ron. 1999. "The New Economic Geography of Money." In *Money and the Space Economy*, edited by Ron Martin. Chichester: John Wiley.

Neff, Gina, and David Stark. 2003. "Permanently Beta: Responsive Organization in the Internet Era." In *Society Online: The Internet in Context*, edited by Philip E. N. Howard and Steve Jones. Thousand Oaks, Calif.: Sage Publications.

Perrow, Charles. 2002. "Disaster Prevention and Mitigation." Unpublished paper. Yale University, New Haven, Conn.

Salgado, Susan. 2002. "Next Door to Disaster: How Participant Observation Changed the Observer." *Journal of Management Inquiry* 11(3): 221–29.

Stark, David. 1999. "Heterarchy: Distributing Intelligence and Organizing Diversity." In *The Biology of Business: Decoding the Natural Laws of Enterprise*, edited by John Clippinger. San Francisco: Jossey-Bass.

———. 2001. "Ambiguous Assets for Uncertain Environments: Heterarchy in Postsocialist Firms." In *The Twenty-first-Century Firm: Changing Economic Organization in International Perspective*, edited by Paul DiMaggio. Princeton, N.J.: Princeton University Press.

Stevenson, Richard, and Jonathan Fuerbringer. 2001. "Nation Shifts Its Focus to Wall Street as a Major Test of Attack's Aftermaths." *New York Times*, September 17, p. A1.

Tierney, Kathleen J. 2002. "Strength of a City: A Disaster Research Perspective on the World Trade Center Attack." Social Science Research Council, After September 11 Archive. Available at: http://www.ssrc.org/sept11/essays/tierney.htm (accessed November 5, 2004).

Weick, Karl. 1979. *The Social Psychology of Organizing*. 2nd ed. Reading, Mass.: Addison-Wesley.

———. 1993. "The Collapse of Sensemaking in Organizations: The Mann Gulch Disaster." *Administrative Science Quarterly* 38: 628–52.

———. 1995. *Sensemaking in Organizations*. Thousand Oaks, Calif.: Sage Publications.

White, Harrison. 1995. *Identity and Control*. Princeton, N.J.: Princeton University Press.

Wolfe, Tom. 1987. *The Bonfire of the Vanities*. New York: Farrar, Straus & Giroux.

Wrzesniewski, Amy. 2002. "'It's Not Just a Job': Shifting Meanings of Work in the Wake of 9/11." *Journal of Management Inquiry* 11(3): 230–34.

CHAPTER 12

Public Deliberations After 9/11

Francesca Polletta and Lesley Wood

IN THE wake of the physical devastation wrought by the terrorist attack on the World Trade Center on September 11, 2001, politicians and planners agreed that rebuilding the site would have to be a participatory process. There was talk of "inclusive" planning and "diverse voices" being heard. What was attacked was American democracy, argued those charged with the key decisions in the rebuilding process, and the response could only be more democracy. "Common ground"—indeed, "consensus" about the most important issues—could be achieved.[1]

One might be forgiven for some skepticism about what such commitments would mean in practice. After all, New York City urban development has long been criticized for being driven by real estate interests (Pedersen 2002) and at the same time paralyzed by battles between community groups and developers (*Gotham Gazette* 2002). In that context, it seemed surprising that the Lower Manhattan Development Corporation (LMDC), an agency led by developers, financiers, and officials for economic development, should talk so enthusiastically about giving power to the people. Yet the rhetoric was matched by action. In the months after the terrorist attack, public forums were organized by a variety of groups. In January, 1,200 people attended a meeting with local officials held in Stuyvesant High School and organized by the community board that represents Lower Manhattan. In February, 600 people talked about their visions for lower Manhattan in a forum sponsored by the Civic Alliance, a coalition of environmental and planning groups. In April the Municipal Arts Society spearheaded a series of 230 "visioning workshops" around the tristate

area, with 3,500 participants generating ideas for memorials, job creation programs, and livable neighborhoods. The LMDC held a public hearing in Manhattan in May and then a series of hearings in each of the boroughs in September. And in July the LMDC collaborated with the Port Authority and the Civic
Alliance to convene possibly the largest "town meeting" ever held in this country. Some 4,500 people met in a midtown convention center to jointly review
the preliminary plans for the World Trade Center site as well as to deliberate
more broadly about the future of lower Manhattan. That event, which attracted international coverage and was credited with sending decisionmakers
back to the design drawing board, was followed by an online dialogue, more
public hearings, an exhibition of new architectural design plans, and numerous
public workshops.

Officials and observers were enthusiastic about the striking level of public
involvement in the design process. Governor George Pataki declared that "ag-
gressive outreach to a broader public" was responsible for the design plan that
was eventually chosen for the site (Wyatt 2003, B1). The designer himself,
Daniel Libeskind, met with a variety of citizens' groups to campaign for his
plan, and he predicted that intense give-and-take with the public would become a standard feature of urban design (Iovine 2003). Commentators hailed
a new responsiveness on the part of public agencies that had long been indifferent to public sensibilities and a veritable "renaissance" in New York City
architecture—all a result of public involvement in the process (Traub 2003;
Muschamp 2002). The enthusiasm was by no means universal, however. From
the beginning, critics complained about the exclusion of elected city officials
from the LMDC board of directors, and many characterized the decisionmaking process as far from transparent (Wyatt 2002a; Sorkin 2002; Russell 2002;
Hetter 2002). Massive town meetings and "listening sessions" were more spectacle than substance, critics charged (Sorkin 2002). Indeed, the civic coalition
that partnered with the LMDC to sponsor the town meeting in July 2002 less
than a year later denounced the LMDC for "closed-door efforts" to alter the
Libeskind plan (Civic Alliance 2003b). Since then, reports have characterized
Libeskind's influence as diminishing still further as the site developer brought
in his own architects to design the new Freedom Towers (Pogrebin 2004).
And the LMDC solicited no public input into its selection of a memorial design
for the site (Dunlap 2003).

Together, then, these developments raise fascinating questions abut the
place of the public in the redevelopment of lower Manhattan. As sociologists
who have studied experiments in radical democracy (Polletta 2001; 2002;
Wood 2004), we wondered how the "public" would be defined in that process
and how its preferences would be balanced with those of family members,
residents, developers, and designers. What would "consensus" mean in a process with high financial stakes and shifting hierarchies of moral authority?

We were especially intrigued by the prominence of novel methods of public deliberation: "visioning workshops," "electronic town meetings," and "online dialogues," among them. We were curious about their relationship to more traditional mechanisms for citizen input into planning decisions. In the context of a recent efflorescence of theorizing about the promise of more deliberative political institutions, were these new forums an indication of the promise of deliberative democracy? Or were they substituting the illusion of public input for real mechanisms of public accountability?

As of this writing, it is still too early to answer any of these questions definitively. However, we can say something about what forms public participation has taken so far, as well as about its initial impacts on both participants themselves and those making decisions about lower Manhattan. This report draws on participant observation and interviews with participants in two public deliberative efforts—"Imagine New York" and "Listening to the City"—to address three questions. One, why did people choose to participate in public forums around the redevelopment of lower Manhattan? Were they advocates pressing for a particular set of interests or a favored design plan? Were they civic stalwarts—the people who always attend community board hearings and city council meetings—or people who do not usually participate but were directly affected by the terrorist attack? Did they come to influence decisionmakers, to process emotionally the events of September 11, or for other reasons? Two, was what took place in the public forums created by Listening to the City and Imagine New York real deliberation? Recent discussions of deliberative democracy have put great stock in strangers' capacity to engage in reasoned dialogue about issues of concern. However, we still know little about the conditions in which organized public forums are likely to foster that kind of dialogue. Our observations of the discussions and interviews with participants offer some insights into that issue. Finally, what short-term impacts have Imagine New York and Listening to the City had on participants and on the development process?

With respect to the first question, we argue that people did not participate in Imagine New York and Listening to the City thinking that either was a pipeline to those in power. In retrospect, they described diverse motivations, prominent among them a sense of obligation to participate and a desire to be part of a process they saw as important. Listening to the City participants became much more confident about their impact on decisionmakers after the original six plans that they were asked to evaluate were scrapped. But what participants liked most about both Listening and Imagine was the opportunity to talk in a mutually respectful way about issues that were important to them with people who were very different from them. With respect to the deliberative character of the discussions, we argue that although the very structure of these efforts sometimes sacrificed the possibility of deliberation in the interests of avoiding conflict, there is some evidence that discussing issues with people with quite different stakes in redevelopment did lead participants to modify or rescale their preferences. Finally, in discussing the impacts of Listening and Imagine, we highlight the tensions between advocacy and deliberation that inevitably mark public deliberative exercises but are little discussed in the literature. The organizations that sponsored Listening to the City and Imagine New York found themselves in an ambiguous position in the wake of those forums—torn between serving as neutral mouthpieces for the public's views and advocating for those views. Their experience in trying to negotiate competing roles suggests an intriguing possibility: civic and advocacy groups, more than decisionmakers, may find political benefit in public forums. We turn to these issues after a brief discussion of current scholarship on deliberative democracy.

NEW FORMS OF DEMOCRATIC DECISIONMAKING

In recent years numerous scholars have championed "deliberative democracy" as an answer to Americans' low levels of participation and trust in the political system (Barber 1988; Dryzek 1990; Cohen 1989; Guttman and Thompson 1996; Fishkin 1991; 1995). Ordinary citizens should be given the opportunity to discuss important political issues, exchange views based on reasoned arguments, and come to recognize areas of agreement as well as the legitimacy of other points of view. Contrary to the assumption that interests are pregiven and fixed, deliberation makes it possible for people to scrutinize and modify their preexisting interests and develop new ones. But for deliberative democrats the object is not necessarily full consensus. Rather, it is the parties' recognition of the validity of a range of arguments, though not all arguments. Once that recognition occurs, people can accept a decision that does not match their preferences exactly (Cohen and Sabel 1997; Shapiro 2002, 198).

Democratic legitimacy, in this view, requires not that every constituent has veto power over decisionmaking, but that he or she has the opportunity to deliberate. In principle, this means that public deliberation can be integrated with existing electoral, legislative, and administrative processes. Those processes should be strengthened by public discourse that avoids polarizing along partisan lines or positions on hot-button moral questions (Fishkin 1995). Participants in deliberative exercises are likely to become more trusting of their political institutions and more informed politically (Cohen 1989; Fishkin 1995; Guttman and Thompson 1996).

Alongside a rich theoretical literature on deliberative democracy, efforts to put deliberative democracy into practice—such as study circles, citizen assemblies, citizen juries, public visioning workshops, national issues forums, and deliberative polls—have proliferated in the last decade (for overviews, see Button and Mattson 1999; Gastil 2000; Passerin D'Entreves 2002). Some research has claimed qualified success for these deliberative forums: participants interviewed before and after their participation in one weekend of discussion gained a greater sense of individual efficacy and trust in government (Fishkin and Luskin 1999), and participants in another forum left more politically informed (Gastil and Dillard 1999).

Still, empirical research on deliberative democracy has not yet caught up with the theoretical claims made for it. At least three areas demand further research. One has to do with the discursive and organizational conditions in which good deliberation is likely to occur in deliberative forums. Theorists have generally seen deliberative discourse as characterized by participants' equality, a diversity of viewpoints, claims that are backed up by reasoned arguments, and, for some theorists, reflexivity—the ability of participants to question the agenda and the procedures for discussion (Cohen 1989; Dryzek 1990; Fishkin 1991; Guttman and Thompson 1996). However, there has been little close empirical analysis of the character of discourse in public deliberative efforts (for exceptions, see Hart and Jarvis 1999; on Internet dialogue, see Stanley, Weare, and Musso 2002). We need to know much more about the organizational conditions and interpersonal dynamics by which people begin to seek out information outside their personal experience, shift opinions on the basis of persuasive arguments rather than subtle coercion, and question the rules of the game.

A second issue about which we lack adequate data is the impact of public deliberation on participants. If research suggests that participants leave study circles, citizens' assemblies, deliberative polls, and issues forums feeling more efficacious, more trusting in government institutions, and more politically knowledgeable, we do not know much about what happens next. Do people then go on to vote, participate in other kinds of political action, pay more attention to political developments, and engage in other forms of social capital formation? Determining whether participation leads to greater trust in government is also made difficult by the generality of the measures of political efficacy and trust. Participants are asked to respond to statements such as, "People like me don't have any say in what the government does," and, "Public officials care a lot about what people like me think" (Fishkin and Luskin 1999, 3). One could imagine that, were participants to feel that their discussions had been ignored by politicians, they might become more skeptical about institutional politics rather than less so (as suggested by the case study in Button and Mattson 1999). We need more research on how participation in public deliberative processes shapes participants' attention to, involvement in, and satisfaction with a policymaking process over time.

If public deliberation has intrinsic benefits for participants, it is also usually seen as bearing on actual policymaking. As Judith Squires (2002) points out, however, deliberative democratic theorists have been maddeningly vague about the normative relationship they envision between public deliberation and conventional political processes of representation, aggregation, and decisionmaking. How is deliberation to be incorporated into political decisionmaking? What makes it difficult to answer empirically the question of how we are to incorporate public deliberative exercises into political decisionmaking is that such exercises have been organized by very different political actors in very different political contexts. Some have been sponsored by government agencies and public commissions (Fishkin and Luskin 1999; Stanley, Weare, and Musso 2002); others have been implemented by local mixes of civic groups and foundations, sometimes with the involvement of local officials (Walters 1998); and still others have taken place entirely outside political institutions (Button and Mattson 1999). This makes it more difficult to assess the political impact of public deliberation in any general sense. But there is another point. Public deliberative efforts usually figure in a policymaking process that includes numerous collective actors: political officials, civic organizations, advocacy groups, influential private groups, foundations, the press, and so on. Many of them claim to speak for the "public." We need to understand better how the organizations sponsoring public deliberation relate to these groups. We also need to understand better how such efforts support, modify, or displace existing mechanisms for citizen input into official decisionmaking. If their appeal is in part as a substitute for such mechanisms, then who wins and who loses as a result?

PUBLIC DELIBERATION AFTER 9/11

Two large-scale efforts to solicit public input into the redevelopment of lower Manhattan offer an opportunity to address these issues. Imagine New York was organized by a coalition of civic, neighborhood, and arts organizations spearheaded by the Municipal Arts Society (MAS). Concerned that early discussions among planners and architects were failing to tap New Yorkers' ideas about and needs for lower Manhattan, MAS staffers Eva Hanhardt and Holly Leicht began to envision a process by which a broad swath of New Yorkers would share ideas about what they wanted not only for the site but for the city and region as a whole. The planner Gianni Longo was recruited to help design the workshops. Longo's public "visioning workshops" in Chattanooga, Tennessee, had been credited with playing a critical role in that city's widely admired revitalization (Walters 1998; Moore, Longo, and Palmer 1999), and he created a modified version of those workshops for Imagine New York.

With the support of the Surdna Foundation, 230 workshops were held in April 2002 around the metropolitan area—in all five boroughs, Long Island, and New York State, Connecticut, and New Jersey—along with a smaller number of more focused design workshops and arts projects for adults and children. The workshops were held in large-scale public venues like the Flushing town hall and Pace University and in smaller venues like a senior citizens' center, a restaurant, and private homes. Participants were recruited through the membership rolls of the sponsoring organizations, outreach efforts by members of the steering committee, posters pasted around the city, some media coverage, and a television spot that ran on several networks.

Trained volunteers facilitated the three-hour workshops. Groups of ten to fifteen people, seated in a circle, were asked to reflect on and then respond to two questions: "What have we lost and how have we changed?" and then, after a visualization exercise, "How can we move forward from September 11?" Participants' round-robin responses were recorded by the facilitator on large sheets of paper taped to the wall. The group was then asked to identify overarching themes in the ideas recorded. Forming small groups around each theme, participants crafted a "vision statement" and a strategy for realizing the vision. The workshop concluded after each subgroup read aloud its statements. All the materials were collected, and a total of nineteen thousand ideas were eventually synthesized into forty-nine draft vision statements by Imagine New York's steering committee. These were reviewed, amended, and ratified by three hundred returning participants at a "summit meeting" (all participants had been invited) on June 1, 2002. The final visions were released to the press on June 10 and submitted to the LMDC and other decisionmaking agencies. An Imagine New York website displayed ideas and designs submitted by people who had not participated in the workshops.[2]

Listening to the City was conceived by the Civic Alliance, a coalition of environmental, planning, and civic groups formed after September 11 and led by the Regional Plan Association (RPA). The July 20 and 22, 2002, events followed a smaller but similar event held in February. Both were designed and run by AmericaSpeaks, a Washington-based organization that specializes in conducting "electronic town meetings." AmericaSpeaks had run a national public forum on Social Security and a forum on livability issues in Washington, D.C., but it was through a friendship with a member of the Civic Alliance that AmericaSpeaks president Carolyn Lukensmeyer came to the attention of the leaders of that group and proposed the idea of a town meeting on lower Manhattan. Members of the coalition were receptive, and the February event garnered the interest and support of the LMDC. That suggested the value and feasibility of a much larger forum in which thousands of New Yorkers would register their ideas about the redevelopment of lower Manhattan and the design of an appropriate memorial. The LMDC signed on, as did the Port Authority, and both committed some funding. The largest share of the estimated $2 million required was raised by the Rockefeller Brothers Fund; additional funding (though less than anticipated) came from corporate contributions.

There were serious conflicts in developing an agenda for the event: the RPA and the Civic Alliance wanted a regional focus and a discussion of economic and social justice, while the Port Authority and the LMDC were determined to concentrate on the site and the preliminary concept plans. Organized family members of 9/11 victims, meanwhile, hoped for a clear signal from the public to slow down the entire decisionmaking. The publicity around the preliminary plans—they were roundly criticized in the press—had made for substantial interest in Listening to the City, and organizers reached their mark of 4,500 participants well before July 20. Some 4,300 people would participate in the daylong event on July 20 at the Jacob Javits Center, and another several hundred in a repeat meeting on July 22. A week later an online Listening to the City dialogue began, with 800 people discussing their ideas for the site in small dialogue groups.[3]

At the July 20 event, the 4,300 participants were assigned to ten-person tables in a giant auditorium. The makeup of the tables was as diverse as possible, with family members scattered throughout the room and translators provided for speakers of Spanish, Mandarin, Cantonese, and sign language. Carolyn Lukensmeyer moderated the event and, after introducing the rebuilding officials, asked participants to enter demographic information about themselves into their keypads. As would be the case for the rest of the day, the polled information was tabulated and projected on Jumbotron screens located throughout the auditorium. The rest of the day's discussion alternated between individual polling and small-group discussions in which table members discussed options for redevelopment. A member of the group typed group responses to questions into the table's laptop computer, along with "minority reports" by dissenting participants. These were then relayed via network to a "theme team," which synthesized responses and projected them onto the screen along with illustrative quotes. Periodically, participants registered individual preferences on their personal keypads on issues such as the importance of housing on the site, how they rated each of the six proposed plans, and how confident they were that decisionmakers would listen to their recommendations.

By the end of the day the six site plans that the LMDC had proposed had been rejected. Participants were uniformly critical of not only the site plans but the proposal to build eleven million square feet of office space on the site. Shortly after the event, which received intense media coverage in New York and across the nation, the LMDC announced that it had scrapped the plans and arranged for a panel of architects and planners to select seven teams of architects, many internationally known, to develop new ideas for the site.

Francesca Polletta joined Imagine New York's steering committee in December 2001 and attended meetings of the Civic Alliance, the group that sponsored

Listening to the City. Those initial contacts made it possible for us to mine several sources of data. We designed a study with four components:

1. A longitudinal study of participants in Imagine New York and Listening to the City, along with those in a control group of people who registered for but did not participate in Listening to the City. The study would allow us to assess whether and how participation in the deliberative exercises influenced people's attention to, involvement in, and views of the development process.

2. A comparison of those who participated in the Listening to the City face-to-face forum with those who participated in the online forum. This comparison would allow us to flesh out profiles of the modal users of the two deliberative forms.

3. A discursive analysis of the twenty-six online discussion groups organized as part of Listening to the City. With this analysis, we could identify the discursive and organizational conditions in which good deliberation occurs.

4. Interviews with the planners of the two deliberative exercises as well as with those charged with decisionmaking in the redevelopment of the site and representatives of advocacy groups. These interviews contributed to our assessment of the impact of these forums on the decisionmaking process overall.

We are at different stages in the four lines of research. In this chapter, we draw on our first round of interviews with fifty participants in Listening to the City and thirty-three participants in Imagine New York; our participant observation of the planning of the forums, their operation, and subsequent efforts to disseminate their results; and our interviews with the events' organizers and the decisionmakers targeted by the forums. Our interviews with participants were open-ended and focused on why and how they came to participate in the forum; how confident they were in the forum's impact on decisionmakers, both before and after their participation; and whether and how their preferences and priorities had changed as a result of their discussions. To collect baseline information for our second round of interviews, we also asked questions designed to assess people's knowledge of and attention to the development process as well as the forms of their civic engagement.

Our interview samples were not as representative of those who participated in Imagine and Listening as we had hoped. Our interviewees roughly matched participants in terms of income level and geographical residence. However, whites, people with advanced degrees, and older participants were overrepresented among our interviewees. One check on our findings comes from the fact that a poll of participants in Listening to the City on some of the questions we asked—for example, about participants' level of confidence in decision-makers and their satisfaction with the discussions—came up with the same results that we did. Still, we treat our statistical data somewhat gingerly.[4]

WHO SPOKE AND WHAT DID THEY WANT?

Who participated in Imagine New York and Listening to the City? Organizers of both efforts sought to secure a diverse cross-section of New Yorkers. Imagine New York drew on its organizational members to do outreach in the five boroughs and the region. Listening to the City relied on an outreach firm to selectively target neighborhoods and demographic groups that were not represented in the pool of early registrants. Neither strategy was entirely successful. Imagine New York had a hard time filling the public venues. Our interviews suggest that people were more likely to be drawn to the event through networks of work, community, and friendship than through media spots and flyers. Forty-one percent of our Imagine respondents heard about the event from an organization of which they were a member, 25 percent through friends or family members, and 22 percent from a coworker. Only 28 percent had heard about the event only through the media. This was true for more participants in Listening to the City: 34 percent had heard about the event only through the media. However, Listening to the City's efforts to reach minority neighborhoods were not especially successful. African Americans and Hispanics were sharply underrepresented, African Americans making up only 7 percent of Listening participants, compared to 20 percent of the region's residents, and Hispanic participants making up only 10 percent of the group, compared to 20 percent of the region's residents.

We noted that many of our participants heard about Imagine and Listening through their social networks. But relatively few of the people we interviewed came accompanied by anyone, let alone in a group. With a few exceptions, which we discuss later, they were not people who had organized to represent their collective interests in the process. Were they then typical civic engagers, the people who always go to community board meetings and city council meetings? Of the thirty-two Listening to the City participants who responded to our questions on this issue, 84 percent had voted in the two years before they participated in Listening to the City, 22 percent had given money to political candidates, 50 percent had given money to advocacy groups, and 63 percent had contacted a public official. Thirty-four percent had attended a community board meeting.

How do these participants compare to Americans generally? Though not exactly comparable, in 2000, a presidential election year, 73 percent of a random sample of Americans said that they had voted. Only 5 percent of the sample had given money to political candidates, 5 percent had given money to advocacy groups, and 22 percent had contacted a public official (Burns, Kinder, and National Election Studies 2000). Another indicator of the high level of civic engagement in our sample was the fact that 38 percent had volunteered on a political campaign in the last two years, compared to 12 percent of a random sample of Americans who had volunteered in 2000 (Lake, Snell, Perry and Associates and the Tarrance Group 2002). Of our Listening sample, 16 percent had a professional or vocational interest in design and planning: they were architects, planners, or amateur designers. Most strikingly, these were people who had been paying attention to the redevelopment process. Twenty-five percent said that in the week before they decided to register this was the top news story they were following; an additional 40 percent said that it was among the top three stories they were following. We asked who currently held the lease to the World Trade Center site, information that was neither provided in the materials available to Listening to the City participants nor mentioned over the course of the day: 64 percent knew that Larry Silverstein held the lease.

Why did people participate? Not because they believed they had a pipeline to those in power. Most people we interviewed said that they had not been very confident that the recommendations that emerged from the forum would be followed by decisionmakers. Forty-three percent of the Listening sample were not very confident, they said; 36 percent were somewhat confident, 11 percent were confident, and 9 percent were very confident. Compare these figures to the level of confidence that most Americans had in local government in 2000: according to an NBC News–*Wall Street Journal* poll conducted in December 2000, only 22 percent had very little or no confidence, 20 percent had quite a bit of confidence, and 18 percent had a great deal of confidence. Listening to the City participants attributed their skepticism mainly to their belief that the important decisions had already been made (31 percent) and/or that developers' interests would ultimately prevail (29 percent). Our respondents may have been exaggerating their skepticism to highlight the change in their views, since fully 90 percent became more confident of the exercise's impact after it was over. However, our figures are not dissimilar to those polled during the event itself toward the end of the day. Asked, "How confident are you that your voice will be heard?" 21 percent said that they were not confident at all, 45 percent that they were somewhat confident, 23 percent that they were confident, and 10 percent that they were very confident (Listening to the City 2002, 21).

So if they were not confident that decisionmakers would listen, why participate? Several reasons were cited. First, many people saw the possibility of influence, slim as it was, as a worthwhile gamble. Forty-seven percent of our Listening sample said that they had participated because they wanted to influence the process or wanted to have "a voice," but they often cautioned that such influence was by no means guaranteed. A rescue worker who participated in Listening to the City explained, "I was a cynic, and I was willing to take a risk. You know the expression: you hope for the best but you expect the worst." A planner said: "I hoped it would have an effect. Believed? No." Fewer of our Imagine New York respondents—28 percent—described wanting to influence the process. This was probably because the timing and agenda of the two efforts were different. While Listening to the City participants spent much of their time reviewing proposed master plans, Imagine participants spent much of theirs giving voice to their feelings of loss as a result of the World Trade Center attack. Forty-seven percent of Imagine participants explained their participation in terms of wanting to process emotionally the events of September 11, compared with only 9 percent of Listening participants who gave this reason.

Both Imagine (25 percent) and Listening participants (34 percent) also talked about their participation as an end in itself, a civic obligation. Our respondents sometimes groped for language to describe this sense of obligation. It was an opportunity "to have my voice heard, whether personal or in terms of planning [the site]," said one. ". . . It's a personal thing, a civic thing." An Imagine participant from Queens noted briefly, "I did what I had to do." Other respondents talked about wanting "to be a part of the rebuilding," wanting to "add a small grain of sand to the system," and wanting to "give an opinion that might be worth something." Still other kinds of motivations appeared in our interviews: 16 percent of our Listening to the City participants said they hoped to learn something about the issues involved or about the deliberative process ("I was fascinated by the process and the electronic stuff—curious about how it would work"), and 12 percent said they had simply looked forward to meeting and talking with other people.

We were struck by the number of people who participated because they wanted "a voice." One can interpret "voice" in political instrumental terms, as synonymous with "influence in the process." But we noticed that respondents often then talked about liking the event because they felt that they were "heard"—by people at their table. This suggests a less political, perhaps even a therapeutic, understanding of voice. However, our second round of interviews sheds more light on the metaphor. When we asked respondents explicitly what they had meant by talking about wanting "a voice," a number said that they had wanted to be heard by "the community" as well as by "decision-makers," or that they wanted to listen as much as to speak. The impression they gave was of wanting to be part of a dialogue involving people with diverse viewpoints, in which they would discover their own views as much as communicate them to decisionmakers.

Can we draw any conclusions from these responses about who is likely to participate in public forums generally? It is hard to imagine that people would be as galvanized by a sense of wanting to participate for its own sake, without the expectation of influence, in discussions of more prosaic matters. On the other hand, when asked, all of our respondents said that they could see this kind of forum being used to discuss other issues, from education to crime to foreign policy. Three respondents suggested that Congress should use Listening's format. And many attested to the utility of the model without our prompting. Indeed, we were struck by how many respondents volunteered that they had contacted friends, acquaintances, and coworkers to tell them about their experiences, sending out group e-mails, for instance, or speaking up in church. A Listening participant who initially believed that the decisions about the site were "a fait accompli," said, "That night in the restaurant I was telling people about it, and it was almost like giving a speech. I told people that it had been unanimous that five thousand people had told [New York Governor George] Pataki where to go." "I'm spreading the word," said another Listening participant, and a third said she had made a point of describing the exercise to members of her small-business association: "It wasn't something I would have done before." A longtime activist "sent e-mails to friends about it, saying that it would shame politicians into acting," and suggested that the exercise could be used to grapple with other issues. "Believe me, the word spread," a teacher assured us. "My big mouth went to my church. . . . We're like little disciples," she concluded. These responses suggest that similar forums on other issues could draw broad participation. Our findings also suggest, however, that if a forum does not exploit ties of friendship, community, work, and church in recruiting participants, it is unlikely to draw a demographically representative group.

WERE THESE PUBLIC FORUMS REAL DELIBERATION?

Participants in both Imagine New York and Listening to the City were enthusiastic about their experience. Strikingly, it was the deliberative character of the discussions they appreciated. "I broadcast this to everyone I knew," a travel writer recounted. "I said, 'The most amazing thing happened: I was in this town hall, and no one argued, and I was listened to, and it was a great day.'" Many of our respondents had anticipated a more conventional public hearing, they told us, in which people would line up behind a microphone to speak for three minutes. Or they expected to be lectured to by public officials—"you know, hearing various pieces of propaganda about how [the WTC site] should be rebuilt without a whole lot of voice." Instead, our respondents said, "people listened to each other" and talked rather than argued. They appreciated that their tablemates were "respectful," that discussion was "calm," that people didn't "rant," and that "there was no shouting and everyone heard us." Thirty percent of both Imagine and Listening respondents referred to the civility of the discussions as what they liked most about the event. Interestingly, a number described Imagine or Listening as not "political"—implicitly associating political discussion with rigidity and contention.

In describing what they liked most about the event, Listening (48 percent) and Imagine respondents (22 percent) also emphasized the diversity of people and viewpoints they encountered. Participants liked being exposed to different points of view that they had not considered. And they liked feeling that they were, as one put it, "a microcosm of New York"—or as another said, "being in a tiny little miniature New York at each table." They liked the sense of being representative of New Yorkers, and they wanted their recommendations to have the prescriptive force of that representation. Several respondents gently complained that the forums were not diverse enough, and they suggested ways to tap underrepresented groups for the next event.

Thus, participants experienced both Imagine New York and Listening to the City as more deliberative than other kinds of forums they had encountered, both those focused on the rebuilding of lower Manhattan and those that dwelt on community affairs. Were their discussions in fact deliberative? Were they characterized by the equality, openness to diverse opinions, validation of reasonable arguments, and reflexivity that scholars have seen as requirements of authentically deliberative discussion? To answer that question would require a close examination of the discussions themselves, which we did not do systematically. However, our observations of the discussions and their planning, in conjunction with our interviews with participants, do permit some observations.

The picture is a mixed one. Imagine's planners self-consciously sacrificed opportunities for deliberation in the workshops in the interests of avoiding conflict. For example, no time for discussion was allowed in the main part of the workshop, and there was only a short period at the end for people to talk in groups of three or four as they worked on their vision statements. For most of the workshop, participants were instructed to register their preferences individually and in turn. Facilitators were told to steer the group back to the individual response format if a group discussion developed. Gianni Longo, who designed the Imagine workshops, said that his usual workshops involved a segment in which participants prioritized their preferences. However, the raw emotions still attached to the World Trade Center site made such an exercise inappropriate.[5]

In fact, our interviews with Imagine participants and our observations of the workshops suggest that some groups adhered to the prescribed format and some did not. When groups followed the format, respondents said that they appreciated the fact that everyone's ideas were heard, recorded, and treated as equal in value. But they also complained about the paucity of discussion, and some regretted the fact that the small-group brainstorming at the end was so brief. "I think the last question really encouraged more interaction between the group than when we were just sort of making lists of things," said one. In other workshops, however, groups refused to be bound by the format, insisting on collectively answering questions and brainstorming solutions. This may account for the fact that several respondents who participated in both Imagine New York and Listening to the City referred to the unstructured and more satisfying character of discussion in Imagine, despite the fact that, formally at least, it had fewer opportunities for group discussion.

In Listening to the City, participants were expected to come up with joint answers to the questions asked of them and, if necessary, a minority report. Was this deliberation? In authentically deliberative discussion, one should expect to see people, if not coming to embrace views or preferences radically different from those with which they began, then at least coming to recognize the legitimacy of other views and preferences. Our interviews with participants in Listening to the City suggest that these kinds of shifts did occur. We developed a scale to capture the opinion shifts that people experienced. Moving from less to more substantial opinion shift, we identified six categories: "I did not change my mind at all"; "I learned new information"; "I came to understand other people's points of view"; "I clarified my own views and values"; "I came to support a practical solution that I had not thought of before"; and "I came away believing something different than I did at first." Respondents often made several kinds of statements in the same interview. Of those we interviewed, 33 percent said that they did not change their minds at all. Twenty percent said that they had not changed their minds but had garnered new information; 20 percent said that they had come to appreciate the views of others; 27 percent said that they had not changed their opinions but had clarified them; and 35 percent said that they had come to agree with practical ideas that they had not thought of previously—that a New Jersey–to–New York subway train could be run downtown, for example, or that West Street, a highly trafficked thoroughfare that cuts the riverfront off from downtown, could be buried. Finally, 32 percent said that they had changed their minds.

Of those who said that they had changed their minds, 84 percent also said that they had come to appreciate the views of others. This figure does not tell us whether there was a causal link or, if so, what it was, but one possibility is that hearing and empathizing with the views of others led people to change their minds. This is the deliberative democratic argument. Our interviews indicate that many people did indeed change their minds about issues because they came to appreciate those holding different views. "We had a family member who had lost someone at our table, and she actually sounded very reasonable, and I guess it made me see how important the memorial really is for people," one interviewee said, concluding that the memorial should be designed before anything else. A Battery Park City resident recounted, "There was one woman who worked at the towers. She educated me about where the money was going and how some people are still having difficulty finding work, and so I learned that we needed to find money for jobs." A woman who once worked in the towers, in turn, was educated by a Battery Park City resident who was concerned that burying West Street would create more security problems. "And I said, 'You know, I didn't think about that.' . . . I thought, wow, security." "I work downtown," said one young man. "I felt very strongly about the towers as symbols of what America was—its wealth and accomplishments. I wanted to restore the ability, the right, to dream big dreams. I hadn't really thought about the people who had died. About their families. After the session, as a result of the people at the table who lost their sons, the people started to matter more. The symbols are still important, but the human factor was stronger." And a Brooklyn resident: "I guess I come from a higher-income family than some of the people at the table, and other people have different priorities. You can't ignore them when there is someone in front of you rather than just a statistic. You have to say, 'I guess they're right, we should compromise on this fact, on affordable housing, and things like that.'"

Note that in these examples people who one might imagine would have a stake in the future of lower Manhattan—a downtown worker and a Battery Park City resident—shifted their preference orderings in response to the information and perspective they gained from other participants. Unsurprisingly, the family members of victims of the World Trade Center attack had a special kind of authority in these shifts. But some participants were pleased to discover that family members were willing to listen to other points of view. "I thought that having a survivor at the table was going to be a real drag," confessed one woman. "I thought that she was going to get p.o.-ed at me, and then I was going to get judgmental against her. And it didn't end up happening that way. She listened to me, and I listened to her." Another respondent said that when relatives of victims introduced themselves at his table, his "first reaction was, 'This is going to be a long afternoon,'" but that when he left he was "surprised with how people could have respect for divergent ideas," and he had new ideas of his own: "I came in with big-picture ideas, and I moved toward thinking more on the individuals."

Respondents referred with pleasure to the experience of being affected by other participants' arguments. One said, "The fact that I was willing to listen to other people's point of view was very exciting, and to really see other people's point of view [was too]." Another reflected: "Much of my thinking prior to the event had been solo thinking. The experience made me aware of other people's experiences. . . . After a couple of minutes of seeing where someone was going, it opened my mind to a different point of view, and perhaps a more valid point of view than what I was holding." A respondent who described herself as politically conservative said she was "amazed at what came out of my mouth. I said there should be low-income housing down there." She explained that the discussion gave her "time to really think about things I've never thought about very much," and she came to believe that "this could be a new beginning for a lot of [people]—for our city and for all of us—and to have low-income and middle-income housing . . . would be a new beginning."

Statements like these suggest that people were redefining their preferences. Was the redefinition subtly coerced? Interestingly, after saying, "I was amazed at what came out of my mouth," the last respondent continued: "There was one man at the table who I thought was a trifle racist, and I was amazed I said there should be low-income housing down there." This suggests that she was coming to see her own preference *in contrast* to that of someone else. Other respondents also emphasized that when the group reached consensus, it seemed genuine. They remarked frequently that group members had strong individual opinions.

In participants' accounts, then, and in our own observations, discussions seemed to be characterized by the equality of participants, a diversity of viewpoints, and in some cases the mutual validation of reasoned arguments. Some deliberative democrats also argue that authentic deliberative discourse should be characterized by reflexivity. That is, participants should be able to revise the agenda and decide on new procedures for discussion. Did reflexivity characterize the discussions in Imagine New York and Listening to the City? Overall, we were struck by participants' desire to follow the prescribed agenda. Imagine New York participants were often given confusing instructions about how to identify a "theme," and yet they struggled diligently to come up with what they believed the facilitator wanted. They refrained from commenting vocally on other people's contributions, instead nodding their heads vigorously. Repeatedly, we noticed that when a participant made a comment that might be interpreted as controversial, other participants either reinterpreted it to sound less controversial or ignored it. In Listening to the City we also noted participants' unease when controversial issues came up, especially about American foreign policy. In interviews, however, some people expressed concern that the format of the questions and of each event made it difficult to depart from the agenda. "The moderators kept telling people to save things for later, so people were basically not allowed to talk," one respondent said of both Listening and Imagine. Occasionally, too, we saw participants collectively altering the rules, as Imagine groups did when they refused to be bound by the round-robin style and instead shifted to a more free-form discussion.

Participants experienced challenges to the rules of the game, our interviews suggest, as opening up new possibilities. When asked whether her discussions had led her to change her mind about anything, one respondent said that before, she would have thought that she had to choose from the six plans. "But then I found that most people were dissatisfied with the plans, and they sort of reflected what I was thinking, and I was like, 'Oh, I guess it's okay not to like any of the plans, and it's okay to not have to pick from a, b, c, d, or e, and [instead] create my own category. And that's what was good about the event. ... I felt as if I could say something different, and I could actually put it out there and not just have to select from what was presented to me." Accounts like this one suggest that we need a better understanding of the conditions in which this kind of challenge to the rules of the game leads participants to feel more empowered rather than unsettled.

WAS THE PUBLIC HEARD?

On December 18, 2002, seven teams of architects presented new designs for the World Trade Center site. Introducing the plans, LMDC president Lou Tomson underscored the "democratic process" that had produced them. "Since the LMDC was created, we pledged that the public would shape the future of lower Manhattan, and today we are honoring that pledge," Tomson declared.

> The seven teams were chosen because of their bold ideas and strong beliefs, but they were not given a blank slate. Instead, they were presented with a program that incorporates a full accounting of the public's comments. It's no accident that every plan attempts to reclaim our skyline with a powerful symbol, and it's no accident that every plan respects the footprints as memorials and as cultural space. As our city heals, these elements are in each plan because that's what we learned the public desires.

Whether the extraordinary level of public commentary on the design process really did influence decisionmakers and designers remains in dispute. Later accounts of the selection of the Libeskind design suggest that agency turf battles, the governor's determination to put his stamp on the process, and the degree to which particular architects seemed willing to alter their plans in line with the Port Authority's objectives played much more of a role than did public input. After that decision, substantial alterations were made to the Libeskind design, without any request for public comment. Those alterations brought the plan uncomfortably close to one of the plans that had been so roundly rejected by Listening to the City participants (Wyatt 2003). Most recently, reports have suggested that almost all of the chief elements of the

Libeskind design have been altered as a design firm hired by the developer Larry Silverstein has taken over design of the major buildings on the site (Pogrebin 2004).

Was Listening to the City simply a feel-good exercise in citizen participation that had no impact? Alex Garvin, former LMDC vice president for design and planning, argues that Listening to the City was critical in giving him the leverage he needed to open up the design process against the original wishes of the Port Authority. "It wasn't just that there was an overwhelming reaction of 'This is not good enough,'" he argues. "There were other things that came out which had a big influence: 'We liked that promenade on West Street. We want our skyline back. We want a street grid. We want a variety of different-sized open spaces, and we want you to treat the footprints with respect.'"[6]

Certainly, public interest in the design process had an effect on the architects competing in the subsequent design study. The finalists, Daniel Libeskind and the THINK team, hired public relations firms, met with family groups and other advocacy coalitions, appeared on the television talk show *Oprah!*, and orchestrated e-mail campaigns in support of their plans. "Architecture will never be the same," Libeskind said, predicting that this kind of interaction with the public "clients" of urban design was likely here to stay (Iovine 2003). Commentators saw another sign of change in the Port Authority's selection of the Spanish architect Santiago Calatrava to design the World Trade Center's new transportation center. "The fact that officials staged a worldwide competition for an architect was almost as astounding as the fact that they chose a figure widely described as the world's greatest architect of transportation," James Traub (2003, F17) writes. "It seems plain that the public demand for meaningful architecture had altered the climate within which the Port Authority operates."

Listening to the City's use by groups critical of the development process should also be entered on the balance sheet of its impacts. The Civic Alliance, which sponsored Listening to the City, called on the LMDC to honor the public's desire for less commercial development at Ground Zero, criticizing its unwillingness to reduce the amount of office space planned for the site (Civic Alliance 2003b). Advocacy groups fighting for towers identical to the height of the originals cited Listening to the City as evidence of the public's desire for the restoration of the towers (Wyatt 2002b).

In contrast to Listening to the City, Imagine New York met with little response on the part of decisionmakers. For Garvin, the fact that Imagine's agenda had not been developed in consultation with the LMDC meant that it was simply "not responsive to the issues in front of us."[7] Garvin attended the June 2002 press conference at which the forty-nine visions were released but made only vague statements about the value of the exercise and pointedly refused to respond to a question about whether the LMDC would follow the recommendations made in the report. Presentations to the LMDC staff were fairly coolly received, as were those made in hearings in December 2002 convened by the State Assembly speaker. On the other hand, Imagine New York's smaller scale and connections to a number of civic groups allowed MAS staffers to turn the project into an ongoing seminar and referendum on the development process, something the organizers of Listening were not able to do. After releasing the project's initial recommendations, Imagine organizers joined with advocacy groups to outline nine principles that had not been addressed by the LMDC's guidelines; invited workshop participants back to comment on the second set of design plans and then presented a summary of those findings at LMDC hearings; convened another set of workshops to solicit public input about transportation issues at the site; and held educational seminars and workshops for people to weigh in on the proposed designs for a memorial at the site. Imagine's lower cost and low-tech format may have made it easier for organizers to maintain an ongoing campaign for public involvement.

This is an interesting possibility because one of the concerns of participants in both forums was whether the recommendations they generated would be implemented. People talked about the project as an ongoing one: they were interested in the next steps, and they wanted the recommendations they made to be *advocated* for. Asked whether he thought Listening to the City would influence decisionmakers, one respondent answered, "It depends on the people who put Listening to the City together, how vigilant [they are]. . . . If they back off and let them maneuver and manipulate this situation, it will be null and void what we did." Another Listening participant said that had he been running the event, he would have pushed LMDC and Port Authority representatives to make a firmer commitment, to "strip them bare," as he put it. "They were still wearing their skivvies when they walked out."

Our respondents thus raised important questions not only about public deliberation's direct impact on decisionmakers but about what role the sponsors of such efforts should play in pressing the recommendations that they generate. Certainly, neither set of recommendations had any formal authority. The LMDC never outlined how it would take into account opinions expressed by the public, nor how it would balance the multiple and sometimes competing voices of the public, groups representing families, small businesses, residents, and its own advisory groups (Hetter 2002). That put the sponsors of the deliberative forums in an ambiguous position. Were they consultants to the LMDC, their job being to tap the public's views, identify areas of consensus, and then stay out of the way? Or were they public watchdogs, charged with determining whether the LMDC and other decisionmakers were following the public's wishes and, if not, trying to publicize where decisionmakers were falling short?

From the beginning, Imagine New York's planners said that they had two goals: "To gather ideas and visions from the broad public [and] to ensure that those voices and ideas [are] heard by decisionmakers who in the months and years to come will be formulating the plans and policies that are critical for the future of the region" (Imagine New York 2002, 5). Those commitments were underscored in statements to the press and in speeches in workshops and at the Imagine summit meeting. But what the second commitment meant—ensuring that the public's ideas were "heard by decisionmakers"—or better, how big a role the MAS should play in realizing that commitment, was unclear. MAS staffers had sought the LMDC's endorsement before the Imagine workshops began. By the summer, however, they had shifted into more of an advocacy role as they joined with groups that had been more publicly critical of the LMDC in order to press for housing, sustainable building, and job creation—concerns that, they said, had received short shrift in the LMDC's planning. At the same time, however, MAS staffers were wrestling with whether their agenda was indeed best served by taking the role of public critic. As MAS's Holly Leicht put it, the question was whether to be "an outside advocate or a monitoring partner." Quiet lobbying was an "MO that MAS uses all the time," Leicht explained. But she confessed that striking a "balance between staying public on issues and having a quiet relationship—influential board members talking to people in LMDC"—was no easy task.[8]

The organizers of Listening to the City confronted similar questions. In February 2002, Civic Alliance head Robert Yaro explained that "our role is not to be directly part of the public process but to be a resource to people who make decisions" (quoted in Pedersen 2002). The Alliance did indeed have a consultative role early in the process, said staffer Petra Todorovich, helping the LMDC to identify development concerns. That changed after Listening to the City was concluded, when neither the LMDC nor the Port Authority made any immediate moves to abandon the plans that had been so soundly rejected. The Civic Alliance issued a press release calling on the LMDC to scrap the plans and from that point on began to take its criticisms of the decisionmaking process to the press, something it had not done before.[9] "Because Listening to the City was such a phenomenal success from a media standpoint, the club we were swinging was bigger than anyone was used to," one Civic Alliance member explained later. Plans to adapt components of Listening to the City for use in LMDC hearings about the new round of designs fell apart in the process. The LMDC ended up relying on a fairly conventional public hearing format, along with staffers' meetings with residents' and families' groups and comment cards that were submitted by visitors to a public exhibition of the nine plans. On December 17, 2002, Listening to the City participants received an e-mail from the Civic Alliance declaring that "the public agencies have ignored our call for a thorough public process" in reviewing the new design plans and urging them to write officials demanding more public input. By that time, according to observers, the Civic Alliance was out of the consultative loop with the LMDC, and its role was firmly critical rather than collaborative.

AmericaSpeaks, which had conducted several public forums before Listening to the City, describes its role as one of "neutral, honest broker" and emphasizes that "any organization attempting to involve the public must position itself so that citizens have confidence that the forums they are participating in are unbiased and meaningful" (AmericaSpeaks 2002, 1, 2). But can "meaningful" forums be guaranteed only if the sponsoring organization is prepared to move from a role as "broker" to one of public advocate for the positions arrived at in the forum? The question has been raised especially sharply in this case, but its relevance goes beyond lower Manhattan.

CONCLUSION

Public forums about the redevelopment of lower Manhattan were convened in a unique set of circumstances. Few development projects are likely ever again to stir the passions of so broad a swath of citizens. Few projects will have to negotiate such a complex process of decisionmaking, involving multiple levels of government, numerous stakeholders, and moral hierarchies of authority as well as political and economic ones. That said, public deliberation around the World Trade Center site may have lasting impacts, not only on the eventual design of the site but on the landscape of citizen participation in urban planning. We conclude this chapter simply by identifying several possible scenarios involving different kinds of longer-term impact.

One scenario, of course, is that the perceived success of public deliberation in rebuilding lower Manhattan will lead to efforts to substitute deliberative forums like Listening to the City for more traditional modes of resident input in other development projects. To critics, city council hearings and community board meetings seem administratively clunky and dominated by advocacy groups rather than ordinary citizens. In fact, our respondents referred approvingly to the fact that Imagine New York and Listening to the City were so unlike the community hearings with which they were familiar. Rather than being required to present fully formed positions, participants were given the opportunity to explore their own opinions and preferences in discussion with people of diverse backgrounds and commitments. Sometimes that discussion strengthened participants' original views; sometimes it altered their views. In their recognition that preferences are rarely fixed or fully informed, forums like Imagine and Listening make it possible for people with very different stakes in development to reach agreement.

In a second scenario, forums like Listening to the City may become institutionalized, but not because they enable the public to control development decisions. Rather, critics worry that forums like Listening to the City give the public the illusion of participation without providing mechanisms for keeping decisionmakers accountable to the recommendations that come out of them. Recall that the LMDC and the Port Authority never made clear how they would incorporate Listening's results. As critics see it, the fact that they eventually did incorporate them—to the extent that they did—was a result of extraordinary media coverage and the fact that LMDC insiders wanted the changes. Rebuilding officials pointedly did not open themselves up to another public referendum when the second set of plans was released. And it is unlikely, in this scenario, that they would do so in the future unless they had firm control of the agenda and/or little responsibility to act on it. By providing the spectacle of democracy—the impressive number of people gathered in one place, the electronic tabulations of individual preferences, the presence of decisionmakers—and by carefully organizing contention out of the process, forums like Listening to the City restyle democracy as consultation. The people get to "speak," but not to "decide," and the former is mistakenly confused with democracy (Sorkin 2002; see also Young 2001).

Whether it is even possible to organize contention out of public deliberative forums is questionable, however, and this insight suggests a third possible scenario. Civic and advocacy groups may have as much to gain from public deliberative forums as decisionmakers do. For groups that claim to represent priorities that are being neglected in the development process, being able to invoke the expressed desires of the public can be powerfully effective. Indeed, it is likely that contention will permeate such forums from beginning to end: rather than accept an agenda and results being controlled by official decisionmakers and their influential allies, diverse groups may mobilize to shape the agenda, composition, and interpretation of future deliberative efforts. Several groups managed to have an informal organized presence at the July 20 Listening to the City forum: small-business people, Chinatown residents, and a group lobbying for rebuilding the towers. They came to get media coverage as well as to raise public consciousness about their concerns, and they were effective in doing so.

What organized efforts to shape deliberative forums means for the *deliberative* character of such forums is an important question. No group at Listening to the City managed to hijack the proceedings. However, some participants in the online dialogues found their groups dominated by advocates for rebuilding the towers. One participant complained that rebuilding advocates made reasoned discussion impossible: "They had their own agenda, and they just storm-trooped the group. They wanted to rebuild the towers. So they spammed the group: 'Rebuild the Towers! Rebuild the Towers!'" Participants began to drop out of this group in frustration. This suggests that maintaining the deliberative character of discussion in public forums like these may be difficult to square with maintaining their openness, since that openness should encompass even organized groups with preexisting agendas. If deliberative forums are institu-tionalized, we may see conflicts emerge as forum organizers try to lessen the influence of such groups, either by screening out participants, spreading them out across tables or online dialogue groups or concentrating them in one, or using facilitators to police discussion.

Together, these scenarios suggest that if it is naive to think that the spon-sors of a deliberative forum can neutrally transmit the unmediated views of the public to decisionmakers, it is just as naive to think that official decision-makers will be the only groups seeking to shape that process. The challenge for champions of deliberative democracy is to figure out how to create forums that are truly open to the public, that maximize deliberation, and that have the cooperation of decisionmakers without being controlled by them. The chal-lenge for students of deliberative democracy is to recognize that the impacts of public deliberation are mediated by complex processes of interpretation and, often, contention.

This research was supported by National Science Foundation grant EIA-03-06868 and by grants from the Russell Sage Foundation and Columbia University's Institute for Social and Economic Research and Policy. Thanks to Iara Duarte Peng, Greg Smithsimon, and Meredith Slopen for their help in conducting participant observa-tion and interviews and in analyzing our findings. Members of the Russell Sage Foundation Social Effects Working Group on New York City's Recovery from September 11 and the Columbia Sociol-ogy Colloquium offered valuable suggestions when Francesca Pol-letta presented our work there. Staffers and volunteers with Imag-ine New York and Listening to the City graciously gave us access to behind-the-scenes planning. Finally, we are grateful to the par-ticipants in Imagine New York and Listening to the City, who were generous with their time, candor, and insight.

NOTES

1. Alexander Garvin (LMDC) and Ron Pisapia (Port Authority), remarks at Imagine New York press conference, June 10, 2002; see also LMDC (2002).
2. See those ideas and designs at the website "Imagine New York: Giving Voice to the People's Visions," www.imaginenewyork.org. The information in this paragraph is based on interviews with Lauren Arana, Darya Cowan, Eva Hanhardt, and Holly Leicht, Municipal Arts Society, New York City, May 14, 2002; an interview with Holly Leicht, October 23, 2002; and notes on the workshops taken by Francesca Polletta, Lesley Wood, Iara Duarte Peng, and Gregory Smithsimon.
3. The information in this paragraph is based on a Listening to the City debriefing on July 21, 2002; an interview with Joseph Goldman, AmericaSpeaks, phone interview,

September 23, 2002; an interview with Petra Todorovich, RPA and Civic Alliance, New York City, June 17, 2003; and the website "Web Lab: Connecting People and Ideas," www.weblab.org.

4. Our fifty-three interviewees were recruited, in the case of Imagine New York, through our attendance at twelve workshops and, in the case of Listening to the City, through participant lists provided us by the organizers. Of those who heard our pitch, 45 percent of the Imagine New York pool were eventually interviewed and 60 percent of those from Listening to the City. Iara Duarte Peng and Gregory Smithsimon also observed Imagine workshops and conducted some of the interviews; Peng and Meredith Slopen conducted some of the Listening interviews.

Whites made up 63 percent of Imagine participants, 78 percent of our Imagine sample, 66 percent of Listening participants, and 79 percent of our Listening sample. Whites make up 64 percent of the region's population. Five percent of our Listening respondents were African American, compared with 7 percent of participants overall and 20 percent of the region's population. Both samples were broadly representative in terms of geographical distribution as well as income level, although a greater proportion of our Imagine interviewees had incomes of less than $34,999 than did Imagine participants overall. However, both our samples were badly skewed on educational attainment. Forty-four percent of our Imagine respondents had a postgraduate degree (compared to 35 percent of Imagine New York participants overall and 13 percent of residents in the region); our Listening sample was even less representative, with 52 percent having a postgraduate degree. Men were underrepresented in our Imagine sample (only 22 percent compared to 49 percent of participants overall). Imagine New York's modal age category was forty-five to sixty-five, as was ours. While our age thirty to forty-four and age eighteen to twenty-nine distributions were roughly similar, we chose not to interview anyone under eighteen. By contrast, 13 percent of Imagine New York's participants were under eighteen. (Listening to the City used different age categories than ours: thirty-five to fifty-four and fifty-five to sixty-four, whereas we used thirty to forty-four and forty-five to sixty-four. However, our forty-five to sixty-four category [57 percent] on its own accounted for roughly the same proportion of participants as their two categories combined [59 percent], suggesting that our sample was skewed upward in terms of age.)

5. Interview with Gianni Longo, ACP Planning and Imagine New York steering committee, New York City, March 9, 2002; see also Carl Moore, Gianni Longo, and Patsy Palmer (1999).

6. Interview with Alexander Garvin, LMDC, phone interview, July 3, 2003.

7. Interview with Alexander Garvin, LMDC, phone interview, July 3, 2003.

8. Interview with Holly Leicht, Municipal Arts Society, phone interview, October 17, 2002.

9. Interview with Petra Todorovich, June 17, 2003; see also Civic Alliance (2003a).

REFERENCES

AmericaSpeaks. 2002. "The AmericaSpeaks Model: Taking Democracy to Scale." Available at: http://www.americaspeaks.org/library/taking_democracy.pdf (accessed November 10, 2004).

Barber, Benjamin. 1988. *The Conquest of Politics*. Princeton, N.J.: Princeton University Press.

Burns, Nancy, Donald R. Kinder, and National Election Studies. 2000. *National Election Studies: 2000 Pilot Study*. Ann Arbor: University of Michigan, Center for Political Studies.

Button, Mark, and Kevin Mattson. 1999. "Deliberative Democracy in Practice: Challenges and Prospects for Civic Deliberation." *Polity* 31(4): 609–37.

Civic Alliance. 2003a. "Civic Alliance Denounces Plans to Dramatically Alter Master Plan for World Trade Center Site." June 11. Available at: http://www.civic-alliance.org/pdf/61103ReleaseLibeskindPlan.pdf (accessed November 11, 2004).

———. 2003b. "Comments on the WTC Site Memorial and Redevelopment Plan Draft Scope." August 4. Available at: http://www.civic-alliance.org/pdf/0804CivicAlliance EISresponse.pdf (accessed November 11, 2004).

Cohen, Joshua. 1989. "Deliberation and Democratic Legitimacy." In *The Good Polity: Normative Analysis of the State*, edited by Alan Hamlin and Philip Pettits. London: Blackwell.

Cohen, Joshua, and Charles Sabel. 1997. "Directly Deliberative Polyarchy." *European Law Journal* 3(4): 313–42.

Dryzek, John S. 1990. *Discursive Democracy: Politics, Policy, and Political Science*. New York: Cambridge University Press.

Dunlap, David W. 2003. "Veil Lifts on Finalists for 9/11 Memorial Design." *New York Times*, November 19, p. A1.

Fishkin, James S. 1991. *Democracy and Deliberation: New Directions for Democratic Reform*. New Haven, Conn.: Yale University Press.

———. 1995. *The Voice of the People*. New Haven, Conn.: Yale University Press.

Fishkin, James S., and Robert C. Luskin. 1999. "Bringing Deliberation to the Democratic Dialogue." In *The Poll with a Human Face: The National Issues Convention in Political Communication*, edited by Maxwell McCombs and Amy Reynolds. Mahwah, N.J.: Lawrence Erlbaum.

Gastil, John. 2000. "Is Face-to-Face Citizen Deliberation a Luxury or a Necessity?" *Political Communication* 17(4): 357–61.

Gastil, John, and J. P. Dillard. 1999. "Increasing Political Sophistication Through Public Deliberation." *Political Communication* 16(1): 3–23.

Gotham Gazette. 2002. "Six Months Later: 11 March 2002." *Gotham Gazette*. Available at: www.gothamgazette.com/iotw/911_sixmonths/ (accessed November 10, 2004).

Guttman, Amy, and Dennis F. Thompson. 1996. *Democracy and Disagreement*. Cambridge, Mass.: Harvard University Press.

Hart, Roderick, and Sharon Jarvis. 1999. "We the People: The Contours of Lay Political Discourse." In *The Poll with a Human Face: The National Issues Convention in Political Communication*, edited by Maxwell McCombs and Amy Reynolds. Mahwah, N.J.: Lawrence Erlbaum.

Hetter, Katia. 2002. "WTC Plan Deadline Extended." *New York Newsday*, December 22, n.p.

Imagine New York. 2002. "Imagine New York: The People's Visions: Summary Report." June 10. Available at: www.imagineny.org/resources/inysummaryreport.html (accessed November 11, 2004).

Iovine, Julie V. 2003. "Turning a Competition into a Public Campaign; Finalists for Ground Zero Design Pull Out the Stops." *New York Times*, February 26, p. E1.

Lake, Snell, Perry and Associates and the Tarrance Group. 2002. "Short Term Impacts Long Term Opportunities: The Political and Civic Engagement of Young Adults in America." Available at www.youngcitizensurvey.org/volunteer.htm (accessed November 10, 2004).

Listening to the City. 2002. "Listening to the City: Final Report." Available at: www.listeningtothecity.org/background/final_report_9_20.pdf (accessed November 11, 2004).

Lower Manhattan Development Corporation (LMDC). 2002. "Principles and Preliminary Blueprint for the Future of Lower Manhattan." New York: Lower Manhattan Development Corporation. Available at: http://www.gothamgazette.com/rebuilding_nyc/topics/governance/principlesfinal.pdf (accessed November 10, 2004).

Moore, Carl M., Gianni Longo, and Patsy Palmer. 1999. "Visioning." In *The Consensus Building Handbook*, edited by Lawrence Susskind, Sarah McKearnan, and Jennifer Thomas-Larmer. Thousand Oaks, Calif.: Sage Publications.

Muschamp, Herbert. 2002. "In Latest Concepts for Ground Zero, It's Reality vs. Renaissance." *New York Times*, December 23, p. E1.

Passerin D'Entreves, Maurizio, ed. 2002. *Democracy as Public Deliberation: New Perspectives*. Manchester: Manchester University Press.

Pedersen, Martin C. 2002. "Missing Persons: Who Will—and Won't—Be Deciding What Gets Built at the World Trade Center Site." *Metropolis* 21(6): n.p. Available at: http://www.metropolismag.com/html/content_0202/ob/ob06.html (accessed November 10, 2004).

Pogrebin, Robin. 2004. "The Incredible Shrinking Daniel Libeskind." *New York Times*, June 20, p. 1.

Polletta, Francesca. 2001. "'This Is What Democracy Looks Like': Decisionmaking in the Direct Action Network." *Social Policy* 31(4): 25–30.

———. 2002. *Freedom Is an Endless Meeting: Democracy in American Social Movements*. Chicago: University of Chicago Press.

Russell, James S. 2002. "How Ground Zero Planning Can Get Beyond Window-Dressing Democracy." *Architectural Record* 190(9): 71.

Shapiro, Ian. 2002. "Optimal Deliberation?" *Journal of Political Philosophy* 10(2): 196–211.

Sorkin, Michael. 2002. "Power Plays at Ground Zero: Backroom Schemes, Laptop Democracy, and a Howl of Protest." *Architectural Record* 190(9): 67.

Squires, Judith. 2002. "Deliberation and Decisionmaking: Discontinuity in the Two-Track Model." In *Democracy as Public Deliberation: New Perspectives*, edited by Maurizio Passerin D'Entreves. Manchester: Manchester University Press.

Stanley, J. Woody, Christopher Weare, and Juliet Musso. 2002. "Participation, Deliberative Democracy, and the Internet: Lessons from a National Forum on Commercial Vehicle Safety." Paper presented to the conference "Prospects for Electronic Democracy." Carnegie-Mellon University, September 20–21.

Traub, James. 2003. "Public Building." *New York Times*, September 7, p. F17.

Walters, Jonathan. 1998. "Cities and the Vision Thing: The Year 2050 Will Be Here Before You Know It. Is Your Master Plan in Place?" *Governing Magazine* 11(May): 32–36.

Wood, Lesley. 2004. "Bridging the Chasms: The Case of People's Global Action" in

Coalitions Across Borders: Transnational Protest and the Neoliberal Order, edited by Joe Bandy and Jackie Smith. New York: Rowman and Littlefield.

Wyatt, Edward. 2002a. "At Trade Center Site, a Wealth of Ideas; Competing Interests Are Fighting to Have a Say in Reviving Downtown." *New York Times*, July 28, p. A25.

———. 2002b. "Longing for a September 10 Skyline: Some Vocal Groups Call for Restoring the Twin Towers." *New York Times*, November 2, p. B1.

———. 2003. "Ground Zero Plan Seems to Circle Back." *New York Times*, September 13, p. B1.

Young, Iris Marion. 2001. "Activist Challenges to Deliberative Democracy." *Political Theory* 29(5): 670–90.

PART V

Epilogue

CHAPTER 13

Epilogue: The Geography of Disaster

Kai Erikson

IN THOSE dark, confused days right after the attacks on the World Trade Center, journalists asked two questions of persons they thought to be expert on human reactions to disaster. The first and most obvious of them was: to what other event can this new horror be compared? This was an effort to identify the genus to which the attack belonged, to locate it somewhere on the scale of human experience so as to give it a recognizable shape.

The bombing of Hiroshima came up frequently in those conversations. That seemed like a natural association, given its size, the volume of death that resulted from it, and the sheer terror it generated. But the dimensions were wrong. Pearl Harbor was another natural association because it, like 9/11, was an act of almost unimaginable treachery, and it had the additional appeal that, unlike the bombing of Hiroshima, we were the victims. But again, the differences were so stark that it was difficult to keep this association in focus for long. It is easy to see why Oklahoma City came to mind, and just as easy to see why it could not serve as a satisfactory comparison. And occasionally one would even hear the dread word "Holocaust." It was harder to follow the logic of that parallel, but what everyone seemed to be looking for was a template against which to measure the terror of that day, and the Holocaust belongs as nothing else quite does at the far outer edges of the humanly explicable.

These events all share in common the fact that they were deliberate acts of malice, even if they were responsible for very different levels of death and destruction. No one asked survivors of the Holocaust or of Hiroshima whether they could see a parallel in these circumstances because that was not the real point. None of us were seeking actual comparisons so much as ways to comprehend the inherently incomprehensible.

In her thoughtful introduction to this volume, Nancy Foner looks at other New York disasters in an effort to see whether they might help locate this one in the history of the city. She mentions the cholera epidemic of 1832, responsible for 3,500 deaths; a fire in 1835 that destroyed most of downtown Manhattan; the *General Slocum* disaster of 1904 that killed 1,000 persons; the Triangle Shirtwaist Factory fire of 1911 that killed 150 people, most of them young women; and the detonation of a bomb on Wall Street in 1920 that caused the deaths of 40 persons. The last of these was most likely the work of terrorists. The only one of these events that approaches the attacks on the World Trade Center in number of deaths was the cholera epidemic of 1832, but that is usually classified as a "natural" disaster, an "act of God" rather than an act of other humans. There may be a minor irony in the fact that the agent of death in three of these events was fire but that in two of the three, the *General Slocum* and Triangle disasters, most of the deaths occurred when people leapt to their deaths from the site of the conflagration—the holiday vacationers on board the *General Slocum* into the waters of the East River, and the young women in the upper stories of the Triangle building onto the sidewalks of Washington Square below. But the collapse of the twin towers, Foner concludes, has a place of its own in any such accounting.

The only other strategy available to the press was to seek comparisons in fairly minor events (as seen on a global scale at least) that involved a good deal of devastation in proportion to the size of the universes in which they took place. The *Wall Street Journal*, for example, drew a parallel on its front page a month later between the terrorist attacks and the Buffalo Creek flood, a disaster I happen to know well and have written about (Erikson 1976). It was an interesting idea. The Buffalo Creek disaster was a relatively small event if one counts only the number of casualties or assesses the volume of damage, but each of the two catastrophes was immense within the borders of its own world. Still, there was little to be learned once the connection was drawn.

The second question many journalists asked in those early days of the crisis was: given what we know about disasters in general, what is it reasonable for us to expect from this one? That was an equally difficult question, at least in part because one needs some kind of answer to the first question before the second can even be approached intelligently. It made sense to assume that a good deal of psychological trauma would manifest itself and that a considerable amount of disorientation, distraction, and flailing about in a dazed way would be a natural consequence of our inability to place this thing in the realm of the recognizable. People everywhere were apt to suffer from something akin to a concussion of the spirit. But how far out into the landscape were those effects likely to reach? What were the dimensions of the universe in which it occurred?

The attack of September 11, 2001, will probably remain without any other name because it belongs on a scale entirely its own. And for that reason, as Foner notes, it is much too large to study in the whole. The chapters that appear here are separate efforts to take the emotional pulse of New York by looking at especially sensitive locations within a terrain that is far too vast and too complex to envision in its entirety. The idea was to take soil samplings, as it were, since there is no way on earth to try to cover that terrain in any inclusive way.

Perhaps the biggest problem in coming to terms with 9/11 is the difficulty of plotting it on any kind of conceptual map. Most disasters have a distinct geography of their own. One can chart the domain in which they took place and in that way at least approximate their size and extent. How far did the earthquake (the storm, the flood, the fire) reach? What was the extent of the underground plume? The toxic cloud? It is never a simple matter to draw a line around a disaster zone, of course, all the more so when invisible substances like radiation and other forms of toxin are involved. But the task is conceptually imaginable, even if difficult to perform.

The geographical dimensions of 9/11, though, appear far more complicated. A map of the disaster would begin simply enough with an epicenter, a point in space called Ground Zero, but from there things spread outward almost endlessly. We might think in terms of concentric circles radiating out from that center like ripples in a pond, each of them describing a ring of receding impact as it moves farther away from the epicenter. They cannot be drawn as neat circles, because human life is never so simple as that, but they can probably be drawn in such a way as to make full circuits—like the lines representing altitudes on a topographical map.

The innermost circle would presumably include those people most immediately affected by the attacks: family members of the persons who died; people injured in the collapse of the towers; rescuers who voluntarily entered Ground Zero from a safe niche outside it; and onlookers who were close enough to the epicenter to feel the flames, hear as well as see the falling bodies, inhale the ashes and fumes, and get caught up in the vortex of fear and horror. I am deliberately using words like *feel* and *hear* and *inhale* because those were the sensations of persons who were actually there rather than of persons who saw it from a distance or on a television screen. These are the true survivors.

The next outer circle would have to include immediately adjacent neighborhoods like Battery Park City and Tribeca, but the perimeter surrounding that zone needs to be drawn with psychological as well as spatial considerations in mind, taking into account levels of involvement and degrees of fragility as well as proximity. Using such criteria as those, the zone would probably include places like Belle Harbor and Jersey City, for example, rather than other neighborhoods that are nearer to Ground Zero as the crow flies. Foner notes that the Upper East Side as well as several neighborhoods in Staten Island and New Jersey lost considerably more than their share of residents, putting them closer to the epicenter in human terms if not in spatial ones. Once we start thinking in this way, we may find that the encircled area includes sensitive locations in the occupational structure or in markets as well as in geographical space, a subject I return to shortly.

Somewhere in this map of concentric circles we cross a perimeter, marked only in people's minds, where the effects of the disaster shade over from states of mind that can legitimately be called "traumatized" to states of mind that are something less drastic. And beyond that perimeter is a vast territory, stretching as far as the mind can see, where people nonetheless feel that they were witnesses *to*, victims *of*, even actors *in*, what Foner calls a "truly global event." Our samplings did not reach that far out into the hinterland, but it is an important part of the story. People felt the shock of 9/11 in Tacoma as well as in Tribeca, in Rapid City as well as in Jersey City. News of it was broadcast so widely, and images of it were so immediate and intimate, that 9/11 became a moment in everyone's history, a part of the national consciousness. The disaster was given official boundaries for compensation purposes, but it had none otherwise.

TRAUMA

Among the problems with drawing the first and second concentric zones, as I was suggesting earlier, is that the *effects* of a disaster on those who experience it cannot be plotted in the same way as the *event* itself. We generally assume that the people most likely to be singed by a flame are the ones nearest to it, but that is not necessarily how trauma and other forms of emotional distress operate. We are dealing with a different geography here, one in which closeness to the epicenter is not measured in yards or miles but in levels of harm sustained.

The most seriously traumatized persons mentioned in the book remain offstage, as it were. These are the men and women whose voices can be heard indirectly in the interviews that Karen Seeley conducted with psychotherapists. Their pain can be felt clearly even at two removes. The next most traumatized persons to appear in the book would seem to be the psychotherapists themselves, many of whom became deeply disturbed by the reports they were hearing from their patients, and the airline workers who had only recently lost their jobs interviewed by William Kornblum and Steven Lang. As a spatial matter, some of the out-of-work airline workers lived and worked as far away

from the epicenter as any persons who figure in this volume, while the therapists may have been as close to Ground Zero as it was possible to get, some
because they were exposed to it themselves and others because they became
so entangled in the lives of patients who had been in the very thick of it that
they felt as though they were sharing the experience with them—caught up
"in the throes of their patients' anguish," as Seeley puts it. One of her interviewees, speaking of both therapists and patients, said simply, "You were all
the same body in some ways."

Seeley heard psychotherapists speak in her interviews of spending their
working hours "dazed, exhausted, and numb" and their evenings "at home in
tears." She heard someone say that "the dead had begun to 'inhabit' her." Kornblum and Lang, in their turn, heard comments that were drawn from largely
the same emotional well. A woman who had been employed as a flight attendant said to them: "This layoff has affected me as deeply as when my husband
passed away ten years ago. . . . The feelings are so similar it's eerie. A sense of
dread, depression, worry, anxiety." A baggage handler told them: "When I'm
alone in the house or in the car, I go into tears thinking how my life just went
into shambles. My manhood, my fatherhood, my dignity was taken away from
me." These are the sounds of trauma, no matter how a clinician would diagnose
the mental conditions of the persons who uttered them. But again, it is important to note that if you tried to guess how close each of these speakers had
been to the site of the attack on that fateful day by the severity of the injuries
they sustained—by how badly they had been singed by the fire—you would
almost surely miss the mark.

The problem with that comparison is that the airline workers were harmed
by an event that could be attributed to 9/11 only indirectly, but I think the
point holds as a general matter anyway. A good example is posed by the very
interesting observations of Philip Kasinitz, Gregory Smithsimon, and Binh Pok
on Tribeca and Battery Park City, although "trauma" is not necessarily what
we are talking about here. Residents of the two neighborhoods lived in the
shadows of the twin towers and were inevitably caught up in the disaster, yet
in the end the people of Tribeca and the people of Battery Park City were
reporting very different experiences of 9/11. The back gate of Tribeca, as it
were, opened onto the World Trade Center, while its front gate faced the rest
of the city, and this had the effect of making downtown Manhattan rather
than the site of the twin towers its main point of reference. Battery Park City
had only one gate, and its point of reference was the World Trade Center.

CITY OF COMRADES

Monisha Das Gupta notes in her chapter on taxi drivers that some of the early
social science research on disasters emphasized the waves of good feelings—of

warmth and fellowship—that were thought to accompany catastrophe. Anthony F. C. Wallace (1956) has written of "a stage of euphoria" that usually wells up in the aftermath of some blow to a community, and others have written in the same vein. Samuel H. Prince (1920), studying a ship explosion in Halifax, talked of a "city of comrades." Robert I. Kutak (1938), studying a flood in Louisville, talked of a "democracy of distress." Charles E. Fritz (1961), studying a tornado in Arkansas, referred to a "community of sufferers." Martha Wolfenstein (1957), reviewing the literature on disasters in general, called the phenomenon "post-disaster utopia," while Allen H. Barton (1969), surveying much the same literature a decade later, referred to an "altruistic community." The earliest of these reports was dated 1920, and the latest 1969.

Newspapers in particular seemed to be very impressed after 9/11 by the masses of New Yorkers who came together in what looked like one vast communion, gathering on street corners, sharing views and information, and generally responding as one might expect in a small town. We all saw it: acts of almost extravagant courtesy and kindness in a city celebrated for its indifference.

If we were asked to point out where those feelings were exhibited most clearly across the New York landscape, judging from the reports that appear in this volume, we might begin by citing neighborhoods like Rockaway, where, in Melanie Hildebrandt's words, the community became "more cohesive, supportive, and unified" in the wake of the attacks and came together in "rituals of gathering" that helped people through difficult times. Or Battery Park City, where residents found ways upon their return to embrace neighbors they had scarcely spoken to before and to "celebrate the community" in new ways.

But I was also taken by the fact that a general sense of fellowship and a desire to become a part of some larger communal whole was apparent in other places as well. The trading room that Daniel Beunza and David Stark studied, for example, had many of the features of a city of comrades, even though the crisis also opened up "dramatic lines of fissure" in the organization. And the ways in which everyday New Yorkers participated in the public forums studied by Francesca Polletta and Lesley Wood seemed to issue from the same feeling. These forums drew tens of thousands of participants, and many if not most appear to have attended not just because they hoped to make some difference in public policy but because they wanted to be a part of the "public," to join ongoing conversations about the future of their community. One gets the sense that the attendees were gathering as if on a village green or an immense street corner. Critics of those gatherings, Polletta and Wood tell us, worried that they might have been "more spectacle than substance"—an altogether reasonable concern if one is interested in knowing whether the public actually makes a difference in these kinds of deliberation. But "spectacles" have a virtue of their own: they offer a way to *be* there, to *belong*.

One might add that the reason so many of those remarkable therapists Seeley interviewed reached high levels of distress was from a powerful feeling of wanting to participate and use their clinical skills to be of assistance. Seeley points out that many of them were "frantically searching for people to help," and it is clear from the rest of her report that this desire to step into the center of the storm and join their fellow creatures there was extremely important to them. The fact that they eventually found themselves members of a "community of sufferers" in doing so, becoming part of "the same body" as their patients, only makes the point stronger. That should give us all hope.

(I would just add a point here that does not quite fit the sequence of the argument I am making. Seeley worries that the "immersion" of mental health professionals "in the anguish" of their patients "puts them at psychological risk." That's a good point. But it may also be the case that some emergencies simply cannot be prepared for and that when the inexplicable does happen, one of the few things we have working for us is minds meeting minds, sensitivities meeting sensitivities, frailties meeting frailties. Judging from what we learn from this compelling chapter, it obviously can work. It might even be the case that the once-wounded have a special qualification for treating the newly wounded. I have always thought it would be a good idea for survivors of a past disaster, who know what trauma looks and feels like, to share their knowledge with survivors of a recent disaster. Such sharing would probably be therapeutic for both groups because, like the therapists and patients we meet here, they are all "of the same body," all part of "a collective nervous system." It would be very interesting to know what these therapists, looking back on the experiences related here, think of this idea.)

THE OPENING OF FISSURES

The reason Das Gupta brings up the early work on "euphoria" and "altruism," of course, is that there is no "city of comrades" where the taxi drivers of New York ply their trade, nor is there one where the Muslims of Jersey City and many other people who appear in these pages live. Indeed, if a single thread can be said to appear and reappear throughout the fabric of the book, it is that the most lasting effects of 9/11 may have been to expose the most insecure fault lines, the weakest seams, in the larger community.

I visited the Japanese city of Kobe not long after a devastating earthquake had done a tremendous amount of damage there, and the image that remained with me was not of the neighborhoods that had been leveled completely but of the neighborhoods in which every third or fourth house had crumpled into a pile of debris while the houses to either side appeared untouched. This should not have come as a surprise: the more unstable a structure is, the more likely it is to collapse, and clearly some were more stable than others. But the image has remained in my mind as a kind of metaphor. In the same way that earthquakes seem to seek out the most vulnerable linkages in physical structures, disasters in general seem to seek out the most vulnerable linkages in social structures. It must sometimes feel to victims as though disasters are like heat-seeking missiles, scanning the landscape for its most precarious workplaces, its least protected persons, its flimsiest connective tissues, and its most badly bruised spirits.

A number of neighborhoods are described in these pages where 9/11 seems to have opened up fissures along fault lines that had long been a part of the community but had never been a source of open division. These fissures may turn out to be permanent, or they may turn out to be temporary. But they ought to be included in any audit we take of the costs of 9/11.

It has been noted for a long time that communities often purchase a new vitality and a new sense of purpose by firming up the boundaries that separate them from neighboring social units. A mild example of that social chemistry appears in the report on Battery Park City by Kasinitz and his colleagues. A form of euphoria emerged among the residents of Battery Park City when they were able to return to their homes. But this was a sense of fellowship that could be shared only among persons who had lived in the neighborhood at the time of the attacks; residents who moved in subsequently almost had to be excluded from that fellow feeling. They did not meet the only qualification for belonging. These things have a way of working themselves out over time, so I only mean to point out here that communities have standards for inclusion, and those standards have as their natural opposite the fact that they exclude others.

It can also happen, in turn, that people excluded by the opening of new fissures within a larger community create a warmer enclave within their own ranks, and in that sense one can say both that community creates division and that division creates community. Jennifer Bryan's report on the Muslims of Jersey City offers a compelling instance of both propositions. It is probably reasonable to suppose that non-Muslim constituencies in Jersey City drew a certain cohesion from the sharpness of their rejection of their Muslim neighbors. Bryan knows the answer to that question, and she may report on it in the longer monograph to follow this preliminary report. But it is clear from what we have here that the Muslim community became stronger—or at least a good deal more self-conscious—as a result of the hostility and mistrust that pressed in on it from all sides. When the fact of being Muslim trumps all other distinguishing characteristics in the minds of the people among whom one lives, it is very likely to have the same effect on one's self. Other ways of identifying one's position in the world—occupational, national, some other— begin to pale in significance because of the sheer weight of the anti-Muslim hostility in the community. Bryan cites the work of Tone Bringa, who, along with many other observers, was struck by the degree to which Muslims in Bosnia, a relatively secular lot on the whole, turned with a kind of inverted passion to the religious traditions of Islam in response to the fact that they were suddenly thought of in that way by the Serbs and Croats with whom they had grown up and with whom they shared the land.

Bryan notes that the Muslims of Jersey City are living in "a state of terror." So were the Muslims of Bosnia. Living like that either crushes people—reducing them to a cowering, inert mass, turned inward on themselves and scrapping with each other for breathing space—or reinforces the identities they share in common. The turn to religion may be a search for individual solace and inner power ("Islam makes me strong," one woman said to Bryan), but it is also a search for community and belonging.

Belle Harbor offers a different case in point. One way of telling the story of that community is to say that it gained strength from having to respond to the horrors of 9/11, and that in doing so even racial and ethnic differences that had long been a prominent part of the local landscape were obscured. But the crash of American Airlines flight 587, in that telling, brought a new set of "internal fissures" to the surface, and at the time Hildebrandt concluded her report, it was not at all clear how matters would eventually be resolved. The community consensus that had emerged from the first disaster seemed to dissipate in the shock of the second. We may never know, however, whether the sense of communality that followed the attack on the World Trade Center would have weakened on its own if nothing else had happened to disturb the peace of Belle Harbor. Hildebrandt reports on two rifts that were beginning to appear in the neighborhood about the time her study came to a close. She was hopeful that the people of Belle Harbor would recover from them, but there are good reasons from the experience of other disasters to be doubtful.

The first rift was beginning to appear when neighbors who continued to mourn the attack on the World Trade Center—to keep it alive as an act of witness—ran afoul of those who wanted to "get on with it" and felt that the time had come to give the disaster an honored place in the past. A second rift began to appear as a result of the fact that a community mourns and commemorates as a unit, but the world compensates those who suffer from a disaster by a totally different set of standards. It happens everywhere. Some members of the community are judged by outside agencies as having suffered enough to deserve compensation, while others, for whatever reason, are judged to deserve less or even no compensation at all. That is both hard for people to understand and hard for them to live with. People who gather together to grieve and commemorate do so as communities, but people who appeal to aid agencies for support (or who mount lawsuits for relief) do so as individuals, and that can be very divisive. William Freudenburg and his colleagues speak of "corrosive communities" as one of the outcomes to expect in such circumstances (see, for example, Freudenburg and Jones 1991). It would be interesting to find out whether something similar happened in Chinatown.

Disasters seem to seek out the softest sectors of the economy as well. This is reflected most clearly here in the reports on occupations. It is not reasonable to insist that the attack on the World Trade Center was responsible in some direct way for what happened to the airline workers or the garment workers who found themselves without employment, the taxi drivers who did not know how to recover from the blow that had landed on them, and the young artists whose already uncertain market deteriorated even further. An econo-mist might well argue that something was sure to happen sooner or later to those insecurely positioned individuals, but that is hardly a source of solace to them. Airline workers must have known that a number of them were sched-uled for downsizing, as Kornblum and Lang suggest. The garment workers must have known that the disaster only "accelerated trends in the garment industry" that were already under way, as Chin puts it. The taxi drivers must have known that 9/11 only "brought to a head preexisting problems in the taxi industry," in Das Gupta's words, and young visual artists were aware, Roth-enberg and Kornblum tell us, that "the economic recession that gripped New York during the months before the suicide bombings had already begun to weaken the art market." But knowing that one lives in a precarious world is very different from knowing that one is no longer employed or can no longer pay the most essential of bills. All of these persons were hurt by events they had no choice but to trace to 9/11. To make matters much worse for them, the media said nothing of their sacrifice or bad luck, and agencies in a position to provide emergency relief funds did not count them as victims of 9/11 or as in any other respect deserving of aid.

This is what Das Gupta may have in mind when she speaks in her report of "the very 'terrain' of disaster" (citing Enarson 1998). Disasters of various kinds spread out to regions of unusual sensitivity in the social order, and in particular to those regions where sharp imbalances in power leave some per-sons susceptible to the ravages of catastrophe and others relatively insulated from them.

I have one last thought that could as easily have been offered at the begin-ning of this epilogue, so it brings us full circle. I am using nothing more than a loose metaphor when I argue that disasters seem to seek the weakest link-ages in human life in much the same way as they seem to seek the weakest timbers in physical structures. Storms do not have intentions, nor can they be accused of malice. Disasters may batter with what feels like vengeance, but they are really a blind lashing-out. If a physical or social structure is damaged because it cannot withstand the battering, that tells us as much about the properties of the structure as it does about the properties of the disaster itself.

But that is not true of acts of terror. The attack on the World Trade Center was a deliberate effort to do harm, and it had much in common with heat-seeking devices in the sense that it was designed to search out sections of maximum vulnerability in the larger landscape. Disasters in general, and perhaps acts of terrorism in particular, are like X-rays that reach through the surface membranes of things and disclose the hidden fragilities within.

REFERENCES

Barton, Allen H. 1969. *Communities in Disaster*. Garden City, N.Y.: Doubleday.

Enarson, Elaine. 1998. "Through Women's Eyes: A Gendered Research Agenda for Disaster Social Science." *Disasters* 22(2): 157–73.

Erikson, Kai. 1976. *Everything in Its Path: Destruction of Community in the Buffalo Creek Flood*. New York: Simon & Schuster.

Freudenburg, William R., and Timothy R. Jones. 1991. "Attitudes and Stress in the Presence of Technological Risk: A Test of the Supreme Court Hypothesis." *Social Forces* 69(4): 1143–68.

Fritz, Charles E. 1961. "Disaster." In *Contemporary Social Problems*, edited by Robert K. Merton and Robert A. Nisbet. New York: Harcourt Brace.

Kutak, Robert I. 1938. "Sociology of Crises: The Louisville Flood of 1937." *Social Forces* 17(1): 66–72.

Prince, Samuel H. 1920. *Catastrophe and Social Change*. New York: Columbia University Press.

Wallace, Anthony F. C. 1956. *Tornado in Worcester*. Disaster Study 3. Washington: Committee on Disaster Studies, National Academy of Sciences—National Research Council.

Wolfenstein, Martha. 1957. *Disaster: A Psychological Essay*. Glencoe, Ill.: Free Press.

INDEX

Boldface numbers refer to figures and tables.

closure, lack of psychological for victims, 274

Cognition in the Wild (Hutchins), 298

cohesion, community. *See* solidarity-unity, community

collective vs. individual trauma, 5–7, 108, 128, 275–76, 353

commercial operations: art galleries, 19, 87, 245–54, 258, 260; dot-com companies, 187, 251; loss of business in Tribeca, 98, 99; Muslims in Jersey City as business operators, 136; and psychological counseling demand, 271; recovery role in Tribeca, 88, 92, 95, 101–2; stratification of art community, 20, 242–43, 249–52, 254, 260–61; Tribeca resident support for, 100, 101. *See also* garment workers; taxi drivers; trading room study

commercial space, use of, 82, 84, 87–88, 187, 251–52. *See also* trading room study

communications disruptions, 195–96, 204n2

community. *See* social-community effects

concentrated vs. dispersed tragedies, 11

conflict avoidance in public forum structure, 334, 337

Consortium for Worker Education (CWE), 175

consumerism as neighborhood rebuilding in Tribeca, 100

corporate welfare for airlines, 164–65, 174, 181

corporations. *See* commercial operations

cosmological events and sensemaking, 299, 300–303

counseling and therapy, 38–39, **40–42**, 124–25. *See also* mental health professionals

covering requirement for Muslim women, 139, 143–45, 152–53, 257

crime levels and well-being effects, 44, 46, **48–49, 67, 69**

CWE (Consortium for Worker Education), 175

data and methods: airline workers, 163, 166; garment workers, 185, 205n9; individual well-being study, 28, 29–30, 31–32, 38, 39, 44, 46; mental health professionals, 265–66; Muslims of Jersey City, 138–39; overview, 4; public deliberation on rebuilding, 323, 329–30, 345n4; Rockaway neighborhoods, 107–8; taxi drivers, 210–12

day care workers, response to 9/11 disaster, 91–92

The Death and Life of Great American Cities (Jacobs), 88

debt, personal, and taxi drivers' difficulties, 221

deliberative democracy in public forums on rebuilding, 323–26, 333–38, 343–44

demographics of effects: and Battery Park City tensions, 95; and Jersey City composition, 135–36, 139; and vulnerable groups, 47–49, 50; well-being study of New Yorkers, 31–38. *See also* ethnic groups

DeNiro, Robert, 87, 100–101

detentions of Muslims, 141–42

development, urban. *See* rebuilding of lower Manhattan

disability and individual well-being effects, 35–36, **40, 49, 54, 58, 62, 66–67, 70**

discrimination against high-skill airline workers, 181–82. *See also* Muslims; taxi drivers

dispersed vs. concentrated tragedies, 11

distributed decisionmaking, 298–300

diversity of views, public forum benefits of, 334, 335–37

Dominican victims of Belle Harbor plane crash, 13–14, 107, 117, 120, 126–27, 130

dot-com companies, 187, 251

drug use, increases in, 42, 264, 270

Durkheim, Émile, 7

dust contamination, 92, 95, 99